Rethinking Nationalism
in the
Arab Middle East

———

D1188400

Rethinking Nationalism
in the
Arab Middle East

———

James Jankowski and Israel Gershoni

editors

Columbia University Press

New York

Columbia University Press
Publishers Since 1893
New York   Chichester, West Sussex
Copyright © 1997 Columbia University Press
All rights reserved

Library of Congress Cataloging-in-Publication Data
Rethinking nationalism in the Arab Middle East / James Jankowski
   and Israel Gershoni, editors.
      p.   cm.
   Includes bibliographical references and index.
   ISBN 0–231–10694–7 (cloth : alk. paper).—ISBN 0–231–10695–5
(paper : alk. paper)
   1. Nationalism—Arab countries. 2. Arab countries—Politics and
government.   I. Jankowski, James, 1937—   . II. Gershoni, I.
DS63.6.R47   1997
320.54'0974927—dc21
                                                              97–12826

Casebound editions of Columbia University Press books are printed on
permanent and durable acid-free paper.
Printed in the United States of America
c 10 9 8 7 6 5 4 3 2 1
p 10 9 8 7 6 5 4 3 2 1

Contents

Acknowledgments

This volume had its genesis in a workshop on nationalism in the Arab Middle East, sponsored by the National Endowment for the Humanities and held at the University of Colorado in September 1994. We wish to thank the Endowment and the Department of History, the College of Arts and Sciences, the Council on Research and Creative Work, and the Committee on the Arts and Humanities of the University for their financial support. We are particularly appreciative of the advice and counsel provided by Dr. David Coder, program officer of the Endowment, and Dean Charles R. Middleton of the College of Arts and Sciences, and for the observations and input of the other workshop participants, Ahmed Abdalla, Amatzia Baram, Joel Beinin, C. Ernest Dawn, Eberhard Kienle, Thomas Philipp, and Robert Vitalis.

We received help from many friends and colleagues. Several contributors offered valuable suggestions concerning the introduction and the structure of the volume, as did Professors Avi Shlaim and Itamar Even-Zohar. In Israel, Robert Jancu and Ursula Wokoeck provided valuable editorial and bibliographical assistance. In Colorado, Professors Steven Epstein and Barbara Engel of the Department of History were most supportive of our efforts, and Pat Murphy a marvelously efficient—and patient—typist of a difficult manuscript. The editorial advice of Kate Wittenberg of Columbia University Press greatly improved the eventual structure and content of the volume. Susan Heath did a splendid job of editing the text, as did Roy Thomas in shepherding the project through the production phase. To all, our most sincere thanks.

As has been the case with our previous collaboration, we are enormously grateful to our families for the support they have given to what they are now terming, with some exasperation but also (we hope) with some affection, "Gershoni-Jankowski Industries."

Introduction

Israel Gershoni and James Jankowski

PERSPECTIVES ON NATIONALISM

Coming to terms with nationalism is a vexing project. Between the totalizing insistence of nationalist ideologues on the immemorial and monolithic reality of their nation, and the expansive and contingent view offered by Zachary Lockman in his contribution to this volume—that "nationalism *always* means different things to different people in different contexts"—a wide range of diverging perspectives about the nature, evolution, and historical role of nationalism exist. In part this is because of the protean nature of the phenomenon; in part it is due to the different prisms through which observers have viewed nationalism over time.

Until recently, scholars have tended to approach nationalism from either of two perspectives. An idealist emphasis on the cognitive and affective aspects of nationalism can be traced back to the time of Ernest Renan's *Qu'est que c'est une nation?* (1882). In Renan's famous phrase, nations are "a daily plebiscite," the product of the subjective collective memory of communities rather than the result of objective "facts" such as kinship, geography, history, language, religion, or economic interests. Renan's positing of "large-scale solidarity" or shared "moral consciousness" as the fundamental criteria of national existence[1] was accepted and reiterated by numerous later writers on nationalism. For Arnold Toynbee in 1915, nationalism "like all great forces in life is nothing material or mechanical, but a subjective psychological feeling in a living people."[2] Hans Kohn's influential *The Idea of Nationalism* (1944) defined the phenomenon as "first and foremost a state of mind, an act of consciousness."[3] When Karl Deutsch's *Nationalism and Social Communication* (1953) redirected scholarly attention to the social dynamics of nationalism—the modes and agencies of communication that create and disseminate national solidarity—he nonetheless remained within the perceptual paradigm.[4] Fully a century after Renan, Benedict Anderson's *Imagined Communities* (1983) continued to treat nationalism in primarily cognitive terms: "Communities are to be distinguished, not by their falsity/genuineness, but by the style in which they are imagined."[5]

The alternative approach to nationalism has been to emphasize its political character. In 1912 Max Weber recognized that, while nationalism was based on "a common bond of sentiment," nationalism's "adequate expression would be a state of its own."[6] Elie Kedourie's *Nationalism* (1960) argued that nationalism had substantively resulted in a "politics in a new style," specifically "an ideological style of politics" that in his view was inherently destructive of civic order.[7] While viewing the genesis and contribution of nationalism in very different terms, Ernest Gellner began his study of the subject with a political definition of nationalism: "Nationalism is primarily a political principle, which holds that the political and the national unit should be congruent."[8] Among recent analysts, John Breuilly has been perhaps the most insistent on the essentially political character of nationalism: "Nationalism is a form of politics. Before trying to theorise about the 'real' purpose or cause of this form of politics—before trying to go 'behind' nationalism in search of some non-political base which supposedly gives rise to nationalism—one should try to work out precisely what is the form of politics we call nationalism, its political context and its political modes."[9]

New Directions in Recent Theory

In the past two decades, an explosion of new theoretical writing on the subject has vastly expanded the analytical framework in which nationalism is considered. The intellectual and political dimensions of nationalism of course continue to receive attention; but the phenomenon has been situated in a wider socioeconomic, cultural, and psychological field. Two sets of contrasting models dominate recent discussion about the nature of nationalism. One pits what has been variously termed a "primordialist" or "perennialist" paradigm against a "modernist" interpretation. Where the former views modern nations as ineluctable outgrowths or adaptations of existing ethnic communities or *ethnies*, the latter model conceives of nations as totally modern constructions, if not inventions, erected *de novo* as a result of the massive processes of change of the past two centuries. Anthony Smith's metaphors of "gastronomy" versus "archeology" capture the distinction between the two approaches: where the modernist model views nationalism as an act of creation analogous to making a "meal out of different ingredients," the primordialist/perennialist model resembles archeology in seeing nationalism as the excavation of successive layers from the past that form the basis for collective identity in the present.[10]

The other set of contrasting models turns on a methodological distinction. The "realist" perspective holds that nationalism is produced by and anchored in objective socioeconomic conditions and material interests; the "semiotic" or "postmodernist" school treats nationalism as a set of signs and an entirely discursive construct. Despite their differences, the primordialist/perennialist and modernist models discussed above are both "realist" in their assumption that nationalism is a tangible reality embedded in concrete historical circumstances (ancient in the case of the former, recent in the case of the latter). Scholars who opt for a semiotic approach interpret nationalism as a continuing discourse about such conditions, and hence resort to hermeneutic tools rather than empirical historical analysis to decipher a nationalism's provenance and character.

Whether primordialist or modernist, realist or postmodernist, recent theoretical analyses of nationalism have unquestionably enriched our understanding of a multifaceted subject. Among modernists, Ernest Gellner's logically compelling if perhaps overschematized explanation of the genesis of nationalism roots the phenomenon in the replacement of older localized and isolated forms of community (village; tribe) by mass urban society, in the spread of literacy among a heterogeneous urban population, and in the inevitable conflicts over resources among differently socialized ethnic groups coexisting in a larger and more complex industrial society.[11] Probably the most widely cited of modernist studies is Benedict Anderson's analysis of the psychological transformations involved in the creation of the new type of imagined community known as the nation. Anderson's complex situating of the origins of modern nationalism in the conjunction of three historical processes—the decline of older forms of broader community (universal religion and dynastic state); the emergence of new ways of conceptualizing time and space (as exemplified in the newspaper and the novel); and the solidification and spread of vernacular languages through print-capitalism—stands as the most comprehensive and stimulating recent etiology of modern nationalism.[12]

The primordialist approach takes much of its inspiration from the emerging subdiscipline of sociobiology, with its emphasis on the role of kinship in determining animal and by extension human behavior.[13] John

Armstrong's detailed analysis of the enduring force of ethnicity in Christian and Islamic history, and Anthony Smith's overview of the character of historical *ethnies* and the ways in which modern nations have built their solidarity on preexisting ethnic ties, represent the more tempered and historically based perennialist variation that draws attention to the importance of communal memory, myth, and symbolism in the formation of modern nations.[14]

Not all recent work fits neatly into the primordialist or modernist categories. John Breuilly's systematic comparison of the political conditions in which different nationalisms have emerged emphasizes how the nature of the state and elite competition for the control of state institutions have shaped the specific trajectories taken by different nationalist movements.[15] Eric Hobsbawm's and Terence Ranger's concept of "invented tradition"—how nationalist ideologues and political leaders consciously create a reservoir of legitimizing symbols and ceremonies sometimes through the reinterpretation of existing beliefs and customs, sometimes out of whole cloth—offers a useful analytical compromise between the extremes of primordialism and modernism.[16] Hobsbawm's more recent historical examination of *Nations and Nationalism Since 1780* provides a subtle discussion of the changing concept of the nation over time, as well as of the complex and not totally polar relationship between class and nation, socialism and nationalism, in modern Europe.[17] Liah Greenfeld's detailed analysis of five major nationalisms (English, French, Russian, German, and American) emphasizes the manner in which these individual nationalisms derived their particular character from the crisis of identity experienced by their elites during the process of modernization.[18] With reference to non-Western nationalisms of the colonial era, Partha Chatterjee's recent work on nationalism in India suggests the need to distinguish between the political realm where nationalist discourse is heavily influenced by metropolitan precedents and where nationalists perforce contend for control of the new colonial state, and the cultural realm where a quite different and more autonomous set of new "nationalist" patterns, institutions, and values can emerge.[19]

The semiotic or postmodernist approach to nationalism assumes the nation to be a discursive entity created by narrativity. As Homi Bhabha writes, "[t]he nation's 'coming into being' as a system of cultural signification, as the representation of social *life* rather than the discipline of social *polity*, emphasizes th[e] instability of knowledge . . . . The emergence of the political 'rationality' of the nation as a form of narrative—textual strategies, metaphoric displacements, sub-texts and figurative strategems—has its own history."[20] Scholars working in this tradition focus on the "narrativistic constituents" of nationalism, the textual structures, tropes, and forms of emplotment characteristic of different nationalist narratives.[21]

Both because the phenomenon of nationalism itself is so varied and because the substantive findings of recent scholarship sometimes pull in different directions, the overall contribution of the new literature on nationalism is difficult to summarize. One clear contribution by modernist writers such as Gellner and Anderson has been to sharpen our appreciation of how intimately nationalism is related to the many sweeping nonpolitical changes of the modern epoch such as printing, literacy, urbanization, changing social roles, and even new ways of comprehending space and time. At the same time, the work of scholars such as Armstrong and Smith provide examples of the indisputable significance of existing ethnic bonds and of the centrality of (reinterpreted) traditions in the construction of modern nations. A less ideologically colored approach to the relationship between the concepts of nationalism and socialism has softened the presumed incompatibility of these two forms of ideology and social organization. The inclusion of non-European (both American and non-Western) examples in recent scholarship has eroded the earlier overemphasis on language as the primary national bond and also points to the need to distinguish between the political trajectory of nationalism on the one hand and its cultural articulation on the other.

More than anything else, recent work has disaggregated nationalism. Concepts such as a nationalist "psyche" or "mind" have been dismissed as essentialist reifications that distort the complexities of history. Quite different causal tracks underlying the emergence and spread of specific nationalisms have been delineated; the presence of numerous and shifting bases for individual nationalisms have been identified. The pretensions of nationalists themselves to speak on behalf of the nation are no longer taken at face value, as such factors as ethnicity, regional loyalty, class, gender, religion and subculture are acknowledged to have produced competing and sometimes drastically different concepts of nationalism within the body of a single "nation." Contingency, multiplicity, and fluidity are the principles underlying contemporary scholarship on nationalism.

NATIONALISM IN THE ARAB MIDDLE EAST

A noteworthy feature of the new scholarship on nationalism is its relative neglect of nationalism in the Arab Middle East. With the partial exceptions of the sociological analyses by Gellner and Smith, which contain occasional references to Arab societies, and the historical discussions by Armstrong and Breuilly, which include specific Middle Eastern case studies, nationalism in the Arab Middle East has received little attention in the recent theoretical literature on nationalism.

For its part, scholarship on modern Arab history has not taken full advantage of the insights offered in recent theoretical work. Accounts of nationalism in Arab Asia and Egypt, the classical centers of "Arab" nationalism, have most often chronicled the evolution of nationalist movements, especially vis-à-vis the backdrop of the struggle against European imperialism, or have described nationalist ideology as articulated by intellectuals and party or regime spokesmen.[22] Models offered to account for the emergence and spread of nationalist sentiment and activism have on the whole been reactive (a response to European imperialism and the collapse of the Ottoman/Islamic order), imitative (the fascination of leading intellectuals with European culture), or diffusionist (the gradual spread of nationalist concepts from their European homeland to the Middle East). Much less attention has been paid to the aspects of the phenomenon that bulk largest in the new theoretical literature (e.g., the social and psychological bases of nationalism; the dissemination of new identities within society; the non-elite dimensions of nationalism).

Only in the past few decades have empirical studies of nationalism in the Arab Middle East begun to draw from the new theoretical scholarship. The main thrust has been to cultivate a polycentric or "peripheral" perspective on nationalism, as scholars attend to the numerous regional, confessional, generational, and socioeconomic factors that have shaped the many temporal and spatial variants of nationalism. As scholars trace the diverse histories of different forms of nationalism in Arab societies, the notion of a homogeneous and hegemonic Arab nationalism so often projected by ideologues is being decentered. The genesis and evolution of nationalism is increasingly being viewed as a multifaceted process whose roots lie in the socioeconomic processes of the modern era and whose meaning extends beyond elites to broader sectors of society.[23]

Temporally, the primary focus of much of the existing scholarship on nationalism in the Arab Middle East has been on its genesis in the late nineteenth and early twentieth centuries. A valuable collaborative volume on this early phase of the history of Arab nationalism was published in 1991.[24] As yet, however, there has been no work of synthesis in which the new theoretical insights have been applied to the broad range of Arab nationalisms as they developed from the World War I period onward.

This volume is an initial attempt to fill this lacuna. The authors of its fourteen essays were invited to rethink their work on aspects of nationalism in the Arab world in terms of the new approaches to nationalism that have been suggested in recent decades. Each essay stands alone as a study of a specific facet of nationalism in the Middle East. Most, however, revolve around certain broad themes. The essays can be read most productively if considered in light of those themes.

NARRATIVITY I
MECHANICS OF HISTORIOGRAPHY:
HOW ACADEMICS CONSTRUCT NATIONALIST HISTORY

Several essays in this volume concentrate on metahistorical issues of historiography and scholarly interpretation of Middle Eastern nationalisms. Israel Gershoni attempts a comprehensive survey of the two successive narrative approaches prevailing in Western scholarship about nationalism in the Arab Middle East, the first in the 1950s and 1960s, the second from the 1970s onward. Employing conceptual tools suggested by Hayden White, Gershoni identifies the main paradigms, tropes, and rhetorical strategies characteristic of the earlier narrative that treated Arab nationalism as a unitary and hegemonic ideology and the later more nuanced peripheralist approach concerned with the detailed analysis of local, regional, and communal variants of Arab nationalism in Egypt and the Fertile Crescent. He also shows how the political fortunes of Arab nationalism itself impinged on its emplotment by academics. When Arab nationalism dominated political discourse and the aspiration for integral Arab unity seemed a realistic possibility in the 1950s and 1960s, essentialist interpretations of the phenomenon as a uniform hegemonic construct were prevalent. With the relative eclipse of pan-Arabism in the 1970s and 1980s, a more pluralist perspective emerged in which localized subnationalisms (territorial, communal, and state-oriented) are discerned as having constituted formidable alternatives to the concept of one indivisible Arab nation. With this demonstration of the inquirer's imbrication in the object of his study, Gershoni calls for greater awareness by researchers regarding their own susceptibility to how contemporary currents can influence their reading of the past. To this end he suggests that a polycentric approach, with its greater attention to communities and movements outside the presumptive mainstream of Arab nationalism, be expanded.

After examining some of the central historiographical debates found in the current theoretical literature on nationalism, Fred Halliday suggests "comparative contingency" as a useful framework for the study of modern nationalisms. Beyond identifying the general historicity of a given nation and understanding both the specific factors contributing to its formation and the specific ideological content of its doctrines, Halliday insists upon the need for close attention to the instrumentality of nationalism; how the nationalism in question corresponded to or conflicted with the values and interests of particular social and political forces, and thus how it was used, resisted, or changed in the hurly-burly of political life. He then applies this approach of comparative contingency to the case of the Yemen. His historical discussion on the one hand demythologizes the essentialist and teleological claims of official Yemeni nationalist ideology; on the other, it demonstrates the manner in which Yemeni nationalism consists of a constantly shifting field of pre-Islamic, Islamic, local, and regional elements that have been utilized in different ways by different Yemenis at different times.

Gabriel Piterberg's contribution focuses on the way in which Egyptian academics have based their nationalist narratives on presumed dichotomies (objective/subjective, material/ideological, content/form, East/West). Drawing on the work of Hayden White, Benedict Anderson, and Timothy Mitchell, he proceeds to problematize the apparently self-evident quality of such dichotomies and thereby to undermine the assumptions underlying much of nationalist historical narrative. The subject of his exercise in deconstruction is the writings of several leading Egyptian historians on Egyptian nationalism. With close attention both to narrative structure and the use of language, Piterberg shows the extent to which their narratives are premised on the culturalist and essentialist axioms of European Orientalism concerning Egypt's Islamic/Ottoman past and are influenced by the assumptions of the territorial nationalism they purport to describe. The Egyptian historical narrative presented by these authors is intended to shape, transmit, and perpetuate a territorialist collective memory and imagined community.

Narrativity 2
Mechanics of Ideology:
How Nationalists Construct History

While the first three essays engage in this self-analysis of the state of the historiographic art, others consider the modes of presentation employed by nationalists to portray history in their own image. William Cleveland reconsiders the foundational text for the study of Arab nationalism, George Antonius's The Arab Awakening (1938), in terms of recent analyses of nationalist narrative, imagery, and symbolism. Although ostensibly a work of scholarship, the book was clearly drafted with an eye to informing British public opinion and thereby influencing British policy towards Arab nationalism. Cleveland's close reading of the text dissects the various ways in which Antonius tailored his historical references and framed his narrative mindful of its impact on this target audience. Postulating three essentialistic criteria for nationhood (ethnicity, shared tradition, and language), Antonius reasons that since the Arabs possess these features they merit national existence, i.e., political sovereignty. Antonius supplies ample "evidence" of the national consciousness of the Arab masses and of their involvement in the national project; his account also makes emotional and effective use of the symbols and tropes of nationhood (maps and flags, martyrs and historical destiny). Cleveland's essay presents *The Arab Awakening* as a textbook example of a historian's imagining of the nation. His concluding section indicates that there is considerable evidence that Western policy-makers were influenced by it and thus that, beyond its historiographical importance, the book also contributed to the later political trajectory of Arab nationalism.

Reeva Simon examines both the intellectual content and the practical aspects of a different attempt at Arab nation-formation—the efforts of the new monarchical regime in Iraq during the interwar period to establish the ideological dominance of a unitary Arab nationalism over an ethnically diverse Iraqi population. She identifies the state educational system as the primary agency through which Arab nationalism was imposed on the populace by an educational establishment which took Sati` al-Husri's twin criteria of nationhood—language and common history—as gospel. Simon emphasizes the failure of this imposition of nationalism from above. Attending to the voices of communal identity ignored in the official Arab nationalist ideology (those of Shi`ites, Kurds, Christians, Jews), she demonstrates the limited and sometimes destructive results of the Iraqi state's attempt to create a hegemonic sense of nationhood in an ethnically divided country.

Beth Baron approaches nationalist imagining from a different angle. The specific concern of her essay is how nationalist iconography in Egypt employed the image of the woman to symbolize the Egyptian nation and what the changing ways in which the image of women were used by nationalists has to say about both nationalism and the position of women in Egypt. She excavates the complex sources of the various images of women found in nationalist painting, sculpture, and caricature and suggests the different ideological purposes that female imagery served (inculcating a romantic attachment by males to the nation when portrayed as a woman; invoking notions of the need to defend the honor of a feminine Egypt). Baron details how the symbolic portrayal of Egypt as woman differed from period to period as well as how it was manipulated differently by sundry groups. Originally the imitation of European examples, the increasing frequency with which Egypt was portrayed as a woman was intimately linked to the social emancipation of women in Egypt, particularly to the unveiling (=liberation) of elite women. By the 1920s, two images predominated. Where the image of Egypt as a peasant woman was wielded to advance a nationalist and populist agenda, the image of Egypt as a modern woman was part and parcel of the Westernizing project of the Egyptian elite of the interwar era. By limning the array of uses and intentions involved in forms of visual nationalist narration, Baron uncovers the dissonance among competing visions of the nation.

DISCURSIVE COMPETITION: THE INTERPLAY OF RIVAL NATIONALIST VISIONS

Baron's essay analyzing the different and sometimes incompatible uses of female imagery by Egyptian nationalists points to a central theme of many of the contributions to this volume. The twentieth-century Arab world provides ample evidence of the coexistence and competition of alternative understandings of communal identity. The narratives that nationalist ideologues create are seldom uncontested. Deployed against rival nationalist visions, they bear the scars of combat. The emphasis on diversity in recent empirical studies of Arab nationalism is an attempt to give full historical weight to the interplay of nationalist discourses both within and among Arab communities.

Two essays have the competition among rival nationalist conceptions as their primary focus. Donald Reid's examination of the scholarly discipline of Egyptology in the early twentieth century analyzes the efforts of indigenous Egyptian students of ancient Egypt to find a place in the Egyptological sun, and the tensions between the national prejudices of Egyptologists and the ostensibly international values of their profession. It is a complex story rich in ironies about both the institutional politics of an academic discipline and the abiding presence of nationalism in the world of scholarship. Reid shows how difficult it was for indigenous Egyptians—presumably the descendants of the ancient Egyptians whose achievements Egyptology extolled—to win the respect of their Western "colleagues" and to rise to prominence in a theoretically internationalist profession. Woven into Reid's analysis of Egyptology is a discussion of the place of Pharaonic referents in Egyptian nationalism itself, how Egyptian nationalists appropriated Egyptological assets in order to build a new community of memory. Many forces in Egyptian society were involved in disseminating an awareness of Pharaonic symbolism in early twentieth-century Egypt: from above, educational works and curricula, museums, stamps, money; from below, tour guides, merchants in archeological artifacts, laborers at Pharaonic digs. Based in the first instance on the results of Egyptology but radiating well beyond the scholarly realm, ancient Pharaonic referents and symbols became an enduring part of the complex national identity of modern Egyptians.

The discursive competition of different national orientations in Egypt in the 1950s are the subject of James Jankowski's essay. Examining first the interplay of Egyptian, Arab, and Islamic strands of identity in the nationalist outlook of Jamal `Abd al-Nasir (Nasser), he argues that the nationalist perspective of the leader of the post-1952 regime remained primarily Egyptianist in the early years of the Egyptian revolution. When a Nasserist commitment to Arab nationalism did emerge (the mid-1950s), it remained closely linked to his anti-imperialism and his perception of the utility—indeed the necessity—of Arab solidarity for the achievement of Egyptian national goals. During the same period, the religious referent was secondary in both Nasser's political vocabulary and his hierarchy of politically meaningful loyalties. Next tracing the political adoption of Arab nationalist policies by the Egyptian government between 1952 and 1958, Jankowski shows the gradual, hesitant, and only partial commitment of the leaders of the new regime to Arab nationalism up to the formation of the United Arab Republic in 1958. He concludes by emphasizing the importance of existing state structures—what Sami Zubeida and Roger Owen have termed the "political field" created by the colonial state—as a determinant of nationalist political behavior in the Arab world.

POLYCENTRISM

One of the key insights of the new theoretical literature on nationalism is an emphasis on the simultaneous presence of various national (and other) identities both in individuals and communities, an idea that challenges the exclusive and absolute claims made by nationalist ideology on identity and allegiance. Rashid Khalidi's contribution to this volume discusses the coexistence of multiple foci of self-definition and loyalty among Palestinian Arabs early in the twentieth century, and goes on to delineate the process whereby a specifically Palestinian Arab identity coalesced and became prevalent as a result of political circumstances during and after World War I. Multiple religious, dynastic (e.g., Ottoman), local/regional, and ethnic Arab affiliations overlapped in the consciousness of articulate Palestinians before World War I. Khalidi argues that it was the political upheavals (Ottoman defeat; the failure of an indigenous successor-state uniting ex-Ottoman Syria to survive; the inauguration of British rule over a territorially distinct Palestine; the intensification of the Zionist presence and challenge under a British umbrella) and the corresponding politicization of Palestinians due to unsettled conditions between 1914 and 1923 that combined to establish the local hegemony of a specifically Palestinian national identity in the wake of the Great War. On the one hand, Khalidi's paper indicates the limitations of a uni-dimensional model of nationalism based on an idealized version of the Western experience prevalent in the older theoretical literature on nationalism; at the same time, its thesis of a paradigm shift in Pales-tinian political consciousness occurring under the impact of a decade of turmoil suggests the kinds of conditions in which national identity undergoes rapid change.

Khalidi's is not the only possible perspective on the evolution of the "peripheral" nationalism of the Palestinians. Musa Budeiri also takes issue with monolithic definitions of identity among Palestinians; like Khalidi, he shows how kin, faction, village, region, religion, and Arabism combined in different quantities at different times to form the multidi-mensional identity of Palestinians. But, viewing Palestinian identity over the (relatively) *longue durée* of the twentieth century, he accords religion, and specifically Islam, a more prominent place in the national identity and political behavior of Palestinians. In his view the symbols and mythology of Palestinian nationalism under the British Mandate were suffused with Islam; even when a discrete and largely secular Pal-estinian national identity did coalesce, a process he dates to the 1960s, it did not replace an Islamic orientation for most Palestinians. Thus the prominence of Islamicist movements today on the West Bank and in the Gaza Strip comes as no surprise; Islam has always provided much of the vocabulary of Palestinian activism. Budeiri's explanation of the persis-tence of Islam in Palestinian nationalism relies in part on the notion of the centrality of the existing "political field," but in the Palestinian case in negative terms. It is the absence of a Palestinian territorial state—both the object and the agent of nonreligious forms of nationalism else-where in the Arab world—that has fostered the continuing salience of Islam in Palestinian political life.

Emmanuel Sivan's contribution addresses a phenomenon in com-parison to which Arab nationalism itself appears peripheral—the con-temporary Islamic movement and how its ideologues view Arab nationalism. His analysis of Islamicist attitudes towards Arab national-ism indicates a visceral rejection of Arab nationalism due to its sec-ularist content, its putative provenance in the West, its quasiracist divi-sion of the Islamic community or *umma* along bogus ethnic lines, and (not least) the persecution its adherents have inflicted on Islamicists themselves. However, Sivan also notes the ways in which Islamicist ideologues partially take account of and allow for identities other than their primary religious one, including state nationalisms and local allegiances. Leading figures in the Islamic movement do acknowledge the value for Arabs in identifying with a specifically Arab culture and history, albeit not with a secular and chauvinist Arab nationalism. This qualified endorsement of plural identities by Islamicist spokesmen testifies to the importance of the polycentric approach in understanding Middle Eastern identity, national and otherwise.

Sivan's contribution is methodological as well as substantive. His primary source for Islamicist attitudes about Arab nationalism is the distinctly contemporary one of audiocassettes. In addition to what these convey about Islamicist ideas, he suggests that this oral medium of communication has added a new dimension to public discourse. Beyond the immediacy and directness of a message delivered via cassette, which increases its affective quality, oral media such as cassettes can transmit concepts of identity and loyalty without recourse to literacy, thereby opening new horizons for the dissemination and popularization of nationalist (or in this case antinationalist) ideas. The emphasis of Gellner and Anderson on the crucial importance of print media and standardized language in the history of nationalism may now have been overtaken by technology. The new oral and visual means of communication developed in recent decades (radio; television; their associated audio- and videocassettes) have created a new non-literate option for transmitting messages that can circumvent the formal literate culture in which nationalism was traditionally expressed. Whether orality is connected specifically to the diffusion of populist Islamic concepts of identity and loyalty while written communication is inherently suited to the dissemination of linguistic (Arabic) nationalism is a possibility that needs further research.

NATIONALIST DIFFUSION FROM THE BOTTOM UP: OTHER VOICES

Previous scholarship on nationalism in the Middle East focused on the role of the elites presumed responsible for the formulation of nationalist concepts and perceived as the agents of nationalism's dissemination. As Philip Khoury begins his essay, "[t]he study of Arab nationalism, as an ideology and as a system of political and social mobilization, has until recently concentrated on grand narratives constructed by and about elites." While summoning scholars to add subaltern groups—

peasants, workers, minorities, women—to the Arab nationalist picture, Khoury also cautions that this must be done appropriately. Rather than aspiring to a new grand narrative in which the histories of subaltern groups are squeezed into a new, seamless, undifferentiated account, he instead urges, in the fashion of Jean-François Lyotard, the construction of numerous micronarratives in which each strain of subnationalism would retain its historical specificity.[25] Family, town, village, religion, class, profession, and gender all inflected Arab nationalism, and thus there is no single nationalist narrative whether elites or subalterns are at issue.

The final three essays of this volume are concerned with the recovery of recessive strains of Arab nationalism emanating from groups below the dominant elite. Thus James Gelvin identifies and dissects populist nationalism in Syria within the new Arab state headed by Amir Faysal in the post-World War I years. Previous studies of Faysal's regime have dismissed the forms of mass sentiment and mobilization examined by Gelvin as "mob" activity; in contrast, Gelvin stresses that what he terms this "other Arab nationalism" was an authentic form of nationalist expression that must be taken into account if nationalism in the Arab world is to be properly understood. He approaches Syrian populism from an unusually broad perspective, placing it in the context of long-term historical change in Syria and evaluating it in the light of recent scholarship on similar populist phenomena elsewhere in the world. Gelvin analyzes how the growth of market relations and rapid urbanization spurred the growth of "horizontal" organizations with improvised egalitarian structures that for the first time gave subaltern strata the power to pursue their agendas. Laboring groups, popular committees, and declining elites such as the `ulama manifested quite a different nationalist profile than the dominant elites; reticent about the benefits of capitalism in light of their own recent experience, they tended to see the future in terms of an idealized communal past. As with other examples of populist nationalism, they constituted themselves as "the nation" as against the more Westernized, politically dominant "antination" represented by the Syrian and Hijazi elite.

Zachary Lockman contemplates the seemingly self-defeating and antinationalist behavior of Arab laborers in Mandatory Palestine as they, against the counsel of Palestinian nationalist intellectuals situated outside the labor arena, periodically sought to make common cause with Jewish labor as represented by the Histadrut labor union. Lockman emphasizes the simultaneity of the disparate and even conflicting identities found in individuals. Borrowing from Michel Foucault, he argues that nationalism is not a thing but a set of forces that derives meaning from its relative position within a discursive field.[26]

Lockman shows that the form of nationalism that emerged among the Palestinian working classes had rather a different cast from that manifested higher on the socioeconomic ladder. Elite formulations of nationalism in Palestine conceptualized Palestinian identity as an absolute category that brooked no divided loyalties and that applied similarly to everyone encompassed by its definition of "Arab." Insofar as working class Palestinians were less influenced by abstruse definitions than by the tangible bonds of kinship, locale, and religion as well as by the imperatives of economic survival, their outlook and behavior sometimes compromised the pristine ideals of Arab nationalism as defined by the Palestinian elite. Thus their sense of nationalism paled before their resentment over the influx of Syrian and Egyptian workers into Palestine who wished to take advantage of the relative prosperity of the Mandate and who threatened to displace local workers. Elitist intellectual constructions of Arab nationalism, univocal and totalizing, brands such Palestinian workers as dupes or collaborators betraying their authentic national interest. In doing so, they provide a measure of the extent to which essentialist constructions make nationalism's "complexity, contestation, and constructedness disappear."

Philip Khoury's own contribution explores the tension and rivalry between older and younger strata within the interwar Syrian elite. Taking the competition among various nationalist organizations and movements in Mandatory Syria in the mid-1930s as his subject, he analyzes the triumph of the National Bloc—a party previously tarnished by policies viewed as collaborationist with the French and whose leadership was composed of absentee landlords and commercial bourgeoisie—over the League of National Action based in a younger and more ideological demigeneration of Syrians. His conclusion is that the National Bloc's pragmatic responsiveness to the needs of the nonliterate urban and rural masses made it more attractive than the doctrinaire League with its ruminations over future Arab unity. In his earlier work Khoury had represented this openness and flexibility on the part of the National Bloc as a deleterious form of "factionalism" that had hampered its effectiveness as a nationalist organization. Khoury has reconsidered this view, now interpreting the Bloc's "factionalism" as a form of pluralism that enabled it to meet the needs of a variety of constituencies. The National Bloc's political longevity was less an indication of the weakness of Arab nationalism in Syria than a demonstration of the complex reality of Arab nationalism. This is a fitting note to end an overview of our collection of essays: the multivalence of National Bloc politics was precisely what enabled it to succeed against rivals wedded to a vision of national homogeneity and uniformity.

BROADER IMPLICATIONS

The essays in this volume are not the last word on the subject of nationalism in the Arab Middle East. Geographically, they focus more heavily on certain regions than on others. Topically, they treat particular nationalist moments or movements while neglecting other, equally worthwhile, dimensions of the subject. Their findings are often suggestive rather than definitive, opening new doors to the understanding of nationalism rather than serving to close debate on the topic.

Nonetheless, beyond their individual value as case studies of specific aspects of the history of nationalism in the Arab Middle East, these essays also serve more general purposes. On one level, their novel approaches and fresh conclusions can make a contribution to defining the agenda for further research on the place and meaning of nationalism in modern Arab history. More broadly, although their purpose is to illuminate the history of nationalism in the Arab Middle East through drawing on insights found in the new theoretical literature on nationalism, they simultaneously contribute to the current scholarly effort to rethink nationalism as a central phenomenon of the modern era.

Considered collectively, the essays indicate the need to question earlier models that framed nationalism in the Arab world in homogeneous terms. Certainly in the Arab Middle East, nationalism has everywhere been layered and inflected by multiple influences and identities. Regional, statal, religious, and class considerations have tugged in different directions, in the process making nationalism in Arab societies a complex field of relations and interactions. The traditional dichotomy of Arab nationalism around two major poles, be they unitary "pan-Arab" versus local or regional nationalisms, religious versus secular allegiances, territorial versus ethnic/linguistic affiliations, or "traditional" versus "modern" forms, by no means exhausts the collage of variants of identity and loyalty found in the Arab Middle East in our century. Such dichotomies cannot reflect the shadings and interpenetration of different kinds of Arab communal expression and action.

Similarly, the essays serve to deflate essentialist notions to the effect that nationalism once constituted stabilizes in a fixed dogma and set of practices. Constantly in motion, Arab nationalism has been incarnated in different modes at different times. The fluidity of national loyalties among Arabs is striking. The relationship among variant forms of Arab nationalism has undergone dramatic shifts from period to period. The story of nationalism in the Arab Middle East is largely one of contestation and the clash of rival national identities and agendas; correspondingly, writing the history of Arab nationalism consists of explicating the interplay among alternative nationalist visions and programs. Arab nationalism was and is a dynamic construct, and is most fruitfully studied as such.

Several essays problematize the premise that nationalism emanates exclusively from elites and is imposed from the top down upon society. They demonstrate the active nature of the reception of nationalism by various non-elite strata and the reciprocal influences in the production and reproduction of nationalist ideas and behavior. They indicate that we have much to learn about nationalism not only through examining elites, regimes, ideologies, and movements but also through studying subaltern groups, popular organizations, and mass culture.

Various essays draw attention to the rich assemblage of agencies through which nationalism is articulated and disseminated. Beyond drawing their data from "canonical" forms of nationalist expression such as nationalist tracts, the press, and speeches by nationalist leaders, contributors demonstrate the importance for our understanding of nationalism of hitherto relatively neglected sources such as visual materials, institutional arrangements in which nationalist attitudes are embedded (e.g., archeology), and newer forms of communication such as audiocassettes. The diverse sources utilized in the essays in this collection do not exhaust the portfolio of relevant sources for the study of nationalism: literature, music, and contemporary popular art forms such as film, radio, and television also have much to say about nationalist imaginings. Just as nationalist attitudes are in constant evolution, so too are the instruments that carry the nationalist message: today spoken Arabic [`ammiyya or other forms of "middle language"] as conveyed by radio, television, cartoons, or cassettes have supplemented and possibly even replaced the paramountcy of the written word [*fusha* or formal literary Arabic] as the main vehicle of collective self-definition in the Arab world.

Perhaps the primary thrust of this volume is to confirm the multi-faceted character of nationalism. Nationalism is simultaneously real and imagined, authentic and invented, concrete and discursive. Through the programs and operations of Ministries of Education and National Guidance as well as via nonofficial organizations, movements, and spontaneous groupings, "imagined" concepts of the nation acquire a tangible existence and a practical character that shape society and inform behavior. The differentiation between imagination and reality in the study of nationalist thought is specious; nationalist imaginings become part and parcel of nationalist reality, and attempts to separate them only obscure an understanding of the phenomenon.

While taking nationalism as their object of inquiry, the essays also point to the need to decenter nationalism within the scholarly enterprise. Now, at the close of a century in which nationalist forms of speculation and activity dominated public life in the Arab world, we are increasingly aware that nationalism has not been the exclusive motor of communal identity and activism in Arab societies. The analysis of nationalism has to be folded into a broader scholarly project that gives due attention to the study of local community structures, class and gender divisions, religious and other forms of communal belonging, and to the interplay among all of these. At the same time that nationalism is a "field," it is part of a larger field that encompasses much that is not explicitly "nationalist." Comprehending nationalism requires situating it in this broader context of only tangentially nationalist or non-nationalist forces.

Thus the essays assembled in this volume do not afford any sense of closure on the subject of Arab nationalism. Rather, they suggest new avenues for research that can contribute to a fuller—but probably never a complete—understanding of one of the most complex and dynamic facets of Middle Eastern history.

Rethinking Nationalism
in the
Arab Middle East

—

PART I

Narrativity I

Mechanics of Historiography:
How Academics Construct Nationalist History

1

Rethinking the Formation of Arab Nationalism in the Middle East, 1920–1945

Old and New Narratives

Israel Gershoni

Benedict Anderson's characterization of nationalism as "an imagined political community" certainly applies to the Arab Middle East.[1] Various forms of "imagined community" have competed for Arab loyalties in the modern era: territorial nationalism, nation-state nationalism, and a broad range of Islamic or religious identities.[2] None of these imaginings, however, seems to have been so successful in proselytizing Arab communities as a nationalism based on the cultural-linguistic dimension of Arabness, crossing geographic and religious boundaries. This "Arab nationalism" [*al-qawmiyya al-`arabiyya*] remains a crucial form of identity and ideology even if it has become fashionable since the end of the 1970s to speak about "the end of pan-Arab nationalism,"[3] and even if its "pan-movement" impulses have faded considerably.[4]

Historically, Arab nationalism emerged and evolved as a theoretical and operative system in the period between the two world wars. It reached maturity at the end of World War II with the founding of the Arab League in 1945. It did not arise ex nihilo in the aftermath of World War I, however. In the latter part of the nineteenth century and the first two decades of the twentieth, it emerged as an opposition movement in the Arab provinces of the Ottoman Empire, for the most part seeking cultural autonomy within the framework of the Ottoman state.[5] An early minority trend espousing Arab national separatism "became the overwhelmingly dominant movement in these [Arab] territories"[6] after World War I, following the final collapse of the Ottoman Empire. Despite the milestone of 1945, the movement's ideological impact and political influence peaked only in the 1950s and 1960s. With Nasserism and Baʿthism, Arab nationalism was transformed into a revolutionary movement, appealing to broad masses by means of a socialist program, populist rhetoric, and a deeper commitment to the idea of establishing a single Arab state.

This essay is concerned neither with that later, revolutionary stage nor with the early, seminal period. Rather, it deals with the interim period of the development of Arab nationalism from 1920 to 1945. This was the era in which it moved from the intellectual periphery to the cultural and political center, being accepted by ruling elites as official ideology and policy. For research on nationalism in the Arab world, this may well be the most interesting period, for it provides an outstanding case-study in processes of intellectual formation, ideological dissemination, social reception, and political institutionalization of an idea.

The focus of this essay is the successive historiographic narratives dealing with Arab nationalism from 1920 to 1945. The study of Arab nationalism can be said to have gone through three stages. The first consisted of contemporary accounts of the aspiration for Arab unity that emerged in the Arab world in the late 1930s and in the 1940s. The sporadic surveys and reports of this stage were a mixture of journalism and scholarship on the state of the pan-Arab movement.[7]

In the second stage, the 1950s and 1960s, the study of Arab nationalism became a scholarly pursuit and achieved academic standing. Serious historical works systematically reconstructed the formation of Arab nationalism in the interwar period and beyond, until the 1950s. These researches into the ideological origins of Arab nationalism constituted a comprehensive narrative that became the canonical framework for further study. In the present essay, the scholarly literature of this stage is termed the "early narrative" or "old narrative."

The main thesis of this essay is the contention that in the early 1970s a new stage emerged in the study of Arab nationalism. This third stage constitutes a distinct narrative that may be defined as the "later narrative" or "new narrative." Its thrust is a systematic reassessment of the formative processes of Arab nationalism in the period from 1920 to 1945. By treating previously unresearched topics, citing new evidence, and employing innovative methodologies, this narrative enables a thorough rethinking of the history of Arab nationalism. Rethinking, however, does not entail revisionism; the new narrative evolved out of the old, refining and supplementing it. Whatever the gradient of change, little if any notice has been paid to the very real transition in historiographic paradigms.[8]

This essay, then, is more concerned with metahistory than history. No "direct" discussion of Arab nationalism itself is offered, though there is an analysis of the modes through which it is represented in both narratives, the old and the new. Our purpose will be to define and characterize the two narratives, to examine the internal discourse unique to each— what Hayden White terms "constituent tropological strategies [that] account for the generation of the different interpretations of history"[9]— and to underline their specific contributions to the study of nationalism in the Arab Middle East. Although our main concern is with "metahistorical" representations relating to the development of Arab nationalism, it is hoped that such a treatment will also shed new light on its "actual history" during its formative period from 1920 to 1945, assuming, optimistically, the tenability of such a notion as "actual history."

THE OLD NARRATIVE

The early narrative was formulated in the 1950s and 1960s as Arab nationalism reached its zenith. In large measure, that narrative was an attempt by scholars to trace, from the present to the recent past, the reasons for the success of Arab nationalism and to explain how it became the premier ideological and political force in the Arab world. To a certain extent, this early narrative is already present in the works of Hazem Zaki Nuseibeh and Fayez Sayegh.[10] However, it was only with the appearance of the influential studies by Elie Kedourie, Albert Hourani, and Sylvia G. Haim that this narrative was fully shaped.[11] Others who contributed to the emergence of the old narrative were Majid Khadduri, Hans Tütsch, Leonard Binder, Anwar Chejne, Bernard Lewis, W. C. Smith, Patrick Seale, Nissim Rejwan, Hisham Sharabi, and Eliezer Be'eri.[12]

Despite individual differences, the scholarship of this era exhibited key commonalities in its approach to fundamental issues. When did Arab nationalism began to flourish as an idea and as a framework for action? In the periodization of the early narrative, the end of World War I, the collapse of the Ottoman Empire and the founding of separate Arab states under British and French Mandatory rule form the context for the transition to Arabism. Moreover, most of the studies that represent this narrative contain the claim that only in the second half of the interwar period, and more specifically in the decade of the 1930s, did a mature ideology of Arab nationalism take shape. " It was not until the 1930s that a serious attempt was made to define the meaning of Arab nationalism and what constitutes the Arab Nation," notes Haim.[13] Hourani likewise states that primarily in the 1930s, there "began to grow up a new sort of [Arab] nationalism, more thoroughgoing than that of the older generation."[14]

What is the essence of Arab nationalism as represented by the old narrative? The studies of this narrative perceived nationalism above all as an idea. The general paradigm that guided its approach to the study of nationalism was that of the "history of ideas." This was a popular discipline in the study of history in the 1950s and early 1960s, propounded most influentially by Arthur Lovejoy and ramifying into derivative modes of intellectual history.[15] The major project of this form of the history of ideas was to reconstruct "unit-ideas" and "mind," individual or collective. In more ambitious cases it assumed that "the largest distinctive aim of the intellectual historian . . . is to describe and explain the spirit of an age."[16] The underlying supposition was that besides the "theoretical" or "philosophical" interest inherent in the ideas in themselves, they were also the expression of whole cultures or societies, constituting the primary force in shaping their historical evolution and in stimulating processes of social and political change.

More specific influences are also discernible. Elie Kedourie's *Nationalism*, itself distinctly a product of the history of ideas and directly influenced by Lovejoy,[17] had an impact on some of the studies of the early narrative. A greater effect was perhaps that had by the Orientalist, textual-philological tradition and the type of cultural-intellectual history written in its light in this period by G. E. von Grunebaum, W. C. Smith, and especially by H. A. R. Gibb.[18] Thus Nuseibeh's aim in his *The Ideas of Arab Nationalism*, "to explore the genesis, ideas, attitudes, and orientations of Arab nationalism;"[19] Hourani's endeavor in *Arabic Thought in the Liberal Age*, emphasizing "those movements of Arabic thought which accepted the dominant ideas of modern Europe;"[20] Haim's anthology *Arab Nationalism*, focusing on its intellectual history;[21] and, more radically, Sayegh's argument in his *Arab Unity—Hope and Fulfillment* that "ideas have a life of their own" and that "the evolution of an idea is in some measure autonomous"[22]—all furnish clear proof of the impact of the "history of ideas" on the old narrative.

A close analysis of the texts produced by Arab nationalist writers constitutes the major part of the old narrative. Some of these early studies, notably Sayegh, make do with a general, somewhat abstract presentation of "the idea of Arab unity."[23] But for the most part the studies deal with specific texts by leading intellectuals, published in the second half of the 1930s and in the early 1940s. Nuseibeh discusses the thought of seven "theoreticians of the Arab national philosophy" (Qustantin Zurayq, `Abdallah al-`Alayili, Raif Khouri, Sati` al-Husri, Niqula Ziyada, Yusuf Haykal, and Nabih Faris);[24] Haim, in what is perhaps the most extensive and detailed analysis, elucidates the writings of eleven prominent "nationalist writers" (Amin al-Rihani, Sami Shawkat, Muhammad Jamil Baihum, Edmond Rabbath, `Abd al-Latif Sharara, `Abdallah al-`Alayili, Sati` al-Husri, `Abd al-Rahman `Azzam, `Abd al-Rahman al-

Bazzaz, Qustantin Zurayq, and Khalil Iskandar Qubrusi) and many other "secondary writers";[25] Hourani analyzes the thought of four "shapers of Arab nationalist doctrine" (`Abd al-Rahman al-Bazzaz, Qustantin Zurayq, Edmond Rabbath and Sati` al-Husri);[26] while Khadduri considers the ideas of five "nationalist thinkers" (Sami Shawkat, Edmond Rabbath, Qustantin Zurayq, `Abd al-Rahman al-Bazzaz and Sati` al-Husri).[27] Thus Rabbath, Zurayq, al-Bazzaz, and especially al-Husri are identified by this narrative as the major theoreticians, those who contributed most significantly to the articulation of the new Arab nationalist doctrine.

According to the early narrative, the central feature of the Arab nationalist ideology of this era was the conviction that the Arabic language was the chief element in forging the Arab nation. "A nation has an objective basis, and in the last analysis this is nothing except language. The Arab nation consists of all who speak Arabic as their mother-tongue, no more, no less."[28] The Arab nation is therefore a linguistic entity, whose spiritual and physical boundaries are those of its tongue.[29]

The adjunct of language is history. The old narrative examines how the nationalist thinkers posited history as the second most important element in the formation of a nation. Arab nationalist theoreticians perceived Arab history as an inexhaustible store of communal heroes, events, periods, traditions, and symbols to be collated in order "to produce a single unified 'past' which gives a convincing and emotionally satisfying account of the present situation of their ethnic kinsmen."[30] Arab nationalist writers went in quest of an erstwhile "golden age" of communal splendor to serve as model for the nation. Reviving classical Arab glory was indispensable for national rebirth. This entailed a systematic historical rehabilitation of the pre-Islamic era, of traditions and civilizations of the ancient Near East, such as those of the Babylonians, the Assyrians, the Pharaohs, the Phoenicians, and sometimes even of Judaism and Christianity. Early Islam was no longer the exclusive primeval golden era, but merely one stage, albeit an important one, in the evolution of the Arab nation.[31]

Although language and history were the primary elements constituting the Arab nation, there were others. Some nationalist writers also noted "religion," "geographical environment," "racial stock," and "common national interests" as "components" of the national community.[32] The precise place and significance of these secondary constituents of nationalism was debated: whereas some writers accepted them as legitimate forces that reinforced language and history in crystallizing the Arab nation, others rejected their role (especially the allegiance to a specific race or territory), arguing that they were at odds with the nation's linguistic-cultural-historical essence and were liable to dissolve it.[33]

Based on this classification of "nationalist components" into legitimate and illegitimate, the nationalist thinkers conventionalized nationalist terminology. The early narrative paid special attention to the creation of "a new vocabulary . . . that took into account, and that would be helpful in coping with, the divergence between the ideal and the reality."[34] At its core, the new vocabulary established the distinction between an affinity for the Arab nation and Arab nationalism [qawm, qawmiyya] and a patriotic affiliation with one's specific homeland [watan, wataniyya]. This distinction was meant to regulate the relations between these two loyalties within one legitimate framework consistent with the aspiration for cultural and political Arab unity [wahda `arabiyya].[35] In contrast, other terms were coined—iqlimiyya (regionalism, provincialism), shu`ubiyya ("narrow chauvinistic loyalty" to Egyptian-Pharaonic, Lebanese-Phoenician, Iraqi-Mesopotamian nationalisms, etc.)—"to denote a reprehensible feeling of loyalty toward a part rather than toward the whole."[36]

Another aspect of the new nationalist theory that was extensively treated by the early narrative concerned the modes in which its proponents portrayed relations between Arab nationalism and Islam. The early studies detail the way in which Arabist writers secularized, modernized, and nationalized Islam so as to make it comport with the postreligious nature of Arab nationalism. They stripped away its universal transcendental and legal dimensions, undermining its status as the supreme arbiter of communal identity. It was relegated to the status of a tool, another "component" to help erect the edifice of Arab national identity. Hourani succinctly describes the metamorphosis that Arab nationalism brought about in the status of Islam:

> The centre of gravity was shifted from Islam as divine law to Islam as a culture; in other words, instead of Arab nationalism being regarded as an indispensable step towards the revival of Islam, Islam was regarded as the creator of the Arab nation, the content of its culture or the object of its collective pride.[37]

External intellectual influences that shaped Arab nationalism were also addressed by the old narrative. In general, most studies of the narrative adopt a diffusionist model whereby nationalism radiated from a European center to a Middle Eastern periphery. They point to a congeries of influences from European philosophies and ideologies absorbed by Arab nationalist thought: German Idealist philosophy from the school of Herder and Fichte; cultural Romanticism of nineteenth-century Germany; the "pan"-nationalist movements of Central and Eastern Europe; the unification of Germany and of Italy, which provided models for founding a single broad nation-state eliminating artificial political entities; the "integral" and historicist nationalist doctrine propounded by French nationalism of the late nineteenth century (notably by Barres and Maurras); and, more immediately, European fascism and Nazism of the 1930s. The impact of liberal nationalism, in its Anglo-Saxon or French form, was, according to the old narrative, overshadowed by the powerful influences originating in Central and Eastern Europe.

In the view of the old narrative, these influences were an important and generally negative contribution to the emergence of the totalitarian, organic, and utopian tendencies in Arab nationalism. Arab ideologists considered nationalism to be a total and exclusive framework for human existence. As a modern substitute for religion, it was to furnish a complete and rounded *Lebenswelt*. Haim remarks on the strong influence that totalitarian conceptions exercised on Arab nationalist ideology, especially in al-Husri's version, in which the nation is consecrated as the natural, total, and sole framework for existence.[38] Khadduri points to the irredentist, integralist, Romantic and populist elements that Arab nationalist doctrine took from Europe.[39] Sayegh is critical of the pan-Arab utopia that aims for an all-embracing Arab unity by refusing to recognize "the real, objective, and stubborn elements of *diversity* in the Arab world." In his view, "the Arab mind had adopted uncritically the European political philosophy of nationalism, and applied it to the Arab situation without adaptation or adjustment."[40] Nuseibeh, for his part, dwells on the great similarity between the use of "historical traditions" by integralist French nationalism and its use by Arab nationalist ideologists.[41]

The old narrative's strength lies in the internal textualist presentation of ideas; it is weak in its external contextualist analysis. Since nationalism was predicated primarily as "ideology," it followed that less, if any, importance should be attached to an examination of external forces that were instrumental in its formation and change. The old narrative rarely offers more than a schematic description of some of the historical developments that stimulated the emergence of Arab nationalism in the interwar period. Arab nationalism, the skimpy historical argument goes, is the response of the Arab elites to the collapse of the Ottoman Empire and the death of the Old Order. It is a quest for a new cultural and political identity to supersede the nonviable traditional one.[42] It was also depicted as a reaction to European colonial domination in the post-Ottoman Arab world, a protest against its arbitrary division into atomized, artificial states.[43] Culturally and psychologically, Arab nationalism was portrayed as an expression of deep-rooted

Arab yearning for renewal via a restoration of the splendid Arab past and classical heritage.[44]

Only on the fringes does the old narrative deal with other factors such as the connections between the growth of nationalism and social change, or between nationalist ideology and specific political interests. Hourani gives an account of the radicalization of "a younger generation" in the 1930s based on its social origins,[45] while Kedourie provides a political etiology of the Hashimite regime in Iraq that gave the "pan-Arabist" current of the post-1930 period its "political base."[46] Such sociopolitical explanations are exceptional in the old narrative.

Even less attention is devoted by the early narrative to the processes of dissemination and reception of the Arab nationalist idea at the different levels of culture and society. The old narrative pays scant attention to whether, in those societies in which Arab nationalism predominated (particularly in the Fertile Crescent), it prevailed among non-elites as well. It typically is content to draw conclusions about the nature and influence of nationalist ideology by perusing "high," "formal" texts produced by a handful of "representative" intellectuals, usually ignoring "nonformal" expressions such as can be found in the press or periodicals. In this respect as well Kedourie is exceptional, as evinced by his pioneering examination of how the Iraqi educational system, set up by the Faysal government and directed by al-Husri, functioned as a primary medium for institutionalizing and transmitting Arab nationalism.[47] Kedourie argues that al-Husri's network of schools was effectively a collection of "seminars for political indoctrination," with a mission "to spread faith in the unity of the Arab nation and to disseminate consciousness of its past glories."[48]

Where the old narrative does attend to the political influence exercised by Arab nationalism, it does not always establish historical connections between idea and praxis. While generally linking the growing strength of pan-Arab ideas and sentiments in the 1930s and 1940s to the increasing interest shown by Arab politicians in forms of Arab unity that generated the inter-Arab system, crowned by the foundation of the Arab League in 1945,[49] the old narrative does not apprise us of how deeply Arab nationalist ideology penetrated the official political mind and to what extent it affected Arab governments and policy-makers. In some cases the studies create the impression that the Arab League was not a culmination of that ideology but either the product of British imperial scheming aimed at consolidating Britain's postwar position in the Middle East or a purely political mechanism intended to alleviate tensions and rivalries among Arab states.[50] Sayegh is perhaps the lone old narrative representative to discern in the League's founding any

causality immanent to Arab nationalist ideology: "[i]nter-Arab cooperation and coordination, of policies and actions, [were] already enjoying
the wholehearted support of the peoples and intellectuals dedicated to
the idea of Arab unity."[51]

A dismissive evaluation of Egypt's position vis-à-vis emergent Arab
nationalism is another feature of the old narrative. Virtually all the early
studies agree that Egypt played almost no role in the evolution of Arab
nationalism from 1920–1945. Arab nationalism, it was argued, pertained
only to the Fertile Crescent, as Egypt was then in the throes of a territorial and Pharaonic-Mediterranean nationalism with radically isolationist tendencies.[52] According to this interpretation, Egypt's transition
to Arab nationalism and to the adoption of a pan-Arab ideology and policy, occurred only with the Free Officers revolution in 1952, and defini-
tively only with the emergence of Nasserism in the mid-1950s.[53] For the
old narrative, the cynical manipulations of pan-Arabist ideology by
Egyptian politicians were not accompanied by a process of ideological
change within the Egyptian public. Egypt remained Egyptian and Arabism remained decidedly foreign.

THE NEW NARRATIVE

The new narrative evolved in the 1970s and 1980s when Arab nationalism was in retreat. Just as the old narrative had developed in the glow of
Arab nationalism's political heyday, contemporary events on the ground
again impinged on historians' reflections on the past. A more generous
view of historians' integrity would attribute the change to the greater
distance from the formative period of Arab nationalism, as well as to the
benefits of a quieter atmosphere enabling a less charged and possibly
more neutral discussion of the subject. In addition, new research sources
were available with the opening of archives in Britain, France, the United
States, Germany, and Israel. These studies also made far more systematic use of contemporary Arab newspapers and periodicals, political and
social pamphlets, memoirs, belles-lettres, and other published materials.

A prominent aspect of the rethinking that characterized the later narrative studies was its decentering of Arab nationalism. It is a viewpoint
that is distinctly "from the periphery to the center," examining the cen-
tripetal momentum of pan-Arabism from the perspective of the particular Arab state or society. The old narrative proceeded in large measure
ahistorically, "from the center to the periphery," placing Arab nationalism at the hub of the historical discussion. The separate Arab countries
and regimes were then examined from this telescoped all-Arab angle.
The fact that the old narrative was composed under the powerful im-

pression of rising Arab nationalism, while the new narrative was composed during its decline and the reassertion of state particularism, may have played a part in promoting a change of perspective.

Rather than leap directly from the eclipse of Ottomanism to the rise of Arabism, as studies of the old narrative had generally done, the "peripheralist" approach lingers over the postwar political entities and local allegiances, treating them as a discrete transitional phase—"the decade of the 1920s"—between Ottomanism and pan-Arabism.[54] Studies of Syria, Palestine, and especially Egypt explore the particularist tendencies that emerged in this decade, such as the National Bloc's policy in Syria of "honorable cooperation" with French authorities so as to win local independence,[55] the introverted Palestinian preoccupation with its double struggle against the British and the Zionists,[56] and Egypt's pronounced territorialist nationalism and explicit rejection of Arabism as alien and reactionary.[57]

Iraq is exceptional in that Faysal's Sunni Arab elite had begun institutionalizing Arab nationalism and transmitting it via official state bodies already by the mid-1920s.[58] In Syria the currents of Arab nationalism circulating beneath the regnant ideologies did not gain the upper hand until 1933–1936;[59] Palestinian Arabs resorted increasingly to pan-Arabism and pan-Islam in the 1930s as their leaders realized that they could not defeat their foes without outside help;[60] and Arabism triumphed in Egypt only in the early 1940s when a generation of middle-stratum professionals who had been alienated from the ruling elites and hence from the established ideologies had matured and occupied positions of power and influence.[61] The new narrative seems to achieve a breakthrough by tracking Arab nationalism's rise from its competition with aspirations to local national independence in the 1920s, rather than deeming it as the direct fallout of Ottoman debility.

This "peripheralism" was closely interwoven with the new narrative's methodological insights. Nationalism was no longer defined as merely an "idea" or a "consciousness." Hence, the historian of nationalism could not confine himself or herself solely to the study of the history of the ideas and the dynamics underlying the evolution of a collective consciousness. Nationalism, rather, was posited as a multidimensional historical movement closely connected with social and economic changes, political and institutional developments, and the specific sociopolitical context of each Arab society individually and all of them together as a cultural unit. Nationalism came to be regarded as no less a political movement, a cultural system, a social phenomenon, and sometimes an economic force as an ideology. Even when studies in the new narrative address the issue of nationalism as a movement for national liberation from colonial rule, they do so within the social, cultural, and political context of each Arab state separately, and of each country as it relates to the all-Arab system.

Consequently, the protagonists of the new narrative are not bodies of ideas or their proponents, a handful of representative writers or intellectuals; they are, rather, national movements subsuming elite and non-elite groups, official and unofficial parties and organizations, as well as economic forces, systems, and institutions. When the new narrative deals with intellectuals as producers and disseminators of a national discourse, it is likely to view them as "secondary intellectuals," a broad "professional intelligentsia," individuals operating in the print media of newspapers, magazines, and books that shape public opinion.

The formal, methodological frameworks that supplanted the "history of ideas" approach included the "new" social history of the Annales school, together with the "political economy" and "world-system" theories. These focused on the study of the "deep" structures of society and the economy, on "the relationships between power and wealth" and "how each of them affects the other."[62] Also influential, albeit to a lesser degree, were the social history of ideas, which endeavors to locate the social basis for ideological change, the contextualist method placing text in sociopolitical context, and anthropological approaches dealing with the study of systems of meaning and collective consciousness.[63] The transition from "idea" to "society" also meant that sociological theories of nationalism and ethnosocial models of "nation formation" became increasingly significant. The earlier work of Karl Deutsch and the more recent studies by Ernest Gellner, Anthony Smith, and Benedict Anderson, although not always tapped directly, provided a general theoretical background for rethinking the sources of Arab nationalism.

Guided by these novel methodological frameworks, scholars now treated Arab nationalism as an agent of modernization and development, as an outgrowth and motor of social mobility, as the product of mass education and acculturation by the new media of "print language," and as a function of the rapid growth of literate consumer publics for that culture. Nationalism was also perceived as an outcome of the disintegration of rural communities, of urbanization and industrialization, the dissemination of modern technology and science, and the expansion of the professional middle classes.

Culturally, the content of the new communal identity was studied not as a purely intellectual construct but as a sociocultural artifact that creates an ethnolinguistic community imagining itself to be homogeneous. The new community was described as "inventing" and "reinventing" its traditions and renovating its collective *ethnie* to comport with modernity. In like manner, the creation of the state or of the nation-state was portrayed not only in terms of political power struggles between the narrow interests of rulers or elite groups but also as an effort to forge a political culture and new patterns of political behavior to meet the needs of the nation. Even when nationalism was studied as an anticolonial movement, it was not grasped solely as a simple mechanical political reaction to the imperialist challenge; it was, rather, understood as a complex national response generated by extensive processes of sociopolitical change that were inherent in the specific cultural context of a Muslim-Arab society.

Thus, the diffusionist model in which nationalism is transmitted as an idea from Europe to the Middle East by individual thinkers (the old narrative) gives way to a more nuanced and comprehensive model. While acknowledging nationalism's external (i.e., European) sources, the new narrative emphasizes the particular cultural-historical experience of the Middle East, with its specific modes of appropriation and reproduction of nationalism that recreate it in "Arab" form. In this regard, nationalism is understood as both a program for modern innovation and an indigenous culture of invented tradition.

Two important works, both published in 1971, on the formation of Arab nationalism as reflected in the life and work of Sati` al-Husri, mark a watershed in the transition from the old to the new narrative. The first, William Cleveland's *The Making of an Arab Nationalist*, remains the most comprehensive biography of al-Husri.[64] The second, *Arab Nationalism: A Critical Enquiry*, by Bassam Tibi, reexamines the development of Arab nationalism since 1920 with a special emphasis on the work of al-Husri as its leading proponent.[65] The two works seem to exhaust the possibilities latent in the old history of ideas paradigm in their detailed analysis of the inner conceptual structure of the ideology of Arab nationalism produced by al-Husri. Yet both depart from the old narrative by placing the nationalist text not only within its own discursive context but also in its broad, sociopolitical context. While Cleveland notes that his "study is primarily concerned with al-Husri's intellectual role in the development of an ideology," nevertheless al-Husri's life and thought are discussed "within the context of the conditions prevailing in the eastern Arab world between the fall of Faysal's kingdom in Syria in 1920 and the emergence of Nasser in 1952."[66] Cleveland also points to the influence of al-Husri's ideas on broad reading publics in Iraq and the Arab world. The systematic analysis of his role in the "institutionalization of Arab nationalism" in Iraq from 1921 to 1941—a theme extensively developed in the new narrative—is especially noteworthy in this connection.[67]

Bassam Tibi, for his part, borrows methodology extensively from the social sciences to stage a critical discussion of the social and political functions of nationalist ideology generally, whereby he can compare the Arab case with that of Europe and the Third World. Tibi's "attempt [at] a definition of nationalism from the point of view of the social sciences"[68] adumbrates the later narrative's methodological axiom that internal textual analysis of Arab nationalist ideology "must be complemented by an analysis of the social structures in which this ideology has emerged."[69]

The rethinking initiated in the work of Cleveland and of Tibi became a full-blown trend since the mid-1970s. The new narrative's reassessment of Arab nationalism encompassed four main areas. First, the causes of its emergence and consolidation; second, the founding "community of discourse" with its media of dissemination and to some extent its modes of reception and consumption; third, the route by which it became politically important; and fourth, a new view of Egypt as integral in all these processes.

The revision begins in periodization. The old narrative dated the mid-1930s as the onset of the intellectual crystallization of Arab nationalism. The new narrative pushed periodization back. It placed the embryonic stage of a meaningful Arab nationalist discourse in the later 1920s and early 1930s. Dawn shows that history textbooks used in the new state-controlled educational system in Iraq in the later 1920s and early 1930s, which were produced in Egypt, Syria, and Palestine as well as in Iraq, already contained "important expressions of pan-Arab thought." Their nationalist themes and their relatively large circulation provide Dawn solid evidence that "[b]y the end of the 1920s, a more or less standard formulation of the Arab self-view had appeared and received comprehensive statement."[70] Simon, in her studies on education in Iraq as primary medium for the dissemination of Arab nationalism; Hurvitz, in a pioneering work on Muhibb al-Din al-Khatib's early (i.e., 1920s) theories on Arab nationalism; Gershoni, who presents incipient intellectual manifestations of Arabist identification in early 1930s Egypt; and more generally Marr and Cleveland in their works, all reinforce the new periodization.[71]

As to the political sphere, the new narrative showed that even though "a system of inter-Arab relations" had "become fully developed [only] after 1945, its major attributes had been adumbrated during the preceding two decades."[72] Gomaa and Porath, in comprehensive discussions of "Hashimite attempts at Fertile Crescent unity" beginning as early as the late 1920s and early 1930s, Rabinovich in his study of political ambitions to the "Syrian throne" in the 1920s and 1930s as a prism through which the emergence of the inter-Arab system "can be most clearly examined," and Khaldun S. Husry in his discussion of King Faysal I's plans for Arab unity in the period from 1930 to 1933, clearly specify the early 1930s as the birthdate of the formation of pan-Arabist political designs.[73]

The new narrative largely followed the old in describing and analyzing the crucial formative forces underlying Arab nationalism. Among these were the collapse of the Ottoman Empire and the recognition that only a new communal identity based on Arabic language, culture, and history would be viable in the post-Ottoman world; the common Arab struggle against Western imperialism fostering political solidarity and boosting of indigenous, non-Western national culture; the reaction against "regionalism" (the European-imposed fragmentation of the Arab nation into artificial territorial entities following World War I); Hashimite political ambitions as a catalyst to strategies for Arab unity, and in counterpoint the attempt by Syria and Egypt to frustrate them via their own plans for promoting unity; the influence of fascism and Nazism as a model for a unifying nationalism based on a "community of strength"; Islamic revivalism in various parts of the Arab world that also advanced identification with the idea of Arab unity; and the exacerbation of the Arab-Jewish conflict in Palestine that fueled powerful sentiments of Islamic and Arabist loyalty. Although these factors had been studied previously, the later narrative drew on abundant new primary sources, enabling a sweeping elaboration and refinement of the old narrative.[74]

One major difference between the two narratives is the new narrative's stress on the socioeconomic engines of Arab nationalism, especially the emergence of new middle-class strata in the large urban centers. This was explained by the rapid urbanization that eroded and uprooted traditional rural and tribal communities; the high social mobility of evolving urban society; and the acculturation of new publics to modern urban life in state schools, the print media, and professional training. In time, the urban, educated middle class, defined as *effendiyya*, became the dominant social force in urban culture and politics. The generational profile of the *effendiyya* was quite young, as it acted as a magnet for pupils and students. The *effendiyya* embraced Arab nationalism partly as a side effect of their alienation from the higher elite groups, as the new professional intelligentsia grasped its socioeconomic power and aspired to political and cultural hegemony. The professional intelligentsia sought a new ideology and political strategy to pursue its interests. They found it in Arab nationalism and in the idea of Arab unity. The new professional intelligentsia did not receive and assimilate Arab nationalism passively, however, but rather imbued it with a far more radical, populist, and politicized hue.[75]

How was the link between the *effendi* professional intelligentsia and Arab nationalism established? The new narrative, although not unaware of this connection, does not always elucidate it. Here recent theoretical work on nationalism is helpful. Ernest Gellner's model emphasizing modern industrial society, massive urbanization, and the new centrality of a uniform culture based on and disseminated through mass literacy, as well as Benedict Anderson's complementary model stressing the nation-building effects of "print-capitalism" in forging linguistic uniformity and a common sense of identity, enhance our understanding of the connection between the Arab professional intelligentsia and Arab nationalism. More than any other group or social stratum in Middle Eastern society, the professional intelligentsia were creatures of the urban print culture, groomed in the state schools to look to it as its fount of information and, in turn, overseeing its content and distribution. In the process, Arabic language and the literate Arab culture became the professional intelligentsia's focus of communal identification. "New media of expression," Hourani notes, "were creating a universe of discourse which united educated Arabs more fully."[76]

Another crucial process, not discussed in the old narrative, is what Anthony Smith has termed "radicalising the intelligentsia."[77] Smith argues that as the professional intelligentsia climb the social ladder en route to power, they are blocked or delayed by certain forces in the society. In their effort to overcome or circumvent these obstacles, they are radicalized in the form of commitment to a nationalist ideology that is particularly nativist, populist and militant.[78]

Three main obstructions engender the professional intelligentsia's radicalization. The first is the educational overproduction of professionals and a paucity of jobs, inducing the intelligentsia to turn to politics in order to initiate policies ensuring their class full employment. The second is the hostility shown the emergent professional intelligentsia by the "old hierarchical bureaucrats," drawn mainly from the established landed elite, which furthered their interests by collaborating with colonial rule. The third hindrance to the professional intelligentsia's rise is competition and conflict with foreign professionals, thought by the "natives" to benefit from preferential employment and the promotional policies of the colonial rulers.

In the Arab case, the professional intelligentsia's struggle against these various obstacles entailed fashioning a political counterculture based on populist nationalism combined with socialist elements as an alternative to the established conservative political culture with its constitutional parliamentary orientation and its links with the West. To foster its cause, the professional intelligentsia sought an alliance with lower social strata, employing nativist rhetoric and presenting themselves as the authentic voice of the aspirations of "the people." Their protest was vented in ethnic and nationalistic forms: as the struggle of the autochthonous (Arab-Muslim) ethnic community against ethnic interlopers (Greeks, Italians, French, British, and in some cases Christians or Jews). In Smith's pungent phrase, the surging radicalization of the new professional intelligentsia is channeled toward an "ethnic solution" in ethnic nationalism.[79] This ethnic solution serves a double function, providing "not only the basis of an alternative status system and power center for an excluded stratum, but a resolution of their identity crisis through a revaluation of their function and purpose."[80]

The new narrative devoted considerable attention to the mediational role of the new professional classes in the dissemination and popularization of their brand of nationalism among broad sectors of literate society. In Iraq, as shown by Cleveland, Marr, Porath, Eppel, and mainly Simon, the state educational system was a prime agent of socialization and acculturation to Arab nationalist culture. The state-controlled system produced, in the 1920s and still more in the 1930s, generations of new professionals (more broadly, urban middle-class *effendiyya*) who soon served in central positions in the state bureaucracy, as young officers in the army, in municipal public life (particularly in Baghdad), in political parties, and as founders and managers of literary and journalistic enterprises. In the 1930s, in an effort to translate their rising social strength into immediate political power, the professionals began accelerating processes of ideological and political radicalization that were channeled primarily into the promotion of ardent pan-Arabism.[81] The Iraqi state-run system also "exported the revolution" happenstantially, for it solved its manpower problem by recruiting educators from abroad, who absorbed the penchant for Arab nationalist instruction during their stints in Iraq and who later dispensed the doctrine upon returning to teaching posts or other positions of cultural influence in their countries of origin.[82]

Pan-Arab radicalism was expressed in diverse forms in 1930s Iraq. In 1935 the "Muthanna Club" was established in Baghdad and rapidly became a forum for the educated from all parts of the Arab world and a center for the dissemination of Arab nationalist propaganda.[83] Nationalist radicalization was also evident in the formation, in the late 1930s, of a paramilitary youth movement [*al-futuwwa*] modeled on fascist and Nazi youth organizations, sponsored by the government and officially instituted in Iraqi schools. Students were indoctrinated to believe that "the youth represented the [Arab] nationalist ideal, the heroic qualities of the Arab, and [that] they were to restore past glory."[84] From 1938 to

1940 the *futuwwa* inculcated a particularly militaristic Arab nationalism into an entire generation of young Iraqis, advocating violent means to realize Arab unity and British withdrawal from the Middle East. The anti-British coup of Rashid `Ali al-Kaylani in 1941, a pro-German and violent expression of Arab nationalism, was the culmination of the process of ideological ferment and political radicalization in Iraq; it was a process generated, primarily, by the new urban middle-class *effendiyya* in their role as shapers of public opinion through state education and the print media.[85]

Similar developments took place in interwar Syria. In the 1930s a new, urban, educated middle class containing a significant professional component sprang up in the expanded cities, particularly Damascus. It constituted the chief social reservoir of a new Syrian political class and culture. Philip Khoury provides a systematic analysis of the social formation of the Syrian middle-class professionals and their entrance as an active opposition force into the political arena; he defines the entire process as "radicalization," and the new forces as "radicalized movements [that] left their mark on the politics of nationalism."[86] These new elements, representing primarily the new, modern middle class of students, bureaucrats, and professionals, entered the political arena "armed with European educations and new, sophisticated methods of political organization acquired abroad."[87] Their political parties, "based on more systematic and rigorous systems of ideas," sought a reformulation of nationalism "that corresponded to and accommodated the structural changes" then underway in Syria. "The language of nationalism itself was refined and altered; these ascendant forces placed more emphasis on social and economic justice for the masses, [and] on pan-Arab unity" as an alternative to "the old nationalist ideas of constitutionalism, liberal parliamentary forms and personal freedoms." The new populist, radical nationalism was designed to bridge the gap between "the nationalism of the upper classes and the nationalism of popular sentiments."[88]

The most important of the radicalized organizations to emerge in Syria in the 1930s was the League of National Action [`Usbat al-`Amal al-Qawmi]. Established in 1933 and operating throughout the remainder of the decade, the League was the mouthpiece of militant, anti-imperialist pan-Arabism. It rejected the National Bloc's opportunist strategy of "honorable cooperation" with the Mandatory authorities, calling instead for mass mobilization and direct action to obtain Syrian independence. Its membership was primarily composed of Syrian youth who had graduated from the state-run school system and entered middle-class professions.[89]

Khoury's view is comprehensive—a rarity among the composers of the new narrative—in plotting Syrian developments in the broader Middle East context:

> In terms of its class and educational background, political style, and ideo-
> logical orientation, this new generation of nationalists in Syria displayed
> characteristics that were remarkably similar to those of an emerging sec-
> ond generation of nationalists in Palestine, Iraq and Egypt. In fact, the
> politically active members of this new generation were able to forge a
> panoply of ties across the Arab world.[90]

Palestine in the 1930s also witnessed a "process of radicalization" and "the rise of radical organizations" among the nationalist public.[91] The unique experience of the simultaneous struggle against Zionism and British rule, together with the new middle class's characteristic alien-ation from the traditional forces and leaders whose conservatism was blamed for all political setbacks, bred ideological and political radicaliza-tion among new, educated, urban middle-class groups in the Palestinian Arab society. Porath and Lesch address this process, demonstrating the analogy with other Arab societies of the 1930s. Porath stresses that the radicalization first appeared in urban centers, leavened by the younger and better educated generation that functioned "as an independent and more radical political force."[92] These young, educated forces established their own political bodies in the early 1930s, such as the "Young Men's Muslim Association," the "Arab Young Men's Association," the "Na-tional Congress of the Arab Youth," the "Patriotic Arab Association" and the "Arab Boy Scouts Association."[93] The party al-Istiqlal became the leading pan-Arab nationalist organization of the period. The founding of al-Istiqlal, Porath writes, "was an outcome of the growth of an educated class of young radicals who saw in Pan-Arabism the panacea for all the illnesses of Arab society." Porath shows that the party's leading activists came from the Palestinian "professional intelligentsia," among them physicians, bank managers and financial experts, journalists and school-teachers.[94] Lesch also contends that the party's support "came primarily from young professionals and government officials."[95] In addition, Porath and Lesch note that the "new professionals" founded and staffed the new nationalist press, of which the leading papers were al-Jami`a al-Islamiyya, al-Wahda al-`Arabiyya, al-`Arab, al-Difa`, and al-Liwa', and impelled the radicalization and more frequent publication of veteran papers such as Filastin, al-Jami`a al-`Arabiyya, and Mir'at al-Sharq. The print media's success in popularizing Arab nationalism in Palestinian society was reflected in the press becoming a significant force in the political struggle against Zionism and imperialism in the 1930s.[96]

In Egypt the rise of the indigenous professional intelligentsia in the interwar years would prove even more consequential. More than any other Arab society, the Egyptian professional stratum was quantitatively far larger and qualitatively more diversified. In addition, because it sprang up against the background of a serious economic crisis that sharply curtailed employment opportunities for high-school and university graduates, it had to wage a more intensive struggle against the established landed elites, their Westernized political culture, and the fierce competition with the "foreign" professionals. The radicalization of Egypt's "new *effendiyya*" was thus bound to leave a deeper impression on Egyptian national life in the 1930s and 1940s.[97]

The professional intelligentsia in Egypt played a pivotal role in steering the country away from territorial nationalism focused on the Land of the Nile, to a supra-Egyptian, Arab-Islamic nationalism assuming Arabic language and culture and Islamic heritage as the primary registers of Egyptian identity. The radicalization of the young, new *effendis* and the transformation they wrought in Egypt's communal identity have been treated extensively by Mitchell, Jankowski, and Gershoni. Their studies have shown that in the Egyptian case, too, the radicalization of the *effendiyya* originated in the unemployment crisis of the educated, overurbanization, disruptions of the parliamentary system, the intensification of the struggle against colonialism, and a creeping fascist influence. This prompted their alienation from the Wafd, the Liberals, the Palace, and the other parliamentary parties. They saw themselves as an "angry young generation" fighting "the corrupt establishment," against whose Westernized, political culture they counterposited nativism, Arabism, Islam, and Easternism.[98]

Organizationally, the familiar pattern of other Arab countries reappears in Egypt. The new social forces established their own political bodies in the 1930s, such as the "Young Men's Muslim Association," "Young Egypt," the "Muslim Brothers," as well as radical student organizations and various intellectual and literary movements, constituting an entire new counterculture. As with its sister movements elsewhere in the Middle East, the Arabism and Islam of Egypt's *effendis* waxed nativist, populist, and militant, endorsing violence against the British occupation and the "foreign" communities allegedly enjoying British protection.[99]

The new narrative also takes note of the Egyptian intelligentsia's distinctive role in the mass dissemination of their radicalized Arab-Islamic nationalism in the 1930s and 1940s. Cairo-based publishing houses owned and operated by *effendiyya* churned out works of philosophy, history, poetry, belles lettres, textbooks, and the popular *Islamiyyat* literature, while new *effendi* periodicals such as *al-Risala*, *al-Thaqafa*, *al-*

Rabita al-'Arabiyya and the "official" journals of the new radical organizations such as the YMMA's *al-Fath*, Young Egypt's *Jaridat Misr al-
Fatah* and the Muslim Brothers' *Jaridat al-Ikhwan al-Muslimin* appealed to a less highbrow readership.[100]

The new narrative also documents the Arabist cultural activity con-
ducted across political borders. The new professional groups created a
pan-Arabist atmosphere with the mushrooming of inter-Arab cultural
associations, especially in the capital cities Cairo, Beirut, Damascus, and
Baghdad. The associations increased literary cooperation among Arab
countries by institutionalizing inter-Arab professional meetings, workshops, and congresses of teachers, university lecturers, students, physicians, engineers, lawyers, journalists, poets, writers, and artists. Other
inter-Arab cultural activity included an Arabist press addressed to reading publics across the Arab world (such as *al-Hadith* in Aleppo, *al-
Makshuf* and *al-Adib* in Beirut, *al-'Arab* in Jerusalem, *al-Risala, al-
Thaqafa* and *al-Rabita al-'Arabiyya* in Cairo), and cultural exchange
delegations comprised of students, journalists, writers, poets, teachers,
university lecturers, politicians, businessmen, and financiers. All these
created a new common universe of Arabist discourse based on a shared
culture and print language. A solid foundation was forged for what contemporaries called the "unity of Arab culture."[101]

No less significant is the contribution of the new narrative to the
rethinking of the political history of Arab nationalism in the 1930s and
1940s. In a number of spheres at least, its reassessment of political processes and events has led to a thorough revision of the old political narrative. A prime case in point is the 1936–1939 Arab Revolt in Palestine
and its impact on the political consolidation of Arab nationalism not
only in Palestine (on this specific point the new narrative presented a
completely new historical portrait) but throughout the Arab world. A
prevalent theme of the new narrative is that

> no event in the 1930s captured the attention of the Arab world as did the
> Arab Revolt in Palestine. Its progress was eagerly followed in the daily
> press of Cairo, Baghdad, Damascus, and in the capitals of North Africa. It
> was also carefully monitored by Arab leaders and regimes. On the one
> hand, the revolt aroused Arab nationalist sentiments . . . ; on the other, it
> alarmed Arab rulers who feared its repercussions on domestic political life
> in their respective countries.[102]

Simon and Eppel show that in Iraq the issue of Palestine in general, and
the Arab Revolt in particular, significantly strengthened pan-Arabist
forces within the Iraqi ruling elite and aroused Arab nationalist sentiments among broad educated segments of the young middle class *effen-*

diyya. The frequent pro-Palestinian articles that appeared in the press, and a series of sympathy protests reinforced the radical political parties that demanded greater Iraqi involvement in Arab affairs and mobilized Iraqi public opinion for pan-Arab causes.[103] In Syria as well the Palestinian Arab Revolt inspired the new urban middle class to maneuver Syrian foreign policy closer to engagement in the Palestinian cause and broader Arab affairs. As Khoury shows, the general public expressed solidarity and offered material aid for the uprising in Palestine. Toward the end of the 1930s the intensification of this unofficial activity, together with the support given the revolt by pan-Arabist politicians, forced the Bloc's government to step up its official support for the Palestinian struggle and beyond that to lay the basis for a continuing Syrian activist policy in Arab affairs.[104]

In Egypt, as shown by Coury, Mayer, Gershoni, Gomaa, and Jankowski, the Arab Revolt rapidly eroded Egypt's traditional isolation from Arab affairs. Even more dramatically than in Iraq and Syria, the radical nationalist urban *effendiyya* of Egypt aroused public support the Palestinian struggle, and skillfully exploited it as an argument for Arab-Islamic unity. By the end of the 1930s radical forces induced the political establishment—the Wafd, the Palace, and the parliamentary parties—to adopt Arabist policies and heighten official Egyptian involvement in the Arab world.[105]

The Palestinian Arab Revolt also spawned a number of inter-Arab congresses and meetings. These were mostly of an unofficial character and demonstrated that Arab nationalism had filtered down to relatively broad popular levels. The general Arab congress in Bludan (Syria) in September 1937, and more tellingly the "Inter-Parliamentary Congress of the Arab and Islamic Countries for the Defense of Palestine," convened in Cairo in October 1938—to cite only two prominent examples—reverberated throughout the Arab world. Hundreds of representatives from various Arab countries participated in the discussions and drafting of resolutions. They clearly reveal how extensive popular support for pan-Arabism had become by the late 1930s, and they augmented this support in turn, so much so that Porath concludes that "the developments in Palestine during the 1936–9 years stand as perhaps the single most important factor which contributed to the growth of pan-Arab ideology, to the feeling of solidarity among the Arab peoples and to the attempt at shaping a unified general Arab position and policy."[106]

There was another central political issue that the new narrative thoroughly revised: the developments from 1941–1945 that culminated in the formation of the Arab League. Where the old narrative found no necessary connection between the Arab nationalist idea that developed in the 1930s and 1940s and the establishment of the Arab League in 1945, the new narrative hypothesized and then proved the connection to be both necessary and immediate. In the latter narrative, the gestation stage of the Arab League, 1941 to 1945, was umbilically linked to the formative years of Arab nationalism in the late 1920s and early 1930s and to the period of its more advanced development after 1936. Thus, according to this narrative, a series of "internal processes"—the Hashimites' repeated efforts to unify the Fertile Crescent; the prolonged crisis in Palestine and the enlistment of broad support for the struggle; and, perhaps above all, "the rise of political pan-Arabism" in the 1930s and 1940s, which soon rallied around Egyptian leadership in the form of Mustafa al-Nahhas' Wafd government—cumulatively led to the establishment of the Arab League.[107]

The role of the British in this process did not escape the attention of the new narrative studies. However, as Porath concludes, "Britain did not create the Arab League, nor did it deliberately encourage its formation; at best it may have indirectly contributed to the process of its formation."[108] According to this version of events, Britain's sole aim from 1943 to 1945 was to further inter-Arab *economic* and *cultural* cooperation. This goal was secondary for the Arab leaders headed by al-Nahhas, whose priority lay in realizing inter-Arab *political* coordination. Hence the bemused reaction of British officials to the formation of the Arab League in March 1945: "a surprising achievement for the Arabs," specifically given its "surprisingly practical" dimensions.[109]

As the above implies, the new narrative depicts Egypt as an integral, often central player in the intellectual and political formation of Arab nationalism. Gomaa, Mayer, Jankowski, Coury, Gershoni, and Porath demur from the earlier view that "politically opportunistic pan-Arabism" had motivated Egyptian politicians rather than "ideological pan-Arabism." Their studies show how Arab nationalism replaced Egypt's territorialist, Mediterranean, Pharaonic, and isolationist orientations, as Egypt evolved from its 1920s self-exclusion from the Arab sphere into deep cultural and political involvement in Arab affairs.[110] Indeed, the consensus of the new narrative holds that Egyptian participation in and ultimate leadership of Arab nationalism was the key to a new phase in its historical evolution.[111]

The new narrative advances a set of novel representations and interpretations of the formation of Arab nationalism from 1920 to 1945. Nevertheless, the new narrative has not yet reached full maturity as a paradigm for research and a new agenda for understanding the roots of modern Arab nationalism. Three weaknesses are particularly noteworthy. First, the new narrative is characterized more by monographs than by synthesis. Its greatest strength seems to lie in case studies that deal with one country, a particular society or individual group of Arab thinkers, but rarely does it endeavor to construct a comprehensive and integrated picture of the region's history of nationalism. The new narrative still awaits the generalizing historians who will take the pieces of the puzzle researched to date with such meticulous scholarship and put them together, producing an overall synthesis of the sources of Arab nationalism. Porath and certain chapters of Hourani's recent book point to possible directions.

Second, the narrative suffers from its inattention to the reception of Arab nationalism among women as well as among subaltern socioeconomic strata such as the lower-middle classes, the working classes, and various levels of the peasantry. Although its discussion of the role played by the new *effendiyya* enormously improves on the old narrative's fixation on a handful of elite intellectuals, the reader is still relatively uninformed as to the modes in which women, the poor, and the illiterate—constituting the overwhelming majority of the societies in question—reacted to the radicalized upper middle stratum's struggle against the Westernized "ancien régime." The new narrative needs further decentering from the already enlarged portrait of *effendiyya* alongside and often supplanting luminary intellectuals in the propagation of the Arab national idea; the narrative must encompass the strains of nationalism from below percolating upward as a supplement to the research on *effendi*-driven nationalism trickling downward.

Third, in overreacting to the reductionist "history of ideas" schema, the new narrative all too often avoids a systematic discussion of ideology and often neglects the intellectual-textual dimension. In many of its studies, nationalism is treated solely as a social and political phenomenon. Nationalist ideas are actually depicted as mere rationalizations for social structures, economic forces, and political processes. There is insufficient appreciation of the integrity of nationalist texts and artifacts at all levels of society. The new narrative has focused on the "history of nationalist experience" and neglected the "history of nationalist meaning."[112] It needs historians who will study the two dimensions both as autonomous and irreducible spheres and as operating through interaction and mutual feedback.[113] The history of nationalism is undoubtedly the history of the national experience; but that experience, to be sure, is "burdened, limited, and shaped by the already constituted, inherited world of meanings in which, and from which, it was constructed."[114] The old narrative still has a certain relevance, after all.

2

The Formation of Yemeni Nationalism:
Initial Reflections

Fred Halliday

Wa ji'tuka min saba' bi-naba' yaqin
And I have come to you from Saba with good tidings
—al-Qur'an, *"Sura of the Ant," verse 22*

The case of Yemen, including that of its nationalisms, has been relatively marginal to the study of the modern history of the Arab Middle East,
which has tended to focus on Egypt and the *Mashriq*. Within writing on
Yemen itself, there is frequent mention of nationalist movements but
remarkably little sustained treatment of this issue.[1] Yet the development
of nationalism in Yemen, in a country of 14 million, is a significant part
of the overall story of nationalism in the Arab world and may also provide the occasion for examining a number of comparative and theoretical questions.

THE DEBATE ON NATIONALISM

Nationalism is both an ideology and a political phenomenon, and, in
these two respects, has been present since the early nineteenth century.
Yet if social science has, late in the day, come to acknowledge the importance of studying this phenomenon in a theoretical or comparative
dimension, much of the writing on specific nationalisms, and hence on
"nations," has remained innocent of it. My own, summary, view of the
debate is that it has in some ways reached an impasse: an array of *general* theories is offset against a mass of *individual* accounts with rela-

tively little interaction between the two. What is needed now is a moratorium on general theories, of which we have plenty, and indeed a questioning, as Sami Zubaida has suggested, of whether a general theory is either desirable or necessary.[2] What we need instead are comparative, individual, histories that are both written in the light of these general theories and that, critically, test them against the historical record.

At the center of much of this debate is the concept of "nation" itself. By the early decades of the nineteenth century, the doctrine of "nations" as historically given, distinct, communities had arrived.[3] As with so many other analytic categories—state, society, economy, market, race— we have now come to accept as natural and eternal what are particular, contingent, definitions.

In addition to a set of normative presumptions about loyalty and the claims of the community, nationalisms themselves seek to suppress debate on historical conditions under which "nations" come into existence and indeed what constitutes them. Nationalism has its answer to this, what can be termed the "archaeological" or "perennialist" theory: nations have always existed, or at least for what is an (undefinedly) sufficient length of time.[4] The history that needs to be written is, therefore, a teleological one, by which they "are born," "emerge," "awake," "arise," etc. In some sense "nations" exist like objects in the ground and the only question that needs to be asked is the supposedly factual one of whether, indeed, such and such a "nation" exists or not.[5] Students of the Middle East will be familiar enough with the consequences of this approach: the arguments on whether there is, or is not, an Arab nation, a Jewish nation, a Turkish nation, and so forth. All supposedly turns on a matter of fact, on accumulating enough evidence to "prove" that such an entity exists or, alternatively, in adducing enough evidence to show that it does not, is "artificial," the result of migration or whatever. The result of such a perennialist scheme is the same as when any optative, ethical, and normative concept is projected onto reality that does not conform: an effort goes into explaining why this reality does not conform to the ideal.

FOR A THEORY OF COMPARATIVE CONTINGENCY

The alternative approach, which Anthony Smith calls "modernism," is to write the history of nations not as teleological and necessary processes but as the emergence of a set of contingencies. Nations are therefore communities that happen to come about through accidents of history, war, and geography and that are one among many other possible such outcomes. Such an approach carries with it the implication of the modernity of nations—i.e., that they cannot be identified prior to the existence of the

ideological and social conditions that give them meaning, namely in the
early nineteenth century. Identifiable linguistic and cultural groups, peoples, or, in a clear pre-nationalist sense, "nations" can be accepted, but
these are not nations in the contemporary sense, nor, it must be emphasized, was it inevitable that they should become so. A range of sociological theories, be they those of Anderson or Gellner, would be variants of
this approach.[6] These differ in the accounts they give and in their normative implications, Anderson being less dismissive of nationalism than
Gellner, but they converge in seeing nations as contingent products of
modernity. Another, well-established, variant of this modernist approach
is the Marxist theory of nations: this relates the emergence of nations
both to the general condition of capitalist modernity and industrialization
and, more specifically, to the development of classes within this modernity for whom nationalism constitutes an appropriate ideology. Much has
been written against Marxist theory, its teleological assumptions and disdain for nationalisms, but some of this could equally apply to nineteenth-
century liberal writing on the subject. The Marxist tradition has, however, the merit of postulating some relationship between nationalism and
socioeconomic change and in suggesting that social groups have differen-
tial relations to the idea of "nation."[7]

This modernist account is, in summary form, the theory that would
be suggested by the writings of sociologists and Marxist historians alike,
but the obstacles to its acceptance are clear enough. On the one hand, it
would undermine much of the historiography, nationalist or other, that
uses some variant of the archaeological approach. On the other hand, the
claim of modernity and contingency is open to misuse: we know this
argument from situations of political contestation, where nationalists
seek to deny not only the claim of another people to territory or whatever but also the very claim that the other side are a "nation" at all. Such
a denial is central in, say, the Irish case, the Arab-Israeli dispute, the
Indo-Pakistani conflict: the modernist argument against perennialism
that denies the reality *and* legitimation of history has become an instrument of polemic and has hence been discredited for this reason. Equally,
any acceptance of the polyvalence of identities, i.e., of the denial of historically constituted and legitimizing essences, would provoke resistance
from within nationalist movements.

One compromise has suggested a distinction between "historic" and
"new" nations; yet in terms of ideology and the role of states in promoting such ideologies they are all modern, products of contingency in
the new international and normative climate created from the early
nineteenth century onward and of the process of state formation that
has accompanied it. The solution to the problem of the history of "na-

tions" is neither to assert a perennialism nor to waste time, political or academic, in boosting or denying the historicity of particular "nations": we can examine how bits of the past have been selected for current uses, but this is not to ascribe causality to this past. The question of the political behavior of "nations," and indeed of the legitimacy of claims to people or territory, can therefore be delinked from that of history.

To write about the nationalisms of any contemporary "nation" is to write within the framework of such a comparative contingency. To suggest a working guideline: nothing more than two centuries old should be of relevance to either history or legitimation. The research agenda that such an approach entails would comprise at four major points. First, it would identify the *general historicity* of this "nation" in the sense of how recently it was formed, and the dependence of this formation on a broader, international, context—it being one of the paradoxes of nationalism that while each claims its uniqueness all are modular variants of a simple code, products of a universal trend of the past century or two. Second, it would seek to identify the *specific causation*, those particular historical factors that contributed to the formation of this nation, with the territory, culture, historical self-image it possesses. Such an account of causation would be antiperennialist in that it would deny any necessary development to this nation. Third, it would be necessary to delineate the *specific ideological content* of this nationalism, not by demanding that it conform to a specific unitary model, based on ethnicity language or anything else, but rather by recognizing, beyond its modular, common, form[8] the diversity and contradictions within it, as well as the changes that could occur in even relatively short periods of time. There would be no place in such an account for discussion of which version of the national ideology is "genuine" or not.

Finally, as part of the investigation of cause and of contingency, this research agenda would examine the *instrumentality* of nationalism, the relation of this nationalism to identifiable social and political groups—in other words the history not of the emergence of a given or an essence but of the creation of both ideology and movement by political forces. If nothing else, this would relate the apparently abstract history of an idea to material and real-world forces, and further preclude any argument to the effect that one group in a society rather than another has a more accurate claim to represent the "genuine" national message. Much of this would involve a study of state-building and of the ways in which those aiming to take power, or retain it, have generated and managed ideas of nation. In Marxist accounts, the role of states would itself be a function of the role of classes. If class has somewhat less of a direct role than orthodox Marxists would suggest, it may provide more of the explanation than idealist or abstracted sociological accounts would claim.

In the Middle East as elsewhere, nationalisms have been modern, contingent, and confused, and the instrumental ideologies and the movements corresponding to them have reflected this. In what follows I shall take one particular nationalism, that of Yemen, and present, in outline form, an account of its formation.

YEMENI NATIONALISM: A SUMMARY ACCOUNT

In the conventional nationalist account, the Yemeni nation is an ancient one, having established a settled civilization in the fertile south-west part of Arabia some millennia ago.[9] The high point of this civilization was comprised by the kingdoms of Ma'in, Saba, and Himyar, which have left extensive archaeological ruins. One example of the characteristically inclusive, "perennialist" claims of Yemeni nationalism to the whole past is to be found in a poster of "South Arabian Scripts" sold in the Salah Museum of Ta'iz, a former palace of the Hamid al-Din Imams. The scripts, designated as "South Arabian" and hence part of the national inheritance, are: Himyaritic, Sabaean, Arabic, Amharic, Hebrew, Greek, and Latin.

These South Arabian kingdoms were significant in the broader history of the Middle East, in part because of the long-distance trade links to India and the states at the top of the Red Sea, in part because migration spread across the Red Sea to Ethiopia, whose languages comprise several descendants of the ancient South Arabian tongues (Amharic, Tigrinya) and use variants of the ancient scripts.[10] With the advent of Islam, Yemen became part of the Arab and Islamic worlds and contributed both militarily to the Islamic conquests and culturally to the mediaeval Islamic period.[11] From the tenth century onward, Yemen seceded from the Abbasid realm and so ceased to be part of the broader Islamic empires: in a more limited space than that earlier denominated by the term "Yaman," it was ruled by a succession of dynasties, controlling more or less of to-day's Yemeni territory. The last of these to control most of to-day's North and South were the Qasimis, who ruled in the mid-seventeenth century. In the early modern period, Yemen fell under various degrees of external influence and control—in the sixteenth and seventeenth centuries the Dutch and the Portuguese yielding to the Ottomans, and in the nineteenth century the Ottomans and the British dividing the country between them. Under Ottoman rule the term "Yaman" came to have its most restricted usage, comprising the *sanjaqs* of Sana`a, Hudeida, and Ta'iz, i.e., the territory that, after

1918, came to be the Imamate of Yemen and, after 1962, the Yemen Arab Republic.

In the twentieth century we can see, so the story goes, the gradual re-emergence of the Yemeni nation within the area of historic "Yemen."[12] Prior to World War I the rule of the Ottomans was challenged by the forces of the Zeidi Imam, and it was he who took over the whole of North Yemen when the Turks departed in 1918. Although at first cautious about challenging the British to the South, the Imam gradually came to assert a claim to the whole of "natural Yemen." In the 1940s there began to develop political oppositions, to both the Imams in the North and the British in the South. The former, the "Free Yemeni" movement, sought to free the North from the dictatorial rule of the Zeidi Imams and in 1948 staged an unsuccessful coup. Its critique of the Imam was initially phrased in religious terms, calling for an end to the Imam's oppression, *dhulm*, through various forms of taxation, and for an Islamic revival to be carried out through a corps of Islamic militants: these, the *shabab al-amr*, would travel through the country mobilizing support for the *nahda* or renaissance and overcoming the ignorance of the population.[13] The aim was as much to establish a truly Islamic Imamate as to replace it. Influenced by the Muslim Brotherhood in Egypt, these Free Yemenis only later turned to a more secular political vocabulary. In the South, political movements in the port of Aden began to articulate the demand for greater self-rule, for Aden itself: the initial slogan, "Aden for the Adenis" was directed both against the British and the more conservative, "backward" rural society of South and North.[14]

By the 1950s, and with the rise of Arab nationalism elsewhere in the region, the predominant politics of the oppositions in North and South was nationalistic, involving support not only for the general goal of "Arab unity" but also for "Yemeni" unity. Nationalists in North and South differed on whether there could be unity under the Imams, but the assumption was that Yemen was one country, wrongly divided by oppressors colonial and dynastic, and that once these oppressors had been removed unity would follow. Following the defeat of the 1948 revolt, the opposition in the North consisted of intellectuals on the one hand and of subterranean officer groups on the other: it was to be the latter who, in September 1962, overthrew the Imam and proclaimed the "Yemen Arab Republic." From the early 1950s onward there was a gradual shift in the language of the opposition, so that when in 1956 the Free Yemenis issued a new set of demands, *matalib al-sha`b*, it presented the Yemeni people as part of the Arab nation, committed to Arab unity.[15] The goal of an Islamic Imamate had gone.

The nationalist opposition in the South was originally based in the trades union movement in Aden and, as part of its support for Arab and Yemeni unity, opposed the British-backed plan for a separate South Arabian state, in which the conservative rural rulers would play a predominant role. Following the outbreak of the revolution in the North, the opposition spread to the countryside of South Yemen and an active guerrilla movement developed. During the period 1963–1967 the guerrilla movement became a major contender for power in both Aden and the countryside, dividing, in the process, into two groupings, a Nasserist FLOSY and a more radical "Marxist-Leninist" National Liberation Front. It was the NLF that then came to power in the South and that, in various guises, was to rule there up to the unification agreement of 1990 and until its defeat in the war of 1994.

The period between 1967, when South Yemen became an independent state, and 1994, when the North conquered the South, was one in which both regimes espoused a nationalist position, asserting their place in the Arab world and calling for Yemeni unity.[16] However, contrary to the expectations of nationalism unity did not follow the departure of the British in 1967; instead the two states set about supporting opposition movements within each other's territory: *both* claimed to be the bearers of nationalist legitimacy and to represent the whole country. As a result no diplomatic relations were exchanged, although, intermittently, political links between them subsisted. On two occasions, in 1972 and 1979, the two states fought short border wars, the first being an attempt by the North, with Saudi and Libyan backing, to conquer the South, the second being an attempt by the South, in alliance with the left-wing guerrillas of the National Democratic Front, to advance in the North. From the early 1980s relations improved and a set of "unity" committees were set up. These made little progress, but in 1989–1990 matters accelerated, as the end of the Cold War and the internal weaknesses of both regimes led them to agree to enter a provisional unification. To much popular acclaim in both North and South, this occurred in May 1990, followed by general elections in April 1993: however, disagreements over the allocation of power within the postelectoral system, and rising distrust between the two leaderships, led to a de facto split in the country in early 1994, followed at the end of April by an outright Northern attack on the South. On 7 July 1994 Northern forces entered Aden, thus effectively unifying the country under one regime for the first time in several centuries.[17]

DISTINGUISHING FEATURES

In broad historical and ideological terms, the nationalism of the Yemen is part of the broader pattern of nationalism in the Arab world, and indeed the third world, delayed somewhat by the region's comparative isolation and later decolonization.[18] Thus it can be seen as having grown in the 1930s and 1940s in reflection of changes in Egypt and Iraq, and as having acquired a powerful impetus from the Egyptian revolution of 1952 and what followed. The emergence of a radical left, in North and South, was a part of the changes within the Movement of Arab Nationalists[19] and, to a lesser extent, of the emergence of Ba`thi and Communist trends. The strength of the left-wing MAN was a result both of the radicalization of the Palestinian movement *and* of the Yemeni situation, where the republican left, increasingly angered by Egyptian compromises with Saudi Arabia, developed well before June 1967 its own specifically Yemeni critique of the "petty bourgeois regimes."[20]

From the 1950s onward the tone and vocabulary of Yemeni nationalism was that of other Arab nationalisms—against imperialism and Zionism and, in its later left variant, against the "petty bourgeois" regimes and their allies. It also reflected changes in colonial policy and administration that were not specific to the Middle East: increased concern in the 1930s to assert control of previously autonomous areas, enhancement of particular colonies for reasons of imperial strategy, the rise of the oil industry, the abandonment by colonial powers of a permanent commitment. The subsequent changes in nationalism also reflect shifts within the Arab context. The use of these apparently universal Arab nationalist terms may, however, conceal more particular local meanings: thus the failure of "petty bourgeois" Nasserism was primarily identified as being a result of Egypt's inability to fight the Yemeni royalists and the Saudis. Hence what might seem to be an exogenous, mimetic, adoption of general Arab nationalist terms concealed a modular, endogenous usage. There are, moreover, a number of other, more specific, features of this nationalism that merit attention.

Double Genesis

In the first place, as a reflection of the division of Yemen into two states, Yemeni nationalism had a *double genesis*, reflecting the different conditions in North and South. In the South nationalism was mainly the conventional third world variant, directed against British colonial rule and in favor of national independence. In the North it was more akin to that of the earlier, antiabsolutist nationalism of Europe, being directed against the Hamid al-Din Imamate and initially aiming not to establish a republican regime but to install a more equitable Imam. But these nationalist strands were not completely separate: while the North also espoused an anticolonial element, insofar as it called for the union of Yemen and the expulsion of British colonialism, the nationalism of the South had its own social radicalism in that it reflected the division within the South between the nationalist movement and the existing political hierarchy of Sultans and tribal leaders within the South Arabian Federation. There was, therefore, both an anticolonial and a politically egalitarian dimension to Yemeni nationalism, reflecting the two sources of the movement.

Social radicalism

The second element of Yemeni nationalism that merits special attention is its *social radicalism*, the espousal of an idea of "revolution" directed not only against colonial rule but also against the indigenous political and social elites. Forms of radicalism could be found in other variants of Arab nationalism, and the word "revolution" [*thawra*] came to have a generic, promiscuous diffusion in modern political rhetoric. In the Yemeni case, however, the role of popular movements, organized by radical political parties, was perhaps greater than elsewhere, in part because of the more rigid social structure in the North and Southern hinterlands, in part because of the absence of that intermediary institution, the modernizing armed forces, which had played such an important role in many other Arab states: to put it in the terminology of the times, it was harder for "petty bourgeois" regimes to establish themselves in Yemen than elsewhere, although in the end they did. Thus in much Yemeni political rhetoric the revolution was as much that of the oppressed poor [*al-kadihin*] as of the Yemeni nation as such.

Yemen and the Arab world

If Yemeni nationalism presented itself as part of the Arab world and of the Arab nationalist movement, it also demarcated itself from this in a specific manner. This was not just a question of the combination of ideological identities, as in the Egyptian or Iraqi cases, but of their being contrasted, i.e., of the Yemeni identity being defined in opposition to that of the Arab world outside. At least three factors can be seen as playing a role here. First, while Yemeni nationalism embraced the country's Islamic identity, the past invoked to justify the "nation" began with the pre-Islamic civilizations.[21] Thus for Yemenis the concept of *jahiliyya*, of the pre-Islamic period being one of "ignorance," is unacceptable, not least because of the contrast that it highlights between what was happening in Yemen and what was taking place elsewhere in the Arabian Peninsula. Yemeni nationalists often set the sons of Qahtan (the Yemenis) against those of `Adnan (the Bedouin, Saudis, etc.). Second, if Yemeni nationalism has been directed against external rule in the form of British and earlier Ottoman colonialism it has also been directed against an Arab neighbor, Saudi Arabia. This is a factor relatively absent in other Arab states and is a reflection of the fact that, in the period in which Arab nationalisms were formed, i.e., after World War I, the Arabian Peninsula was the only area where independent Arab states existed and could engage in interstate, nationalism-provoking activities. The clashes in the 1920s and early 1930s with Saudi Arabia have been compounded by the treatment of Yemenis in Saudi Arabia during the oil boom and by the ongoing political, including border, disputes between the two states. It could be said, with only a little simplification, that *the main "national" enemy of Yemen is a neighboring Arab state*. This sense of contrast with other Arab states is further compounded by the experience of the Egyptian military presence during the 1960s: even among those republicans whom the Egyptians were supporting, there was a strong sense of antipathy to the supposed liberators, one amply reciprocated, as is well known, by the Egyptians themselves.

This uneasy relation to Arab nationalism is well illustrated in the documents of the Southern nationalist movement. In the NLF's founding document of 1965 the Arabs are referred to as the people [*sha`b*] to whom the Yemenis belong, but by the 1970s the Yemenis were to become the *sha`b* and the Arabs the looser *umma*. Similarly, while in the 1970 South Yemeni constitution Yemen is a district [*iqlim*] of the Arab world, by 1978 Yemen itself is the *watan*, the homeland.[22] Thus while the Arab identity was in no sense rejected or overtly challenged, the Yemeni dimension came be given greater centrality.

Yemeni "Unity"

The role of "unity" within Yemeni politics reflects both a general Arab aspiration and a particular Yemeni one. Thus the support for Arab unity, from the 1950s onward, served not only to express Yemen's membership of and participation in the Arab world but also to attract to Yemen support—military, political, financial—from other Arab states: it reflected Yemen's relative isolation and poverty. However unity also meant the resolution of a specific more local problem, the fragmentation of Yemen itself. Most obviously, this pertained to the division between North and South, ascribed, as we have seen, to the policies of colonial powers. Prior to the 1950s the area now known as South Yemen was known as "Aden," or "the Protectorates," later as "South Arabia" [*Junub al-Jazira al-`Arabiyya*] or the "Arab South" [*al-Junub al-`Arabi*], and it was only from the late 1950s that terms such as "Yemeni

South" [al-Junub al-Yamani] or "South Yemen" [Junub al-Yaman] came into political usage, alongside that of South Arabia.[23] A proper charting of the shifting denomination of the "Yemeni" area in the writing and political rhetoric of the period remains to be written: the most cursory review indicates, however, a fast, politically inspired shifting of nomenclature, with at any one time frequent uncertainties and alternative usages.[24] But there were further elements to this call for unity: the demand for the return of the three provinces occupied by Saudi Arabia in 1934; hostility to political movements in the South, be they Aden-based or more broadly "South Arabian,"[25] which wanted to maintain the inherited divisions of the country; and, implicitly, support for the idea of national integration and centralization in the face of a highly fragmented, regional and tribal society. This assertion of a Yemeni national identity was also designed to preclude emergence of other, potential, contemporary "nationalisms"—Adeni, Hadrami, `Asiri.

CONTINGENCY AND INSTRUMENTALITY

In comparative annals of modern nationalism, the Yemeni case may appear to be more historically rooted than that of many others, including some in the Middle East.[26] Yet, even if this is so, this historical overview, and the discussion of particular ideological elements in Yemeni nationalism, provides the raw material for recognition of the contingent formation of Yemeni nationalism. In the first place, the *general historicity* of Yemeni nationalism, i.e., the role of the international and universalizing context, can be analyzed in terms of a number of processes: changes in international trade and strategy in the nineteenth and twentieth centuries, the impact of changes in colonial administration on the South, the introduction of ideas of social and political organization from the Arab world and elsewhere (including the British trades union movement and Indonesian politics, the latter mediated via emigres in South-East Asia), and the political evolution of the Arab world from the 1940s onward. Thus the particular history and formation of Yemeni nationalism took place within a broader, universalizing context.

Analysis of the *specific causation* of Yemeni nationalism would encompass both the preexisting social and political structures in the country and the impact on Yemen of external events, including the rise of Saudi Arabia in the 1920s, the explosion of the Palestine question in the 1940s (with the very specific impact on Yemen of the departure of the Jewish community hitherto seen as part of the Yemeni people),[27] and the Egyptian revolution of 1952. It would, however, also address the contingency of this nationalism taking the form it did. In the first place there is the contingency of space: there was nothing inevitable in "national" Yemen either comprising or excluding the territory that it did. Given the divisions within Yemeni society prior to, and indeed accompanying, the rise of the nationalist movement, other outcomes are more than conceivable: Aden could have remained separate, becoming eventually a separate cosmopolitan nation-state, an Arab equivalent of Singapore to the rest of the Yemen's Malaysia, a Qatar or a Kuwait; the Hadramaut could also have broken away as could any of the other seventeen political entities in the South or the Zeidi parts of the North;[28] political Yemen could have extended to include the southern, Dhofar, region of the Sultanate of Oman, an area historically claimed by Yemenis and with more geographic and social continuity with the Mahra province of Yemen than with the rest of Oman.[29] Had the Saudis pursued their conquests in 1934, the whole of North Yemen might have been incorporated into Saudi Arabia and Yemen would today have the status of Hijaz, an entity with some historical distinctiveness but with, in Anthony Smith's terms, an unrealized substratum. Equally, had the British not been there, the Saudis might have annexed Hadramaut, a region where "Yemeni" sentiment is intermittent at best and that would have given them direct access to the Indian Ocean.[30]

This contingency extends to that of ideology. We see in Yemeni nationalism the combination of elements found in other Middle Eastern nationalisms—pre-Islamic, Islamic, Arab, third worldist, local, in this case, Yemeni: far from these being set by history, or necessarily contradictory, they are combined in a mutually supportive, and changing, manner. The history textbooks used in schools stress a "people" in continuous time and without tribal or other fragmentary characteristics who have acted to create the modern Yemen.[31] In declarations of state each of the four elements is deployed to endorse the existence of a historic, natural, Yemeni "nation," with changing emphases reflecting changing circumstances: thus when Yemen faces conflict with Saudi Arabia, it is conventional to appeal to "the sons of Saba and Himyar"; when Yemeni politicians respond to events in Palestine, or the Gulf, their "Arabness" is highlighted; in times of rapprochement with Saudi Arabia, emphasis is given to Islamic fraternity and the contribution of Yemen to Islam. On the other hand, the varying emphases also reflect shifts in the political situation within the country: thus the "Islamic" element has been prominent in two periods, in the 1940s, with the rise of the Free Yemeni opposition, and again from the late 1980s, with the emergence of an Islamist current, *al-Islah*. Again, there are no constraints on the combination, or adjustment, of these different ideological components.

Behind such accounts of ideology, and of definitions developed and changed, lies the question of *instrumentality*, of the use of these ideas by political leaderships, in or out of power, to serve their particular ends. Much of the discourse of nation and nationalism revolves around the state, not least through the efforts of states to promote a specific "national" awareness against external and internal, centrifugal forces. Nowhere is this more so than with regard to the question of "unity" itself. While this corresponded to a widespread popular sentiment, one that combined easily with support for Arab unity, it was articulated by political leaderships for their own, instrumental, reasons. Thus in the 1950s the Imam used "Yemeni unity" as a means of advancing his dynastic claim to influence in the South and to the territory occupied by the British. After the revolution of 1962, the Sana`a government used "unity" as a means of enhancing their domestic legitimacy, countering British involvement in support of the royalists in the North and mobilizing support for their own regime from the population in the South. Once two Yemeni states came into existence in 1967, "unity" became an instrument for conducting relations, mostly of rivalry, between the two regimes. While on the one hand "unity" reflected some common interests between the two states, in matters of economic development and tourism, little progress was made in this regard; more substantively, the two regimes used "unity" to legitimate forms of pressure on the other.

For much of the late 1960s and 1970s this involved support for guerrilla opposition within the other state, but on two occasions it led to war. Both wars, those of 1972 and 1979, were attempts by one regime, using the slogan of "unity" and in alliance with opposition forces within the other state, to advance their interests. For the South unity had long been, and remained, part not only of the reintegration of the Yemeni homeland but of the transformation of the North as well. Thus in the aftermath of independence South Yemeni officials insisted that "Yemeni unity . . . is a unity of the toiling people, and must be made by them. . . . This unity must be progressive and must not be racial or regional in character, and must be hostile to colonialism and reaction."[32] The pre-1962 argument, that there could not be unity until there had been a transformation in the North, now became one that unity would be achieved by promoting such a transformation.

This instrumentality remained central in the period of unification itself, 1990–1994. Each regime hoped that it could use unification both to enhance its own position within its respective area of power and advance it in the area of the other. Unity was, therefore, not a policy aimed at fusion but an instrument for inter-regime competition. If, at first, it appeared as if this was not a zero-sum game, and that both sides could benefit from and live with the unity agreement, the elections of 1993 showed that, in reality, each was bent on consolidating within its own territory: however, the situation had so changed that the North now believed it could impose its will on the South, a goal that, after some months of preparation and misleading negotiation, it proceeded to meet. Yemeni unity was thus achieved by the successful imposition of the Northern regime's power on the South, in alliance both with Islamists in the North, and with dissident exiles from the South.[33]

As already noted, both between and within states "unity" reflected another, more general, goal: namely that of state-building. North Yemeni society is more socially fragmented than that of any other regional country, with the exception of Afghanistan, a fragmentation reflected in the lack of influence of the central government outside the major cities, and the widespread distribution of arms in society. In most discussion of Yemen, by Yemenis and others, this armed rural population is referred to as "tribal": few of these inhabitants of the rural areas are nomadic, and the term "tribe" is used in a number of senses, but the fact of such diffusion of power, arms and identity is clear enough.[34] In the South, British rule made some impact on the tribal system, and the Socialist Party went much further in the direction of centralization. Advocacy of "unity" entailed both the creation of a single "Yemeni" political culture and the strengthening of the powers of the state itself. At the ideological level, this involved a denial, with mixed impact, of the "tribal," regional, and sectarian differences within Yemen, and hence an assertion of the legitimacy of the central state.[35] In practice, it meant that both states sought to reduce the power of the armed rural population, the South more successfully than the North. In the North during the 1970s the regime of President Ibrahim al-Hamdi promoted closer ties with the South as part of an attempt to strengthen the central government.[36] Probably one of the main considerations of the Sana`a regime in entering the unity process in 1990 was its hope that it could use the Southern army and administrative apparatus to strengthen itself in the North. The irony was that, when it came to the war of 1994, Sana`a could only prevail by making significant concessions to the centrifugal forces.

To this discussion of the instrumentality of unity as far as states are concerned can be conjoined that of the instrumentality of classes. It is not difficult to write a history of Yemeni nationalism in "class" terms, seeing nationalism in general, and the idea of unity in particular, as the ideologies of particular classes seeking to advance their interests against the prevailing, fragmented, state structures. Thus in the North unity was espoused first by dissident *sada* or chiefs and merchants, denied their proper status by the Imams, and then by the newly rising social groups—intellectuals, educated technocrats, and army officers and, later, the incipient trades union and peasant movements. The radical left in the North, which clashed with the regime in the late 1960s, and that waged guerrilla war between 1978 and 1982, saw itself as the vanguard of a mass movement that would bring about unity through overthrowing the military and tribal forces dominating the country.[37] In the South it was the rising trades union movement in Aden, later backed by a radicalized rural population, that pioneered unity against those social interests, merchants in Aden, and Sultans in the countryside, whose interest lay in preserving a separate, and itself fragmented, South.

Such "class analysis" may often have taken a simplified, crude, form, one that would have been inappropriate not just for any country in the Middle East but for any more developed society as well. To reject such reductionist use of class analysis is not, however, to preclude that there was a wide-ranging and multiple interaction of classes with ideas of nation and nationalism, and that any history of nationalism in Yemen, as elsewhere, must take such an interaction into account. Here again comparative contingency may be a suitable guideline: the question is not whether nationalism was determined by class, or unrelated to it but how, within the general context of modernity and under the impact of exogenous political and social change, specific articulations of class and nationalist ideology occurred. All may not be the work of the undifferentiated "proletariat," "petty bourgeoisie," or, in the Yemeni case, *sayyadin* (fishermen), and all resistance did not come from *iqta`in* (feudalists) but these forces certainly played a part.

This essay has attempted to provide an analysis of nationalism in Yemen within the framework of "comparative contingency."[38] The aim has been to show not how a Yemeni "nation" has existed for centuries or millennia, or how such a preexisting "nation" has "arisen" or "woken up" but, rather, how a set of recent processes, some international, some within Yemen, have combined to produce a nationalist movement and discourse and to give them their particular content. That, in accordance with the universal pressures operating on it, Yemen would have had to produce some form of "nationalism" by the middle of the twentieth century was inevitable (even Qatar has been able to do so), but that it produced the particular form it did, and in the time it occurred, reflects a set of contingent events and processes. Equally, while the population as a whole has been involved in this diffusion of a nationalist ideology, the actual content and emphasis of this ideology has varied between time and place, reflecting the instrumental usage of nationalism by aspirant political leaderships and established regimes alike. It follows that the Yemenis had to be part of some nationalist process, in the conditions of the modern world; that they were incorporated into *this particular nationalism* was a result of the multiple contingencies already discussed. In neither case was the outcome the result of a historical determination derived from the existence of this "nation" nor was the outcome predetermined as to the geographical context or ideological content of this nationalism. Nor indeed is the process yet over, as tensions between secular and religious forces in Yemen, as elsewhere in the region, demonstrate. All of which is without prejudice to claims about contemporary belief or political legitimacy.

3

The Tropes of Stagnation and Awakening in Nationalist Historical Consciousness

The Egyptian Case[*]

Gabriel Piterberg

For me, a child of a successful anti-colonial struggle, *Orientalism* was a book which talked of things I felt I had known all along but had never found the language to formulate with clarity. Like many great books, it seemed to say for the first time what one had always wanted to say. The force of the argument made its impact in the first few pages, and halfway through the book I found my thoughts straying beyond the confines of Said's discussion. I was struck by the way Orientalism was implicated in the construction of not only the ideology of British colonialism which had dominated India for two centuries, but also of the nationalism which was my own heritage. Orientalist constructions of Indian civilization had been avidly seized upon by the ideologues of Indian nationalism in order to assert the glory and antiquity of a national past. So Indian nationalists had accepted the colonialist critique of the Indian present: a society fallen into barbarism and stagnation, incapable of progress and modernity.
—*Partha Chatterjee, "Their Own Words? An Essay for Edward Said"*

A METHODOLOGICAL INTRODUCTION

This article is the product of my interest in the relationship between modern historiography and nationalism and more generally, in the construction of narratives of identity in modernity. The topic discussed here

[*]While researching and writing this article I was a fellow in the Middle East Seminar, the Van Leer Jerusalem Institute. I benefited greatly from the seminar's discussions. I am particularly indebted to the wisdom, scholarship and friendship of Azmi Bishara, Rivka Feldhai, Adel Mana, Amnon Raz-Krakotzkin and Ursula Wokoeck.

is the perplexing, yet patently evident, presence of the Orientalist discourse[1] in non-European nationalist historiographies. Modern Egyptian historiography is examined as a case study. The morphology and function of Orientalism in the construction of a national-territorial narrative are considered with regard to the representations of a specific referent: Ottoman Egypt in particular, and the Ottoman Empire and its rule over the Arab Middle East in general. Two sorts of texts are read: works by professional historians, and school textbooks used for the teaching of national history and civic studies.

On the basis of this reading, I put forth the following argument: (1) In terms of morphology, Egyptian historiography adopted, lock, stock and barrel, the Orientalist narrative of the "decline" and "stagnation" of the Ottoman Empire and its provincial rule from the middle of sixteenth century on, with special emphasis on the year 1798 as the turning-point in modern Middle Eastern and Egyptian history. (2) In terms of function, the Orientalist discourse underlies the portrayal of a stereotypical—and foreign—ancien régime, on the ruins of which the dormant nation emerges as congruent with modernity and as a modernizing force. Put differently, the Orientalist discourse underlies the familiar nationalist narrative of the protagonist (the nation) that transfers itself from stagnation and medieval slumber into awakening and modernity.[2]

Before proceeding with the case study, I wish to set forth the basic components that stimulate my reading of nationalist historiography, and situate this reading within the context of a larger debate within the social sciences on the nature of modernity; though of pivotal importance, nationalism is only a constituent part in this debate.

The framework within which I read nationalist historiography is an attempt to amalgamate Hayden White's understanding of modern historiography and Benedict Anderson's understanding of modern nationalism, or, to be more precise, modern "nation-ness."[3] What makes this amalgam possible—and from my perspective, appealing—is the fact that both White and Anderson challenge, in a radical and fundamental fashion, the most persistent orthodoxy in the social and human sciences. Their challenge is accompanied by the alternatives they offer; these pertain to different issues but are philosophically analogous.[4]

Instead of labeling the orthodox paradigm I prefer to identify it by its underlying premise, namely, *dichotomism*. According to this premise the human world, especially in the age of modernity, can be observed and explained through a prism that consists of a series of analogous dichotomies: objective/ subjective, reality/language, material/ideal (or ideological), content/form, West/East, society/state, history/myth (or fiction), and more. In the last two decades this dichotomism has been acutely undermined by several scholars who, each taking on a polarity pertinent to her/his interest, have, in effect, deconstructed these alleged-ly timeless truths by showing that they are historical and discursive. Peter Novick's work on the concept of objectivity in American histori-ography is a good example of the critical power of rendering historical something that is constructed as eternally valid.[5]

A more explicit deconstruction of dichotomism in a particular context is Timothy Mitchell's work on the phenomenology of the modern state and its appearance in the Middle East.[6] Tackling the state/society di-chotomy, Mitchell perceptively notes, first, that debates among different schools in conventional political science have always remained within the confines of dichotomism: society is always grasped as an objective content and the state as a subjective form, and the main endeavor is to arrive at a finite definition of the elusive line that separates state and society. Mitchell then argues that the modern state is not a found enti-ty, unproblematically distinguishable from society but an assembly of social practices that, through various means and technologies, appear to constitute an entity that is external to society. The modern state, in Mitchell's words, is a "discursively produced effect."

Mitchell's approach undermines this particular dichotomy by radically altering questions and categories. The latter are no longer two entities, occupying spaces the boundaries between which must be identified, but social and other practices. The focus is the historical processes through which some of these practices are constructed as "the state"; and the ques-tion of whether the state is "real" ceases to be interesting. "Real" is no longer posited as a dichotomous opposite to "fabricated."

White and Anderson do something rather similar. White's work on the narrative in modern European historiography is a complex under-taking that I cannot seriously claim to discuss here. I focus on the two pairs of related dichotomies that White deconstructs: content/form and history/literature (especially the modern novel). Orthodox scholarship reads the historical narrative on the basis of two assumptions. One, termed by White *coherence*, presupposes that past reality offers itself in coherent structures. According to the other assumption, *correspondence* in White's terminology, the narrative is seen as an indifferent form that, if competently written, merely mimics the content of its referent, that is, the coherent way in which historical reality already offers itself.[7]

On the basis of these two assumptions a twofold dichotomy is then drawn: between a content (which is self-offered) and a form (which is transparent and merely mimics what is already offered by the content); and between the imaginary narrative and the historical narrative. It implies, White contends, "that the form in which historical events present themselves to a prospective narrator are found rather than constructed."[8] Moreover, the form of the historical narrative "adds nothing to the content of the representation."[9] White's fundamental rejection of this double dichotomy is premised on the view that reality as it occurs is formless and meaningless, and that making a narrative sense of it is a product of human consciousness expressed in a certain form of language. It follows that the representation of a past reality through a historical narrative is not an indifferent form, which, at best, is an adequate mimesis of how the content offers itself, but a form that constitutes content and is indistinguishable from it.[10]

The twin dichotomy of content/form is that between history and fictional literature, especially the kinds of literature that employ narrative discourse (the modern novel and the epic are good examples). The proponents of this dichotomy base it on the argument that the contents are dichotomous: the historical narrative refers to events that really happened whereas fictional literature's referents are imagined or invented events. In the historical narrative, therefore, form need not seriously influence the truthful and realistic reflection of its subject matter. Language is transparent. White undermines this in two ways. First, he convincingly shows that when the reader comprehends the meaning produced by a historical narrative, his/her comprehension depends on the recognition of the narrative's form as much as it does on its content; further, in this process of comprehension the content and the form are inseparable.[11] Second, White renders historical the dichotomous pair. He shows that the premise by which historical discourse need not, and should not, resort to any literary strategies in order to reflect truthfully and realistically its subject matter has a history and a context. It was part of the professionalization of history in the nineteenth century, and ought to be set against the ideological and political controversies in that period about the upheavals of the French Revolution, and who and what caused them.[12]

Since the publication of the first edition of his *Imagined Communities* in 1983, the impact of Benedict Anderson on the study of nationalism has been, paradoxically, immense and limited.[13] As Alon Confino puts it: "Since 1983 Anderson's fascinating notion of the nation as an imagined community has become a household term in the way we think and talk about nationalism; but we still await a study that explores the process—social, political and cultural—by which people come to imagine a distinct nation."[14] There are, I think, three reasons for this perplexing paradox. The first is the nature of Anderson's work: it has tremendous explanatory force and a host of stimulating ideas but, at the same time, it does not easily lend itself to direct and specific applications as, for instance, White's concept of historiography or Weber's of bureaucracy do. Second, the two chapters that are of a more applicable nature have appeared relatively recently, in the revised edition (1991).[15] The third reason is the reluctance of historians in particular—for historians are the chief suppliers of case studies—seriously to consider theoretical issues as part and parcel of their applied work, in a manner that is neither instrumental nor eclectic. The consequence of all this is that in many studies of particular nationalisms we find openings that praise Anderson's "apt coinage" or "refreshing concept;" there, however, the mutual relevance between Anderson's model and a given nationalism abruptly ends.

What has gone largely unnoticed in Anderson's concept is its potential to transform the debate over the modern nation in a radical fashion. This radical transformation is, in my understanding, analogous to those put forth by Mitchell and White with regard to the modern state and modern historiography respectively: Anderson acutely undermines yet another variant that comprises the paradigm of dichotomism.

The point can be clarified through a common and well-known classification of the scholarship on nationalism offered by Anthony Smith. He identifies two types of scholars: modernists and primordialists.[16] Smith's discussion on these approaches to nationalism reveals two things. One is that the debate safely remains within the confines of dichotomism: the polarity is essentially whether modern nations are "really real" and genuine collectives, with empirically verifiable premodern lineages, roots, and origins, as the primordialists—and, albeit more crudely, the nationalists themselves—say; or whether they are strictly modern creatures, with an invented, falsified, or fabricated (according to taste) genesis in the past as the modernists maintain. The other thing is that Smith's reference to Anderson as one of the two most important proponents of the modernist school (the other being Gellner) is typical of the way in which the radical potential in Anderson's work is time and again overlooked if not missed altogether.[17]

True, within the confines of a dichotomistic discourse it is fairly reasonable to understand Anderson's approach as modernist. The point is that the concept of imagined communities *transcends* the premordialist/modernist polarity, in the same way as Mitchell's concept of the modern state as a "discursively produced effect" transcends the state/ society polarity. Anderson himself, in the revised edition (1991), seems to be aware that his approach is fundamentally different.[18] The radical potential, however, already exists in the original edition (1983), and it lies in Anderson's disagreement with Gellner and his insistence on the nation as an *imagined* rather than *invented* community. It is quite puzzling that Smith, while unproblematically attaching Gellner and Anderson to the same "school," fails to see the significance of the following passage:

> With a certain ferocity Gellner makes a comparable point [comparable to Renan's] when he rules that "Nationalism is not the awakening of nations to self-consciousness: it *invents* nations where they do not exist." The drawback to this formulation, however, is that Gellner is so anxious to show that nationalism masquerades under false pretenses that he assimilates "invention" to "fabrication" and "falsity," rather than to "imagining" and "creation." In this way he implies that "true" communities can be advantageously juxtaposed to nations. In fact, all communities larger than primordial villages of face-to-face contact . . . are imagined. Communities are to be distinguished, not by their falsity/genuineness, but by the style in which they are imagined [emphasis in original].[19]

Anderson not only casts aside the above polarity, he also makes it clear that in his model "imagined" should not be construed as dichotomous to "real." The modern nation (and any other large form of collectivity for that matter) is inseparably and simultaneously imagined *and* real: it has to be imagined because it is not a tangible thing and because all of its members will never meet each other; it is at the same time real because, paradoxical as it may seem, the imagining is real, that is, most people really think and act as members of nations. Consciousness itself, once adopted, circulated, and reproduced, becomes a "real fact."

There is another way in which Anderson's work is capable of transforming our understanding of nationalism: the fact that it tries to disentangle what can be termed nationalism's black box, that is, the cultural process in which people come to make a nationalist sense of themselves and the world around them. This unraveling of the sense of nationness starts from Anderson's explicit view that the nationalism is first and foremost a "cultural artefact."[20]

The significance of the emphasis Anderson lays on nationalism as a cultural sense-making phenomenon may be better appreciated through another analogy. The impact that Anderson's cultural emphasis may have on the study of nationalism resembles the impact on the study of ideology that Clifford Geertz's famous essay had more than twenty years ago.[21] What seemed to have motivated Geertz to apply his general model of culture to the concept of ideology was the inadequacy of the then prevailing theories: the Marxist (the interest theory in Geertz's terminology) and the Behaviorist (the strain theory). The former viewed ideology as a reflection and reproduction of class interests, whereas for the latter ideology was functional in managing and alleviating modernity's strain. While these theories are not without merits, they have a fundamental flaw that Geertz perceptively pointed out: they go from what might be the source of ideology (Marxism) to what might be its effect (Behaviorism), and the complicated process, cultural in essence, of the production of meaning (i.e., ideology itself), is left idle like an unopened black box. Be the merits and demerits of Geertz's approach what they may, its great contribution has been in drawing attention to the ignored process of cultural signification. The analogy between Geertz's and Anderson's insights may be more than coincidental, for both approach their respective topics—ideology and nationalism—from the vantage point of sociocultural anthropology.[22]

THE EGYPTIAN HISTORIOGRAPHICAL DISCOURSE

This section is concerned with the representation of a certain portion of Egypt's past, the Ottoman portion, in a host of modern Egyptian historical texts. These comprise works by professional historians, as well as three textbooks selected from the project entitled *al-Tarbiyya al-Wataniyya.* Though the corpus under consideration may not be a perfect reflection of Egyptian nationalist historiography from the 1920s on, it is sufficiently substantial to sustain the chief argument I put forth.[23]

Despite the fact that I have intentionally selected texts from different historiographic generations, texts that reflect varied interests and views, their representations of the Ottoman Empire, its Arabic-speaking provinces, and Ottoman Egypt in particular have several fundamental features; it might even be tentatively suggested that these historical representations constitute a uniform approach. The uniformity of this corpus stems from the fact that its constituent parts display a simultaneous and perhaps unselfconscious acceptance of two powerful discourses: the Orientalist and that of territorial Egyptian nationness as it was shaped in the 1920s. What these two discourses have in common is a cultural-essentialist perception of history, and strong, at times vitriolic, anti-Ottoman judgments and views.

The emphasis laid on the territorial nationalist discourse requires some explanation. The most authoritative works on the history of nationalist culture in Egypt, by Israel Gershoni and James Jankowski, identify at least two, possibly three competing nationalist discourses: the Egyptianist-Pharaonic and the Islamic-Arab;[24] to these it is possible to add, as Ursula Wokoeck does, the radical Islamic discourse.[25] Moreover, according to Gershoni and Jankowski, whereas the Egyptianist concept prevailed until roughly the early 1930s, it was gradually marginalized by its Islamic-Arab challenger (which became more Arab than Islamic) from the mid-1930s and thereafter.[26]

I do not wish to contest this thesis, supported as it is by impressive and varied data. My point of departure is, however, somewhat different. My reading of nationalist historiography ought to be placed within the context offered by Sami Zubaida and Roger Owen.[27] Separately but in a related way, they argue that from the 1920s on the "colonial state," later the territorial nation-state, became the most irreducibly basic unit in the Middle East in terms of both politics and what Edward Said terms "identitarian thought."[28] According to Zubaida and Owen, the modern state and the territorial nation as an imagined community created a new and different "political field," under the rules of which politics—including the politics of collective identity—had to be played. What this means, as Zubaida in particular argues convincingly, is not that radical Islam or Arabism were meaningless alternatives to, say, Egyptian Pharaonism, but rather that their imaginings too were subordinated to the model of the territorial nation. This perspective, I think, does not contradict the Gershoni-Jankowski thesis of two national cultures; it simply sees them as two discourses that contest the power to shape Egyptian nationness.

The texts in question being historical, I shall examine first the representation of time, where the Orientalist discourse is emphasized; then the representation of space and subject, where the Egyptian nationalist discourse is evident; and, finally, the explicit and formal explanations these texts offer. The neat attribution of one discourse to one dimension is obviously dictated by analytical convenience and clarity of presentation.

The temporal definition of a historical topic, "periodization" in the professional jargon, evinces the historian's interpretation and sometimes may even surrender her/his worldview. In our case the periodization touches upon what since the 1970s has become an intensely debated bone of contention in Middle East studies, namely, the beginning of the modern era in the region's history.

The position of the Egyptian historians on this issue is decisive, and justifies a view of them as, to use the late Albert Hourani's formulation, "Near Eastern historians looking at themselves with eyes given their direction by the West." Clearly implying adherence to the Orientalist discourse, their position is that the year 1798, in which Bonaparte invaded Egypt, erected a barrier between the eighteenth century and the Ottoman period in general on the one hand, and the nineteenth century on the other.

For Shafiq Ghurbal, the doyen of twentieth-century Egyptian historiography, the five centuries that preceded the French invasion are not worthy of serious consideration. In the preface to his published Masters thesis, *The Beginning of the Egyptian Question* (1928), Ghurbal declares that the nineteenth century opened a new era in the history of the Middle East and Egypt in particular. The Westernization of the East was, according to Ghurbal, the history of the nineteenth century. In this process the French invasion was a hallmark, and the intervention and cultural influence of the West played a major role. Indicative in this respect is the citation with which Ghurbal opens his Preface: " 'L'Organisation de l'Orient,' wrote M. Lavisse, 'est en somme, la fait capital de la periode moderne.' "[29]

Though a detailed analysis of Ghurbal's historiography cannot be ventured here, it should be pointed out that he most probably absorbed the Orientalist discourse through his supervisor at the University of London, Arnold Toynbee. Consider for instance the following short passage from Toynbee's forward to Ghurbal's book. In it Toynbee illustrates his version of the "Occident-Orient" encounter, as it was embodied in the Mamluk beys riding to intercept the French force in the summer of 1798:

> and they encountered not men (as human capacity was conceived of by Orientals in 1798), but creatures armed with all the incomprehensible and irresistible powers of Mr. Well's 'Martians.' At the first onset, these Occidental 'Martians' carried all before them, and Oriental mankind was stunned. Egypt became a battleground on which superhuman Frenchmen and superhuman Englishmen fought one another."[30]

One of Ghurbal's outstanding disciples, Jamal al-Din al-Shayyal, further reinforces the acceptance of Orientalism in the discourse of modern Egyptian historiography. He contributes to this discourse the term *"rukud"* (stagnation), as something that incarnates and sums up what is for him three centuries of Egyptian history under Ottoman yoke.[31] The original feature in al-Shayyal's work that reveals how Orientalism and territorial nationalism are inextricably intertwined is his thesis of *al-nahda al-tilqa'iyya* (the spontaneous awakening). This awakening, al-Shayyal observes, occurred in the second half of the eighteenth century and was authentically Egyptian, innocent of either Eastern or Western influence. The interesting point for the present discussion is, however, al-Shayyal's assertion that the casting aside of this authentically Egyptian awakening by what he calls "the movement of translation and imitation in the nineteenth century" was not only inevitable but *desirable*.[32] The reason for which "the spontaneous awakening" was bound to come to a halt, al-Shayyal explains, was that the French introduced in Egypt "Manifestations of a scientific awakening that were in fundamental contrast to those of the Egyptian awakening in every field" (note how through the same word—*nahda*—modernization and nationalism are rendered two analogous parts of the same whole). The result was that Egyptian scholars "began to compare the knowledge they possessed with that possessed by these Frenchmen." The imprint left on Egypt by the French expedition, al-Shayyal concludes, was ineradicable. Therefore, the reforms Muhammad `Ali Pasha carried out "required the imitation of the West, if Egypt desired a real awakening, [one] that would conform with the [awakening] in the world."[33]

Al-Shayyal's colleague, Ahmad `Izzat `Abd al-Karim, reiterates the Orientalist notion, argued as it is on a cultural-essentialist premise, that the nineteenth century marked an abrupt change, but does so in a more narrowly defined context. He contributed an essay that forwards al-Shayyal's book on Egyptian historiography in the nineteenth century. Concentrating on the great historian `Abd al-Rahman al-Jabarti and entitled "The Historical Writing at the End of the Eighteenth Century," the essay is thus concluded by `Abd al-Karim:

> It is therefore evident that we see in al-Jabarti the last disciple of the school of Muslim historians in the Middle Ages, and we do not see in him the first disciple of the nineteenth century school. For Egypt of the nineteenth century was something different, which al-Jabarti did not know, and had he known he would not have understood it. The fact that culture was to be developed in Egypt by those who desired renovation . . . was inevitable. The [historical] writing of the nineteenth century drew the sources of its formation from this general cultural awakening.[34]

The work of Muhammad Anis is particularly significant to my tentative argument that at least with regard to the Ottoman past the approach of modern Egyptian historiography shows uniformity, and that this uniformity consists of the Orientalist and territorial nationalist discourses. The significance lies in the fact that in almost any classification of Egyptian historians Anis would not be classified with those I have thus far discussed. He is not a disciple of Ghurbal's, he belongs to a later generational group, he propagated the use of scientific socialism and dialectic materialism (as distinguished from Ghurbal's diplomatic historiography or Shayyal's adherence to the "old" history of ideas and culture), and ideologically he was a Nasserite.[35] To return to the Gershoni-Jankowski thesis, Anis should have been a clear proponent of the secular Arab alternative; as I will show, however, he abides by the discourse as it was shaped by Ghurbal and al-Shayyal.

The first thing to note is that Anis dedicates his book on the Ottoman period "ila faqid al-ta'rikh al-ʿArabi al-hadith ustadhina Muhammad Shafiq Ghurbal."[36] More important, like Ghurbal, al-Shayyal, ʿAbd al-Karim, and others, he draws a clear line between two periods. The first, from the Ottoman conquest in 1517 to the eighteenth century, he identifies by the term "*iflas*," that is, the bankruptcy of the Ottoman system at the center and in the Arab provinces. The second period is characterized by Anis as the era of *al-ittijahat al-jadida* (the new orientations) that spread throughout the Middle East: Muhammad ʿAli's reforms and—fantastic as it may seem—the Wahhabiyya in the first half of the nineteenth century, and the inception of Arab and Turkish nationalisms in the second half.[37]

Though the formal explanations offered by the historians will be presented later, it seems necessary to comment here on how the periodization is justified. This justification brings to the fore a fundamental Orientalist premise embedded in the discussion hitherto: the superiority of "Western culture" and its sine qua non status for generating change in a stagnant society. In this respect the historiographic discourse considered here is not only uniform but unanimous.

Al-Shayyal for instance, in order to account for the alleged *rukud*, quotes lengthy passages extracted from Ghurbal's preface to the book *The Islamic East* written by another colleague, Husayn Muʿnis. One of these passages, underlined in al-Shayyal's own text, reads as follows: "The stagnation stemmed from the fact that the Ottoman force doubtless prevented the contact of the peoples of the [Ottoman] state with foreign cultures in general . . . and European culture in particular."[38] Anis offers a similar argument. The isolation imposed on Egyptian society, he explains, "turned Egypt—indeed the whole Arab East—into a stagnant region [*mintaqa rakida*], which was not affected by the cultural developments undergone by Europe from the Italian Renaissance to the French Revolution."[39]

ʿAbd al-Rahman ʿAbd al-Rahim also accepts this periodization and justification. His case is interesting for two reasons. One is that the work by ʿAbd al-Rahim referred to here was published relatively late (1977). Another reason is that ʿAbd al-Rahim is a socioeconomic historian, and socioeconomic history is a scholarly quarter out of which emanated most serious doubts about the validity of the 1798 narrative; further, and in a clearer way than any of the historians mentioned thus far, his specialized topic is Ottoman Egypt in the eighteenth century. Yet ʿAbd al-Rahim, perhaps even more blatantly than his colleagues, sees nothing but decay, stagnation, and exploitation in the pre-1798 period. For him, as for so many Orientalists, the accounts of European travelers (the famous Volney in this case) are authoritative reflections of socioeconomic realities.[40] In his summary of how Egypt was socially and economically affected by Ottoman rule, the social domain is thus portrayed as follows by `Abd al-Rahim:

> This was [then] the social situation under Ottoman rule which went from bad to worse. A comprehensive change had to be found. But things remained as they had been until the arrival of the French expedition (1798). A new page was then opened in the history of modern Egypt.[41]

While the representation of time reveals the uniformity with which the Egyptian historical texts follow the Orientalist discourse, the representation of space and subject brings to the fore the acute impact on this historiography of another discourse: territorial Egyptian nationness as it was shaped between the 1890s and the 1920s.[42] The crux of this discourse's impact is what might be called the "Misrification" [*tamsir* in Arabic] of space and subject. It is in this dimension that the writing of "Egypt" as a modern historical subject comes to the fore in a concrete, tangible fashion.

At a more general level this phenomenon corresponds with a key argument through which Anderson understands the nation as an imagined community. He perceptively notices several related processes from the sixteenth century on, which resulted in a major metamorphosis in the conception of time and space. The gist of it was that time came to be conceived of as empty, homogeneous, and simultaneous. Nationalism as cultural artefact is one, albeit central, derivative of this metamorphosis. Further, a nationalist mode of collective imagining is possible only within this sort of time conception, for it facilitates the nation's representation as a sociological-organic essence that floats in its territory in an empty, homogeneous time and manifests itself in a variety of ways.[43]

The process of the Misrification of space and subject correlates with one of several possible classifications of twentieth-century Egyptian historians.[44] The criterion adopted by this particular classification is the nature of the protagonist each group of historians selected as its subject. For the first group, best represented by Ghurbal, the protagonist was the *dawla* (dynastic state) and its enterprising and determined ruler. Its proponents wrote political-diplomatic history, desired that Egypt would become a member in the community of nation-states as an independent state led by the Muhammad `Ali dynasty, and that it would adopt Western culture so as to become part thereof. This is well illustrated by Ghurbal's work mentioned earlier, *The Beginning of the Egyptian Question and the Rise of Mehmet Ali* (1928), a work whose title surrenders its central thesis. For if the French invasion and, more important, Muhammad `Ali Pasha's enterprising rule founded a separate Egyptian political entity, then it was only natural that such an entity should have had distinct political and diplomatic concerns. Thus the Eastern question, at the center of which stood the Ottoman Empire as a whole, is Misrified by Ghurbal.

The second group comprises Ghurbal students, among them al-Shayyal, Mu'nis, and 'Abd al-Karim. The major change they introduced was the shift of the protagonist from *dawla* to *sha`b* (people). By *sha`b* it was not meant that historiographic emphasis had to be laid on the wider strata of society instead of the elite, the ruler and his household. Rather, it was *sha`b* in the sense of a collective whose long, incessant interaction with its geopolitical and climatic environment had distilled an organic-territorial nation. Henceforth other types of protagonists of a similar vein appeared: *al-shakhsiyya al-Misriyya* (the Egyptian personality), *al-hadara al-Misriyya* (Egyptian civilization), *al-thaqafa al-Misriyya* (Egyptian culture), and so on.

Al-Shayyal, for example, contends that Egypt's location on the junction of three continents, its eternal river, creative inhabitants, and florescent culture had distilled an Egyptian personality that "preserved its independence and distinctiveness throughout history."[45] Particularly telling is what according to al-Shayyal the Egyptians could turn to in a dire circumstance such as the "nadir" of Ottoman rule:

> But at that point something was [found] which Egyptians had not forsaken for generations, and this was their consciousness of themselves and their country, Egypt [*shu`urahum bi-anfusihim wa bi-biladihim Misr*]. This consciousness left its trace on Egypt's cultural life, for Egyptians always turned to their very own history, rulers, `ulama, cities, temples, Nile, festivities and so forth. And from this enduring effort we have gained the chain of *khittat* and history books which it contains. It commences with the writing of Ibn `Abd al-Hakam on the conquest of Egypt and ends with `Ali Mubarak's *Khittat al-Tawfiqiyya*, Amin Sami's *Taqwim al-Nil* and `Abd al-Rahman al-Rafi`i's *Ta'rikh al-Haraka al-Qawmiyya*.[46]

An important comment must be made on al-Shayyal's passage. It will be recalled that the passage is extracted from the elaboration of his "spontaneous awakening" thesis alluded to earlier, which occurred in the latter part of the eighteenth century, the nadir of Ottoman yoke. This passage is, I think, a perfect example of the nation as an organic essence that floats in an empty, homogeneous time, from an immemorial past to the present and thence will continue to float ad infinitum. Second, consider the sentence around which the whole passage is constructed, that the Egyptians, whenever they found themselves in dire circumstances always turned to *shu`urahum bi-anfusihim wa bi-biladihim Misr*. This sentence, indeed the whole passage, could have been neatly inserted into Renan's famous lecture "What is a nation?" There may be, in other words, what might be called a "grammar" that underpins all modern, nationalist historiography. The following short passage from Renan's text illustrates this basic grammar, for it shows that Renan's imagining of the nation in general and al-Shayyal's imagining of a particular nation are in principle identical:

> A nation is a soul, spiritual principle. Two things, which in truth are but one, constitute this soul or spiritual principle. One lies in the past, one in the present. One is the possession in common of a rich legacy of memories; the other is present-day consent . . . the will to perpetuate the value of the heritage that one has received in an undivided form. Man, Gentlemen, does not improvise. The nation, like the individual, is the culmination of a long past of endeavours, sacrifice and devotion.[47]

The third group in the classification employed here is one under the roof of which reside, not unproblematically, both socialist and Arab nationalist tendencies. My point concerning this group, as was shown in the discussion on the periodization and will be further shown with regard to the formal explanations, is that in this case also the territorial nation-based discourse prevails. Historians of this group stress the centrality of social and economic processes at the expense of other protagonists, outstanding personalities first and foremost; they also pay much attention to the lower classes—the peasants and urban masses. My point is borne out by the new protagonists introduced by the historians who fall into this group. These widen the social scope of a horizontally imagined community in the historiographic discourse: this "horizontality" means that the peasants embody the national communion no less than Muhammad ʿAli or al-Shayyal's champions of Egyptian culture. The widening of the imagined community does not mean, however, that the hegemony of territorial-nationalist discourse is broken, for all these new protagonists share a common feature with their predecessors—they are all Misrified.

Thus in Anis's work on the Ottoman period *al-mujtamaʿ al-Misri* (Egyptian society) becomes a meaningful subject. Anis explains, for instance, that Jabarti's distinction as a historian, to the extent he cannot be compared to his contemporaries, stems from the fact that Jabarti "gives a comprehensive description of Egyptian society during the Ottoman period," whereas the works of his contemporaries are confined to the traditional elites.[48] The same is true for the term "*al-iqtisad al-Misri*" (the Egyptian economy).[49] The clearest evidence for my observation is ʿAbd al-Rahim's concise structuring of the society in eighteenth-century Ottoman Egypt. This structural depiction appears as a statement of fact, and class and national criteria are woven together in it. Most significantly, the latter criterion overwhelms the former: "Society became one of classes; there was, first, the class of Ottoman rulers, then the Mamluks and finally the Egyptian people, among whom both rich and poor could be found."[50]

An examination of the formal explanations offered for the Ottoman *rukud* by three historians—Ghurbal, al-Shayyal, and Anis—brings us back to Orientalism. These explanations adhere to Orientalist fundamentals in two ways: in all of them the empire is grasped as a monolithic, self-contained entity embodied in the term *al-Dawla al-`Uthmaniyya*; all are cultural-essentialist explanations that at times resort to characterizations of mind and mentality.

The explanation of Ghurbal and al-Shayyal for the alleged *rukud* is one and the same for a prosaic reason: as mentioned earlier, seeking to account for the stagnation, al-Shayyal inserts a long quotation of Ghurbal's preface to Husayn Mu'nis's book, and confirms that this is the quotation's function.[51] In the first reason of his explanatory scheme Ghurbal resorts to cultural-mental argumentation. He asserts that the rukud stemmed from the fact that "the Ottoman rulers were of a *qawm* which in its nature was inclined to conservatism. The Ottomans did not consist of one *qawm*. Ottomanism was nothing but a criterion for belonging to the ruling elite."[52] I should note here that as the internal logic of Ghurbal's argument is rather vague (was Ottomanism the essence of a ruling class or something else?), it is difficult to ascertain what he means by *qawm* in this particular context.

Ghurbal's recommendation for how the East ought to have extricated itself from its stagnant predicament is strikingly condescending:

> The fair researcher cannot assume that the Europeans, from the sixteenth century on, were willing to grant the Eastern Christian and Muslim subjects of the sultan the fruits of their cultural renaissance as a mere present. . . . And if this was the case then it cannot be argued that the Ottoman East could have benefitted from the European renaissance without relinquishing its *masculine honour and freedom* [*rujulatihi wa hurriyyatihi*, emphasis added].[53]

The last reason Ghurbal puts forth is deemed finite and, again, resorts to essentialism and collective mentality:

> The truth about the question of stagnation is that the Ottoman state ruled over degenerated peoples, and the Ottoman rule was incapable of altering

this. Because the Ottomans were a *qawm* that takes and not [one] that gives, and their *khittat*, belief and culture testify to that. They organized whoever they ruled under their comprehensive possession, and made sure that no change or transformation would reach them.[54]

Anis's explanation is intriguingly similar, not so much because it is also essentialist and the *Dawla `Uthmaniyya* is the same self-contained entity, but because where one would expect to find essentialism of the Marxist variety one encounters in this case too, for the most part, the more common Hegelian variety. Thus, pondering the alleged deterioration under the Ottomans of *al-`ulum al-`aqliyya* (the rational sciences) in general and "the science of history" in particular, Anis identifies the familiar culprit: "The Ottomans did not possess any cultural capital [*rasid hadari*] which they could transfer to and invest in Egypt's cultural life." On another occasion Anis offers a fuller explanation. The following passage seems to encapsulate E. H. Carr's definition of history as a dialogue between the present and the past. In the background looms the Nasserite state, grasped as centralized and modernizing, as the diametrical opposite of the *Dawla `Uthmaniyya*:

> The Ottoman rule of Egypt—and the other provinces—was based on the principle of leaving things as they had been. . . . For this reason Ottoman Egypt inherited most of the arrangements that had prevailed in the previous period, chiefly in terms of . . . the structure of society itself. Because the Ottoman rule was a weak feudal rule which did not radically altered the life of Egyptian society even though it lasted nearly 300 years. Whether the Ottoman rule was direct or indirect, whether this was an Ottoman intention or international circumstances, this rule caused the political and economic decline of Egypt. To what extent did this occupation leave its imprint on Egypt's intellectual and ideational life? The truth is that the imprint of the Ottoman rule was so insignificant that mentioning it is not worth the bother.[55]

Turning now to school textbooks, I should point out that my reason for discussing these texts separately is somewhat prosaic: my research on Egyptian school textbooks is preliminary. This separation should not be taken, however, to imply that the particular "genre" of school textbooks ought to be examined in isolation from other components of nationalist historiography, or that they are of secondary importance for the construction of this historiography.

There are, nonetheless, two related features that distinguish the school textbooks from the professional historical works. One is the degree to which the textbooks are so much more condensed. Since these books are clearly intended for the nonspecialist, and since they cover a wide range of subjects and periods, the space allocated to a given subject is limited. The consequence is that in these texts the production of meaning through literary and rhetorical means, even through basic syntax, is that much more ostensive; this adds an interesting dimension to the task of interpreting them.

The other feature is the problem of intentionality. This is an intensely debated problem among interpreters of texts, but it is compounded with regard to the textbooks for two reasons. The first is that each of them is part of a project or a series—al-Tarbiyya al-Wataniyya in this particular case. A basic characteristic of such a project is that in its diachronical evolution each specific item draws heavily on its predecessor(s). It therefore seems to me that in this case intentionality has to be sought in the context of the institutional history of the project (something I have not yet investigated), and that trying to ascribe intentionality to the author(s) of a particular item might not be very fruitful.[56] The second reason is that ascribing *self-conscious* intentionality to meanings produced through, for instance, syntax is highly speculative. In what follows, therefore, I show that meaning is certainly produced in the school textbooks, but I avoid discussing the intentions of their authors.

Essentially, the three samples of al-Tarbiyya al-Wataniyya examined here perpetuate the nationalist historiographic discourse I have already presented and display adherence to its two chief components: Orientalism and territorial nationness.[57] The basic narrative is a familiar one: the Ottoman "subordination" of Egypt was a sorry—but external and insignificant—stage in the nation's history. The only consequence of the Ottoman conquest to which the textbooks allude, indeed stress and formulate identically, is that "Egypt lost its independence and became a subordinate Ottoman province." The Ottoman rule, however, soon became merely nominal and power was wielded by the Mamluk beys. The dawn of the nineteenth century, epitomized by the French invasion and the ascendancy of Muhammad `Ali Pasha, ushered in a new era in Egypt's history—the modern era.[58]

This narrative is underpinned, first, by the space allotted to the Ottoman period (1517–1798, according to the Orientalist periodization) in comparison to other episodes. The insignificance of that period is fundamentally conveyed by the fact that three centuries of Ottoman rule and three years of French rule are given the same space (two pages) and that the space occupied in these textbooks by the ventures of the great Pasha is larger than both. Equally meaningful are the brief descriptions of the Ottoman period itself. Though these sections ostensibly look as no more than chronological-factual accounts, they severely reduce the importance of the Ottoman period through a representation of time in which the whole period appears shrunken and redundant: the descriptions start with the story of the Ottoman conquest and thence, abruptly and directly, jump to the second half of the eighteenth century where the extent to which Ottoman presence was nominal is illustrated through `Ali Bey al-Kabir; the conspicuous silence over the period 1520s-1760s signifies its importance, or lack thereof.[59]

Another interesting feature in the school textbooks is what might be termed Orientalism-through-syntax. By this I mean the construction of sentences and headings that refer to two sorts of relations: between the Ottomans (or "Turks" in these texts) and Egypt (as a communion of an imagined community and a territory), and between the French and Egypt. What the syntax of these formulations does is to depict the Ottomans as passive vis-à-vis Egypt and the French as active. Among the various cases in which this syntax occurs, the most striking examples are two consecutive subheadings within a large section that presents, in effect, Ghurbal's Misrification of the Eastern Question. These subheadings are even more striking when they appear in the contents, simply because there, one is seen immediately beneath the other. They read as follows (the translation is on purpose as literal as possible):[60]

"*Dukhul Misr taht hukm al-Atrak* (The Entrance of Egypt under the Rule of the Turks)."

"*Dukhul al-Faransiyyin Misr* (The Entrance of the French into Egypt)."

What brings to the fore so powerfully the meaning produced by the syntax is, I think, the proximity: within two lines (in the text) or three centuries (in "history") Misr turns from a subject that "enters" under Ottoman rule into an object into which the French "enter." It is difficult not to recall in this respect Toynbee's phrase cited earlier, whereby "Egypt became a battle-ground on which superhuman Frenchmen and superhuman Englishmen fought one another."[61] A similar sort of syntax abounds in the narrative itself. The syntax conveys the decline-narrative by the following pattern, which is true for all three texts examined here. The "Turks," or Ottomans, are invariably the active subject of the sentences that describe the process of the Ottoman conquest in 1516–1517. As soon as the narrative abruptly turns to the late eighteenth century, however, these "Turks" become the sentences' object, the passive recipients of other agents' acts, be they `Ali Bey al-Kabir or the French expedition.

The most outstanding illustration for this syntax lies in a single sentence, the function of which in the narrative is to see the reader through the brief period of "interregnum" between the French evacuation and the rise of the Pasha. This sentence appears in nearly identical formulations in all three texts. It, too, displays the power of proximity, for the French are rendered an active subject and the Ottomans a passive object within a single sentence: "When the French had left Egypt, the country returned to Ottoman sovereignty nominally and to Mamluk rule actually."[62] Note also how the syntax changes Egypt's status within the sentence: it is an object before the comma, and the subject (as "the country") thereafter.

The importance attributed to the impact of the French occupation in the textbooks is similar to al-Shayyal's explanation of why "the spontaneous awakening" had to give way to Western culture:

> The French occupation left in Egypt an imprint which the passage of time did not erase, for their entrance was the beginning of the country's awakening from the slumber of the middle ages and the opening of the modern era, and of a novel civilization that unfolded ideas . . . and knowledge with which Egyptians had been unfamiliar until then. The expedition also . . . exposed their [the Mamluks'] weakness and impotence in front of the Egyptians for the first time.[63]

One of these textbooks goes farther than al-Shayyal and manifests not only appreciation of French culture but also familial affection. This affection is expressed after the text has "conceded" that in the rivalry between Britain and France over the "Egyptian Question" the former gained the upper hand. The following statement is a tangible reminder of the fact that until today the French of many upper-class Egyptians is as fluent as their Arabic: "However . . . the bond that tied France to Egypt became one which resembles the bond that ties the master to his pupil [al-ustadh bi-tilmidhihi]."[64]

In 1996, as part of an undergraduate seminar titled "Cairo: A History of a City," my department organized a trip to Cairo. Our group comprised thirty-five students and six faculty members; we enjoyed the overwhelming beauty and historical and cultural variety of Cairo for two weeks. One of the most striking features of that tour, conveyed by the tour's "plot," the tour-guides, the students' Arabic teachers, and the Egyptian intellectuals we met (among them Lutfi al-Khuli, `Ali Salim, and Ahmad Khamrush), was the extent to which, from the vantage point of 1996, the Egyptian territorial-organic narrative has prevailed and triumphed, including its Orientalist facet. For many of the students this particular feature also served as a critical mirror of their own nationalism/historiography.

Though not wishing anachronistically to argue that the eventual prevalence of this narrative is a fair reflection of the options that may have existed along the way, I do think that nationalist narratives, once formed, leave little room for pluralist contestation. This is particularly the case when such a narrative becomes that of a strong, centralized nation-state. The unanimous nature of the Egyptian historical discourse with regard to the Ottoman past, despite the changing historical circumstances that have surrounded this discourse, illustrates the endurance and tenacity of nationalist, territorial historical consciousness.

PART II

Narrativity II

Mechanics of Ideology:
How Nationalists Construct Nationalist History

4

The Arab Nationalism of George Antonius Reconsidered

William L. Cleveland

I

"Arise, ye Arabs, and awake!" With the placement of this line from Ibrahim al-Yaziji's poem beneath the title page of his book, *The Arab Awakening: The Story of the Arab National Movement*, George Antonius launched his successful "imagining" of the modern Arab nation.[1]

We tend to think of *The Arab Awakening* as a work of history and its author as an amateur though gifted historian. Most of the attention that has been directed at the book since the early 1960s, when it came under renewed scholarly scrutiny, has concentrated on its historical interpretations: the role of Christian missionaries and Christian Arabs in the awakening; the Arab secret societies and the extent of their influence and membership; the extent of support among the urban Arabs of Greater Syria for the revolt of Sharif Husayn; and the contents and outcomes of the British promises to Husayn. It is entirely proper to view George Antonius as the pioneering historian of a controversial subject. It is also entirely proper to regard him as a historian-advocate who had a case to make.[2]

Until receiving the invitation to participate in this volume, I thought I was thoroughly familiar with all aspects of *The Arab Awakening*. I considered it a brave and groundbreaking work, but one that was now more representative of its era than of evidential value. However, it appears that Antonius's book is far from being consigned to the category of outmoded classic. Fouad Ajami and Edward Said—to pair two rather different Arab-American perspectives—have recently extolled the book's significance for understanding Arab nationalism. Ajami called it "Antonius's manifesto" and asserted that it foreshadowed "all the grand themes of Arab nationalism."[3] Edward Said proclaimed that "Antonius's *The Arab*

66   WILLIAM L. CLEVELAND

Awakening remains *the* classic and foundational book on Arab national-ism."[4] These contemporary appreciations of the nationalist thrust of the book, in combination with some of the questions posed by the editors of this volume, have led me to re-evaluate Antonius's contribution to Arab nationalism.

In the first part of this essay, I attempt to examine *The Arab Awakening* in the context of certain recent theoretical works on nationalism. I also use evidence from Antonius's testimony before the Peel Commission as an additional source for his ideas on the development of the Arab nationalist movement. I am primarily concerned with Antonius's use of language, his manipulation of symbols, and his construction of the foundations of Arab national identity. Because Antonius's language is so crucial to his message, I have not paraphrased him very often, preferring instead to use direct quotations. The second part of the essay examines, in an admittedly preliminary manner, the diffusion of Antonius's ideas.

I should emphasize from the start that I am not concerned here with testing the accuracy of Antonius's historical interpretations. Rather, I wish to examine, in the company of Benedict Anderson and others, Antonius the nationalist. I should also acknowledge that there is possibly something contrived about this exercise. Antonius was, after all, engaged primarily in writing a work of history and did not set out to validate Anderson's hypotheses, to become a subject of Edward Said's "the voyage inward," or to be a reference point for Anthony Smith's "dual dichotomy." It is entirely fair to ask whether the examination of a work on the basis of analytical categories developed decades later does not threaten to misrepresent the original contribution. Yet it may also be argued that if a work is to endure, it must stand up to new readings and convey its core message to later generations. So, while I recognize Antonius first and foremost as a historian, I also think it is legitimate to read him as a nationalist author and to examine his presentation of nationalism in the light of contemporary insights.

Background

George Antonius (1891–1942) brought a formidable combination of skills and experiences to his self-proclaimed task of telling a story, not the least of which was his ability to communicate with the particular audience of British policy-makers he had targeted for *The Arab Awakening*. By virtue of his own background, he was well-suited to present the history of the Arab national movement in language that such an audience could understand.

Educated at Victoria College in Alexandria and King's College, Cambridge, Antonius served as an official of the British government from 1915 to 1930, first in Alexandria and then for nine years in Palestine. He circulated among and formed friendships with members of the British cultural and political elite both within and outside the Middle East. Whether guiding E. M. Forster around Alexandria, lunching with Sir Herbert Samuel at the latter's London club, or serving as first secretary on Sir Gilbert Clayton's missions to Arabia, Antonius was thoroughly familiar with the outlook of British policy-makers. However, during his service in Palestine he was confronted with personal and professional discrimination and learned, if he had not previously known, that he would never fully transcend the status of native in the eyes of most of his British colleagues.

Antonius was as fluent in Arabic as he was in English, and he built up an extensive network of friends and associates in Cairo, Beirut, Damascus, and Jerusalem. His access to leading participants in the Arab movement, especially Sharif Husayn and his sons, not only opened unparalleled research opportunities for him but also enabled him to pass judgment on matters Arab from the position of authoritative insider.

In *The Arab Awakening* his vocabulary and reference points are attuned to the literary expectations of his readers, and he ushers them gently into the Arab world with occasional references to classical Greece. Describing the tortuous verbosity of Sharif Husayn's Arabic notes to Sir Henry McMahon, he helpfully suggests to the reader that in comparison to Husayn's prose, "the style of *Euphues* seems Attic" (p. 167).[5] The anguish of the harassed Jamal Pasha in 1915, surrounded by rumors of Arab nationalist agitation but unable to identify the participants, is amplified with this reference: "Like Polyphemus, he wanted to strike but did not know at whom" (p. 186). That Polyphemus was a crude and violent Cyclops may have been as much an inspiration for Antonius's choice of analogy as the situation itself. Even an Arab tradition that Antonius regards as something of a shortcoming can, through a contorted comparison with the golden age of Greece, be made to appear not so weak after all. Commenting on the positive achievements of the Society of Arts and Sciences founded in Beirut in 1847, Antonius notes that its idea of promoting the spread of knowledge through an organized collective effort "was foreign to the individualistic nature of the Arab whose method of approaching higher learning was akin to that of Plato's Greece" (p. 52). In 1938 what well-placed graduate of the Oxbridge system could fail to appreciate the customary Arab method of approaching higher learning as set forth in this brief aside?

In his exposition of Arab nationalism, as with his general references, Antonius uses concepts that are likely to be familiar to his readers. He wraps these concepts in a powerful narrative that leads inexorably to the conclusion that an Arab nation exists and that it, like other nations, ought to be independent and unified.

Components of Nationhood:
History, Ethnicity, Language/Culture

It is a given among students of nationalism that the modern nation is often constructed around myths of heroic achievements from earlier times. Antonius engages only sparingly in this practice, possibly because he chooses not to focus on accomplishments associated primarily with Islam. Nevertheless he manages to equate the conquests of the seventh and eighth centuries with revitalization and progress, writing that the twin processes of Islamization and Arabization acted as forces of "cultural evolution" in the conquered territories whose culture at the time was "hybrid and debilitated" (pp. 15–16). Evolution is an important concept for Antonius, and he uses it frequently in describing the stages of the Arab national movement. However, he does not, either in his background chapter or in later sections, draw on a specific *mythomoteur* of the type Anthony Smith posits.[6] Readers learn that a rich civilization, which Antonius defines as Arab, came into existence, flourished (until the sixteenth century in his account), and was then eclipsed by the Ottoman conquests.

But in subsequent passages, Antonius suggests that the qualities of the earlier Arab entity remained latent. Thus he attributes to Muhammad `Ali's son, Ibrahim Pasha, an intent "to *revive* Arab national consciousness and *restore* Arab nationhood" (p. 29, emphasis added). His terminology may be anachronistic, but his intent is clear—to implant in his reader's mind the idea of a connection between the modern Arab national movement and the glories of the Arab past.

Antonius uses the term "Arab world" to introduce his definition of nationalism. As he explains it, the Arab world was made up of individuals "whose racial descent, even when it was not of pure Arab lineage, had become submerged in the tide of arabisation; whose manners and traditions had been shaped in an Arab mould; and, most decisive of all, whose mother tongue is Arabic" (p. 18). These are Antonius's three main components of Arab nationalism: ethnicity, shared traditions, and language. Throughout most of his book, he fails to define the first, ignores the second (except for the final section on Mandate Palestine), and places most of his emphasis on the third.

Antonius frequently refers to the subjects of his book as "the Arab race." In part the term may be merely a stylistic convention, but, given the definition of Arab cited above, it should also have specific meaning for Antonius. He clearly equates race and nation. For example, another of the objectives he assigns to Ibrahim Pasha is an effort "to regenerate the Arab race," and one of his several charges against the Committee of Union and Progress (CUP) is its assertion of Turkish racial supremacy within the Ottoman Empire (pp. 28, 105). In a more complex usage, Antonius writes that the agitation caused by the appearance of posters in Beirut in 1880 demanding Arab independence served to "translate racial sentiment into a political creed" (p. 89). This passage implies the existence of a prenationalist ethnic identity that becomes true nationalism only when it adopts political objectives. Aside from these selections and the ongoing references to the Arab race, Antonius does not use the concept of ethnicity to further his case for Arab nationalism. This may be because he was either uncomfortable or unfamiliar with theories of race; or because he recognized that Englishmen might be more amenable to cultural than to racial examples of nationhood.

Antonius regards language as the most decisive feature of the Arab nation, and his analysis of the twin concepts of language and culture serves as the foundation for his claims that an Arab nation exists. The contents of his presentation of the Arab awakening in Greater Syria is well-known and need not be reviewed here. However, it will be useful to examine the method by which Antonius builds his case and the emphasis he places on the emergence of a national language.

His starting point is the debased state of the Arabic language in the late eighteenth century and the general "retardment of cultural development" among the Arabs (p. 38). Outlining the lack of educational facilities and the absence of printing presses in Syria, Antonius skillfully sets the foundation for his nationalist argument: "Without school or book, the making of a nation in modern times is inconceivable" (p. 40). Obviously, the converse is also true—with school and book, the making of a nation is possible, and Antonius sets out to demonstrate that the Arabs acquired, in abundance, these two essential building blocks of nationhood. In his treatment of the Arab literary awakening, he might well have been writing a primer for the analyses of Hobsbawm, Smith, and others. Anderson stresses the importance of "national print languages" in the emergence of nineteenth-century European nationalisms, while Hobsbawm argues that the forcing of a common language into print gives it permanence and makes it more eternal than it might actually have been.[7]

Antonius presents the Arabs' acquisition of school and book as a mutually reinforcing process, with assertions that from 1834 onward "the spread of education progressed by leaps and bounds," driven in part by Ibrahim Pasha's desire to sow "the seed of Arab national conscious-ness" in his school system and by American missionaries who not only founded dozens of schools but "gave pride of place to Arabic" in their instruction and thus contributed to an indigenous "cultural efferves-cence" (pp. 40, 43). For Antonius, educational expansion represents far more than an increase in literacy; it is the cornerstone of a specifically Arab literary awakening. Moreover, education is, itself, evolutionary and suggests progress. Through their immersion into "school and book," the Arabs were advancing, moving forward to a level of shared cultural con-sciousness from which they could legitimately aspire to the final rung of communal evolution—nationhood.

A similar emphasis on the centrality of language and its linkage with communal self-consciousness runs through Antonius's treatment of other facets of the awakening. A noteworthy example is the role he as-signs to Butrus al-Bustani. In addition to his other achievements, al-Bustani provided order and conformity to the national language by pro-ducing a dictionary and an encyclopedia, precisely the tasks required for the standardization of a modern print language. And, for good measure, Antonius makes sure his readers are aware that Bustani's work was modern by reminding them that the encyclopedia "made full use of the available European sources" (p. 49). For all his emphasis on the indige-nous roots of the Arab revival, Antonius at times found it useful to asso-ciate the movement with European science.

In his explanation for the impulse that culminated in the formation of the Syrian Scientific Society in 1857, he stresses the members' love of the emerging national language and their desire to express new ideas in that language. But in describing the significance of the society, he takes a sudden leap from literature to nationalism. He claims that the society brought members of various sects together "in an active part-nership for a common end. An interest in the progress of the country as a national unit was now their incentive, a pride in the Arab inheritance their bond. The foundation of the Society was the first outward mani-festation of a collective national consciousness" and the society itself was "the cradle of a new political movement" (p. 54). In this brief pas-sage, Antonius manages to inject the society with national self-aware-ness and to equate the emerging national consciousness with the notion of progress.

I should like to make one final point regarding Antonius's stress on language as the primary component of nationhood. As it is Butrus al-Bustani's devotion to Arabic that earns him praise, so it is T. E. Law-rence's failings in the language that merit criticism and, ultimately, exclusion. Edward Said is correct to note that *The Arab Awakening* is intended to counteract Lawrence's account and to provide a Western audience with "a native point of view."[8] But Said overlooks the main criterion that Antonius uses to marginalize Lawrence and his work. Gloating twice in the same paragraph over new evidence he has found in Arab sources, Antonius pointedly explains that the faults and inconsistencies contained in *Seven Pillars of Wisdom* are due to "the inadequacy of his [Lawrence's] knowledge of Arabic and of his acquaintance with the historical background of the Arab Revolt" (p. 320). What could be more exclusionary, more culturally unauthentic, than an inadequate knowledge of the national language and of the story of its revival that Antonius has painstakingly recreated? The achievements of the Arab revolt were the achievements of Arabic speakers, not of an outsider whose accent and use of words ("to say nothing of his appearance") would never enable him to pass as an Arab among Arabs (p. 321). Although Antonius is appreciative of many of Lawrence's talents, Lawrence the impostor masquerading as an Arab is a usurpation that he will not tolerate. Language is too important.

The literary revival was, in Antonius's view, part of a larger nineteenth-century Arab cultural awakening. He is at great pains to portray the original impulse behind this awakening as totally devoid of political objectives. It is as though he was trying to establish the indigenous roots of the Arab cultural movement, to free it from any association with external influences, and thus to show its absolute authenticity. In his testimony before the Peel Commission in 1937 he stated: "It may be of interest to know that the national movement, the Arab national movement, began as a cultural movement, which had nothing to do with politics in its early days or with any of the concepts of nationalism which had begun to appear in Europe. It began entirely independently, as a cultural revival."[9] Antonius reasserted this principle in his book, stating that the forces that had set the Arab movement in motion "were not only of a moral order, unaffected by economic needs or political theories; but they were also forces of spontaneous origin, generated by emotions from within. The movement had derived its ideas from the familiar sources of its environment, long before it took to borrowing the Western notions of political evolution" (pp. 85–86). Later in the same paragraph he writes that the Arab national movement "had sprung in a soil of its own making [and] derived its main sustenance from the earth in which it had roots." Only in the last quarter of the nineteenth century did the "Western concept of nation-state graft itself on the indigenous tree of Arab nationalism." This is a fascinating mixture of terminologies as Antonius attempts to persuade outsiders of the genuineness of the Arab movement by anchoring it in its own environment and demonstrating its original cultural purity. The movement was authentic because it was untainted with political or material motives. However, once it became fully developed culturally, Antonius allows it to borrow "Western notions of political evolution" as it progressed to a higher stage.

The Transition to a Political Movement: Freedom, Independence, and Unity

By presenting the Arabs as possessing a fixed literary language and a mutual awareness of their shared culture, Antonius shows them to be a nation with legitimate aspirations to the requisites of nationhood—freedom and independence. In his approach, the words "freedom/liberation" differ slightly from the term "independence." The latter is a political definition and refers to a sovereign nation state. But freedom/liberation imply a release from oppression, a desire to break free from an imposed culturally alien rule, an act that is in itself an integral stage in the step toward political independence. I do not wish to stretch this terminological distinction too far; of course Antonius employs freedom/liberation and independence to mean similar conditions. But he also makes subtle distinctions between them, always playing to a readership that is likely to be receptive to notions of freedom/liberation in the sense of Delacroix's "Liberty Leading the People" or to an Arab spirit moved by a "passion for freedom" (p. 60).

To justify the Arabs' struggle for freedom, Antonius presents a relentlessly dark image of the forces of oppression from which they suffered. There are no nuances—no politics of the notables—in his view of the Ottoman Empire. It is neither a dynastic nor a multiethnic state; it is only Turkish. And to Antonius, it is self-evident that Turks should not rule Arabs, especially Arabs awakened to their own national identity. From the very beginning, The Arab Awakening views Turkish repression of Arabs as an established characteristic of the Ottoman Empire. Thus Ibrahim Pasha was "a champion of Arab liberation" who inspired the population of Syria with "the prospect of liberty" from "the detested rule of the Turk" (pp. 26–27). Antonius's portraits of the Hamidian and CUP despotisms—which he juxtaposes with accounts of the Arab cultural/political awakening—urgently convey a need for liberation. He views Abdul Hamid's reign as a tyrannical era "scarcely surpassed in history" and further blackens the sultan by listing the failings of his regime in terms that would be particularly repugnant to British readers: corruption of the judicial system; stifling censorship; and a close association with Kaiser Wilhelm II to whom the sultan "held out his hand" and to whose kisses he "lent his cheek" (pp. 64, 78).

The CUP's greatest prewar misdemeanor was its policy of Turkification. I have previously noted how crucial language and culture are to Antonius's argument for the existence of an Arab nation longing to be fulfilled. The CUP's attempt to force the Arabs "to abandon their cultural aspirations" was, then, tantamount to denying Arab nationhood and made the need for freedom all the more pressing and all the more obvious (p. 107). Confronted with CUP Turkification and centralization, patriotic Arabs formed secret societies that sought "liberation from Turkish or any other alien domination," the latter phrase serving as a reminder that the postwar Mandates constituted a denial of long-standing Arab aspirations for freedom (p. 111). A masterful linking of Arab freedom and Arab independence appears in Antonius's description of the full meaning of Faysal's entry into Damascus in October 1918. It is an especially vivid passage, connecting a number of themes, and shows Antonius at his narrative and nationalist best:

> Damascus was in a frenzy of joy and gave itself over wholly to its emotion. . . . It seemed as though the sufferings of the four hideous years, sharpening the city's capacity to feel, had intensified its passion; and that the nightmare of Jemal's tyranny had quickened its instincts. The climax occurred when Faisal entered the city and appeared as the embodiment of freedom to a people to whom freedom meant, not merely an escape, but also a long-dreamt fulfillment. (p. 238)

Antonius leaves unstated the full meaning of the "long-dreamt fulfillment," trusting that his readers will be able to make the connections he wishes them to.

Unity of purpose, action, and sentiment are among the principal criteria by which nationalist movements are justified from within and assessed from without. Antonius the historian and Antonius the nationalist are occasionally in conflict on the question of unity. He is too responsible a historian to overlook the fractious tribalism of the Arabian peninsula and Iraq or the sectarian tensions of Greater Syria. But he is too committed to the unifying power of language and culture to allow regional or personal differences to dominate his discussion, and he manages to portray the Arab revolt as a unified national movement of all the Arab regions east of Egypt.[10]

He does this by insisting over and over again that the political objectives of the Arab revolt were identical with the larger goals of Arab independence and unity. At one point he argues that despite the existence of certain social and confessional differences between Syria and Iraq, the two regions were unified by virtue of "a common language and culture" (p. 248). To divide them, as the postwar settlement had done, "was in conflict with the natural forces at work," forces that had made the national movement inseparable from the twin forces of Arab unity and independence (p. 249). In this version of the nationalist program, Arab independence was only one part of the intended outcome of the revolt—political unity was equally vital to the participants and "was implicit in the very origins of the national movement" (p. 303). According to Antonius, "that movement was never a regional movement in which Syria wanted independence for Syria, or Iraq wanted independence for Iraq." It was a "movement of the whole Arab race working together to free themselves from Turkish rule and establish the Arab life."[11] In the chapter of *The Arab Awakening* that treats the postwar settlement, Antonius joins together the words "independence" and "unity" at least a dozen times, never letting his readers forget the full objectives of the revolt or the full dimensions of the Allied betrayal.

Another of his techniques for emphasizing the unity of the Arab movement is to provide the leading members of the founding "national" dynasty, the Hashimites, with impeccable nationalist credentials. He downplays Sharif Husayn's local and personal ambitions and elevates him to the level of selfless leader of the Arab movement at large. From this perspective, Kitchener's vague message to `Abdullah in 1914 becomes, in Husayn's mind, "an unmistakable invitation to foment a revolt of all the Arabs" (p. 133). In his testimony to the Peel Commission, Antonius completely disassociated Husayn from his local environment and from any personal involvement with Great Britain. He explained that although the Arab revolt started in the Hijaz, it "was not a Hedjazi revolt. It was really a revolt of the countries of Syria, Iraq and Palestine. Primarily it was made, prepared and instigated in these countries, and for various reasons the leadership was entrusted to King Hussein, who was then Sherif of Mecca."[12] It is important for Antonius to locate the origins of the Arab revolt among the bourgeoisie of Greater Syria, the center of the Arab awakening. But it is equally important for him to find a way to tie Husayn to Syria and thus to project a semblance of unity to the revolt.

Antonius views Amir Faysal as both symbol and creator of Arab unity. In one of several compelling episodes featuring Faysal, Antonius portrays him as single-handedly persuading the tribal factions of the peninsula to sink their differences in pursuit of the common goal of emancipation: "infected with his faith," the tribesmen took "an oath to serve as brothers in arms under him for the liberation of all Arabs" (p. 220). Even later in his life, when he was thrust into a narrower role as king of Iraq, Faysal remained attuned to the sentiments he had aroused years earlier and "never lost sight of the broader aims of the Arab Movement" (p. 360).

In addition to portraying a unified leadership in quest of commonly held objectives of political independence and unity, Antonius buttresses his claims for the Arab revolt as a nationalist undertaking with assertions of mass support. It should be noted that he does not, with the exception of a few references to the bedouins' natural love of freedom, emphasize a *volk* component of the Arab awakening, probably because he is so concerned with establishing the importance of a shared literary language. However, he has no reservations about offering up a background chorus of mass involvement, especially when describing pivotal moments in the movement's history. For example, when the Beirut-based Committee of Reform published a program requesting autonomy for the Arab provinces in 1913, the plan was "greeted with demonstrations of popular favor" in Iraq as well as Syria; and when the leaders of the committee were arrested, popular agitation in Beirut "evoked demonstrations in other parts of Syria" (pp. 113–114). At another crucial juncture toward the end of World War I, when the British Foreign Office issued the so-called Declaration to the Seven pledging support for the independence of the Arab provinces, Antonius claims that "a wave of jubilation swept the Arab world" and that the pledge had a profound impact on "the fervour of the Arab participation in the final offensive" (p. 273). And finally, in his description of popular sentiments on the eve of the announcement of the Mandates in the Treaty of San Remo, Antonius reports the General Syrian Congress's proclamation of the independence of Greater Syria and a similar proclamation for Iraq by Iraqi leaders residing in Damascus. These proclamations, Antonius asserts, "were an expression of the popular will, giving voice to the tenets of the Arab national movement and to the wishes of the populations concerned" (p. 304).

In the examples already cited, Antonius suggests that from the first demands for autonomy in 1913 to the final last-gasp effort to preserve independence, the Arab masses were involved in the movement. He gives the masses agency if not identity, and endeavors to show the existence of a popular will that found fulfillment in the actions of the nationalist leadership. This is a revealing instance of Antonius inventing the nation, of offering the reader "evidence" of mass consciousness of belonging to a nation.

A subtheme of unity is organization and intent. Benedict Anderson notes that nationalist myth-makers sometimes engage in a process of modular transfer, ascribing to their national movement the characteristics of other, previously successful, movements. One of the characteristics frequently transferred is the notion of planning.[13] Antonius draws no direct parallels between the Arab national movement and others.

However, he does appear to believe that independence movements possess a greater degree of legitimacy if they are planned than if they are spontaneous, and he goes to considerable lengths to portray the Arab movement as a deliberately organized endeavor. In so doing, he grants the Arabs initiative and separates the authentic historical movement from any association with opportunism created by the wartime circumstances. Thus the formation of a secret Arab society in Beirut in 1875 represents "the first *organized* effort in the Arab national movement" (p. 79, emphasis added). In an overview of developments following 1908, Antonius writes that "the seed of Arab consciousness which had taken root in Syria, threw out shoots into the neighboring Arabic-speaking countries, and finally blossomed forth . . . into *a deliberate and widespread agitation*" (p. 62, emphasis added). And when he states that during the Arab drive to Damascus in 1918, "the whole countryside had risen on a signal from Faisal," he conveys the impression of an organized network and elaborate advance planning (and of Faysal's unquestioned authority) (p. 237). In another of his several attempts to link Husayn with the larger Arab movement, Antonius relates that Fawzi al-Bakri conveyed to the Sharif an invitation on behalf of "the nationalist leaders in Syria and Iraq" to lead the revolt for "the attainment of Arab independence" (p. 149). This passage implies planning, organization, and intent.

Maps and Borders

Anderson offers a fascinating analysis of the role that "cartographic discourse" can play in the creation of nations.[14] The establishment of borders on paper can lead to the acceptance of them on the ground. Among the most famous sections of *The Arab Awakening* are those dealing with borders. On the surface it may appear that these frontiers are no more than political bargaining chips or objects of dispute between Sharif Husayn and the Allies. But Antonius is a master at cartographic discourse, and his selection of maps combined with his persuasive text conveys the portrait of an Arab nation in which geographical and cultural space are in total harmony.

Pages 78 and 79 reproduce two of the maps from *The Arab Awakening*. Their significance is that both maps show identical shaded areas east of Egypt. The eastern Arab world of 1915 covers precisely the same space that it did in the middle ages. The modern nation is rooted in the historical reality of distant centuries. But Antonius goes even further—by captioning the 1915 map with mention of Sharif Husayn's note, he not only shows that the modern nation is an existing entity bordered by the limits of the Arabic language, he also indirectly reminds the reader that this was the nation whose independence Britain promised to recognize.

In the text itself Antonius exercises the full range of his narrative powers to make two main points about the shaded area of map 2: first, that it coincides perfectly with the borders of Arab cultural dominance; and second, that it was defined as the Arab nation by an indigenous historical process, not by the political ambitions of Sharif Husayn or the imperial machinations of Great Britain. Antonius presents these points in four interrelated incidents.

First, he argues that the distribution of a "revolutionary" placard by members of the Syrian Scientific Society in Beirut in 1880 defines the moment when the Arab awakening made the transition from a purely cultural to a nationalist liberation movement. This particular placard is significant because it put forth a political program that included a demand for the independence of a unified Syria and Lebanon. The indigenously driven cultural movement had now produced an indigenously driven demand for political space. In this context the 1880 program was the first manifestation of "a politically independent state resting on a truly national basis" (p. 86).

Antonius finds echoes of 1880 in the program of a later secret Arab society, *al-Fatat*, founded in 1911. According to his analysis, *al-Fatat*'s objectives were "to work for the independence of the Arab countries and their liberation from Turkish or any other alien domination." This program represented "an unconscious return to the ideals of the Beirut secret society" (p. 111). The spatial demands have been expanded from a unified Syria and Lebanon to the Arab countries. But as Antonius explains the two programs, they appear historically sequential and generated by similar requirements and individuals: patriotic young Arabs fully awakened culturally and politically.

Cartographic discourse becomes more specific with Antonius's introduction of the Damascus Protocol of 1915, the document outlining the territorial demands of the Arabs in exchange for a revolt and an alliance with Britain. Antonius uses the Damascus Protocol to make a number of points, only two of which concern us here. First, he implies that the area of desired Arab independence coincided exactly with the shaded area of map 2; that is, with the natural borders of the eastern Arab world. Second, he claims that these territorial demands were drawn up in Damascus by members of *al-Fatat* and *al-'Ahd*. Sharif Husayn's role at this stage was simply to convey the document to the British. Thus it was not Sharif Husayn who defined the frontiers of the Arab nation, but the Arab leadership as a whole. And, as map 2 again shows, Husayn's first note to Sir Henry McMahon requested the

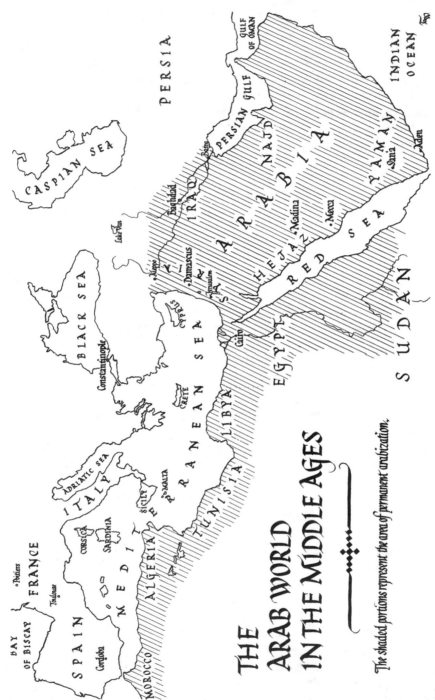

THE
ARAB WORLD
IN THE MIDDLE AGES

The shaded portions represent the area of permanent arabization.

Map 1

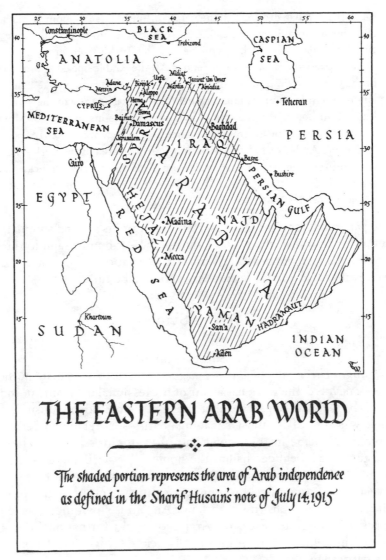

THE EASTERN ARAB WORLD

❖

*The shaded portion represents the area of Arab independence
as defined in the Sharif Husain's note of July 14, 1915*

Map 2

independence of precisely the same territories that were defined in the
Damascus Protocol.

The fourth development in this sequence, and the culmination of Antonius's depiction of the convergence of territory and culture, is found
in the majestic opening paragraph of chapter 14.

The war was won, and for the first time in its history the Arab national
movement stood abreast of its destiny. Victory had carried its standard as

far north as it had dreamed, to the very confines of its kingdom. Syria had
been freed, from Sinai to the Taurus; so had Iraq, up to Mosul; while in
the Peninsula itself all that remained of the Turkish power were a few
helpless garrisons doomed to surrender. All the Arabic-speaking provinces
of the Ottoman Empire in Asia were at last rid of the alien yoke that had
lain on them for four stifling centuries. It seemed as though the war-god
himself, in homage to the role of language in the history of the Movement, had stayed the northward advance on the very watershed of speech,
just where Arabic ceased and Turkish began. The area of the Turk's defeat
was precisely the area of Arab aspirations, and its frontiers coincided exactly with those defined by the Sharif Husain as the natural limits of Arab
independence (p. 276).

The paragraph requires no gloss. Here is Antonius's grand summary, his
hymn to the role of the Arabic language, to Arab unity, and to the har-
monious balance of borders and culture. The nation defined in map 2 had
been realized; historical destiny was about to be fulfilled.

Various Symbols

The Supreme Sacrifice

Although *The Arab Awakening* argues a case to which its author is
deeply devoted, the work has an air of professional detachment. Indeed,
an early reviewer suggested that the "gentle cosmopolitanism" of the
book was one of its most engaging features.[15] Yet death becomes a
prominent theme in the second half of Antonius's history. These are
not gory battlefield deaths but the noble self-sacrificing acts of moral
grandeur that Anderson and others associate with the supreme patriotic sacrifice of dying for one's country.[16] In showing that groups of secure, bourgeois Arabs (my terms, not Antonius's) willingly made such
a sacrifice, Antonius places the Arab movement for national liberation
within the context of other historically acknowledged incidents of selfless patriotism.

   This is most evident in his recounting of the executions carried out
on the orders of the Ottoman governor, Jamal Pasha, during World War
I. Antonius, more I think than any other author, has contributed to the
notion of the martyrdom of innocent young Arab patriots at the hands
of Jamal Pasha. Although he makes certain to present Jamal Pasha as an
instrument of "Turkish" brutality, he is even more concerned with
drawing attention to the victims' attitudes. Of the group hanged in Beirut in August 1915, Antonius writes: "most of them were young and

died well," adding that their compatriots exalted "their last words at the gallows into a stirring message of patriotic faith" (p. 187).

The second group of victims was no less heroic in accepting its fate for the cause of the Arab movement. As they were driven from Damascus to Beirut for execution, they "whiled the hours of darkness away with hymns to Arab freedom, one cabload answering another, until, as dawn was breaking, the convoy came to a halt in Liberty Square" (p. 189). This is highly romanticized and surely imagined. But it is effective and entirely consistent with the message Antonius wishes to convey—Arabs, like other patriots in the Western tradition, went to their deaths with praises of their country's freedom on their lips. The inspiration for such pure and selfless behavior could only be love of the nation; and for such love to exist, the nation had to exist.

Antonius transfers the aura of individual self-sacrifice into the mainstream of the Arab revolt in his account of Amir Faysal's reaction to the second round of executions. Faysal was in Damascus at the time (early 1916) and, in Antonius's lush depiction, on hearing of the executions uttered a cry of revulsion that "became the battlecry of the Arab Revolt" (p. 190). We learn a few sentences later the details of the battle cry: "Faisal leapt to his feet and, tearing his *kufiya* from his head, flung it down and trampled it savagely with a cry: `Tab al-maut ya `arab!' " (p. 191). Antonius professes that the phrase is virtually untranslatable but suggests that it "amounts to an appeal to all Arabs to take up arms, at the risk of their lives, to avenge the executions in blood" (p. 191). Put another way, the battle cry of the Arab revolt was a call for the same kind of selfless patriotic act in which the martyrs of Beirut and Damascus had engaged. This message was understandable to Antonius's intended readership.

Was an Arab Flag Flying There?

The Arab Awakening mentions an Arab flag three times. The first is completely rhetorical but nonetheless significant. Writing about the 1880 program for independence demanded by the Beirut society, to which I have already referred, Antonius proclaims that the society's program "had not merely unfurled a flag, but, what was more needed still, had set an arrow to point the way" (p. 89). Even if this passing reference to an unfurled flag is only a rhetorical flourish, one can argue that by employing it Antonius, consciously or unconsciously, establishes a marker for the beginning of the existence of an Arab nation. If a flag, even an imagined and purely literary one, exists, so does the nation that it represents.

The second reference to a flag is more pointed and more directed at the independent state that the Arab movement seemed to have achieved. The situation is the eve of the Arab entry into Damascus in October 1918. Antonius carefully prepares the reader by explaining that the Arab forces chose not to take the city at night but instead sent in an advance guard to instruct the city's leaders to set up an Arab government. However, according to Antonius, the advance units had been preempted: an Arab government was already in place and, as the units reached the main square, they "beheld the Arab flag flying. Four hundred years of Ottoman domination had passed into history" (p. 238). The juxtaposition is superb; the Arab flag *was* flying there and it meant that Arab sovereignty had replaced Turkish.

The final flag reference takes place in the context of the Anglo-French agreement to allow France to occupy the Syrian coast, including the city of Beirut. Antonius offers an account of the proclamation of Arab sovereignty and the raising of the Arab flag in Beirut in October 1918. He goes on, however, to recount that the presence of the flag irritated the French and their complaints prompted Allenby to order "the flag to be removed" (p. 275). This, in turn, caused "an incipient mutiny" among Faysal's troops in Damascus, which the amir put down only with great difficulty.

The literary sequence of the three references is powerful even if unintended—a flag unfurled, a flag flying, and a flag removed—removed by the imperial forces that would, in the end, remove all semblance of the sovereignty symbolized by the flag flying in Damascus. Antonius never describes the flag and does not need to. All that is necessary is to mention its existence and explain the actions that its presence inspired. His readers will know what he means—a flag inspired loyalty and sacrifice because it represented the nation.

Destiny

Antonius employs the term "destiny," with its evocation of the fulfillment of a historical process, to reinforce his claims for the existence of an Arab nation. In an early section on the merger of cultural and political currents, he proclaims that the Arab national movement was "borne slowly towards its destiny on the wings of a renascent literature" (p. 60). In this case, "destiny" can only mean an independent nation-state. Describing Faysal's efforts to persuade the tribes of the Hijaz to terminate their blood feuds and cooperate in the revolt, Antonius claims that Faysal appealed to them in the name of "the destiny of the Arab race" (p. 219). The most powerful image of destiny on the verge of fulfillment is conveyed in the passage opening chapter 14. Here, Antonius links the word "destiny" with specific territory and nationalist terminology. There can be no question as to the nature of the destiny that the Arab movement was about to fulfill.

To interfere in the course of history by denying destiny the chance to run its course is one of the offenses with which Antonius charges Great Britain. To be sure, he also attacks Britain's betrayal of the Arabs on grounds of morality and honor, but his narrative has so carefully set forth the stages of the Arab movement's march toward independence that Britain's intervention can be seen as more than duplicity—it is a disruption of natural historical forces. Had the promises to Sharif Husayn been kept (as Antonius interprets those promises) and the Arabs allowed to govern the territories in which they were culturally dominant, they would have achieved their rightful destiny—"to be like all the nations."

II

From the 1950s through to at least the 1970s, the words "the classic study by George Antonius" adorned the bibliography of any work aspiring to scholarly status—and many that did not—on a broad range of Middle Eastern topics. What was the process by which *The Arab Awakening* become so firmly entrenched as an essential source on modern Arab history? How were Antonius's ideas on Arab nationalism absorbed and transmitted? I am not in a position to provide full answers to these questions, but I can present some evidence on how the book was received and offer some suggestions about the channels through which its message was diffused.

In order to appreciate what a revelatory work *The Arab Awakening* was, it is necessary to imagine a British scholarly and political world in which the contents of the Husayn-McMahon correspondence were largely unknown. It is also important to recall that the book appeared on the eve of the London Conference of 1939. In this setting *The Arab Awakening* arrived like a bombshell. Within British foreign and colonial office circles as well as among certain members of parliament, it immediately became a cause célèbre and led to a whirl of official activity, including the secondment of Antonius to a special subcommittee of the London Conference to assist the British government in producing a definitive English version of the correspondence for publication. As Elizabeth MacCallum concluded in her review, Antonius's work was a text that "has made history as well as recorded it."[17]

I admit that this discussion examines *The Arab Awakening* more in the context of its impact on policy than as a presentation of Arab nationalism, but the two go together. If Antonius's claim that the Arab national movement was cut off at the knees by Britain's betrayal was to acquire credibility, those responsible for the betrayal had to admit some prior knowledge of the agreement with Husayn. Once the correspondence was officially released, thereby verifying one of the crucial but most contentious of Antonius's claims, then his version of the early history of the Arab national movement was more likely to gain acceptance. And, if my arguments in part I of this essay are valid, Antonius's talents as a communicator only enhanced the appeal of his book as the definitive account of the Arab national movement.

In addition to its immediate impact in London, *The Arab Awakening* received official attention in British and U.S. diplomatic circles. During the early 1940s the Foreign Office provided copies of *The Arab Awakening* to all British consuls in the Arab world with instructions that they read the book. Antonius was as well-known to U.S. diplomats in the Middle East as he was to the British, and his opinions carried considerable weight with such long-serving U.S. consuls as Paul Knabenshue, Ely Palmer, and George Wadsworth. Knabenshue, the consul in Baghdad, was so impressed with *The Arab Awakening* that he sent an official dispatch to the Secretary of State urging the State Department to purchase a copy. Drawing on his twenty-seven years of experience in the Arab Middle East and his own extensive research, Knabenshue wrote: "I unhesitatingly pronounce Mr. Antonius' book the best work which has ever been produced on the subject." He praised the book's fairness but also noted its skill in presenting the Arab case, concluding: "It is so thorough and well presented that the Arab delegates at the forthcoming conference in London might well with impunity place it upon the table and rest their case upon it."[18]

This is only one opinion and one incident, but I suspect that further research will show that *The Arab Awakening*, and the perspective it advocated, permeated the circles of U.S. foreign service Arabists over the ensuing decades. In his sensationalist book, *The Arabists*, Robert Kaplan explores the influences on and attitudes of several generations of American Middle East hands. One of them, Michael Sterner (Harvard class of 1951), recalled in particular the impact of "Antonius's *The Arab Awakening*, a political classic that got into the bloodstream."[19] Foreign service officers who were inclined to view the Middle East from the Arab perspective were drawn to Antonius's interpretations and may have served as an influential source for the continued diffusion and acceptance of his book.

Another way of testing the success of an author's ability to convey an argument is to examine the book reviews. Such an exercise can be useful because it involves contemporary responses to a work rather than historical revisionism. On the basis of the reviews of *The Arab Awakening* that I have consulted, Antonius was largely successful in transmitting to his audience the portrait of Arab nationalism that he wished to present. Certainly, the book's reception in Great Britain and the United States assured it wide exposure. It was reviewed in the *Times* (London) and the major British weeklies, and both the *New York Times* and the *Herald Tribune* featured full-page reviews in their weekend editions. In addition, scholarly journals such as *The American Historical Review* and *The American Political Science Review* also carried timely reviews.

A few of the reviewers writing for newspapers or weekly magazines tended to assess the book in terms of their own positions on the Arab-Zionist conflict and therefore devoted more attention to Antonius's final pages than to his chapters on the cultural awakening. But in most instances even pro-Zionist reviewers acknowledged Antonius's achievement as a historian and thus implicitly accepted his version of the early Arab national movement. For example, Albert Viton, writing in *The Nation*, vigorously refuted Antonius's interpretation of events in the Palestine Mandate but nevertheless acknowledged: "Never has the story of the origin and growth of the Arab national movement been told with such brilliance or such a wealth of detail."[20]

Some British reviewers with experience in the Arab world, among them H. A. R. Gibb and Freya Stark, regarded the book's documentary revelations with their exposure of Britain's duplicity as Antonius's "greatest service to history."[21] However, Gibb also pointed out the originality of the book's account of the Arab national movement and demonstrated his acceptance of Antonius's version of it by deploring Britain's betrayal of the Arab ideals of unity.

The scholarly reviews were generally insightful and less concerned with current events. William Yale grasped Antonius's central argument, writing that *The Arab Awakening* was "a valuable contribution to the knowledge of the rise of Arab nationalism" and commending its author for his objectivity in writing of "his people's struggle to attain national freedom and unity."[22] Hans Kohn described the theme of the book as "the early history of Arab nationalism" and called it an "indispensable study."[23] Philip W. Ireland's review made all the connections Antonius would have wished. According to Ireland, the author's "account of Arab nationalism" showed that the movement has followed familiar patterns. Revival of language and literature, fallen into a state of decay and degeneration, preceded national consciousness. Secret societies, ostensibly for literary or scientific purposes, became forcing beds for nationalism. . . . Attempted forcible Ottomanization by the Young Turks brought resistance, fanned Arab particularism to white heat, and sent the movement underground into secret societies with varied objectives. Arabs executed by the Turks became martyrs to the nationalist cause.[24]

In this instance, Antonius had clearly conveyed his message. He also conveyed it to the unnamed reviewer in *Foreign Affairs* who wrote that Antonius "has written the first comprehensive history of the Pan Arab movement, and he has done it with such thorough scholarship that there will be little incentive for anyone else to seek to cover the same ground."[25]

Although later scholars found incentives aplenty to cover the same ground and to offer revisions to Antonius's interpretations, his book quickly became accepted as the standard work on the history of the Arab national movement. In this brief account of the reception of *The Arab Awakening* in England and the United States, I have tried to show that the book was given sufficient, and sufficiently enthusiastic, publicity to enable it to reach a potentially wide audience; and that Antonius had persuaded at least some of his reviewers to accept his version of the rise of Arab nationalism. These are necessary first steps for the wider diffusion of a work and its ideas.

Another important channel for the transmission of ideas is published scholarship. Although scholars eager to disprove Antonius's suggestion that the Arab national movement had any claim to Palestine attacked his book from time to time, his interpretation of the linkage between Arab cultural and political nationalism was largely accepted, or at least largely unchallenged for nearly twenty-five years. One has only to read the contributions in the recently published work, *The Origins of Arab Nationalism*, to realize the centrality of *The Arab Awakening* to scholarly discourse on the early history of Arab nationalism.[26] The contributors to that volume do an admirable job of reviewing Antonius's interpretations and offering correctives to them, and I do not intend to repeat their task here. I would, however, like to suggest that the discussions in *The Origins of Arab Nationalism* stand as an important contemporary testament to George Antonius's achievements as a skilled communicator, an advocate of Arab nationalism, and a dedicated historian.

5

The Imposition of Nationalism on a Non-Nation State

The Case of Iraq During the Interwar Period, 1921–1941

Reeva S. Simon

An obvious example of an artificially created state, Iraq came into existence at the end of World War I at the behest of the British. New borders had to be created in the Middle East after the dissolution of the Ottoman Empire. As the victors, the British directed territorial design according to their own strategic concerns that now required a shift in policy. In order to protect their interests in India and later to control the oil discovered in Iraq, the British were determined to dominate a swath of territory from the Mediterranean to the Persian Gulf.[1] They drew the new lines at the conference in Cairo in 1921 that created the country of Iraq out of the former Ottoman provinces of Baghdad, Basra, and Mosul.[2]

The new country of Iraq was a fragmented society, a territory of ethnic and religious diversity, where some groups worked for independence and some paid nominal allegiance to whoever collected the taxes. The Arab Shi`i of the central and southern part of the country were the largest group. Organized in tribes and tribal confederations, they made up 53 percent of the population in 1919 and 56 percent in 1932.[3] Recent converts to Shi`ism, the Iraqi Arab Shi`is by 1920 had developed a political ideology that promoted independence from foreign rule and an Islamic state from Kurdistan to the Persian Gulf.[4] The Kurds of the Mosul region, non-Arab Kurdish-speaking tribes were in a constant struggle for cultural autonomy at the minimum, with an independent Kurdistan their ultimate goal. Apolitical, the Jews traced their domicile in Iraq to ancient times. Most of the Jewish population lived in Baghdad by the 1930s, where they were the majority, had already begun the Westernization process, and filled the civil service jobs under the British and the early monarchy. Approximately 2 percent of the population, Christians who were Nestorians and Chaldeans for the most part, looked spiritually to Rome and lived in the Mosul area. They remained out of politics, unlike the Assyrians, non-Uniate Nestorians who, encouraged by the British during the war to attempt a rebellion against the Turks, fled to Iraq when it failed and remained under British protection. The Arab Sunnis of the Baghdad area, although not the majority, were first backed by the Ottomans and then supported by the British as the ruling political elite of the new country.

The British placed a monarch of their choice on the throne of the kingdom. Faysal, leader of the Arab revolt, respected by his Arab nationalist army officers, and by both Arab Sunnis and Shi`is for his religious lineage and his Arabness, came to Iraq after ignominious betrayal by the British and defeat in Syria at the hands of the French. Iraq was a consolation prize for him, and although most of his retinue consisted of Iraqi former Ottoman officers, the political situation in Iraq differed from that of Syria. Where Damascus was the center of Arab nationalism during the war, Baghdad remained a backwater province, its fate to be decided by the British as they advanced up the Tigris. Faysal's goal in Iraq was to create a nation while advancing Hashimite dynastic goals, both of which were incorporated into the pan-Arab ideology he and his successors imposed on the indigenous population. As late as 1933, just before his death, he wondered whether or not the creation of an Iraqi nation was really possible.

The question we can still ask today is whether or not he and the Arab nationalists were successful. Can a nation be forged from so many disparate elements or is a nation a natural configuration? Must a "nation" evolve or can nationalism be imposed from the top down?

Recently published theoretical studies of nationalism provide paradigmatic typologies that facilitate analyses of the creation and propagation of nationalist ideologies in newly emergent states. Iraq, for example, is a case study whose historical narrative meshes neatly with the theories of both Benedict Anderson and Anthony Smith.[5] Iraq's "imagined community" was that of the Arabs, rather than Iraqis or Mesopotamians, Arabs whose identity and history were fashioned by Arab nationalist ideologues. These new elites, or "priesthood," teachers who taught from the textbooks commissioned and prescribed by the Ministry of Education in Baghdad, attempted to amalgamate the Sunni minority elite with the ethnic and religious minorities and the Shi`i majority via the glue of Arab nationalism in order to forge a pan-Arab identity for the Iraqis.

What needs to be examined in order to attempt an answer to the question of whether or not an imposed nationalism is possible is first, an analysis of the specific ideology or "imagined community" that the Sunni Arab elite created in an attempt to unify Iraq and the methodology they used to impose this dominant ideology.

Monitoring the politicization process, however, is more problematic. For the purposes of this essay, assessing the impact of the process of implementation of a nationalist ideology on Iraq in the short term—namely, during the interwar period—is possible. If we designate the "Rashid `Ali coup" and the war with Britain in 1941 as the chronological end point of the study, we can monitor the impact of the propagation of Arab nationalism on Iraq by looking at first, the attempt to implement Arab nationalist goals via an activist pan-Arab foreign policy and the British reaction to these events. Second, we can look at the reactions of two non-Sunni groups in Iraqi society to the imposition of pan-Arabism as the dominant ideology for Iraq. The Shi`i majority and the Jewish minority, both subordinate populations, emerge from the interwar period with different reactions to Arabism.

The Sharifians arrived in Iraq with a definite, though not completely worked out political ideology of nationalism that drew upon a number of European models. From the nineteenth-century Italian and German political experience came the view that the Arabs, too, could unite around a powerful core. Iraq, because of its good prospects for early independence, could draw Syria, Palestine, and Transjordan around it like a strong magnet. In this scenario Faysal's dynastic goals of Hashimite unity based on British wartime promises to the Arabs coalesced with pan-Arab dreams of Arab unity.

The definition of "Arab nation" was provided by Sati` al-Husri, who became the primary ideologue of Arab nationalism. Adopting a view of history common in the 1930s, borrowed from the German "volk" historians, the theory of a primeval ancestor nation that transmitted civilization to the rest of the world during its meanderings from an original homeland to its present abode was Arabized. The nationalists extolled the historic role of the pre-Islamic Arabs and then looked to the geographic unity of the territory that was to incorporate the modern Arab nation. Its boundaries were the Taurus Mountains and Kurdistan, Iran, the Arabian Sea, the Indian Ocean, the Gulf of Suez, and the Mediterranean Sea—or, the Arabian Peninsula and the Fertile Crescent. Palestine and Syria were integral parts of this area. The Semites were the progenitors of the modern Arabs.[6]

Husri was concerned less about borders than national identity. In short, his philosophy was that a common language and a common history were the basis of nation formation and nationalism. He maintained that

> The union of these two spheres leads to a union of emotions and aims, sufferings, hopes, and culture. Thus the members of one group see themselves as members of a unitary nation, which distinguishes itself from others. However neither religion nor the state nor a shared economic life are the basic elements of a nation, and nor is common territory. . . . If we want to define the role of language and history for a nation we can say in short that the language is the soul and the life of the nation, but history is its memory and its consciousness.[7]

The history of the Arab nation was the history of the Arabs, not of Islam; Islam's role in history was to spread Arabism, to help to preserve the Arab identity of the Arabs. It played a subordinate role in the history of the Arabs, which began in pre-Islamic Arabia and spread with the Islamic conquest throughout the Middle East and North Africa. Thus, Arabism— or the acceptance of Arab culture and the history of the Arabs as the focus of loyalty despite one's religious belief—transcended religious and communal ties.[8] It could be accepted by Sunni and Shi`i, Christian and Jew. How the Kurds could become Arabs was an issue that did not seem of concern. Iraqi governments have always maintained that Kurdistan is part of Iraq.

Faysal and his followers worked throughout the 1920s to dissipate both Sunni and Shi`i local Iraqi political leadership in order to ensure that the king and the Sharifian military that had begun to integrate with the landowning elite, though numerically a small number of individuals, achieved political dominance. Once the military-backed regime was in power, ethnic and religious minorities were subjugated via military suppression, cultural denigration, discriminatory legislation, or exile in order to ensure an Arab nationalist Sunni dominance.

At the same time the regime worked assiduously through the institution of state education both in military and government civilian schools to propagate Arabism as the locus of ideological conformity and the method for assimilation of the various groups into the Arab nationalist body politic. Teachers and textbooks were the vehicles for the transmission of nationalism; the military was to implement the goal of pan-Arabism through an activist foreign policy enacted once Iraq became independent.

The local allegiances and political aspirations that existed in the Ottoman provinces of Baghdad, Basra, and Mosul did not disappear with the lines drawn in Cairo. There remained strong opposition to Faysal as king by politicians who had first lobbied for local independence and then rebelled against British and British-imposed Arab Sunni rule. During the prewar period and the war years, there was no overwhelming support for the Arab nationalist cause, despite the propagation of *al-'Ahd* propaganda disseminated by Iraqi Ottoman army officers stationed in Iraq or on home visit. Many of the Iraqi officers who joined Faysal did so after they were captured by the British as they advanced from Basra to Baghdad. Given the choice of the Arab army or a British prisoner of war camp, some one hundred and thirty officers opted for Faysal.[9] Faysal's local competition, Sayyid Talib of Basra, for example, was summarily exiled by the British when his protests against Faysal became too overt.

The tribes and the Shi'i were another story altogether. Comprising more than one-half of the population in central and southern Iraq during Ottoman rule, the tribes of the south, mostly Shi'i, were organized in loose confederations headed by *shaykhs* who led these self-governing units that interacted with other tribes over control of trade routes and land.[10] Increasingly, the tribesmen became more an economic than a tribal base. The *shaykhs* joined the political elite when their goals converged, and a rift between the tribesmen and their leaders developed as the *shaykhs* were coopted by the government that provided them with seats in parliament (21 percent in 1933[11]), tax immunity, and legislation passed for their benefit.[12] No longer dependent upon the tribesmen, the greater *shaykhs*, through the system of land tenure and parliamentary seats, became part of the ruling elite.

The method of divide and conquer so aptly described by specialists on tribes and class in Iraq cut more than one way. In Shi'i areas in particular, Faysal and his successors were also determined to destroy any real Shi'i political opposition. They tried to destroy any common purpose between the Iraqi Shi'i *shaykhs* and the Shi'i *mujtahadin* of al-Najaf and Karbala, and then, using the ethnic card, they called into question the loyalty of Shi'i Iraqis to the Iraqi state. These measures were designed to ensure that any effective Shi'i/tribal leadership would become neutralized and that the Sunni Arab minority operating out of Baghdad would control the country and become the focus of popular loyalty. Ironically, the successful suppression of the Shi'i was achieved despite the fact that it was Shi'i-Sharifian unity of purpose in the 1920 revolt that led to Faysal's accession of power.

The actual evaporation of Shi'i political power need only be summarized here. Faysal was alarmed at the prospect of Shi'i solidarity, the apex of which came during the war and the revolt against the British in 1920 that followed. By then the Shi'i *mujtahidin*, having developed a political program that opposed any foreign occupation of Iraq, called for an Islamic state, controlled al-Najaf and Karbala, and worked with the Sharifians. They opposed the British mandate and the Anglo-Iraqi treaty that was negotiated in 1922 and was due to be ratified in the Constituent Assembly. Angered by the lack of government response to Saudi *Ikhwan* incursions into southern Iraq and by a perception that Faysal, because of the treaty, was a British agent, the *mujtahidin*, headquartered in al-Najaf and Karbala, issued *fatwas* against participation in the elections. The Shi`i greater *shaykhs* had already been coopted by the government and supported the treaty. Frustrated with the inability to hold elections, Faysal had the *mujtahidin* arrested and exiled to Iran. He allowed them to return in 1926; but by that time all effective Arab Iraqi Shi`i leadership had been broken as the *mujtahidin* had taken up residence in Iran and there was no "premier *mujtahid*" to follow.[13]

Faysal was also able to thwart any overt Shi`i rebellion by the force of his personality and his ability to balance off the different groups in Iraqi society. He felt comfortable with the tribesmen and visited the tribal areas where he could function as a safety valve for Shi`i grievances. After his death this mechanism ceased, for his son, Ghazi, disliked this aspect of kingship and was rarely seen in the company of tribesmen. From 1933 on any effective Shi`i opposition to government policies could only be articulated by joining the opposition, which was ready to use tribal dissatisfaction as a means to gain power. The tribal rebellion of 1935, for example, was incited by opposition politicians Yasin al-Hashimi and Rashid `Ali al-Kaylani in their attempt to come to power.

What rankled the Iraqi Shi`i more than the loss of political power was the ethnic denigration that was a natural concommitant of the imposition of the Arab nationalist ideology. The publication of Anis al-Nasuli's Sunni text, *al-Dawla al-Umawiyya fi al-Sham* (The Umayyad State in Syria), which glorified the Umayyads, sparked Shi`i demonstrations in 1927 and the demand that the Syrian teacher be relieved of his post.[14] With the publication of `Abd al-Razzaq al-Hasani's *al-`Uruba fi al-Mizan* (Arabism on the Scales), anti-Shi`ism became more blatant when the author criticized Shi`i Persian and sectarian loyalties. Fear over Iranian designs on the Shi`i holy sites and Shi`i opposition to pan-Arabism led to discriminatory practices against them. The Iraqi government forbade Shi`i proselytization, reduced the economic significance of al-Najaf by limiting its grain exports to Saudi Arabia, and passed Nationality Laws in 1924 and 1927 that prohibited employment by non-Iraqis in certain jobs generally held by Shi`is.

The Kurds and the Assyrians, both deemed political threats to the regime, were suppressed militarily. Incorporated into the new Iraqi state despite their own nationalist aspirations, the Kurds rebelled against Iraqi authority from the early 1920s and were held in check during the 1920s and 1930s by the RAF planes that the British provided the Iraqis in order to maintain control of the north.[15] Once Mosul and its oil potential were absorbed into the Iraqi state, there was no possibility of an independent Kurdistan. Kurdish rebellions against the Baghdad government have occurred throughout most of this century, ceasing for short periods of time when cultural autonomy and political inclusion seemed possible.

The Assyrians, protected by the British, were seen as a thorn in the side of the Iraqi Arab nationalists and were dealt with in 1933. Bakr Sidqi's military campaign, resulting in the decimation of the inhabitants of the village of Symayl, was viewed as a nationalist enterprise and was accompanied by demonstrations and fundraising. In May—June 1933, the Ministry of Education solicited funds from students and teachers to purchase a tank and the Ministry of Defense requested employees to donate two days of salary to a fund to buy a plane. Nationalists in southern Syria, desiring to express their appreciation for the Iraqi military, proposed to donate to the Iraqi army a tank or a plane to be named "Southern Syria."[16] Bakr returned to Baghdad a national hero.

Faysal understood that the political trappings of the state—king and parliament—were the "democratic" facade that the British had imposed on Iraq so that their Mandate could pass muster as an example to the world of enlightened tutelage. Faysal also recognized that education and control of the military were the keys to the creation of a nation. The education portfolio, always given to a nominal Shi`i, was, in reality under the direct control of Arab nationalists within the ministry, who wrote and imposed the curriculum, imported and hired Arab nationalist teachers from Syria and Palestine, and directed the publication of course syllabi and textbooks that would be used not only in Iraq but throughout the Arab world.

Faysal invited Sati` al-Husri to direct education in Iraq. A renowned Ottoman pedagogue, Husri became an Arab nationalist just before the war and joined Faysal in Damascus. In Iraq it was Husri's job to work out accommodation to League of Nations requirements for the inclusion of ethnic and religious diversity within a national education system while at the same time pursuing an Arab nationalist agenda under the nose of the omnipresent British advisors. Husri came into conflict with the Shi`i, especially with Muhammad Fadil al-Jamali, who succeeded him as Director General within the Ministry of Education and whose goal was the advancement of Shi`i education and the decentralization of authority. Ironically, however, both Husri and Jamali pursued a pan-Arab goal in education.

During his tenure in Iraq from 1921–1941, Husri remained aloof from local party politics and attended to what he considered to be "higher politics" or the achievement of fundamental national goals, among them the fostering of patriotism and nationalism. "I will employ every means," he said, "to strengthen the feeling of nationalism among the sons of Iraq to spread the belief in the unity of the Arab nation. And I shall do this without joining any of the political parties which will eventually be formed."[17]

The school, instead of the home and family, would become the social and cultural educator. It would teach the superiority of the community, order, discipline, cooperation, love of fatherland, and the role of the individual in service to the nation. The school was to be not only a place for study but also the theater of a new life, the mechanism for social change, by which Husri meant the indoctrination in an Arab nationalist culture. To Husri, compulsory education and universal military conscription were the two most important mechanisms for the cohesion of the nation, military service being a further stage in the assimilation process of the individual to the nation.[18]

Military conscription was to be used not only as a means to strengthen the army but also as a method to achieve national cohesion. It also became the "litmus test" for nationalist allegiance. During the parliamentary debate on the issue of conscription in 1927, Ja`far al-`Askari, took conscription past military defense when he said that an army based on universal military conscription "will be more inclusive of the racial qualities and national virtues with which the Iraqi nation is graced than an army built on any other basis." Yasin al-Hashimi advocated induction as cheaper than a volunteer army and maintained that, in theory, conscription did not have to be limited to those under twenty for military service but could be applied equally to all citizens for the exploitation of natural and industrial resources.[19] Despite Shi`i contributions to Ottoman paramilitary forces during World War I, to them the army remained a Sunni preserve. Officers remained Sunni and conscripts were drawn from Shi`i tribesmen from the south.[20] Shi`is saw national conscription as means for the Sunnis to dominate and to increase the Baghdad central authority's control. During the turbulent year of 1927, and again in 1932, the Shi`i opposed military conscription legislation that was to be passed in 1934. They could not sustain their opposition after Iraq became independent when conscription became a key nationalist issue.[21]

When the army advocated that the military was to be a school for the nation, guided by an Arab nationalist officer corps,this was a natural extension of the ideology developed by the Prussian officer corps, adopted by the French, and later transmitted to the Iraqi Arabs via German military advisors at the Ottoman military academy.[22] The officers who came to power after 1936 were of a generation that did not go through the process of national self-definition while in the Ottoman army but were trained in nationalism by officers who had undergone the throes of Ottomanism versus Arabism.

The pan-Arab military was buttressed by the schools that mandated the teaching of nationalism. Husri's curriculum, like the French model he incorporated into the Iraqi version, emphasized the study of language and history. Arabic, Middle Eastern, and European history, as well as geography and civics, accounted for about half the hours the Iraqi child spent in primary school.[23] Intermediate and secondary school curricula were not completed until the mid 1930s, but throughout the interwar period, despite the plethora of subjects in the course of study, more than 15 percent of the curriculum was devoted to history, geography, and civics.[24] There was no compulsory education law in Iraq, so Husri took into account the strong attrition rate as the students progressed via the state-administered examinations at every level and designed his program to inculcate nationalism in primary school and reinforce it in the upper grades. Like the French curriculum, nationalist subjects in the Iraqi course of study were presented in simplified narrative in the early grades with more detail added as the students progressed.[25]

Husri left the Ministry of Education in 1936 because of disagreements over method and altercations with subordinates, but his work was continued by his successors Muhammad Fadil al-Jamali and Sami Shawkat, who retained and expanded on Husri's curriculum. Jamali actively recruited Syrian and Palestinian teachers in the 1930s, placing them in administrative positions, appointing them as history teachers, and commissioning their history textbooks for use in Iraqi schools.[26] In Iraq the pan-Arabs emphasized Arab political issues rather than Iraqi local concerns.

History was the most important tool used to inculcate national awareness in the younger generation. "History for history's sake," Shawkat preached to a meeting of history teachers in Baghdad, "has no place in our present society: it is a matter for the specialist and for those who devote themselves to learning alone. The histories which are written with this aim in view are buried and nobody reads them."[27] Teachers were provided, therefore, with explicit instructions on how to teach history detailed in the curriculum guides provided by the Ministry of Education. The "study of history is glorious," they were told, "filled with life, great and exciting tales, sentiments to awaken national pride, free from complexities, not loaded with names, dates, and facts which oppress the memory in such a manner as to restrict the understanding of the course of history."[28]

The Iraqi curriculum used biographical sketches to introduce elementary school children to the history of the Arabs. Heroes were to be taught in terms of their "glorious historical exploits through bravery, courage, determination, endurance, and noble deeds"[29] and teachers were to emphasize the virtuous and pious characters of the personalities and their service to the nation. It is worth taking a detailed look at the personalities chosen, as the lists of heroes change throughout the 1930s. It is illustrative of the shift from an inclusive Arab nationalism imposed by Husri to a more secular Syrian/Palestinian approach that became law by 1940.

In the curriculum for the 1920s there were twenty-eight names on the list of heroes, including six women.[30] In 1936 the number increased to forty and included such modern personalities as King Ghazi, Faysal, King Husayn of the Hijaz, and recent Middle Eastern rulers or Muslim leaders from the Middle East and North Africa who led revolts against the Europeans. The Kurd Salah al-Din al-Ayyubi was studied as were the significant Abbasid and Umayyad Caliphs, governors of Iraq, the Four Righteous Caliphs, and the Prophet Muhammad. In addition, students were to know of the deeds of pre-Islamic heroes that included the Jewish poet, al-Samwa`il, and important women: Khadija, `Aisha, al-Khinsa, Bilqis, and Zenobia.[31]

From 1936 to 1940 a change occurred that emphasized the pan-Arab and more secular nature of the curriculum. The heroes became "Arab" heroes, non-Arabs and North African personalities were replaced by Arab conquerors of Syria and Palestine, and there was a change in the description of Muhammad. In 1936 the syllabus referred to "The Prophet Muhammad, God bless him and grant him salvation," while in 1940, conforming to Akram Zu`aytir's nationalist text, *Ta'rikhuna bi Uslub Qisasi* (Our History in Story Form), which teachers were advised to use for reference, Muhammad was identified as Sayyidna Muhammad ibn `Abdullah. In their instructions, teachers were told to stress to the students the greatness of the Prophet Muhammad, the "Commander" [*za`im*], emphasizing, in a departure from the norm, the historical Muhammad, the "leader of the nation and the source of its power in the past, in the present, and in the future."[32]

By the end of the 1930s there was a definite shift away from the treatment of the Islamic and the multiethnic composition of Iraqi society to the emphasis on an Iraq that was part of an anti-British, pan-Arab union. During the 1920s when he was implementing the educational system, Husri dithered over the establishment of teaching in the vernacular in Kurdish areas, a requirement of the League and a criticism the American observers of the Monroe Commission noted in their report on education in Iraq issued in 1932. He opposed opening a secondary school in al-Najaf and a teacher training school in Hilla and decided to abolish the Directorate of Education for the middle Euphrates region in 1925.[33]

The nationalists' control over education was capped by the Public Education Law of 1940 advocated by Jamali, which was the culmination of the "pan-Arabization" policy initiated in the schools during the 1920s. Its object was to synchronize by law the teaching of "nationalist subjects"—history, geography, the Arabic language and literature—in nongovernment schools. The goal of the policy was to ensure that students received information in a prescribed manner from a pan-Arab nationalist approach, delivered by teachers appointed or approved by the Iraqi Ministry of Education. By the mid 1930s, many of them were Syrians and Palestinians, who were strong advocates for Palestine within the context of the Arabism they were teaching.

This law, like similar laws passed during the interwar years in Argentina, Japan, Germany, and long in effect in France, was to be the means of assurance that in the multiethnic and multireligious state of Iraq, nationalism could be fully propagated. Any deviation in curriculum, textbooks, or teaching not in the spirit of the law was prohibited.[34] Budgets of all private schools had to be cleared with the Ministry of Education, and every student took the same mandated state-administered examination.

This legislated conformity to Arab nationalist goals in the curriculum coincided with political events that put the implementation of the nationalist ideology to a real test. Iraqi foreign policy at the end of the 1930s, when the government was dominated by political and military pan-Arabists, was directed along the lines already set in motion by Faysal. The "Rashid `Ali Coup" and the war with Britain in 1941 were the practical culmination of the designated ideological process.

Faysal initiated an activist approach to Arab nationalist aspirations through his involvement in Syrian politics during the 1920s in attempts to convince politicians of the efficacy of Hashimite unity. With Iraqi independence in 1932, plans for a pan-Arab congress backed by Syrians and Palestinians who had supported Faysal in 1918–1920 to be held in Baghdad were underway. Though his death in 1933 delayed the Hashimite approach to Arab unity, the pan-Arab policy was taken up by the military that had been politicized during the 1930s and resulted in the hostilities that broke out between Iraq and Great Britain on May 2, 1941.

The war that resulted lasted until May 30, when, as British troops were on the outskirts of Baghdad, the military leaders sued for peace and fled the country for Teheran, Istanbul, and Berlin. In an attempt to bring to fruition the goal of Arab unity under Iraqi hegemony by aligning with the Axis powers when Britain, in the spring of 1941, seemed on the verge of defeat, the pan-Arab military officers who had taken control of the government, together with the Jerusalem Mufti, Hajj Amin al-Husayni and his Syrian and Palestinian supporters who followed him to exile in Baghdad after 1937, sought to oust the British not only from Iraq but from the Middle East entirely.[35]

These were the officers, exemplified by Salah al-Din al-Sabbagh, who attended the Baghdad Military College in the 1930s where Arabism was the mark of solidarity. Although theoretically the military college was open to all ethnic and communal groups, more and more entering cadets were from Arab Sunni backgrounds; fewer non-Sunnis attended as cadets and were gauged on their feelings of "`Uruba" (Arabness). And while the totalitarian regimes of Europe in the 1930s certainly impressed the officers, they had no interest in social or economic reform.[36] Their goals were to rearm Iraq and to achieve Palestine's independence from British control. To that end al-Sabbagh joined the pan-Arab clubs like *al-Muthanna*, was one of those who trained the paramilitary *Futuwwa* units in Iraqi schools, and became the leader of the "Golden Square"—the officers who backed the Mufti and Rashid `Ali in their abortive war against the British.

The British and the restored Hashimite regime understood the war to be an Arab nationalist attack on the British; the subsequent government report, which assessed blame for the war and the attack on the Jewish community of Baghdad by retreating Iraqi soldiers, bedouin, and youth gangs, focused on the politicization of the military through the education process in Iraq during the interwar period.[37]

As a result officers suspected of harboring pro-Axis sentiments were pensioned off or interned in camps located in southern Iraq while older, demonstrably promonarchy officers were brought out of retirement. Rashid `Ali and the Golden Square were tried in absentia and, as the military perpetrators of the war were gradually extradited, they were returned for execution in Iraq. It was not until the end of the war that Nuri al-Sa`id, prime minister since the fall of 1941, realized that the future security needs of the country required a revitalized army and a British military mission was brought in to provide training.

But military activists were a small minority in Iraq. The tribes did not participate in the revolt and though the hostilities reached the capital, the war was short-lived. Iraqi casualties were some five hundred officers and enlisted men. Thus the British, who had relinquished all authority to Iraqis in the Ministry of Education in the 1920s, now undertook to repair the damage in what they saw as the anti-British, Arab nationalist institution.

Though the British had warned of the danger of a politicized student body as early as the late 1920s and had foreseen the consequences of lenient punishment meted out to students demonstrators, no prophylactic action was taken. Those who demonstrated at the Ministry of Education against the expulsion of Anis al-Nasuli and the retraction of his pro-Syrian Sunni history of the Umayyads in 1927 were duly noted by the British. The police dispersed the student agitators. Student leaders and their mentors, among them Darwish al-Miqdadi, were expelled from school. Nevertheless, despite Shi`i grievances, when tensions subsided all were reinstated. The British commented that "the Ministry of Education must apparently reconcile itself to the fact that in a crisis, it cannot trust either the commonsense or the loyalty of teachers."[38]

Teachers encouraged students to give eloquent anti-British speeches, especially on national holidays such as Renaissance Day, which commemorated the Arab Revolt against the Ottoman Turks. In the 1930s the British government became the target of the rhetoric, which extolled the virtues of all who opposed the Anglo-Iraqi treaty and now condemned politicians such as Nuri al-Sa`id and Ja`far al-`Askari who, despite their sponsorship of the treaty, had actually participated in the revolt on the Arab side.

The anti-British political climate, partly derived from anti-British sections in al-Miqdadi's texts that stressed themes such as British imperialism and noted that it was British cowardice as opposed to Iraqi bravery in the revolt of 1920 that resulted in Iraqi independence. These ideas were reinforced in the classroom, a student wrote to the British, so that one retained the view that the British "cried during the battles like children," that they "won the war only through their money and mean diplomacy." The Arabs, on the other hand, "captured British cannons and artillery when they were armed only with clubs" and "machine-gun nests . . . with sticks only."[39]

In 1941–1942, the British and Nuri's government specifically ordered the alteration of textbooks and the expulsion of nationalist teachers. Although the order to excise anti-British material from the end of Darwish al-Miqdadi's text was given almost as soon as Nuri returned to power in the fall of 1941, in February 1942 the British lamented the noncooperation of the civil servants and the teachers in the Ministry of Education. Not until both Jamali and Shawkat left the ministry and a British advisor was installed in 1942, however, did the process of decentralization within the ministry begin and the installation of new cadres of teachers take place.

But, in a comment noted on a "Security Summary," the author noted that in reality it was "almost impossible to insist on the suppression of all anti-British references in school books objectionable as these are, the interference involved in their enforced suppression would possibly be more to our disadvantage than their remaining." He noted that anti-British teachers were stated

> to have shed tears when pausing at a deleted passage, the effect being more impressive than the reading of the passage! There is no escaping the fact that we and the French in Syria, are not popular in Arab nationalist circles, and no amount of censoring schoolbooks will alter the fact. What we can justly object to is Arab discrimination in favour of the Axis in such books: condemnation of our methods in Palestine and the French in North Africa and Syria without mentioning the Italians in Libya.[40]

Despite Sati` al-Husri's policy of benign neglect in Shi`i areas and the anti-Shi`i tone of the Sunni/Syrian authored texts, Shi`i began to attend government school in larger numbers due for the most part to the championing of Shi`i interests by Jamali.[41] As young Shi`i realized the importance of secular education in achieving goals of equal opportunity, power-sharing in a Sunni dominated state, and working toward the eradication of the belief propagated by Arab nationalists that Shi`ism was a subversive heresy motivated by Persian hatred for the Arabs and a threat to Arab nationalism,[42] the curriculum became less of an issue. The religious dilemma inherent in cooperating with a political regime deemed illegitimate by orthodox Shi`ism, however, remained below the surface.[43]

Jamali, a Shi`i and an ardent and outspoken Arab nationalist, used his tenure in the Ministry of Education for the advocacy of Shi`i mobility. It was largely due to his efforts that Shi`i inclusion into the Iraqi socio-political mainstream already became evident in the mid 1940s. He encouraged and accepted more Shi`i students as foreign mission students; assured their entrance into the Higher Teachers Training College, which charged no tuition; established a secondary school in al-Najaf; and eased requirements for students in the provinces to enter secondary schools.[44]

Shi`is began to attend government schools in order to prepare themselves to fill government posts in proportion to their numbers in the Iraqi population. They were concerned with the nature of education in the state school system and many went on to become professional educators, where after World War II, they entered the teaching profession in large numbers.[45] Between 1930 and 1945 the number of students in Iraqi schools tripled and there were secondary schools in all of the districts. Much of the expansion, including an increase in the numbers of foreign mission students and those attending the Higher Teachers Training College, came from Shi`i areas.[46]

Many intellectuals submerged their Shi`i identity and became Arab nationalists. The historian `Abd al-Razzaq al-Hasani rarely mentions Shi`i grievances in his multivolume history of Iraqi cabinets and was a supporter of the Rashid `Ali government, whose failure resulted in Hasani's incarceration for four years in an internment camp in southern Iraq. Young Shi`is used education in order to fit into Iraqi society, for to become professional Shi`i smacked of sectarianism [*al-ta'ifiyya*] and diluted their loyalty to the regime. These were the young men who began to fill the government posts after 1945, became teachers, and who, by the early 1950s, filled the middle-class slots left vacated by the Jewish emigration in 1950–1951.[47] Physical hostility by the regime against the Shi`i would come under the Ba`th.

For the Jewish community, the Public Education Law of 1940 brought out into the open basic questions of the relationship between the Jewish community and the Iraqi regime. What the law actually did was legalize nationalist conformity and, by doing so, expose Jews in all Iraqi schools to the inherent political conflict between Zionism and Arab nationalism.

The community was divided in its approach to the government of the new state. Those who had developed commercial links with British interests welcomed the Mandate, while Jews who served as professionals and civil servants under the Ottomans looked forward to an Iraqi regime. Political communal solidarity also began to weaken as Jews began to attend government schools to receive a completely secular education and acquired aspirations for full social, intellectual, and political participation in Iraqi society.

Groups of secularly educated Jewish youth identified themselves as citizens of Arab Iraq, loyal to the country of their birth. They became part of the newly emerging Iraqi Arab intelligentsia of the interwar years. They edited books, started Arabic literary journals and newspapers, and wrote poetry extolling their homeland. Murad Michael's first poem, published in 1922, was an ode of praise and love for Iraq. Many also joined liberal opposition movements. To these Jews there was no conflict between the Jewish religion and Iraqi nationality. They considered themselves to be Jewish Arabs and did not identify with Zionism.[48]

Jews began attending government schools in large numbers during the 1930s even if there was a Jewish school in the area. School was free and government schools had night classes. A high school diploma from a government school was the ticket to a job in the civil service or teaching, guaranteeing economic security. Husri's Arabization curriculum meant an emphasis on Arabic and preparation for the government administered examinations required for entrance to high school. So long as the government needed Jews to fill government posts, Jews attended and completed secondary school in numbers far exceeding their proportion of the population.[49] A diploma was also the gateway for study at the Law College and admission to the American University at Beirut. For those interested in a

European university education, the Alliance school, because of its strong English component, was the track to study in England.

Matriculation in a government-accredited secondary school also meant exemption from military conscription. Though there were Jews in the police force and in the army in the mid 1930s, educated Jews, like the Shiʿi, tried to avoid military service that would place them in the army as inductees under Sunni Muslim officers. In order to counteract the flow of Jews to completely secular schools, the Jewish community established a number of Jewish secondary schools that provided religious instruction, were staffed by Jewish and Muslim teachers, and were accredited by the state. These, too, came under the jurisdiction of the 1940 education law.[50]

The distinctions made by early Arab nationalists between the Jewish religion and political Zionism began to blur in the early 1930s, especially after 1936, with the infiltration of Nazi propaganda and when Iraqi support for the Palestine Arabs coalesced with its pan-Arab foreign policy. During this period, al-Samawʿil, the pre-Islamic Jewish Arab, was dropped from the list of heroes taught in Iraqi schools. Jews were requested to openly declare their loyalty to the Iraqi regime, which they did: "We are Arabs before we are Jews," Ezra Menahem Daniel proclaimed in 1936 after a bomb exploded in a Jewish area on Yom Kippur.[51] Anwar Shaʾul and other literary figures published notices of their loyalty to the Iraqi regime in the press, which elicited a response from Palestinian Akram Zuʿaytir who was visiting Baghdad. He approved of Shaʾul's views but pressed him to be even "more emphatic in his condemnation of Zionism."[52]

Though officially apolitical with regard to the events in Palestine and evincing little to no support for political Zionism, the Jewish community had to walk a fine line after Faysal's death in 1933. By the mid 1930s Zionist activity was officially banned in Iraq, the importation of Hebrew books and newspapers from Palestine was interdicted, and the last Jewish teachers of the Hebrew language who had come from Palestine were expelled.[53] The Iraqi government also forbade the teaching of Jewish history and the Hebrew language in Jewish schools under the pretext of nondissemination of ideology of Zionism.[54] Prayers and the Bible could be read in the original Hebrew but not translated into Arabic for discussion. When Ezra Haddad, headmaster of the Shamash School, tried to obtain permission to publish a handbook for the teaching of the Bible, he was refused. Studying a version of history in which teachers railed against Jews in Palestine during the fighting there from 1936 to 1939, and attending classes where funds and support were solicited actively for the Palestine Defense Fund whose monies were allocated for Arab martyrs in Palestine, caused serious conflicts for the Jewish students who saw matriculation as the only means to remain economically secure in an increasingly volatile political atmosphere. They accommodated themselves to the political situation by closing schools when demonstrations were expected to occur and by conforming to government regulation to the letter. As Iraqi Muslims became available for civil service positions, they began to replace Jews working for the government. Layoffs of Jewish civil servants in the Ministry of Economics began to occur in 1934. Jews found jobs in the private sector.

So long as the community was not physically threatened, Jews could live with the political exigencies. Everyone, however—Jews, the British, and Iraqis—was shocked by the *farhud* in Baghdad that occurred in June 1941 when more than one hundred and fifty Jews were killed and Jewish property was looted.[55] More than any other event, the *farhud* resulted in a new phase of Jewish history in Iraq, which led to an obfuscation of the Jewish role in Iraqi society by implying doubts about Jewish loyalty. For many who rode the waves of sporadic anti-Jewish feeling in Iraq during the 1930s, not questioning their loyalties and allegiances, the events of 1941 caused a shift in thinking. Insecurity and doubt about their future role in Iraq politicized the community. Jews joined liberal opposition groups, the Communist Party, and the Zionist movement. Ultimately, virtually the entire Jewish population of Iraq emigrated.

The attempt to impose nationalism from the top down by the Iraqi Arab nationalists during the interwar period resulted in foreign policy operations that failed to implement the goals of Arab unity. After Faysal's death, the flag of Hashimite hegemony over the Arab world was transmuted into a program for a pan-Arab [Iraqi, Syrian, Palestinian] union dominated by Iraqi pan-Arab military officers and the Jerusalem Mufti. When it was clear that the Iraqi-British War of 1941 had ended in defeat for the nationalist cause, the Hashimite banner was passed to Trans-Jordan. As heir to the legacy, `Abdullah began to the reconstitution of the Arab monarchy in 1948 through his acquisition of the old city of Jerusalem and the West Bank. But Syria would lie beyond his grasp. Meddling in Syrian politics during the 1950s became the idée fixe of the Iraqi regent `Abd al-Ilah, who needed assurances of a throne once Faysal II reached his majority.[56] The revolution in 1958 ended Hashimite unity goals. The pan-Arab ideology, however, would be reconstituted by the Ba`th party.

The Arab nationalists also failed to create a coherent inclusive ideology that could weld the fragments of Iraqi society to the Sunni Arab nationalist regime in Baghdad. As a secular umbrella, the ideology of Arab nationalism could theoretically accommodate sectarian ethnic and religious identification so long as the adherents professed loyalty to the state and adopted "Arab culture" as their own. There was room for separation of religion and nationality. The definition of Arabism, however, became narrower as Iraqi foreign policy adopted the Palestinian Arab cause. With Syrian and Palestinian emigres in charge of education and the means of dissemination of political discourse through the schools, pan-Arabism took on a Syrian "Umayyad" caste in opposition to an Iraqi "Abbasid" definition that could incorporate Shi`is and Jews. Because of Palestine, religious and political identification blurred and Jews, no matter how vociferous their loyalty as Jewish Iraqi Arabs and denials of Zionist partisanship, were the targets of anti-Zionism and anti-Semitism—the latter disseminated through the German legation in Baghdad.

Kurds, Jews, and Shi`i found themselves excluded from social and political incorporation in the new Iraq. For Kurds the response would be almost continuous rebellion against the regime in power.[57] For Jews the political solution to exclusion meant emigration.

By 1944 Shi`i schools in the south were overcrowded, the Shi`i leadership was demanding more government schools in the area, and parents pushed their children to prepare for government positions. The Sunni government responded to Shi`i demands for inclusion of more Shi`is in government by expanding the numbers of bureaucratic and government posts to allow for more Shi`is but also to ensure Sunni dominance of the state mechanism. By 1949 the Shi`i had their first Iraqi prime minister, Salih Jabr, but not only was his tenure short-lived, he spent the rest of his political career in opposition to the perennial prime minister, Nuri al-Sa`id. Shi`i frustration over their inability to achieve political parity in Baghdad and failure to have their needs addressed led many to join opposition movements. Both the Communist Party and radical Islamic groups that would play a greater role after the revolution of 1958 attracted Shi`i adherents during the last years of the monarchy.[58]

Thus Arab nationalism in Iraq during the early monarchy failed to translate the political legacies of the Ottoman Empire—ethnicity and communal identity—into an operative nationalist concept that could incorporate the indigenous ethnic and religious fragments within the borders of the territory allocated to the the new state into an inclusive nation.[59]

6

Nationalist Iconography

Egypt as a Woman[*]

Beth Baron

A nation is an abstraction. That is, it has no material form. Yet from the rise of nationalism, the nation has been represented visually.[1] The purposes of such representations are clear. Images of the nation are meant to reaffirm the unity of the nation and give the concept of nationhood greater immediacy. In societies such as those of the Middle East, where large segments of the population remain illiterate, they are also meant to disseminate the idea of nationalism. The nation is thus an "imagined community"[2] that is sometimes imagined in human or other form. When the nation has been personified, it obviously appears as either a male or female figure. The selection and subsequent attributes associated with the chosen figure give insights into a particular nationalism and illuminate gender roles in a new nation-state.

This essay analyzes the visual representations of the Egyptian nation from the 1870s through the 1930s. A variety of forms will be examined, including paintings, sculptures, and cartoons. Images were generated under diverse circumstances by a variety of artists and others for different audiences. We will consider the context of creation of these works, their intended meanings, and their reception by Egyptian audiences. We will see that over time, and with few exceptions, Egypt came to be depicted as a woman.[3]

It could be argued that the idea of representing the nation as a woman,

[*]Special thanks to the workshop participants as well as Ami Ayalon and Arthur Goldschmidt, Jr. for comments on this article.

like the idea of nationalism itself, had come from abroad. Derived from the European model in general or the French precedent in particular (Marianne), it would thus be one more example of an almost universal practice. Yet local traditions had a significant impact on the production of images of the nation, making the indigenous imprint extremely important and the nationalist iconography of Egypt at times unique.

First, Egypt came to be represented as a woman in a process that coincided with the unveiling of Egyptian women. This was not a self-evident or seamless process but, rather, one that took time. Egypt could not effectively be represented as a woman until the debate on unveiling had advanced in the early 1900s and the urban elite women who wore a face covering had begun to unveil in the century's teens and twenties. Unveiling then became a metaphor for independence. Second, this female image was not a mere importation of the French Marianne or of other European representations. The images of the Egyptian nation as a woman reflected something of the social situation of Egyptian women and of the local discourse on their place in society. Unlike the barebreasted Marianne, Egypt only bared her face, and in general she respected local customs pertaining to modest dress. Third, no one image of the nation emerged. Rather, there was a multiplicity of images, of young and old, healthy and ailing, Pharaonic and Islamic, urban and rural women. The multiplicity indicated a measure of confusion about the content of Egyptian nationalism and its direction. It suggested that the notion of "nation" in Egypt was still fluid and that Egypt was not yet a coherent collective.

NINETEENTH-CENTURY DEPICTIONS

Some of the earliest images of the Egyptian nation came from the pen of Ya`qub Sanu`a, an Egyptian nationalist educated in part in Italy and no doubt influenced by the arts there. Sanu`a was a man of many talents who in the early 1870s wrote and produced plays, founding native Egyptian theatre. In 1877 he started a satirical weekly called *Abu Naddara Zarqa'* (the man with the blue glasses). Only fifteen issues of the handwritten journal appeared before an angry Khedive Isma`il expelled Sanu`a from Egypt. Sanu`a took up residence in Paris, where he continued to produce his journal under various titles for decades, adding French to the colloquial Arabic.[4]

Sanu`a's journal circulated widely in its early days, according to contemporary observers. Blanchard Jerrold wrote that the satire in the second issue "was so thoroughly to the taste of the public, that the paper was sold in immense quantities. It was in every barrack, in every Government-office. In every town and village it was read with the liveliest delight." Jerrold claimed that the journal subsequently "found its way into every village, and was read universally." If they could not read, he explained, the *fallah* "learned to listen with delight to the satire of the Abou Naddarah."[5] Once Sanu`a moved overseas, he had the banned journal smuggled back into Egypt using various devices. Copies were hidden in the pages of art books and large journals or in the luggage of Egyptian travelers. One poverty-stricken woman carried the journal home in her bedding.[6] Circulation figures for *Abu Naddara* have been variously estimated, the most reasonable being 3,300 per issue.[7] Because papers were passed from hand-to-hand and read aloud, scholars of the Arabic press suggest that circulation numbers ought to be multiplied for a more accurate accounting of distribution.[8] And to readers and listeners, we must add viewers, for Sanu`a introduced cartoons to the Egyptian public.[9]

Sanu`a himself often appeared in the cartoons, in the garb of a *shaykh* or otherwise dressed and always wearing glasses, the perennial observer. Unlike cartoons of the 1920s and 1930s, which spared the monarch, Sanu`a's cartoons incessantly attacked Khedive Isma`il and his successors as well as ministers and foreign officials. John Bull and representations of other European nations made frequent appearances in the pages of *Abu Naddara*. Convenient symbols for the great powers, they could be easily caricatured.[10] Sanu`a also depicted the Egyptian nation in various guises. One series of cartoons showed Egypt as a cow (occasionally with the head of the Sphinx) being milked dry by ministers and by the European powers, or actually sucked by foreigners. Fat or lean, the cow appeared as a passive victim.[11] Egypt also appeared as a donkey: Isma`il sat astride the animal as his sons and associates beat it in an attempt to steal it.[12]

Sanu`a represented Egypt as a woman from time to time. In the early 1880s Egypt appeared twice as an ailing Pharaonic queen (figure 6.1).[13] European excavators had begun to unearth Pharaonic treasures from the mid-nineteenth century, providing artists and intellectuals with new motifs and designs. The decision to depict the nation in Pharaonic garb thus reflected the impact of Egyptology on Egyptians. But there were also few female alternatives. Sanu`a showed Egypt as a fully veiled woman in 1894; the woman representing Egypt stands next to women representing France and Russia and in front of a female Britannia (figure 6.2).[14] The contrasts are compelling and suggest the artistic and ideological limitations of depicting Egypt as an Islamic woman with no visage. Nationalism was meant to be a modernizing force, but a fully veiled woman in the mid-1890s did not represent modernity. Sanu`a himself was a man of liberal ideas who had critiqued the situation of women in Egyptian society in his plays and attacked institutions such as polygamy.

Fig. 6.1   The Assassination of a Nation. [*Abu Naddara* 8, no. 3 (1884), 142]

Yet until the debate on unveiling had begun, he could not easily use contemporary women as representations of Egypt. This image, in any case, was not repeated in the pages of *Abu Naddara*.

The importance of visual matter in *Abu Naddara* should not be underestimated, given the low literacy rates of the day. But would viewers have easily understood the cartoons? A knowledge of Egyptian and European politics would seem important, and the captions in Egyptian dialect (and French) under the cartoons no doubt clarified meanings. But the cartoons could have been appreciated on a number of levels. They caricatured familiar figures and drew on local humor. Verbal antecedents to the cartoon could be found in indigenous Egyptian humor: folktales (in particular the Goha repertoire), proverbs, *zajals*, (rhymed prose), and *nuktas* (verbal cartoon or joke).[15] Still, one should not assume that illiterate Egyptians had a visual literacy and understood the signs and symbols used in cartoons. Reading pictures was a skill that had to be learned.[16]

Ya`qub Sanu`a followed events of the 1881–1882 `Urabi Revolt closely, commenting upon them both editorially and visually. In the period following the exile of many of those who had backed `Urabi, Sanu`a continued to articulate and illustrate a pro-French nationalist position. His significance diminished with the emergence of Mustafa Kamil and a younger generation of nationalists. These men developed their own organs, such as the newspaper *al-Liwa'*, which did not favor the cartoon as

ILLUSION DÉTRUITE

Fig. 6.2   A Veiled Egypt. [*Abu Naddara* 18, no. 12 (1894), 50]

a political expression (given its pan-Islamic bent, it avoided human images altogether). With the odd exception, the cartoon seems less con-spicuous in the press.[17] This may have been a matter of Mustafa Kamil's style, the simple absence of illustrators with a bent toward humor, or a focus on a narrower, more literate audience. For early images of the nation, we must turn toward other art forms.

Mustafa Kamil's initial strategy, like that of Sanu`a, was to appeal to the French to pressure the British to leave Egypt peacefully. When Mustafa Kamil presented the president of the French Chamber of Deputies with a petition in 1895 requesting French aid in evicting the British from Egypt, he also gave him a painting (figure 6.3). This work, reproduced in `Ali Fahmi Kamil's biography of his brother and later in `Abd al-Rahman al-Rafi`i's book on the nationalist leader, depicts Egypt as a captive of the British. In the foreground an Egyptian with clothes stripped to the waist sits with back to the viewer and hands chained; the chains are held in the claws of the lion of Great Britain lying to the right; to the right of the lion sits a barechested soldier, sword in hand and eyeing Egypt suspiciously. Behind this group an Egyptian wearing European dress and a *tarbush* (fez) hands a document to an allegorical woman symbolizing France and justice. To his left a group of male Egyptians stands in *tarbushes* and tur-bans, waving the Ottoman-Egyptian flag; to the right women represent-ing nations that the French had helped to achieve independence observe the scene.[18]

Appel au secours du Peuple égyptien à la France libératrice des nations.

Fig. 6.3   Picture presented to the French Chamber of Deputies (1895).

The figure representing Egypt is ambiguous. The physique appears to be that of a man. Yet 'Ali Fahmi Kamil writes that it is a woman.[19] Whether he makes that claim because he knew the original intent of the work, or because by the time he published his book over a decade later, Egypt was consistently depicted as a woman, is unclear. If it is a woman (as it probably was meant to be), it is consistent with the other nations rendered as women in the picture. Although her partial nakedness might be considered shocking, it is only implied and not revealed, as her back is towards us.

It is unlikely that this work was painted by an Egyptian, as the first generation of modern Egyptian painters were still in their infancy. It was therefore almost certainly painted by a Frenchman commissioned for

تمثال مصطفى كامل - ميدان مصطفى كامل

Fig. 6.4   Statue of Mustafa Kamil (1914).

this job. How widely viewed was this image? Mustafa Kamil presented the original painting to French officials, but thousands of copies were made of the picture and distributed to the international press.[20] Presumably some copies circulated in Egypt, appearing in the press there. Would those Egyptians who saw this picture have comprehended the symbolism? The law students who comprised an important segment of Kamil's followers might have; the uneducated would not have read the signs so easily. It seems, in any case, to have been primarily intended for a foreign audience.

MONUMENTAL WORKS

After Mustafa Kamil died in 1908, a committee was formed to commission a statue of the youthful nationalist. Since the School of Fine Arts had opened in Cairo only that year, no local artist yet had the requisite skills to create a monument in metal. The memorial committee thus chose a famous French sculptor based in Paris to cast the work in bronze.[21] But when we examine the monument, we can probably assume that the sculptor had to comply with the committee's design for the work or at least with their expectations for it.

The statue shows Mustafa Kamil standing erect delivering a speech (figure 6.4). He places his left hand on top of a bust of the Sphinx, which evokes Egypt's past glory, and points down with his right hand. The extended forefinger of his right hand draws us to the pedestal of the statue, which proves most intriguing for our purposes. A raised bronze shows a seated peasant woman of about the same dimension as Mustafa Kamil. Entrapped in the square space, the peasant woman represents Egypt under British occupation. She listens to the speaker and with her right hand implores that others do the same. Her left hand draws aside her veil in a gesture that signifies a desire for liberation.[22]

That the monument to one of Egypt's earliest nationalists depicted the nation as a peasant is not surprising. Many nationalisms celebrate male and female peasants as "culturally authentic." Peasants have a concrete tie to the land, which is, after all, central to the claims of territorial nationalists. In the case of Egypt, depicting the nation as a peasant emphasized the agrarian nature of society. Yet the celebration of Egyptian peasants shows a significant break with earlier elite attitudes toward them. The Turco-Circassian aristocracy had despised the peasantry, and the elevation of the peasant as the embodiment of the nation coincided with the former's declining influence. Moreover, the generation that was coming to the helm of Egypt prided itself on its "peasant" (that is indigenous Egyptian origins) as opposed to the "foreign" Turco-Circassian elite, even though the men on the rise were landowners rather than laborers on the land.

The statue of Mustafa Kamil was delivered to Egypt in 1914 in the midst of a debate on whether or not Egyptian women ought to remove their face coverings. Unveiling meant different things to proponents and opponents of the step. Writers in the journal al-Sufur, founded in 1915, argued for unveiling (this is the meaning of al-sufur) whereas those in the weekly al-'Afaf (Virtue), founded in 1910, opposed the greater mixing of men and women that unveiling would inevitably bring. The cover of the latter journal had initially carried the picture of an Egyptian peasant woman with an opaque head scarf drawn across her face, but the editor subsequently blotted out the woman's facial features below her eyes. Both sides of this debate had come to see women as symbols of the nation, either of its backwardness, as in the case of the intellectuals around al-Sufur, or of its purity, as in the case of those writing for al-'Afaf.[23] The appearance of a woman as the representative of Egypt on the ped-

estal of the statue commemorating Mustafa Kamil expressed this sentiment artistically. The irony is that Mustafa Kamil was not a proponent
of unveiling. To be sure, peasant women had never worn the same sort
of face covering [*hijab*] that elite women had. They dressed modestly
and covered their heads, and if they needed to they drew the head scarf
across their faces. Their work in the fields and elsewhere made strict
veiling and the seclusion that it suggested impractical. The differences
between the veiling practices of rural and urban women were pointed
out in the press. Still, a peasant woman unveiling came to represent the
nation in its struggle for independence in a conflation of symbols.

By the time the monument arrived in Egypt, Kamil's successor, Muhammad Farid, had gone into exile and his party had fragmented.
Although the statue was originally intended as an official memorial, it
was barred from public exhibition. Neither the British nor the Khedive
would have permitted this in 1914. Instead the statue was erected in the
courtyard of the school Kamil had founded, where it no doubt became a
familiar sight to schoolboys. Set as it was on private grounds, the statue
did not have nearly the size audience that it later gained when it was
moved to a public square in 1938.[24]

The spread of renderings of Egypt as a woman was impossible until
the debate on unveiling had reached a certain level. Yet it was no accident that debates on unveiling coincided with the rise of nationalism.
Both were tied to the question of modernity. Moreover, the endeavor of
building a nation-state required the mobilization of the entire population, male and female, and women had participated in the nationalist
movement from its rise. In the 1890s they started journals promoting a
domestic ideology posited on women's role as "mothers of the nation"
whose job was to inculcate their sons and daughters with patriotism.
They formed charities pioneering social reform in the name of national
revival. Decades of organizing prepared elite women for public action,
and in 1919 they marched in protest against British policy in Egypt, taking a visible role in the 1919 Revolution.[25]

Inspired by the events of that revolution and influenced by the Mexi-
can muralists, Muhammad Naji painted a vibrant tableau in 1919. The
monumental oil on canvas bears the title "The Awakening of Egypt
[*Nahdat Misr*], or the Procession of Isis" and contains Pharaonic and
rural motifs. Here Egypt is represented as the queen-goddess Isis. She
rides alongside the Nile in a chariot drawn by a water buffalo surrounded by male and female peasants. The procession is slow and colorful,
suggesting historic motion and the march toward freedom. Naji's mural
has hung in the hall of the Egyptian National Assembly since 1922.[26]
Although displayed in a public building, one cannot presume all Egyp-

tians could view the work. Women were denied access to the parliament in its early days, and the parliament was closed even to its own members under certain cabinets.

Images of women representing the nation multiplied in the 1920s as Egypt gained quasi-independence. This trend can be partially attributed to the proliferation of one specific image: Mahmud Mukhtar's "Nahdat Misr." As a village youth, Mukhtar had shown a talent for sculpting. He became one of the first graduates of the School of Fine Arts and went on to Paris to continue his studies. There in 1920 he won a prize for a model of "Nahdat Misr." Enthusiasm for his success abroad resulted in a campaign to have the sculpture enlarged and erected in the square in front of the Cairo train station. Pink granite quarried in Aswan was floated down the Nile in conscious imitation of the production of Pharaonic monuments. It took Mukhtar almost until the end of the decade to complete the costly project, but finally in 1928 the sculpture was presented to the public with great fanfare (figure 6.5).[27]

The work juxtaposes two images: the Sphinx rising and a peasant woman unveiling. Both the Sphinx and the woman represent Egypt, one the ancient civilization, the other the modern nation. The Sphinx rising suggests a rebirth of Egypt's ancient grandeur; the peasant woman lifting her veil symbolizes the liberation of the nation. The linking of the two figures—the woman's hand rests on the Sphinx's head—connects antiquity to the present.[28] Some of the elements of the Mustafa Kamil statue are thus repeated, only the man himself is missing.

Critics acclaimed Mukhtar's "Nahdat Misr." Since the sculpture was erected in a busy square through which all those who came to Cairo by train had to pass, it had a captive audience. Even foreign travelers noticed the sculpture. "The visitor to Cairo is greeted on his arrival, as he passes out of the station, by a statue on the Station Square called *The Awakening of Egypt*," reported the American tourist Ruth Woodsmall. "On his departure from Cairo this statue remains his last impression."[29] Yet well before the final work was unveiled, the model had become familiar to many Egyptians. The journal *al-Nahda al-Nisa'iyya* (the Women's Awakening), founded in July 1921, often carried a picture of the model in profile on its cover.[30] Cartoons in *al-Kashkul*, a satirical journal also founded in 1921, parodied Mukhtar's effort to complete and display the statue through the decade.[31]

CARICATURES OF THE NATION

The 1920s witnessed the reemergence of the cartoon as an important medium for conveying political and social critique. Two journals domi-

Fig. 6.5   The Awakening of Egypt (1928).

nated the field, offering contrasting caricatures of national types. In *Ruz al-Yusuf*, a pro-Wafd weekly founded in 1925 by the actress Fatima al-Yusuf, the Egyptian character al-Misri Effendi became quite popular. A short, rounded figure, he wore a European-style suit and a *tarbush* (symbol of the new middle class) and carried prayer beads. However, this character represented "Mr. Average Egyptian" rather than the nation per se (which was occasionally depicted as a woman).[32] Launched in 1929, the character al-Misri Effendi soon spread to other periodicals. According to the cartoonist Muhammad Rakha, who helped to create its successor, in 1941 the chief editor of *al-Ithnayn* and the editorial staff of Dar al-Hilal decided that the caricature no longer symbolized the Egyptian character because, as Rakha relates, "it represented the lowest class of government official, that is the *effendi* class, or petty bureaucrats." They concluded that "the personality of an *ibn al-balad* [son of the people] represented a more independent and emancipated personality and one which really represented the Egyptian."[33] Rakha's comments shed light on the process by which certain caricatures were created. Decisions about what images to present to readers and viewers were often taken at the highest level by the editor and staff.

Whether this was the case at *al-Kashkul* (Scrapbook), a major rival of *Ruz al-Yusuf*, is not apparent. Edited by Sulayman Fawzi from the time it first appeared in May 1921, *al-Kashkul* introduced a new sort of satirical political journalism into Egypt.[34] It lampooned the government, assailing its weakness in dealing with the British, and condemned corruption in the Wafd. The paper appeared weekly, with a format of four full-page color cartoons in each issue of sixteen or more pages in its first decade, and ran until after World War II.[35] *Al-Kashkul*'s cartoons played on familiar themes and were probably comprehensible to many Egyptians. The caricatured figures were generally well-known, and the captions were in colloquial Arabic and could have been read aloud to the illiterate. Among the most popular weeklies in the interwar period, *al-Kashkul* had a circulation estimated at ten thousand in 1927–1928.[36] This was considered sizable at a time in which high illiteracy rates and the cost of ten milliemes per issue (or just over fifty piastres a year) would have precluded mass distribution. Its broad circulation and stinging satire no doubt irritated those government officials who came under attack, and upon at least one occasion the editor was arrested for insulting public officials in the pages of his paper. On that occasion a cartoon had shown the then Prime Minister, Sa`d Zaghlul, as an organ-grinder.[37]

A series of cartoons in *al-Kashkul* depicted Egypt as a woman. The image was not fixed, however, and several "Egypts" ran through the 1920s and early 1930s, differing in age, size, and attributes in spite of the fact that most seem to be by the same hand. The most prevalent image of Egypt in the cartoons is that of a young woman (figure 6.6). She wears contemporary European dress, gloves, and high-heeled shoes along with a head scarf, a very light face veil, and a cloak. Her clothes change over the course of the decade: her cloak and dress become shorter, the gloves come off, the veil is removed, and she carries a clutch pocketbook. She even sports a fur wrap, indicating an elite background. That she oversees the cook, but does not cook herself, confirms this status. She travels, drives a car, and mixes with men. In short, she is the "new woman" of the age, educated and sophisticated, the counterpart to *al-Kashkul*'s al-Misri

Fig. 6.6   The High Commissioner and Egypt.
[*Al-Kashkul* 5, no. 233 (1925), 20]

Bey, who occasionally appeared, and a step above *Ruz al-Yusuf*'s al-Misri Effendi.[38]

A second image shows a younger Egypt. She wears bows in her hair and bows on her dress, which is often decorated with the stars and crescent of the Egyptian flag. She is not just younger but smaller and appears weak and prone: she plays on a beach when suddenly the peace is disturbed by British planes and warships; she is accosted by foreign men (John Bull and others) who grab her; and she is befriended by Egyptian politicians (figure 6.7). Whereas British personalities and Egyptian politicians appear sinister and devious, she represents innocence and purity.[39] A third image is that of a rural woman, wearing a peasant scarf, ankle bracelets, and no shoes. Less sophisticated than the "new woman," she is more sensual. She is also more abused: she appears tied to a chair and gagged (figure 6.8), and in chains and blindfolded. In addition, she conveys more emotion: in one cartoon she wails at the side of a grave.[40] Yet the cartoonist at *al-Kashkul* did not tie himself to these sets of images, and he continued to create new ones. Egypt gives birth to the constitution, lies in a sick-bed attended by male politician-doctors, and appears weak and emaciated with a walking stick.[41]

Fig. 6.7   Egypt and the Negotiations. [*Al-Kashkul* 7,
no. 328 (1927), 1]

These are political cartoons concerned primarily with critiquing
government policy. Yet we cannot ignore other levels of meaning.
These cartoons convey their messages through caricatures that are
based on widespread perceptions about gender and power, and they
rely on sexual illusions as metaphors for politics. The sexual innuendo
gives the artist almost unlimited opportunity for political critique.
Egypt as a woman plays opposite to England's John Bull (figure 6.9),
who is preferred to the female Britannia, as well as to Egypt's male
politicians (there are no female ones). The Egyptian nation is wooed
and pursued, and occasionally punished. In this way, the cartoons provide an outlet for expressions of sexuality that would be proscribed in
other media, and they give a running commentary on contemporary
gender relations. Because of her status in society, a woman could easily suggest the attributes associated with colonial occupation: as occupied as opposed to occupier, she was passive, prone, and weak. She also

Fig. 6.8   A Gagged Egypt. [*Al-Kashkul*, no. 34 (1922), 16]

represented powerlessness and purity in the face of the corruption of Egyptian politicians.

The cartoons also contain explicit and implicit messages about race and class. Egypt almost always appears with a fair complexion, whether she is a young girl, "new woman," or peasant. By comparison, the Sudan—depicted as a nearly naked woman and in other guises—has darkened skin and exaggerated facial features. The Egypt of *al-Kashkul* is clearly not akin to territories to the south and of the African continent but closer in resemblance and style to European neighbors to the north. Egypt is also, with some exceptions, depicted as a woman of means. This is not surprising, as notables—lawyers and landowners—dominated Egyptian politics in the 1920s and 1930s. One wonders what appeal an elite woman of this sort would have had as a symbol of the Egyptian nation to a broader audience. Would she have evoked sympathy? Perhaps she would have in an age of paternalistic politics and of a different class consciousness.

Fig. 6.9   Egypt and England. [*Al-Kashkul* 5, no. 250
(1926), 1]

In any case, it was convenient for the cartoonist at *al-Kashkul* to depict
Egypt as a woman at a time when women had not been elected to the parliament or entered the cabinet. It was unlikely that she would be confused,
as a male figure might have been, with a living personality. With the
notable exceptions of Huda Sha`rawi, Nabawiyya Musa, Safiyya Zaghlul,
and Fatima al-Yusuf, few real women appeared in the cartoons.

PRODUCERS AND CONSUMERS

Not surprisingly, those sculptors, painters, cartoonists, and others who
depicted the nation as a woman in various media were mostly male.
While they presented the typical Egyptian—such as al-Misri Effendi—
as male, they rendered the collective female. The man was the citizen;
the woman was the nation. The artists who produced these images of the
nation probably imagined their audience as male as well. Representing

the nation as a woman was meant to tap notions of honor and instill in male viewers the sense that they had the duty to support, protect, and defend it.[42] Yet honor was not the only sentiment at stake. These images were intended to generate a romantic attachment to the nation and encourage a fusion with it. By depicting the nation as a woman, nationalists hoped to stimulate love for the nation and draw male youth to the cause. The images thus drew on emotions associated with gender and sexual relations. The man was the actor, the speaker, the lover; the woman was the acted upon, the listener, the beloved.

The audience of these images differed in size and composition. The paintings had the most limited consumption, hung as they were in restricted quarters. Yet replications circulated. The sculptures that appeared in public squares had a wider audience, though one of a limited circumference. Cartoons could have been consumed by the illiterate, who often gathered around newspaper readers to hear sections of a paper read aloud and would have seen the pictures. Seeing did not necessarily guarantee visual literacy, however. Visual representations have their own signs and symbols, which may not be apparent to all viewers. Even if understood, an image may not have resonated with its audience. Still, visual representations would have reached a much broader segment of the population than print culture and would have operated on a more visceral level.

Women did not seem to protest the nationalist iconography representing the nation as a woman. The women's journal *al-Nahda al-Nisa'iyya* had carried a picture of the model of Mukhtar's sculpture in profile on its cover from its inception. That Labiba Ahmad, its editor and president of the *Jam`iyyat Nahdat al-Sayyidat* (Women's Awakening Society), chose to feature this image on the front of her new journal suggests a certain pride in the connection made between women and the nation. This fit well with the argument that the nation could not advance until women had progressed, which female intellectuals had used to legitimize such demands as expanded education and marital reform.

Yet the audience for most of these images was meant to be male. In 1928 when the monumental version of "Nahdat Misr" was unveiled in front of an audience of thousands, among them the country's male notables, the only women allowed to attend the ceremony were three or four members of the press corps. King Fu'ad had apparently blocked the participation of other women.[43] Initially, women could not enter the building where Naji's painting hung. Some women could, of course, buy *al-Kashkul*, but they were not the intended audience of most of these images of the nation. In short, women's inclusion in the nation was in question. Male Egyptians made the transition from subjects of a colonial state to cit-

izens of a semi-independent nation-state with certain rights and responsibilities, while women became second-class citizens with far fewer rights.
Some protested against this exclusion. The irony remains that although a
woman symbolized the nation, women were kept to the perimeters of the
public stage when it came to their actual roles as citizens.

CONCLUSION: A CONSENSUS

One of the most important ways of transmitting the idea of nationalism
beyond literate circles was through visual representations of the nation.
From the 1870s the Egyptian nation was depicted in human form in
sculpture, painting, and cartoons. Taken by itself, any one of these visual images could have been the whim of an artist or a patron commissioning art. Taken together they form compelling images of the nation as a
woman, or rather as a variety of types of women. A consensus had
arisen, even among opposing forces, over nationalist iconography. Egypt
might be young or old, healthy or ailing, urban or rural, Pharaonic or
Islamic, but she was a woman. Only on very few occasions (such as one
or two cartoons out of thousands printed in *al-Kashkul* in its first decade) was the nation represented as a man. The spread of women as symbols of the nation corresponded with the effort of nationalists to broad-
en their movement and also corresponded with the movement toward
the unveiling of women. This is not to say that all images were well
received. Some of them had broader circulation than others, and some
were more easily understood than others. Moreover, not all nationalist
iconography targeted the same audience or had the same meaning.

Depicting the nation as a woman was favored over showing it as a
man for several reasons. Arabic is a gendered language and Misr (Egypt)
is gendered female. Depicting Egypt as a woman thus had a certain linguistic logic. It also gave intellectuals and artists a rich field for political
commentary through sexual innuendo and gendered metaphors. French
cultural influence no doubt played a role as well. Those Egyptian intellectuals and artists who had spent time in France (Sanu`a lived there in
exile, Mustafa Kamil was a frequent visitor, and Mukhtar and Naji studied there) had most likely seen Delacroix's "Liberty on the Barricades"
and become acquainted with Marianne as a symbol of the Republic (although she was not uniformly admired). These Egyptians did not all
choose to make Egypt a woman. For those who did, there were important differences between Marianne—an ideal woman derived from ancient allegorical female figures[44]—and the images of Egypt as a woman.
First, Egypt almost never appeared naked, bare-breasted, or only lightly
clothed like Marianne. Second, different images of Egypt proliferated,

varying in age, size, outlook, attire, and origin, as opposed to the one female representation of France. Finally, just at the time when Egyptians began representing the nation as a woman, French and other European iconography of insurgency began to shift from female to male figures.[45]

In spite of the multiplicity of images, two types prevailed by the 1920s: the peasant and the "new woman." In sculpture, the *fallaha* (peasant woman) emerged as a representation of the nation. The process of celebrating Egyptian peasants probably began in the 1890s.[46] By the 1920s peasants had become prized as the soul of Egypt: "the repository of all that was virtuous and noble in the Egyptian nation."[47] The selection of the peasant—male or female—as the embodiment of the nation and the emphasis on agrarian roots contrasted with the predisposition of Arabs to the east to favor nomads and the desert. Egypt's sedentary population had always been much larger than her nomadic one, and her record of settlement had been much longer and continuous than that of her neighbors. Ennobling the peasant thus reinforced Egyptian identity over Arab, Turkish, or Islamic alternatives.

Cartoons of the 1920s and 1930s, on the other hand, tended to depict the nation in urban garb. *Al-Kashkul* mostly chose a "new woman" type to represent the nation. Urban characters were presented in multiple situations, showing the realism and dynamism of the contemporary city.[48] That is not to say that *al-Kashkul* ignored the countryside. But the focus was urban, since politics were centered in the city and city folk gave the cartoonists greater range for political commentary and antigovernment critique.

The media used for nationalist iconography obviously differed in their characteristics. By nature, cartoons were much more timely, allowing a rapid response to a current political drama. They had a fluid nature, but were also quite ephemeral as each week new cartoons appeared. Statues take much more time in the making and as a result tended to be more idealized. The meanings of the nationalist images discussed here should be understood in the context of the media in which they were portrayed.

If certain images prevailed in the nationalist iconography, others were noticeably lacking. Egypt is, in popular parlance, *Umm al-Dunya* (Mother of the World), yet there was no "Mother Egypt" in art, akin to Mother India. Rendering such an image would have been emotionally powerful. One explanation for the absence of such an image might be the presence of *Umm al-Misriyyin* (the Mother of Egyptians) in the person of Safiyya Zaghlul, the wife of the nationalist leader Sa`d Zaghlul. Her photograph appeared in the national press in the 1920s, and she was caricatured, as were a few other women, in the pages of *al-*

Kashkul. But there was no artistic representation of an abstract Mother Egypt.

While artists, intellectuals, and others came to agree that Egypt should be represented as a woman, they had different notions about what sort of woman she should be. What did this multiplicity of representations of the nation mean? These images did not grow out of a timeless perception of Egyptian womanhood. Rather, they were very much tied to debates by and about women on veiling and other topics from the 1890s, and they reflected the fluidity of women's roles and a blurring of gender boundaries during this period. This explains in part why so many sometimes seemingly contrasting images of woman were used to represent the nation. The multiplicity of images also showed a diversity of views regarding the direction Egypt should take among various groups of nationalists. Thus it reflected the fluidity of the notion of "nation" as well—not a coherent collective but rather one typified by a variety of values.

PART III

Discursive Competitions

The Interplay of Rival Nationalist Visions

7

Nationalizing the Pharaonic Past

Egyptology, Imperialism, and Egyptian Nationalism, 1922–1952*

Donald Malcolm Reid

Science neither has nor should have a country, for it is the fruit of efforts made by human thought for the welfare of humanity. It must have no geographical boundaries and must be free from local or national prejudices. Nevertheless we cannot avoid expressing admiration for Professor Selim Hassan on his archaeological skill and his continuous finds, the last of which was the fourth pyramid. . . . It is indeed a matter of deep regret that the monuments should be ours and the history should be ours, but that those who write books on the history of ancient Egypt should not be Egyptians.

—*al-Balagh, 1932*[1]

The writer of these lines was proud of pioneering Egyptologist Selim Hassan and believed it urgent to reclaim the pharaonic past from the Westerners who had rediscovered and appropriated it during the nineteenth century. He felt compelled, however, to follow the convention of wrapping his particularist nationalism in the rhetoric of universal science. In this he had plenty of company, for British, French, and German Egyptologists had long been declaring their devotion to objective science and to their countries in almost the same breath, suppressing any misgivings that the two might be incompatible.

*My research in Egypt in 1987–88 was funded by grants from the Fulbright Hays Faculty Research Abroad program and Georgia State University. It was sponsored by the Fulbright Binational Commission, the American Research Center in Egypt, Cairo University, and Ayn Shams University.

This article examines the ways in which Egyptian Egyptologists[2] "nationalized" their field between 1922 and 1952. To do this, they had to struggle on two fronts. On the first front they gradually dismantled foreign control over the Egyptian Museum, the Antiquities Service, excavations, and the export of antiquities. This paralleled, and was part of, the simultaneous fight to win complete national independence from Britain. In order to strengthen their case for national control in archeology, Egyptian Egyptologists engaged in an uphill struggle to establish their credentials in a discipline created, defined, and dominated by Westerners. On the second front Egyptologists worked to persuade their compatriots to take pride in ancient Egypt as an essential component of modern Egyptian identity. This effort paralleled, and was part of, the national struggle to rally the entire public behind the demand for full independence. Egyptian Egyptologists succeeded, but only in a qualified way, on both fronts.

Like their Western colleagues, Egypt's Egyptologists often felt misgivings when nationalist readings of ancient Egypt slipped over into chauvinism. Egyptologists not could afford to ignore either the "imagined communities" of the nation states in which they lived or the universal fellowship of their discipline. Though in fact deeply nationalistic, German professorial "mandarins" struck a responsive chord in Europe, the United States, and Egypt with their invocation of "science for science's sake."[3] Belief in Egyptology as an objective, progressive, and universal "science" was more than lip service. For Egyptians, the dilemma was this: if they embraced universal standards and values in Egyptology, how could they escape a hegemonic Western discourse that might well doom them to perpetual inferiority?[4] How could they ever hope to compete as equals in a field whose international languages were—and still remain—English, French, and German? "For the native," complained Frantz Fanon, "objectivity is always directed against him."[5]

Insiders often idealize their profession or discipline, suppressing scandals and rivalries, whether national or personal, which might tarnish the "noble dream"[6] of objectivity. Eulogists produce sanitized histories of selfless saints as unconvincing at one extreme as debunking biographies, retailing scandal for its own sake, can be at the other. Dawson's and Uphill's indispensable *Who Was Who in Egyptology*, for example, omits or minimizes national and personal feuds. This may be justifiable in a reference work, but it makes for sanitized and misleading cultural history. Their entry on Selim Hassan conveys nothing of the lively mix of personal ambition and nationalism that brought him into conflict with the French Antiquities directors or of the charges that tragically derailed his career.[7] John Wilson's carefully nuanced accounts, while still suppressing a good deal, do better. While taking national feuds in Egyptology into account, he suggests that competition for jobs in Egyptology may have made feuds within nations even worse than those between them.[8]

The 1922–1952 period serves our purpose well. Nineteen twenty-two represents the chance conjuncture of partial Egyptian independence and the discovery of Tutankhamun's tomb; Egyptology and nationalism became more tightly intertwined than ever before. British excavator Howard Carter looked to Britain for imperial support of his claims, while the Egyptian government insisted on Egypt's total control of the tomb and its treasure. The discovery hastened the establishment of Egyptology in the Egyptian (now Cairo) University and intensified demands for national control of the Antiquities Service, excavations, and the export of antiquities. Thirty years later in 1952, national politics and Egyptology just as clearly converged when the Free Officers' revolution abruptly ended ninety-four years of French domination of the service.

In Egypt and around the world, nationalists who rallied the people against Western imperialism expected to continue to lead after independence. Similarly, Egyptian Egyptologists set out to persuade their countrymen that pharaonic remains were more than treasure troves of buried gold, quarries for building stones and fertilizer, charms to cure infertility, relics of an idolatrous past, and lures for Western tourists. Pharaonic discourse redefined antiquities as sacred relics of a glorious past, priceless evidence for modern science, and inspiration for a national renaissance. If this discourse carried the day, Egyptologists would be indispensable in the new order of things.

Anthony Smith notes that modern national pride in ancient Greece, Egypt, and Iran appealed to intellectual elites in the three countries, while Orthodox Byzantium, Arabism, and Islam respectively had more popular appeal. Gershoni and Jankowski have traced the rise of "pharaonicist" nationalism in the 1920s and early 1930s among the Westernized Egyptian elite and its waning thereafter before a more populist Arab and Islamic discourse. While generally valid, the thesis may underestimate the persistence and perhaps even the social depth of an admittedly watered-down pharaonism. The 1930s and 1940s saw the permanent establishment of Egyptian Egyptology as an academic and professional field; an irreversible drive to Egyptianize the Antiquities Service; and the rewriting of Egyptian history, which gave the pharaonic past a seemingly permanent place in school textbooks.[9]

WESTERN IMPERIALISM AND EGYPTOLOGY, 1822–1922

A century before the discovery of Tutankhamun's tomb, Jean François Champollion opened the door to hieroglyphics. By 1900 scholars in

France, Germany, and Britain led the emerging discipline of Egyptology, Italy and smaller European countries had joined in, and Russia and the United States were waiting in the wings.

In the West, popular accounts of Egyptology play up flamboyant personalities and the romance of excavation, while scholarly accounts trace the steady accumulation of positive knowledge and highlight the occasional dramatic breakthrough. Neither the popular nor the scholarly accounts linger long on the imperialist context within which Egyptology grew up. The imperialist context of the discovery of the Rosetta Stone and the production of the great *Description de l'Egypte* is unmistakable, of course. But less attention is given, for example, to the imperial context within which Auguste Mariette founded the Egyptian Antiquities Service, Flinders Petrie excavated, and Frenchmen dominated the service for ninety-four years.

Western imperialism sometimes put on a monolithic face, with Europeans joining together in self-congratulation on their civilizing mission or white man's burden. In the rarified world of Egyptology too, scholars and excavators relished their membership in an avowedly international—but in practice long exclusively Western—fraternity. (The fraternity also long remained exclusively male, with females such as Amelia Edwards[10] being accepted only in supporting roles.) Western Egyptologists encountered modern Egyptians as officials, laborers, and servants but could hardly imagine them as potential colleagues.

Behind the facade of international science, Western Egyptology seethed with national rivalries. The Anglo-French Egyptological rivalry, which was bound up with the two powers' imperial ambitions in Egypt and the Eastern Mediterranean, spanned the nineteenth century and persisted well into the twentieth. Franco-German Egyptological rivalry was already taking shape by the time of the two nations' fateful clash on the battlefield at Sedan in 1870. By the turn of the century, Americans had begun bringing their own national and scholarly perspectives to Egyptology.[11]

These intra-European Egyptological rivalries were not mere petty sideshows to the onward march of science and progress; they were integral to the manufacture of knowledge itself. They are important to this study not only because they show that Egyptians had plenty of company in infusing nationalism into the discipline but also because these Western rivalries opened up cracks within which Egyptian Egyptology tried to grow. Similarly in national politics at the turn of the century, Anglo-French imperial rivalry led some Frenchmen to encourage Mustafa Kamil's nationalist movement in Egypt despite the dangerous implications of this for France's relations with its own colonized Muslims and Arabs.

AHMAD KAMAL AND THE LOST GENERATION OF EGYPTIAN EGYPTOLOGISTS

It was just such a crack in Western solidarity that gave Ahmad Kamal (1849–1923) his start on the road to Egyptology. Such cracks were narrow, however, and he alone of his generation managed to parlay that start into a full career in Egyptology.[12]

Egyptology was not high on the agenda of Egypt's sovereigns in the century leading up to 1922. To Muhammad `Ali (r. 1805–1848), antiquities were bargaining chips with the British and French consuls as he pursued military and political ambitions. Nevertheless, one potentially fruitful result was his antiquities decree of 1835. Following up on a suggestion by Champollion, it outlawed unauthorized digging and export of antiquities, named an antiquities inspector, and provided for Rifa`a al-Tahtawi to collect antiquities in a Cairo storehouse. Tahtawi had discovered the lure of ancient Egypt while studying in France, where he visited the collection Champollion had organized at the Louvre.

European cupidity and Egyptian indifference aborted this embryonic antiquities service and museum, and in 1855 Sa`id (r. 1854–1863) presented the remnants of the collection to Archduke Maximillian of Austria. Auguste Mariette, fresh from the discovery of the Serapeum at Saqqara, played on imperial rivalries in persuading Sa`id that France, in the person of Prince Napoleon, deserved an equivalent gift. In 1858 the francophile Sa`id, deeply enmeshed in Ferdinand de Lesseps' Suez Canal project and eager to ingratiate himself with Napoleon III, authorized Mariette to create and direct an antiquities service and museum.

A decade later, in the fall of 1869, even as French influence in Egypt peaked with the opening of the Suez Canal, Prussia got a toe in the door with Heinrich Brugsch's appointment as director of a tiny School of Egyptology ("School of the Ancient Language") to train Egyptians in Cairo.[13] Mariette, the French Director of the Antiquities Service, feared the School as a possible German wedge to challenge his control of antiquities. To Egyptians, the School of Egyptology was one facet of a cultural florescence under Khedive Isma`il (r. 1863–1879), which included rapid expansion of schools and literacy, the birth of a private press, the founding of the National Library and Khedivial Geographical Society, an opera house, and urban renewal *à la Parisienne*. Minister of Education `Ali Mubarak, who like Tahtawi took a lively interest in ancient Egypt, worked out the arrangements for the Egyptological school with Brugsch.

Twenty year-old Ahmad Kamal leapt at the chance to join nine other Egyptians in studying Arabic, French, German, Egyptian, Coptic, and Ethiopic at the new school. But the school collapsed after several years. Ignoring the German-French tension, Brugsch lamented:

> The Viceroy was highly satisfied with my work, the minister of education was delighted, and the director of government schools almost burst with envy. . . . my old friend Mariette worried that it might lead the Viceroy to have it up his sleeve to appoint officials who had studied hieroglyphics to his museum. No matter how much I tried to set his mind at ease, he remained so suspicious that he gave the order to museum officials that no native be allowed to copy hieroglyphic inscriptions. The persons in question were thus simply expelled from the Temple.[14]

Mariette refused to hire Brugsch's graduates, and Kamal and his colleagues had to fall back on jobs as teachers, translators, and clerks. A later nationalist wrote,

> With foreigners wanting to monopolize Egyptian antiquities, the former students of the School of hieroglyphics had to enter teaching like Ahmed Bey Naguib and Mohammed Effendi Ismat or teach calligraphy like Ibrahim Effendi Naguib. . . . All these Egyptians passed like shadows. Unfortunately they were Egyptians.[15]

With Britain occupying Egypt after 1882 and Germany concentrating on Istanbul rather than Cairo in its Ottoman policy, Anglo-French rivalry occupied center stage in Cairo, both in Egyptology and in general affairs. Furious at losing Egypt to the British, the French fought a long rearguard retreat as the British tried to whittle away at their influence in the Antiquities Service, the Mixed Courts, and the schools. In 1899 the French were disappointed at being forced to admit two British inspectors into the Antiquities Service.[16] Five years later they were relieved when the entente cordiale formally recognized French directorship of the Antiquities Service.

With French fears of a German archeological coup in Cairo allayed, Maspero proved to be more cordial than Mariette had been to the alumni of Brugsch's school. With the backing of the Egyptian prime minister (Riyad Pasha) himself, Ahmad Kamal first obtained a post as secretary-translator at the museum, then joined the regular cadre of the service as an assistant curator. Maspero encouraged Kamal to relaunch the school of Egyptology by teaching five Egyptians at the museum.

During an interim when Maspero was absent in France, Kamal's petition for promotion over less senior Europeans was rejected,[17] and one of the French directors even tried to fire him. Over the years Kamal worked on the museum's published catalogue, translated Maspero's guidebook into Arabic, published short notices in the service's *ASAE*, taught at the private Egyptian University, and worked on a huge twenty-two-volume Egyptian-Arabic dictionary. His stress on the Arabic-Semitic affinities of ancient Egyptian had obvious nationalist implications. Kamal had not advanced beyond assistant curator when he retired in 1914, with no prospect of an Egyptian successor in sight. Arrangements to publish his dictionary fell through after his death.

THE TURNING POINT: NATIONALIZING TUTANKHAMUN

Howard Carter's discovery of the tomb of Tutankhamun a few months after Britain's unilateral declaration of limited Egyptian independence in 1922 set the stage for a showdown between British Egyptologists and Egyptian nationalists over control of the find. American Egyptologist James Henry Breasted, a coworker and ally of Carter's, had nothing but contempt for the nationalists. His son and biographer, Charles Breasted, conveyed the prevailing British and American view:

> To the Egyptians in general the significance of Tutenkhamon's tomb was entirely political and financial. It was further proof of their past and present glory, and it offered a superlative excuse for another burst of crowing over their newly acquired independence. Most important of all, it contained golden treasure and attracted great crowds of tourists to be bled of their cash. This was something the Egyptians could understand; whereas the proper salvaging of the objects in the tomb, the solicitude of the entire scientific world, and the legal rights of the discoverer and his late patron were wholly academic matters which they neither comprehended nor cared about.[18]

Herbert Winlock of the Metropolitan Museum of Art, whose staff assisted Carter on the tomb, held similar views. He would "certainly not" take an "educated, high class Egyptian" on a dig because millennia of foreign rule had made "an intellectual facility to twist facts . . . an integral part of the Egyptian character." Although they would not steal [!], and "many of them are delightful, cultivated people," the problem was "intellectual gymnastics,"

> *facility* of mind, which enables an Egyptian, or any Oriental for that matter, however cultivated, to see the thing as he *wants* to see it. . . . when some relic was discovered, supposing that I was in need of more evidence

to prove something, say that Rameses III. ruled before Rameses II., he would do everything he could to prove it—in order to please me.

Winlock clinched his case by ridiculing Sa`d Zaghlul's deviousness in Anglo-Egyptian negotiations.[19]

Ignoring the imperial context that had influenced Egyptology for a century, Carter and his Anglo-American team presented the struggle over Tutankhamun's tomb as one of selfless Western science against greedy and ignorant Egyptian nationalists. The prevailing practice had been a fifty-fifty split of most archeological finds between the foreign excavators and the (foreign-run) Antiquities Service. Before his sudden death in the spring of 1923, Carter's patron Lord Carnarvon had insisted on his share of the finds. He also angered the Egyptians by awarding the London *Times* exclusive press coverage of the tomb without consulting them.

The Tutankhamun affair also reopened the old Anglo-French rivalry, which worked to the Egyptians' advantage. With no Egyptologists of their own who could speak with scholarly authority after Kamal's death, the nationalists found a perhaps unexpected ally in Pierre Lacau, Maspero's successor as director-general of the Antiquities Service. In January 1924, Sa`d Zaghlul's proudly nationalist Wafd government had come to power, and Lacau had to answer to it. Lacau peppered Carter in Luxor with instructions for work on the tomb and for receiving official dignitaries. Two American and two British Egyptologists helping Carter warned Lacau in an open letter: "you, as Director General of Antiquities are failing completely to carry out the obligations of your high office to protect scientific procedure in this all important task."[20]

The last straw for Carter was an order from Lacau's superior, minister of the interior Murqus Hanna, forbidding Carter to show his coworkers' wives and families the tomb. Carter locked the tomb in a fury, returned to Cairo, and sued the government in the Mixed Courts. Zaghlul's government struck back—canceling Carter's concession (held in the name of Carnarvon estate) and dispatching Lacau to saw off the locks and seize the tomb. Carter had foolishly chosen as legal counsel the very lawyer (F. M. Maxwell) who had demanded the death penalty in prosecuting Murqus Hanna and other imprisoned Wafdists not long before! Maxwell denounced the government for breaking into the tomb "like a bandit" and all negotiations collapsed.

Treating the tomb as a national shrine, Murqus Hanna led parliamentarians on a pilgrimage there in March 1924 to celebrate the inauguration of Egypt's new parliamentary era. In the Arabic press only Muhammad Husayn Haykal's Liberal Constitutionalist *al-Siyasa*, sharply at odds with Zaghlul and the Wafd, bucked the nationalist tide to side with Carter. The Wafdist *al-Balagh* flung the Western rhetoric of selfless science back in Carter's face: "European and American archaeologists should work for the sake of science, and not expect profit or fame," it intoned: "Egypt has suffered enough from this foreigner, who, under the nose of the Egyptian public and of a high official of the Government, closes the tomb of Pharaoh as though it were the tomb of his own father."[21]

The nationalists won, and the undivided contents of the tomb went to the Egyptian Museum. But the antiquities law that Lacau helped draft and the parliament passed in these circumstances was so draconian that it largely dried up foreign excavation in Egypt for a generation. Even the French government distanced itself from Lacau, noting that he had been acting only in his capacity as an Egyptian official.[22]

In January 1925, however, the Ziwar government quietly readmitted Carter to work on the tomb. In November 1924 the British had seized on the assassination of Sir Lee Stack (the Sirdar, commander of the Egyptian Army and governor-general of the Sudan) to dismiss the Wafd and install Ziwar's compliant palace government. Carter blamed the service for having left Tutankhamun's unique pall out in the sun all summer, ruining it: "Mr. Carter was profoundly moved, but managed to restrain his comment to 'Well, anyway, it's your pall.' "[23]

It was in this overheated atmosphere that the Rockefeller Foundation's offer of a magnificent $10,000,000 new antiquities museum for Cairo foundered. The University of Chicago's James Henry Breasted was the moving spirit behind the proposal, which might have established American dominance of Egyptology. The fatal flaw proved to be a proposed international board that would control the museum during a thirty-year transition while Egyptians were being trained to take over. Egypt, Britain, France, and the US would each have two seats on the board. Those who read archeology as politics variously perceived a scheme to perpetuate Western control at Egyptian expense, a bid for American leadership in Egyptology, and a blow to entrenched French interests in the service. Eighty years later the old Egyptian Museum has yet to be replaced.[24]

AN EGYPTIAN SCHOOL OF ARCHEOLOGY ON THE FOURTH TRY

Ahmad Kamal undertook to explain the significance of Tutankhamun's tomb in the Arabic press, but his death the summer following its discovery left Egyptians profoundly embarrassed at their lack of Egyptologists. Two of Kamal's former pupils, his son Hasan Ahmad Kamal and Selim Hassan, wrote about the tomb in Arabic,[25] but the former was a medical doctor and the latter had only recently resumed Egyptological studies. All the professionals on Carter's Tutankhamun team were foreigners, which was usual at the time.

It had been Westerners who forced the three schools of Egyptology with which Kamal had been associated to close. Kamal's passing in 1923 after fifty years in Egyptology went unremarked at the time in the service's *Annales*. Shortly before his death, Kamal pled with Lacau—twenty-four years his junior—to hire Egyptians. Lacau retorted that few besides Kamal himself had shown any interest. "Ah, M. Lacau," came the reply, "in the sixty-five years you French have directed the service, what opportunities have you given us?"[26]

Yet the tide was already turning. In 1921 Kamal had persuaded Sultan Fu'ad (r. 1917–1936, king from 1922) to arrange for the selection and training of three Egyptian assistant curators for the museum.[27] Taha Husayn, then professor of ancient history at the private Egyptian University, recommended making the selection from graduates of the higher schools under the age of twenty-six, apprenticing them at the museum, then sending them to Europe for advanced study.[28]

The three winners became the core of Egypt's scant second generation of Egyptologists (counting Kamal's largely lost generation as the first). In the event, none of the three—Selim Hassan (1886/87–1961), Sami Gabra (1893–1879), and Mahmud Hamza—was under twenty-six. Hassan and Hamza had studied at Kamal's 1910–1912 Egyptology school before drifting off to teaching; Gabra held a *licence* and *doctorate* in law from Bordeaux. Now Hassan headed for Paris to study Egyptology, while Gabra and Hamza studied at Liverpool before moving on to Paris. They returned to the Antiquities Service about 1928 and published their first articles in its *ASAE* shortly thereafter.[29]

Meanwhile, Egypt's fourth school of Egyptology had begun molding a third generation of Egyptian Egyptologists. In 1923—reportedly on the day Kamal died—a decree founded Egypt's fourth school of Egyptology. Kamal was to have been its director. Like its prewar predecessor, the school began as a section in the Higher Teachers College. With Kamal gone, European professors were the only option; they directed the program until World War II. Vladimir Golénischeff, an elderly expatriate Russian nobleman who divided his time between Nice and Cairo, was the first.[30]

In 1925 the Egyptology program was transferred to the new, state-run Egyptian University. Lord Cromer had vetoed a university as a likely center of nationalist unrest, but his successor, Sir Eldon Gorst, allowed the small private Egyptian University to open in 1908. (Kamal taught an Egyptology course there one year). By 1914 the British had decided to allow a state university and appointed a University Commission to draft a plan. Lacau, Institut Français d'Archéologie Orientale (IFAO) director G. Foucart, and Ahmad Kamal sat on a subcommittee for archeology, which recommended chairs in Egyptology and Islamic archeology, with chairs in ethnography (Foucart's enthusiasm) and Coptic archeology to be added later. Instruction via English and French was prescribed to discipline student minds, as Greek and Latin were presumed to do in Europe. German was also required, but Arabic was mentioned only as a medium for lectures to the general public.[31]

The postwar independence movement derailed the University Commission, and in 1925, with the Wafd in eclipse, King Fu'ad and the Liberal Constitutionalists designed the new Egyptian University. The Egyptological section at the Higher Teachers College was upgraded into a department in the new Faculty of Arts. In the early 1930s K. A. C. Creswell took up the new chair of Islamic archeology, and a graduate-level Institute of Archeology replaced the undergraduate department. Despite France's long archeological presence in the Antiquities Service and IFAO, the British managed to exclude them from University chairs in archeology. The British had no objections to letting Golénischeff occupy the Egyptology chair at first; Russian influence in Egypt was nil, and he was an emigré in any case. Another Russian expatriate who never received a chair, Victor Vikentiev, also taught Egyptian there.

Labib Habachi, a member of the third generation that began graduating from the Egyptian University in 1928, had begun archeology at the Higher Teachers College and followed the program into the University. He regretted never having met Ahmad Kamal but reminisced about studying hieroglyphics with Golénischeff, Arabic literature with Taha Husayn, and Coptic and a little demotic with Georgi Sobhy and Ahmose Labib (also a Copt, and one with a pharaonic name, Habachi pointed out).[32] Sobhy served as advisor to the students' Egyptology club, which brought out several issues of a magazine, *al-Qadim*, in 1925.

PHARAONISM AND NATIONALISM IN THE 1920S AND EARLY 1930S

Tutankhamun's tomb quickened the interest of upper- and upper-middle-class Egyptians in the pharaohs. "Prince of Poets" Ahmad Shawqi and Khalil Mutran composed patriotic odes on Tutankhamun.[33] In 1933 Tawfiq al-Hakim's *Return of the Spirit* used the resurrection of Osiris from the Book of the Dead as a metaphor for Egypt's "awakening" in 1919 and Zaghlul's return from exile and prison. Hakim has a French archeologist lecture a skeptical British irrigation engineer on how the fellahin retained the deep intuitive wisdom of the ancients throughout centuries of invasion and foreign rule.[34]

In 1929 the shift of the Antiquities Service from the ministry of public works to that of education suggested a wider mission than shoring up monuments and excavating dirt; schools would educate modern Egyptians about their pharaonic heritage. School field trips to sites such as the Giza pyramids and Luxor impressed Husayn Fawzi (the author of *Sindibad Misri* [1961]) and future sociologist Sayyid `Uways, whose headmaster always plied his pupils with dynastic charts of the pharaohs.[35]

The paintings of Mahmud Sa`id, the sculptures of Mahmud Mukhtar, and neopharaonic architecture of the 1920s caught the same mood. Mukhtar's granite "Awakening of Egypt," now in front of Cairo University, shows a sphinx rising as a peasant woman removes her veil. Mukhtar's monumental statures of Sa`d Zaghlul in Cairo and Alexandria include pharaonic motifs, and Zaghlul's mausoleum epitomizes the pharaonic revival in architecture. Secularist Muslims and Copts won out in the pharaonic design for the mausoleum; others had advocated a traditional mosque-tomb for the national hero. Isma`il Sidqi's palace government mockingly packed Zaghlul's unfinished tomb with royal mummies from the Egyptian Museum, but in 1936 the Wafd returned to power and triumphantly reburied their hero in the finished tomb.[36]

Liberal Constitutionalists and their forerunners among the intellectuals and landlords of the Umma Party tended to be even more pharaonist than the Wafd. As the editor of the Umma's *al-Jarida* before 1914, Lutfi al-Sayyid implored the youth to visit pharaonic and Islamic sites and the Egyptian Museum, "For the truth of the matter is that we do not know as much about the stature of our fatherland and its glory as tourists do!"[37] As university rector after 1925 he nurtured the Egyptology program, yearned for the day when Egyptians could learn about their ancient forebears from fellow countrymen, and approved the addition of "Arab archeology" at the university. Lutfi's protégé Muhammad Husayn Haykal, editor of *al-Siyasa*, became the leading political-literary pharaonist in the 1920s. The Watani Party of the late Mustafa Kamil included a sphinx's head in the statue of their founder, and Ahmad Husayn's Young Egypt began with a strong pharaonist tint.

King Fu'ad harnessed pharaonism to his pursuit of legitimacy and royal power. Shawqi's Tutankhamun ode presented Fu'ad as a benevolent constitutional monarch(!) and worthy heir to the pharaohs, countering Western depictions of them as brutal oppressors.[38] Seven of nineteen stamps issued during Fu'ad's reign (1922–1936) used pharaonic motifs. On one set, the god of wisdom Thoth carves "Fu'ad" in a hieroglyphic cartouche. Neopharaonic buildings in Egypt peaked in the late 1920s. Yet when occasion demanded, King Fu'ad posed as a pious Muslim, courting al-Azhar and aspiring to be caliph.

PHARAONISM FROM BELOW? DIGGERS, DEALERS, AND DRAGOMEN

On a practical level, tourism and work with archeological expeditions gave many Egyptians a material stake in the pharaonic legacy. For over a century and a half, Alexandria, Cairo, Luxor, and Aswan have presented opportunities for guides, guards, donkey boys, felucca sailors, carriage or taxi drivers, archeological laborers, hoteliers, and peddlers of real and fake antiquities. The as yet unwritten histories of the town of Luxor and villages such as Qurna (opposite Luxor), Mit Rahina, Saqqara, and Nazlat al-Samman (at the foot of the Giza Sphinx) would have been totally different without Western Egyptology and tourism. A multigenerational biography of Qurna's `Abd al-Rasul family, who discovered the cache of royal mummies at Deir al-Bahri about 1871 and mined it for a decade before being caught, could make an illuminating social history. So could the century-old guild of skilled archeological laborers from Quft whom Petrie first recruited in the 1890s.

An incurable romantic, Egyptologist Sami Gabra believed that "The poor villages of Egypt, near the excavations, have never forgotten the solicitude of these great foreign masters so humane to the peasants and their offspring."[39] But Western exploration, archeology, and tourism were immensely destructive of local customs and economies. Benedict Anderson remarks that "the reconstructed monuments, juxtaposed with the surrounding rural poverty, said to natives: Our very presence shows that you have always been, or have long become, incapable of either greatness or self-rule."[40]

Qurna villagers met eighteenth-century Western travelers with stones, and Bonaparte's savants surveyed Egypt only at bayonet point. To many nineteenth-century villagers, archeology meant unpaid forced labor (corvée) for European consul-collectors and later for Mariette's Antiquities Service. Archeology cleared the way for excavation and tourism by evicting villagers from homes in the temples of Luxor and Edfu. In the 1940s the inhabitants of Qurna sabotaged a project to move them from amongst the Tombs of the Nobles down to Hassan Fathi's utopian "New Qurna" in the floodplain; and they are currently resisting another scheme to transfer their village. The uneven personal and regional benefits and costs of tourism, the tensions between insensitive tourists and conservative villagers, folk-beliefs about the fertility-inducing power of antiquities, and the antipharaonism of Islamist purists are all pieces of an as yet little-known puzzle.

EGYPTIANIZING THE ANTIQUITIES SERVICE: SAMI GABRA AND THE COPTS

Britain began its long and intermittent retreat from domination of Egypt in 1922. The nationalization of the Egyptology and Islamic archeology at the Egyptian University and the Antiquities Service were similarly drawn out. Sometimes the ideal of scholarly internationalism smoothed the transition; at others the inherent conflict between imperialism and nationalism made the change more abrasive. Personalities, on both sides of the Egyptian-Western divide, also helped at times to account for the difference between friendly accommodation and outright confrontation.

Egyptology in those days held special appeal for Copts. The great German Egyptologist Adolf Erman had first greeted Sami Gabra with a hearty "You are a Copt . . . of the blood of Amenophis III, that dear Pharaoh whom I would like to see in another age."[41] Copts latched onto the Western belief, often couched in the racialist idiom of the day, that they were the truest descendants of the ancient Egyptians. Claudius Labib (1868–1918), who ran the press at the Coptic Patriarchate and taught Coptic and some Egyptian, gave his children pharaonic names and insisted they speak only Coptic—a dead liturgical language—at home. His son Pahor Claudius Labib (b. 1905) followed him into Egyptology and Coptology, becoming director of the Coptic Museum. George Sobhy (1884–1964) joined his surgeon colleague Elliot Smith in dissecting mummies at the Cairo School of Medicine and taught Coptic and demotic on the side. Sobhy's student Girgis Mattha (d. 1967) succeeded him as the University's demotic and Coptic specialist. Copts constituted only 6 to 10 percent of Egypt's population, but two of seven graduates in the first Egyptology class of 1928 (Mattha and Labib Habachi) were Copts, as were over 40 percent of the Egyptologists graduated between 1928 and 1950.[42]

For Sami Gabra the 1930s were "the golden age" of Egyptian archeology, as savants from all over the West dug away "under the desert sky." Lacau had hand picked Gabra in 1929 to excavate a site at the Coptic Village of Deir Tassa, near Gabra's hometown. After years of American, French, and British schooling, Gabra was so Westernized that he wrote his memoirs in French instead of Arabic. He relished scholarly congresses in Europe and welcomed Western colleagues who visited his excavations at the Greco-Roman necropolis at Tuna al-Gabal. Even his Egyptian nationalism had a gallic twist, as when he praised Lacau's determined resistance to attempts to enrich European museums at Egypt's expense. Gabra hailed "the first pioneering genius" Champollion and the "noble line of his successors: Mariette, Maspero, Loret, Lacau, Drioton. One cannot forget these noble figures, these men always ready to serve science and Egypt with rectitude and modesty."[43]

In national politics too, many Copts would look back on the 1920s and early 1930s as a golden age. The Western-educated upper and upper-middle classes—like many of their Muslim counterparts—felt at ease in the cosmopolitan circles of Cairo and Alexandria. For Copts who took their nationalism seriously, the relative secularism of the Wafd offered a chance for full participation unmatched in either the nineteenth century or after 1952.

EGYPTIANIZING THE ANTIQUITIES SERVICE: SELIM HASSAN AND THE FRENCH

Congenial as Gabra was to Westerners, he lived in a cosmopolitan world that not many Egyptians could share. Selim Hassan was less at home in English and French, his personal ambition and his nationalism put him at odds with the French Antiquities directors, and his prickly personality compounded the friction. in 1912 Maspero had blighted Hassan's career for a decade by refusing to hire Kamal's Egyptology students. When unforeseeable events opened an apprenticeship to him in the Antiquities Service a decade later, he resented having to pay his own way to attend the Champollion centennial celebrated in Grenoble in 1922. R. Engelbach, Chief Inspector of Antiquities for Upper Egypt, reportedly barred him from Tutankhamun's tomb until Carter intervened.[44]

Cracks in the solidarity of Western Egyptology, along both national and personal lines, helped Selim Hassan advance his career. British Egyptologist P. E. Newberry, who had succeeded Golénischeff, welcomed Hassan to the Egyptian University, but his most important patron was Hermann Junker, an Austro-German Egyptologist from the University of Vienna. In 1929 Junker had reopened the German Archeological Institute in Cairo under Austrian auspices. Founded in 1907 under Ludwig Borchardt and sequestered during World War I, the Institute remained frozen until 1929 because of charges that Borchardt had smuggled Nefertiti's famous bust out of Egypt.[45] When Hassan switched from the Antiquities Service to the Egyptian University (about 1931), Junker took Hassan under his wing, providing him with a three-month archeological apprenticeship digging at Giza, offering advice when Hassan began his own excavations for the Faculty of Arts, and guiding him to a University of Vienna doctorate in 1935.

Hassan also benefited from friendly advice from an American, George Reisner, whose Harvard-Boston Museum of Fine Arts expedition was also excavating at Giza. Reisner had broken with his American colleague Breasted, siding unequivocally with the Egyptian government in the Tutankhamun affair.[46] Reisner also endeared himself to Egyptians by training them as archeological photographers and record keepers, treating them as much like colleagues as possible, and helping arrange schooling for sons of his crew.[47]

Nearly fifty when he obtained his doctorate in 1935, and with mandatory retirement looming at sixty, Hassan was a man in a hurry. He set his sights on replacing Lacau as director-general of Antiquities. Lacau had considered retiring as early as 1923 but was warned that the English, Americans, or Germans might snatch up his post.[48] He soldiered on for another dozen years "at head of this service so important for science and for French influence."[49] Georges Foucart, director of IFAO from 1915 to 1928, failed to groom a French heir apparent to Lacau.[50] No help could come from the University either, where a bid to slip Raymond Weill into Junker's chair in 1934 failed.[51]

The gratitude Lacau earned from Egyptian nationalists for his role in the Tutankhamun affair was short-lived. In 1930 nationalists in the Egyptian parliament denounced his six-month summer leaves.[52] In the mid-1930s the nationalist press blamed both Lacau and Pierre Jouguet, Foucart's successor at IFAO, when antiquities from an IFAO dig at Deir El Medina surfaced for sale abroad. Jouguet wondered if Hassan, Newberry, or Junker might be the insider fueling the attacks, but he could not rule out disgruntled French scholars such as Mme. Gauthier-Laurent, who was rumored to have put Selim Hassan's Paris thesis into French.[53]

Early in 1936 Lacau retired at last, and Miles Lampson, the British High Commissioner, hoped that in the absence of an obvious French successor, Chief Curator Engelbach might move up: "My own inclination is to get such things for our own people whenever we properly can! It's always a little galling to me that the Antiquities here should be French run."[54] (A dozen years earlier Lord Allenby had worried instead that an Egyptian, "however incompetent," might follow Lacau.[55]) But when the French did settle on a candidate, the Abbé Etienne Drioton from the Louvre, Lampson felt bound by the 1904 entente to support him.

Egypt had not been a party to the entente cordiale, of course, and the nationalists demanded an Egyptian director. Hearing that Gabra might be named, Mahmud Hamza scrambled to present his own credentials.[56]

But it was Selim Hassan who emerged as the Egyptian candidate. Presumably because of personal rivalries, Gabra mentions neither Hassan nor Hamza in his memoirs.

Nahhas's new Wafdist government was nationalist enough, but an Egyptian director of Antiquities was not its top priority. Anglo-French solidarity prevailed and Drioton won out, though the French Ambassador reported: "Nahhas pacha (whom I suspect of not knowing very well what the "Rosetta Stone" is) answered me that the nomination of the Abbé Drioton was decided in principle six weeks ago . . . but that in view of public opinion the Wafdist govt. was obliged to create for Selim Hassan a post as sub Director."[57]

The Liberal Constitutionalist *al-Siyasa* hailed Drioton, but other Arabic papers protested: "l'Abbé Drioton au Service des Antiquités. Une colonisation française perpetuelle" and noted the irony of "the [Wafdist] Government of the people" appointing "this French priest," a mere "assistant conservator" at the Louvre with credentials allegedly inferior to Hassan's.[58]

In their private dispatches the French and British embassies closed ranks and vilified Hassan. Conceding only his skill in excavation, the French dismissed him as "a rather mediocre student of the Abbé Drioton"[59] with "merely elementary" education. The Rosetta Stone itself would done him no good since he lacked Greek and Latin, whereas "L'Abbé Drioton himself, knows—like Champollion—besides Greek, Hebrew, Chaldean, Arabic, Syriac, and Coptic."[60] The British Embassy was equally vicious:

> For a number of years he [Hassan] has been employed by the Egyptian University who, nonetheless, dislike him cordially. . . . Selim has always been disliked by the majority of Egyptians who regard him as an ignoramus and self-advertising humbug but [he] seems to be feared and is said to be able to count on the support of Nokrashi Pasha.
>
> Selim is the creation of Professor Newberry who has now left Egypt for good. Like his master Selim was always bitterly anti-French who [sic] in his opinion had not appreciated his merits as the one and only Egyptian savant. . . .
>
> He is, I think probably a little mad and most certainly dangerous and malevolent. If unchecked he will end by wrecking the department.[61]

At the museum, the atmosphere turned poisonous. As deputy director-general, Hassan leap-frogged Secretary-General Gauthier, who left the fray by retiring at sixty in 1937. Lampson approved Drioton's tactic of giving Hassan "enough rope to hang himself." Drioton warned Lampson that he was afraid to go on summer leave before the contracts of his European subordinates were renewed; Hassan might fire them. Lampson marched straight to the prime minister himself to obtain the renewals.[62]

As the June 1939 expiration date of Drioton's three-year contract neared, press attacks on the Europeans in the service intensified. Hassan might have won, wrote the French ambassador,

> if archeological science and its representative in Egypt [Drioton] had not found an unexpected, determined, and persistent champion, in the person of King Farouk. . . . He inherited from his father the conviction that Egyptian antiquity is one of the key sources of modern Egyptian brilliance, and that without foreigners, Egyptians are not yet capable of conserving and bringing it to light.[63]

"The Sovereign of Egypt and the able Canon of the Nancy Chapter [Drioton], successor of Mariette and of Maspero,"[64] had hit it off on a royal tour of Upper Egypt. Frustrated by Selim Hassan's poor English—so the gossip went—the princesses of the party had turned with relief to Drioton's French. (Ironically, Arabic was not even considered for these communications between Egyptians.) Hassan reportedly had confused the Apis Bull with the sacrificial bull, and at Asyut he authenticated as ancient a modern necklace presented to Faruq.[65] With the British, the French, and the king in his corner, Drioton stayed on until 1952. One necessary price was silence when antiquities vanished into Faruq's palace collections.

With his 1939 contract renewal in hand, Drioton turned on Hassan, who was suspected of embezzling funds, smuggling out antiquities to Germany, and pulling strings to avoid prosecution. When the royal jewels of Psusennes were stolen in 1940, the British suspected that Hassan had the incident "deliberately framed in order to discredit and expel all Europeans from the Service."[66] Drioton scoffed that though Hassan had charged 26,000 objects were missing from the museum, an inventory showed only three or four mislaid since 1914. "I agree with Selim Bey Hassan," declared Drioton wryly," on the necessity of protecting Egyptian antiquities, not only from foreign hands, but from Egyptian hands as well!!!"[67]

PHARAONISM AND THE ARAB AND ISLAMIC TURN, 1930S–1952

Gershoni and Jankowski have shown that pharaonism faded before more populist Arab and Islamic themes in the 1930s and 1940s. Pharaonic revival buildings became rare, and Haykal dropped the winged sun from the masthead of *al-Siyasa al-Usbu`iyya*.[68] Only six of thirty-six stamp sets issued under Faruq had pharaonic motifs, compared to seven of nineteen under Fu'ad.

Yet the retreat of pharaonism was not a rout. As a youth Nasser had thrilled to the pharaonist patriotism of al-Hakim's *Return of the Spirit*. Young Egypt continued to extol pharaonic as well as Arab and Islamic greatness. In the late 1930s and early 1940s Najib Mahfuz set his first three novels in ancient Egypt, and four of eighteen novels in the Arabic Language Academy's 1941 "best novel" competition had pharaonic settings.[69]

The "Unity of the Nile Valley" slogan appealed across the political spectrum in the 1940s and 1950s, for Egyptians feared Britain's intentions for the Sudan with its vital Nile waters. The slogan had no Arab or Islamic appeal but fit well with pharaonism. Egyptian Egyptologists, historians, geographers, and Africanists rushed to make the case for Egyptian-Sudanese unity.[70] If white Westerners erred in whitening the ancient Egyptians and distancing them from black Africa, American Afrocentrists in our own day often go too far in the opposite direction. Neither position much interests modern Egyptians, whose proverb simply declares Egypt (or Cairo) *Umm al-Dunya*—the Mother of the World.

Nationalists of the 1930s and 1940s might have written the Antiquities Service off as a foreign institution dealing with an alien pre-Arab and pre-Islamic past. Instead they made its nationalization, like the retention of Tutankhamun's treasures and the return of Nefertiti's bust, a touchstone of national pride. With each passing year the small but steady output of Egyptology graduates enlarged the reservoir of professionals with a vested interest in ancient Egypt.

The Museum of Egyptian Civilization, opened in 1949, presented an official version of a secular worldview that still attracts many educated middle-to-upper-class Egyptians. The distinguished modern historian Shafiq Ghurbal, who had begun as a student of Ahmad Kamal's, oversaw the project. The Egypt-centered dioramas progress from prehistory through the pharaonic, Greco-Roman, Coptic, Arab, and Ottoman eras. The French Expedition marks the start of the modern era. The sections on "the modern age," including one on Egyptian expansion into the Sudan, glorify the Muhammad `Ali dynasty.[71] If one elides the prehistoric stage into the pharaonic, follows the progression through the Greco-Roman and Coptic eras, folds the Ottoman into the Arab (or Islamic) period, and marks off the nineteenth and twentieth centuries as the modern period, the result is a five-stage paradigm of Egyptian history still popular today. It is often trumpeted as "7,000 years of civilization." Each of Egypt's four main historical museums (the Egyptian Museum, the Greco-Roman and Coptic museums, and the Museum of Islamic Art) represents one period of the first four in the paradigm.

The retreat from the exaggerated pharaonism of the 1920s helped the more far-sighted members of the Westernized elite keep in touch with the more pragmatic religious leaders of al-Azhar and with the middle and lower-middle classes in the burgeoning towns. Perhaps because no political group of the old regime staked its fate on pharaonism as the Pahlavi dynasty had on ancient Iran, the 1952 revolution felt no need to assault the pre-Islamic past as did Iran's Islamic revolution of 1979. Current Islamist challenges to the Mubarak regime may reopen the question, however.

THE CHANGING OF THE GUARD: 1939–1952

While Drioton's political skills and scholarly stature kept him in office until 1952, Egyptianization proceeded around him in the University and the Antiquities Service. When the British finally drove Junker out of the Egyptian University (for his alleged Nazi sympathies), they were embarrassed to find that they could not come up with a British replacement. The British never had an archeological base in Egypt comparable to IFAO (they were less committed than France to a state-supported *mission civilisatrice*), or even one to rival the German Institute or the American's Chicago House at Luxor. (The British School of Archaeology was merely Petrie's name for his camp wherever he was digging). Sami Gabra became the first Egyptian director of the university's Institute of Archeology by default.[72]

As for the Antiquities Service, Muhammad Husayn Haykal as minister of education almost continuously from 1938 to 1942, searched for a compromise. He proposed placing a single Egyptian administrator-general over the museums of Egyptian, Greco-Roman, Coptic, and Arab Art and reclassifying Drioton and other Europeans as "technical" or "scientific" advisors.[73] The British Embassy, Drioton and the French, and the king joined together to scuttle the plan, but the Psusennes theft gave the government the opening to reclassify Chief Curator Engelbach in 1942 as a technical advisor, with Mahmud Hamza becoming the first Egyptian chief curator. A British maneuver to move in a British understudy to Assistant Curator Guy Brunton failed, so Engelbach's death in 1946 and Brunton's retirement in 1948 quietly ended nearly half a century of British presence in the service.[74]

H. W. Fairman sounded the despairing cries often heard as colonial officials depart: Mahmud Hamza was a "lazy, ignorant intriguer," and

[t]here are a crowd of Egyptian excavators working at Sakkara, ruthless-
ly opening tomb after tomb, and leaving no record of their work except
the obvious. Many will not be published, some will only be published
inadequately and all are rigorously prohibited to the Egyptologist to visit.
Egyptology has been built up by the efforts of scholars of all nations and
has been a truly international science, with the exception that the
Egyptian contribution has been nil.[75]

Engelback found Fairman's charges exaggerated and unfair to Hamza,
who had turned against the French only because of Drioton's "hatred."
Engelbach also defended the scholarship of his Egyptian colleagues, saying that he corrected their manuscripts only for English.

Meanwhile the third generation of Egyptians were moving up. Abdel
Moneim Abu Bakr, Labib Habachi, Girgis Mattha, and three future direc-
tors of the Coptic Museum (Togo Mina, Pahor Labib, and Victor Girgis)
were among those who earned their B.A.s between 1928 and 1933.
Thereafter undergraduate Egyptology was dropped at Cairo University
until 1957 and replaced with a graduate-level Institute of Archeology.
During the 1930s Abu Bakr, Pahor Labib, and Ahmad Badawi overcame
the language barrier and earned Egyptology doctorates in Germany;
Ahmad Fakhry and Anwar Shukri were on the same course when World
War II forced them to return home. Shukri received Fu'ad I (formerly the
Egyptian) University's first Egyptology doctorate in 1942; Fakhry and
seven others had followed him by 1966.[76]

Nationalist pressures had the upper hand in 1945, when Chief Curator Hamza issued a list of American institutions, including the Oriental
Institute, which had not returned objects loaned for study. The implication was that new permits for archeological work would not be forthcoming until their return. French Egyptology had difficulty healing the
wounds of the Vichy/Free French divide, and the Cold War produced
new challenges to scholarly internationalism. The International Association of Egyptologists, which met in 1947, was still-born, though Dutch
scholars salvaged an important annual international bibliography, which
still appears.[77]

Drioton was summering in Europe in 1952 when the revolution
came. The friend of the king knew he could not return, and ninety-four
years of French domination of Antiquities Service came to an end.

AFTER 1952

Early in 1953 Mustafa `Amr (1896–1973) was brought in from the out-
side to become the first Egyptian director-general of the Antiquities

Service. He had come up through the Higher Teachers College (although not its Egyptology section) and taken a geography M.A. at Liverpool. As a geography professor in the 1930s he excavated a prehistoric site at El Maadi. Moving into administration, he had reached the rectorship of the University of Alexandria by the time of the revolution.[78]

Gabra reluctantly retired from the university at sixty in the spring of 1952 and paid a nostalgic visit to the deposed Drioton in France that summer. In 1954 Gabra and medievalist ʿAziz ʿAtiya reaffirmed their Coptic roots by founding the Institute of Coptic Studies at the Patriarchate.

Selim Hassan spent his last twenty years struggling to rehabilitate himself. His ten-part *Excavations at Giza* runs over 3,000 pages! In Arabic his works include a two-volume *Literature of Ancient Egypt*, and a six-volume history of *Ancient Egypt from Prehistoric Times to the Age of Rameses II*. In the 1950s he advised on the Nubian salvage campaign and an inventory at the museum. After his death in 1961 he was honored with a commemorative volume of *ASAE* and a bust in the pantheon of Egyptologists enshrined behind Mariette's garden monument. The street before the museum was renamed in his honor. A full and fair critical assessment of his career has yet to be made.[79]

Nasser's turn toward Arabism and the rise of Islamism under Sadat and Mubarak has overshadowed the persisting interest of modern Egyptians in the pharaohs. Muhammad Husayn Haykal did shift from pharaonist to Islamic themes in the 1930s, but his daughter Fayza Haykal became an Egyptologist. Nasser's regime erected one of the Memphis colossi of Ramses II in the vast square before the Cairo train station, and the square and the street linking it with Maydan al-Tahrir still bear that proud pharaoh's name. For a few years the sphinx replaced King Faruq's portrait as the national symbol on coins. Eighty years before, the pyramids and sphinx on Egyptian postage stamps had reflected European ideas of what should symbolize Egypt. But Europeans, the wealthy, and the government were the early patrons of the postal system, and stamps hardly touched the lives of most Egyptians. It was quite another thing in the 1950s to affirm the sphinx as a national symbol on coins, which circulated daily through the hands of nearly every Egyptian.

Patriots were proud that it was Egyptian archaeologists who made the twin sensational discoveries of 1954—the boats south of the Great Pyramid and Sekhemkhet's unfinished pyramid at Saqqara. Egyptologist Gamal Mokhtar took charge of rewriting school textbooks in an "our ancestors the pharaohs" vein,[80] and Husayn Fawzi's autobiographical *Sindibad al-Misri* (1961) glorified the pharaonic past its author had treasured since the 1930s.

With the confidence born of full independence and control of its

Antiquities Service and museums, Egypt reached out for indispensable international aid to salvage the antiquities of Nubia from the waters of Lake Nasser. Even as he rode the crest of Arab nationalism, Nasser appealed to internationalism through the UNESCO-sponsored salvage campaign, declaring that the High Dam would be for the benefit of Egypt but that the antiquities were the heritage of all humanity.[81] Foreign institutions were allowed to keep half of their Nubian finds and became eligible to excavate elsewhere later on the same generous terms. The rancorous Egyptological feuds of the interwar years faded as expeditions from around the globe joined the international campaign.

Retreating from the disappointments of Nasser's Pan-Arabism, Sadat promoted both local pride in Egypt's civilization through the ages and Islamic revival. A current of identification with ancient Egypt, which Egyptology and pharaonism sometimes extravagantly promoted, seems to have become an independent and self-sustaining element of modern Egyptian identity. Saddam Husayn's Iraq and Asad's Syria, more Arab nationalist and secular then Sadat's Egypt, similarly stressed the pre-Islamic civilizations that had flourished within their modern boundaries. Territorial patriotism, Arabism, and Islamism are incompatible only in the abstract and unreal world of ideal types. What does it mean that Sa`d Zaghlul, an alumnus of al-Azhar, lies in a pharaonic mausoleum and that Nasser, a pragmatic secularist, is buried in a mosque-tomb? Or that "believer president" Sadat, who fostered Islamism but perished at the hands of assassins who shouted "we have killed Pharaoh," rests beneath a pyramid-shaped monument decorated with a Qur'anic quotation?

This essay has stressed the clash of Egyptian nationalism with Western imperialism in Egyptology while keeping in view the persistence of an internationalist ideal of objective scholarship. Internationalist rhetoric often cloaked Western imperialism, but cracks in the solidarity of Western Egyptology sometimes gave Egyptian Egyptology a chance to sprout. Some Western Egyptologists freely shared their expertise with Egyptians, and some Egyptian Egyptologists acknowledged their debt to the West without sacrificing their nationalism. In independent Egypt today, a street bears the name of Selim Hassan, but Champollion, Mariette, and Maspero also live on in the names of Cairo landmarks.[82] Near the end of a lifetime in Egyptology, John Wilson wrote: "We still say wistfully that matters of culture should not be affected by politics. We must continue to act in that hope so that it may be partially true."[83]

8

Arab Nationalism in "Nasserism" and Egyptian State Policy, 1952–1958

James Jankowski

The 1950s were a tumultuous period for Egypt. A military coup in July 1952 overthrew the Egyptian monarchy and established a new republican order. After decades of effort, Egyptians finally realized the termination of the British occupation. Political and economic links with the West were eroded and/or severed; at the same time a new relationship with the Soviet Union was established. In the world arena Egypt became a leader of the nonaligned movement of Third World states. Closer to home, Egypt adopted a policy of involvement in and leadership of the Arab nationalist movement. The culminating event of the latter development was the integral union of Egypt and Syria in the United Arab Republic in 1958.

At least in terms of state policy, Egyptian nationalism moved into new channels over the course of the 1950s. This essay examines that process. First, it discusses the nationalist outlook of the central figure in the new regime, Jamal `Abd al-Nasir (Gamal Abdul Nasser). Second, it investigates the revolutionary regime's involvement in Arab nationalism from its assumption of power in 1952 to the creation of the United Arab Republic in 1958. What considerations and calculations lay behind the Egyptian government's assumption of a leadership role in the Arab nationalist movement?

THE NATIONALISM OF GAMAL ABDUL NASSER

A central theme of recent research on nationalism has been to emphasize the contingent, fluid, and multivalent nature of national identity. This perspective is certainly borne out by the nationalist views and orientation manifested by Nasser in the 1950s. To focus on the two national allegiances most salient in his own case, Nasser himself repeatedly emphasized the coexistence as well as the compatibility of his Egyptian and Arab loyalties. "Arab Egypt" was used in his public rhetoric from an early date;[1] later addresses declared Egypt to be "a member of the greater Arab entity"[2] or maintained that "by our country I mean the whole Arab world."[3] The Egyptian National Charter of 1962, largely drafted by Nasser himself, provides the most authoritative Nasserist statement of this folding of Egypt into an Arab loaf, referring in its opening to "the Arab people of Egypt" and later explicitly asserting that "there is no conflict whatsoever between Egyptian patriotism and Arab nationalism."[4]

Despite his assertion of both a narrower Egyptian and a broader Arab national allegiance, the two were not equal loyalties for Nasser. Nasser's identification with Egypt clearly developed earlier and, at least through the 1950s, took precedence over any Arab affiliation. Egypt lay at the center of Nasser's emotional universe. Once asked whether his sense of collective identity was more Egyptian or Arab, his response was an unreserved expression of his self-definition as an Egyptian coupled with a more contingent sense of Arab affiliation: "I am Egyptian. And I feel Arab because I am deeply affected by the fortunes and misfortunes of the Arabs, wherever they may occur."[5] The primary formative influences on Nasser's emerging political consciousness derived from the Egyptian nationalist context. The specific course of his politicization as a youth— membership in the Young Egypt movement and participation in student demonstrations in the mid-1930s—imbued him with a fierce Egyptian patriotism. The writings of Tawfiq al-Hakim, one of the more territorialist of Egyptian interwar intellectuals, were of particular importance in the development of the political outlook of the young Nasser. He himself attempted a novel modelled on Hakim's ʿAwdat al-Ruh (Return of the Spirit) when in school, and years later acknowledged the importance of Hakim's writings to his intellectual formation.[6]

Echoes of the exclusively Egyptian nationalist outlook that flourished in Egypt in the 1920s and 1930s are visible in some of Nasser's declarations and writings of the 1950s. His introduction to Husayn Muʾnis's Egypt and Its Mission (Misr wa Risalatuha) manifested much the same tone of pride in Egypt's national distinctiveness and world-historical role as had characterized the writings of an earlier generation of Egyptian territorial nationalists. Egypt was "the center from which civilization had radiated throughout the world," the source of human knowledge in areas as diverse as religion and literature, medicine and engineering; later it had become the leader of Islamic civilization; it was "the genius nation (*al-umma al-`abqariyya*)."[7] However, Nasser did not go as far as as to assert Egypt's "Mediterranean" or Western character, the position that marked the extreme edge of Egyptian territorialist thought. In his view the Egypt=Mediterranean/Western equation was "a fundamentally mistaken theory;" Egypt's "spirit" was Arab rather than Western.[8]

The systematic analysis of several of Nasser's major addresses undertaken by the Egyptian scholar Marlene Nasr has demonstrated the centrality of Egypt in Nasser's rhetoric. Phrases referring to Egypt were usually unqualified in Nasser's speeches (e.g., "*al-watan*" meant the land of Egypt; "*al-umma*" meant the Egyptian nation); phrases referring to the Arabs were qualified (e.g., "the Arab homeland/*al-watan al-`arabi*;" "the Arab nation/*al-umma al-`arabiyya*") and appeared later in time.[9] In moments of tension or crisis it was references to Egypt that predominated in Nasser's public addresses. Whereas his three-hour speech of 26 July 1956 in which he announced the nationalization of the Suez Canal gave considerable attention to Arab nationalism and its benefits in its early passages, its emotional peroration defending the nationalization of the Canal and asserting Egypt's determination to control its own resources had Egypt and its people, rather than the Arabs, as its sole referents:

> Now, while I am speaking to you, Egyptian brothers of yours are taking over the administration and management of the Canal Company. At this moment they are taking over the Canal Company, the Egyptian Canal Company not the foreign Canal Company. They are taking over the Canal Company and its facilities and directing navigation in the canal, the Canal which is situated in the land of Egypt, which cuts through the land of Egypt, which is a part of Egypt and belongs to Egypt.[10]

In contrast to the primary place held by Egypt in Nasser's hierarchy of national loyalties, his identification with the Arab nation and Arab nationalism emerged later in time; it was also a more intellectual phenomenon lacking much of the emotional resonance that he expressed towards Egypt. According to the account in his autobiographical tract *The Philosophy of the Revolution*, "the first elements of [Nasser's] Arab consciousness" began to develop only in the later 1930s through participation in demonstrations in support of the Palestinian and Syrian nationalist movements.[11] At first no more than "the echoes of sentiment,"[12] Nasser's Arabism began to acquire an intellectual rationale in the 1940s through his military studies when his analysis of World War I campaigns in the Middle East made him aware of the strategic importance of Palestine in the defense of Egypt.[13] By the time of the war for Palestine in 1948, he had come to realize that "the fighting in Palestine was not fighting on foreign territory. Nor was it inspired by sentiment. It was a duty imposed by self-defense."[14] His participation in the war solidified his conviction of the integral political link between Egypt and Arab Asia:

> After the siege and battles in Palestine I came home with the whole region in my mind one complete whole. . . . An event may happen in Cairo today; it is repeated in Damascus, Beirut, Amman or any other place tomorrow. This was naturally in conformity with the picture that experience has left within me: One region, the same factors and circumstances, even the same forces opposing them all.[15]

Ideological influences were secondary in the development of Nasser's identification with Arab nationalism. He appears to have read the writings of several Arab nationalist or protonationalist writers—'Abd al-Rahman al-Kawakibi, Jamal al-Din al-Afghani, Muhammad 'Abduh, Shakib Arslan—during the course of his education. But these formed only a minor component of his reading when in secondary and military school, the bulk of which concerned Egyptian, modern European, and military history.[16] He is reported not to have read the leading contemporary Arab nationalist ideologue Abu Khaldun Sati' al-Husri until after the Revolution of 1952. When he did, he was impressed enough with Husri's views to arrange a meeting with him.[17] According to his confidant Muhammad Hasanayn Haykal, Nasser paid little attention to Arab politics in the early years of the revolution; even from 1955 onward, when Arab issues assumed more importance for his regime, his reading on Arab affairs remained sporadic.[18]

The key Arabist terms in the Nasserist lexicon were "the Arab nation/*al-umma al-'arabiyya*" (first referred to in 1954), "Arab nationalism/*al-qawmiyya al-'arabiyya*" (1955), and "Arab unity/*al-wahda al-'arabiyya*" (1956).[19] Nasser's earliest usage of "Arab nationalism" referred to the Arab nationalist movement in Western Asia and did not include Egypt.[20] A benchmark in Nasser's rhetoric occurred in July 1954, when he asserted that "the goal of the government of the Revolution is that the Arabs become a united nation (*umma muttahida*), its sons cooperating for the common good."[21] His identification with Arab nationalism was much stronger by 1956. In the early passages of his speech of 26 July announcing the nationalization of the Suez Canal, the referent "Arab nationalism" assumed the inclusion of Egypt in the movement. Now it was "our Arab nationalism" and "our Arabism" that was at stake in the imminent confrontation with the West, and resistance to the West was couched in the Arab terms of the need to "defend our freedom and our Arabism."[22]

What were the reasons articulated by Nasser for his belief in the Arab nation, Arab nationalism, and Arab unity in the mid-1950s? When Nasser first declared that "the goal of the government of the revolution is that the Arabs become a united nation" in July 1954, his rationale was a blend of historical and contemporary considerations:

> It [the revolutionary regime] believes that the place occupied by the Arabs between the continents of the world, their great contribution to culture, their valuable economic resources, and their connection with the Islamic East and the East as a whole nominates them for a great place and destines them for influence in the affairs of the world.
>
> The revolution also believes that the problems of the Arabs are the problems of Egyptians. If the problem of the [British] occupation has until now absorbed the greatest part of the effort of Egyptians, it has never distracted them from participating in every Arab effort expended for the sake of the liberation of the Arabs.[23]

It was the common problems of Egyptians and Arabs and the practical utility of solidarity for both that Nasser emphasized as the motive force behind Arab nationalism over the next few years. A frequent theme in Nasser's understanding of history was that, from the Crusades through the Egyptian Revolution of 1919 (which had only limited success because its leaders "failed to extend their vision beyond Sinai") to the first Arab-Israeli war, Arab disunity guaranteed Arab defeat; concomitantly, Arab unity was the path to victory.[24] Both history and contemporary experience taught the same lesson: "it is not possible to assure their [the Arabs'] security save if united with all of their brothers in Arabism in a strong cohesive unity."[25] Arab cooperation was a necessity for self-defense: "if the Arabs cooperate, it will be possible for them to defend themselves; if they are divided, others will dominate them."[26]

Arab nationalism meant Arab effectiveness: "our strength is in this Arab nationalism, the Arabs sticking together for the benefit of the Arabs."[27] Various phrases were used to illustrate the practical reasons for Arab nationalism and unity: Arab nationalism was "the protective armor" of each Arab state against both imperialism and Israel;[28] it was their "weapon," even their "principal weapon," in the struggle against foreign domination;[29] it was "strategic necessity" or more fully "a defensive necessity, a strategic necessity, and common interests" which impelled the Arabs towards unity.[30] Arab nationalism was thus justified in terms of its pragmatic utility in the achievement of the parallel nationalist aspirations of the different Arab lands. The conclusion of Nasser's speech of 26

July 1957 celebrating the nationalization of the Suez Canal a year earlier made the link between Arab nationalism and Egyptian national interest explicit:

> Our policy is based on Arab nationalism because Arab nationalism is a weapon for every Arab state. Arab nationalism is a weapon employed against aggression. It is necessary for the aggressor to know that, if he aggresses against any Arab country, he will endanger his interests. This is the way, oh brotherly compatriots, that we must advance for the sake of Egypt, glorious Egypt, independent Egypt.[31]

If Nasser's nationalism consisted of an original Egyptian patriotism overlaid in time by a more contingent sense of the benefits of Arab solidarity, what was missing from his portfolio of politically meaningful identities? A striking feature of both Nasser and his regime in the 1950s is the rejection of religion as a political referent.

Nasser's only occasional public discussions of religion in the 1950s clearly indicate a personal preference for the separation of religion and politics into distinct spheres of human activity. Although *The Philosophy of the Revolution* makes the "Islamic circle" the last and largest of the three arenas in which Egypt had to find its proper role, it also speaks of Muslim "cooperation" in looser and less vital terms than those employed for the Arab and African circles.[32] In an interview with Jean Lacouture early in 1954, Nasser was careful to disavow religion as the basis for state policy: "after eighteen months in power, I still don't see how it would be possible to govern according to the Koran. . . . The Koran is a very general text, capable of interpretation, and that is why I don't think it is suitable as a source of policy or political doctrine."[33] This was not just a placebo tailored for foreign consumption; he offered a similar analysis of the desirability of separating religion from politics in a press conference of 1956 when asked whether Muslims had a particular aversion to foreign rule: "all peoples wish to live free, independent, and equal. This is not a religious question but a political question. . . . For *the Muslim is a human being before he is a Muslim.*"[34]

Marlene Nasr's analysis of several of Nasser's major addresses bears out the marginality of religion as a political referent for Nasser. It was language and culture, not religion, which were the primary criteria for membership in the Arab nation; in his view "membership in the Arab nation was independent of any religious affiliation."[35] Whereas he eventually came to speak the desirability of Arab "unity," his use of the word "cooperation" for Muslim interaction implied a weaker bond.[36] Nasser's speeches were not usually couched in terms of concepts such as "Islamic education" or "Islamic society"—at most, they used the vaguer phrase "the Islamic spirit."[37] Nasser used the word "nation/*umma*" first for Egypt, later for the Arabs, but not in its traditional meaning of the community of believers in Islam; similarly, "unity/*wahda*" was applied only infrequently to the Muslim community, and then only in combination with "Arab unity" and "Asian-African unity."[38]

Much the same dismissal of religion as a bond of political affiliation is found in Nasser's policy positions. By the 1950s the concept of an Islamic Caliphate was a dead issue for Egyptian policy-makers. Nasser bluntly told the Iraqi Regent `Abd Il-Ilah as much when the latter inquired about the possible revival of the office in 1954: "we believe that the Caliphate is an historical stage whose purposes have come and gone, and any discussion of it in current circumstances is a waste of time."[39] Muhammad Hasanayn Haykal reports Nasser telling Nuri al-Sa`id of Iraq that "the holy bond of Islam is one thing, unity of interest and security another, particularly if it is based, in addition to religion, on a unity of history, culture, language, and geography."[40]

On the level of policy the revolutionary government largely ignored Muslim solidarity as a tool of state policy. The major "Islamic" initiative of the Nasserist regime in the 1950s was its sponsorship of the "Islamic Conference [*al-mu'tamar al-Islami*]" in 1954. First discussed with the Saudis by Salah Salim during a trip to Saudi Arabia in June and launched by Nasser when on Pilgrimage in August, the initiative for an international Islamic coordinating office centered in Cairo was at least partially inspired by the the regime's current political struggle with the Muslim Brotherhood in 1954.[41] Headed by Anwar al-Sadat advised by a board of `ulama, its official aims were promoting international Muslim education and interaction, the propagation of the message of Islam, and the establishment of Islamic cultural centers.[42] It appears to have received little attention from the regime after the crushing of the Brotherhood late in 1954. By 1957 a British evaluation of Egyptian regional policies estimated that "Egyptian endeavors to obtain hegemony in the Moslem world have been relatively unsuccessful," and went on to observe that by that date (1957) Egypt had become "relatively inactive" in propaganda efforts in other Muslim lands.[43]

The Nasserist regime's disavowal of religion as a political referent for Egyptian policy of course occurred in a particular context. In the initial years of the revolutionary regime in the early and mid-1950s, its most serious domestic challenge came from the Muslim Brotherhood. The regime's rejection of a religious basis for national politics was at least in part produced by the need to distinguish its programs and appeal from that of the Brotherhood.[44] Yet the consistent marginalization of religion in both the rhetoric and the policies of Nasserist regime in the 1950s seems to indicate that this dismissal of religion as a political bond was more than just a tactical maneuver. The disavowal of religion as a political referent had marked the dominant strain of Egyptian territorial nationalism prior to 1952. On the whole, Nasser and his colleagues seem to have absorbed and to have remained faithful to a secular and a religious perspective on Egyptian national identity after they came to power. As Nasser himself put it in a speech at the end of the decade, using the same secularist terminology that had been employed by the previous generation of Egyptian nationalists, "religion belongs to God; the *watan* belongs to each individual living in it."[45]

ARAB NATIONALISM IN EGYPTIAN STATE POLICY, 1952–1958

Two generalizations are often made about the initial policy orientation of the new regime that came to power in Egypt in July 1952. One is the pragmatic and nonideological outlook of its leaders. As a group, the army officers who made up the Free Officers movement and who dominated Egypt through the mechanism of the Revolutionary Command Council in 1952–1954 were military technocrats, not intellectuals. Other than a sense of frustration with the deteriorating socioeconomic conditions of Egypt, a commitment to rooting out political corruption, and a determination to achieve complete Egyptian independence—what an early speech of Nasser termed the "hateful trio" comprised of "social injustice, political despotism, and British occupation"[46]—they had no detailed plan for the development of Egyptian society. It is in part this lack of a blueprint that explains their extended arguments as to whether to restore parliamentary rule and their vacillating treatment of existing political forces in the early years of the revolution.[47]

The second generalization is the Egyptian focus of the new regime. The original concerns of the Free Officers were primarily domestic rather than foreign. American diplomatic reports in 1952–1953 stressed that the regime was "concentrating . . . on domestic problems" and spoke in terms of its "preoccupation with domestic affairs."[48] In as far as the new government had an international agenda, it related primarily to Egypt: retrospective evaluations of the thrust of the new government by former members of the Free Officers emphasize British evacuation from Egypt as the central concern of the revolution in its initial phase.[49] Nasser's public statements through 1953 spoke in the same Egypt-oriented terms of the goal of the revolution being "the liberation of the *watan* from imperialism" (his first public address, November 1952), that the "chief goal" of the Free Officers movement was "seeing their country achieve full, complete independence" (January 1953), or that "this revolution was staged to liberate Egypt and drive out the occupation forces" (June 1953).[50] *The Philosophy of the Revolution* codified the Egypto-centric thrust of the revolution in its early days: "What is is we want to do? . . . There is no doubt that we all dream of Egypt free and strong."[51]

In as far as the new government had foreign policy concerns in 1952–1953, they were Egyptian and Nile Valley issues such as the negotiations with the British over the status of the Sudan (concluded in February 1953), the on-and-off negotiations with the British over British evacuation from the Suez Canal zone (concluded in October 1954), and the convoluted and ultimately unsuccessful discussions with the United States concerning American military aid. According to General Muhammad Najib, even the issue of the status of the Sudan was a secondary concern for the new regime's leadership: reports on the Sudanese negotiations went unread by Revolutionary Command Council (RCC) members, and Nasser himself at one point is stated to have referred to the Sudan as being "a burden upon Egypt which it is better to abandon."[52] Through 1952–1953 issues related to Egypt took precedence over Egyptian relations with its neighbors.

The first effort at developing a new regional foreign policy stance for Egypt on the part of the revolutionary government came in early 1954, in the form of a new policy of Egyptian "neutrality." In December 1953 key Egyptian ambassadors were summoned home to discuss the formulation of a policy of neutrality. As summarized by a source close to Nasser, the thrust of the new approach was (1) a formal Egyptian declaration of neutrality; (2) efforts to persuade other Arab states to follow the same line; (3) an attempt to strengthen Egyptian ties with the Asian-African bloc of states.[53]

By early 1954 these deliberations resulted in the articulation of a policy of declared Egyptian neutrality. That "neutrality," however, was clearly based on its utility for the achievement of Egyptian national goals, particularly the conclusion of a satisfactory agreement with Great Britain over the termination of the British base in the Suez Canal zone. As the government daily *al-Jumhuriyya* explained the policy in January 1954, "Egypt's new foreign policy position will not be one of 'neutrality' in the general sense but will be based on the principle that Egypt will not cooperate with anyone unless her rights and sovereignty are recognized."[54] Regime spokesman Salah Salim defined Egyptian neutrality in much the same terms a few days later: "Egypt's policy is hostility and non-cooperation toward any nation which infringes (on) Egypt's dignity and freedom, but cooperation with all countries both east and west which extend the hand of friendship."[55] Nasser was more ambivalent about a neutralist policy: while asserting his personal conviction that "neutrality (is) of no avail, especially in wartime," he nonetheless declared that Egypt's policy henceforth would be one of "non-cooperation with those who encroach on her sovereignty."[56]

Foreign observers also noted the instrumentalist thrust of this new policy. The British Ambassador Sir Ralph Stevenson termed Egyptian neutrality a "tactical move . . . to impress the Americans and ourselves."[57] US Ambassador Jefferson Caffery's evaluation of Egyptian neutrality was that " '(n)eutrality' as they see it is a policy of non-cooperation and not a commitment to any theory of foreign affairs. To them neutrality is the position of being able to play the field without commitments. . . . (T)he elite of the RCC conceive of 'neutrality' as an entirely controllable instrument of Egyptian foreign policy which can be turned on or off at will."[58]

Egyptian neutrality blossomed into something meaningful only in 1955, when external stimuli such as the Bandung Conference provided new opportunities for Egyptian assertiveness in the international arena. In the interim a specifically Middle Eastern policy of greater importance took shape. This was the struggle against Western-aligned regional pacts and the concomitant effort to promote greater inter-Arab cooperation as an alternative to alliance with the West. In essence, it was opposition to a Western-linked system for Middle Eastern defense in 1954–1955, which sparked a policy of augmenting Arab solidarity under Egyptian initiative and in the process set the revolutionary regime on the path of Egyptian leadership of the Arab nationalist movement.

Through the intermittent discussions between Egypt and the Western powers in 1952–1954 concerning the creation of a regional defense organization, the Egyptian government's consistent position was that regional defense needed to be the collective prerogative of the Arabs themselves.[59] The issue acquired new urgency early in 1954, when it appeared that Iraq might break with formal Arab solidarity and join Turkey and Pakistan in a Western-oriented defense grouping. Such a prospect was repeatedly condemned by Egypt's leadership in 1954. Both government spokesmen and the Egyptian press repeatedly cautioned Iraq against being enticed into a Western-linked alliance that would weaken the Arab League and Arab solidarity.[60] The operative motive for this position as articulated by Egyptian spokesmen was primarily what such a Western-linked defense arrangement would mean for Egypt—its isolation in regional politics. Thus in April Nasser publicly warned that "any policy aimed at isolating some Arab states from the others would be strongly opposed" by Egypt.[61] Other Egyptian sources reiterated Nasser's belief that recent Western maneuvers were "designed [to] isolate Egypt."[62] In place of a Western-linked defense agreement, the Egyptian preference was for the strengthening of the Arab Collective Security Pact.[63] As Nasser put it to a Western journalist in August 1954, "the most effective way of defending this area is to leave it in the hands of the area's people."[64] Egyptian propaganda outlets emphasized this theme from mid-1954 onward:

> The "Voice of the Arabs" calls on the Arabs to stand in one rank in the face of imperialism, to expel the British, to cleanse the land of Arabdom from this plague, to obtain with their own money and to make for themselves arms which will repulse aggression, and and to maintain peace and justice. . . . This, O Arabs, is the policy of Egypt.[65]

The demand for an independent Arab defense arrangement "based upon indigenous factors" rather than tied to the West was reiterated by Nasser and other spokesmen for the regime through the rest of 1954.[66]

The crisis over the issue of independent versus Western-linked collective defense arrangements came in early 1955, when despite vehement Egyptian opposition Iraq formally aligned itself with pro-Western regional states and Great Britain in the Baghdad Pact. Egypt's reaction—propaganda attacks on Iraq and the Pact; hastily concluded defense agreements with Syria and Saudi Arabia; encouraging internal forces in other Arab countries, particularly Syria and Jordan, to resist efforts to bring these states into the Baghdad Pact system—marked the effective beginnings of the "Arabist" phase of Egyptian foreign policy during the Nasserist era.[67]

Why this vehement opposition to the Baghdad Pact? The contemporary American interpretation of Nasser's and Egypt's motivation in opposing the Baghdad Pact upon its conclusion in early 1955 was that Egyptian opposition was prompted less by abstract devotion to the principle of Arab unity than by the practical concern that the Iraqi initiative was an attempt to isolate Egypt within Arab politics. As Ambassador Henry Byroade evaluated the Egyptian position in March 1955, "Nasser was not greatly upset by (the) fact that Iraq joined in (the) pact with Turkey;" what did upset him was the Iraqi attempt to draw other Arab countries into the arrangement, which Nasser viewed as both a step towards the longstanding goal of Iraqi-Syrian union and simultaneously an attempt to "isolate Egypt" in the Arab world.[68] "He saw Egypt eventually isolated. . . . He admitted (the) man in the street had no feeling about all this but Egypt under his leadership would not be so isolated."[69]

It was Nasser's perception of Egypt as "the victim of a Western policy designed to separate her from the Middle East" which Byroade credited with prompting Egypt's vehement opposition to the Baghdad Pact.[70]

In a speech before a group of Army officers in March 1955, Nasser himself explained the new policy of regional assertiveness his government was developing in similar terms. The point of his remarks was that the realization of complete Egyptian independence was dependent on the achievement of a position of regional influence:

> All we want today is to create for ourselves an independent personality which will be strong and not dependent, which will be free to direct its domestic policy the way it wants and (to) direct its foreign policy in a way which serves its interests. . . .
>
> If, God willing, we want to have an independent personality and develop it in the critical period we are in, we must steel ourselves. Our revolution calls for liberation and independence. This means liberation internally and externally, and that we must have an entity [sic] and an influence on what goes on around us.[71]

Byroade's commentary on this speech found it "not surprising that Nasser as an Army officer places first and foremost in his foreign policy thinking the need for Egypt to develop its military and political 'personality' so that it can be truly 'independent'—i.e. can it achieve such a position of internal and external strength that it will never again be subject to big-power 'domination.' "[72]

A parallel interpretation of the genesis of Egyptian regional activism in the mid-1950's has been voiced retrospectively by some of Nasser's associates who participated in the development of that policy. According to Muhammad Hasanayn Haykal, it was during the negotiations with Great Britain over evacuation from the Suez Canal zone in 1952–1954 that Nasser came to the realization that genuine Egyptian independence depended not only on the withdrawal of all foreign forces from the Nile Valley; it also required preventing the perpetuation of foreign hegemony in the alternative form of a regional defense pact.[73] As Haykal phrased it, it was Nasser's concern for Egyptian independence which led him "to define the identity of Egypt in the environment in which it lived."[74] Egypt's Ambassador to Syria Mahmud Riyad has explained Nasser's regional thinking in much the same terms. Although Nasser had no definite Arab policy from the start, he became convinced in time that "the liberation of Egypt was connected with the liberation of the Arab states" and that Arab liberation would "aid Egypt" in its own struggle for national independence.[75] Thus to both Nasser and his closest associates involved in the formulation of Egyptian foreign policy in the mid-1950s, the adoption of an Arab nationalist orientation was a policy choice rooted in the utility of Arab solidarity for the achievement and maintenance of Egyptian independence.

The touchstone of the practical Egyptian position on Arab nationalism in the 1950s was the stance taken by the Egyptian government in regard to various proposals for Arab federation or unity. Egypt's leaders viewed proposals for Arab federation or unity with considerable skepticism in their early years in power. Muhammad Najib records that he regarded Iraqi suggestions concerning Arab federation in 1953 as "a fairy-tale" and that he told the Iraqis that "it is necessary [first] for us to unify our thoughts and our interests—then we can unify our countries."[76] In an interview of late 1953 Nasser similarly stated that he did not believe that current projects for Arab federation were realizable in view of Hashimite-Saudi historical enmities as well as the current foreign domination existing in many Arab countries.[77] When the Iraqis floated the idea of a formal Iraqi-Jordanian union before the Egyptians early in 1954, Nasser's view was that this was "premature"—foreign policy and defense coordination had to come before efforts at closer federation would be successful.[78] `Abd al-Latif al-Baghdadi similarly expressed skepticism when asked about the prospects for Arab federation early in 1954.[79] A few months later Nasser publicly spoke against the idea of Fertile Crescent unity on the grounds that it would isolate Egypt within the Arab world and thus "render the Arabs asunder."[80]

It is in the regime's response to periodic Syrian efforts to establish closer links with Egypt in the mid-1950s that the practical Egyptian reserve about Arab unity can be seen most clearly. Fuelled primarily by the competitive dynamics of Syrian politics at the time, various Syrian leaders and parties put forth proposals for closer Syrian-Egyptian political integration in 1955–1956. The Egyptian response to these proposals was consistently negative. The first Syrian approach for Egyptian-Syrian union apparently came from Syrian Prime Minister Khalid al-`Azm early in 1955, in the context of Egyptian-Syrian collaboration in opposition to the Baghdad Pact. According to Mahmud Riyad, "there was absolutely no thought in my mind, or in Abdul Nasser's, in attempting constitutional union between Egypt and Syria at that time in the manner which `Azm was calling for."[81] When later in 1955 the Syrian Parliament requested a secret commitment that Egypt would automatically come to the aid of Syria in case of attack by Israel as the price for the creation of a joint Syrian-Egyptian military command, Egypt refused to accede to the Syrian demand.[82] In August 1956 the Egyptian government declined to receive a Syrian delegation that wished to visit Egypt to discuss Egyptian-Syrian union. As relayed from a Syrian source, the reason given to the Syrians was the impeccably Egyptianist one that "Egypt has too many other pressing problems now."[83]

Late 1956 was indeed a time of other pressing problems for Egypt. The momentous events of that year—Western refusal to support construction of a new dam at Aswan; the consequent Egyptian nationalization of the Suez Canal; the international crisis that ensued; and the combined British-French-Israeli military operation against Egypt of late 1956—fall outside the scope of this essay. But these events were not without major consequences for Egypt's relationship to Arab nationalism. By consolidating Nasser's personal prestige and position as unrivalled leader of the Arab world, the Suez crisis of 1956 moved Arab nationalist aspirations to a new level and led to the more intense efforts to attain meaningful Arab unity that marked the later 1950s.

Yet in retrospect Suez did not bring an immediate change in the regional stance and policies of the Egyptian government. Two detailed reports on private conversations with Nasser in the months after Suez had catapulted him to a position as hero of Arab nationalism show little change in the emphases of the Egyptian government from what they had been prior to the events of 1956. In December 1956 Nasser held a three-hour meeting with US Ambassador Raymond Hare.[84] According to Hare's record of this conversation (in which Nasser had been "just about as frank as we could expect"), Nasser told the ambassador that his first priority was to "build up (the) domestic economy" of Egypt; in Nasser's view "preoccupation with foreign affairs" only detracted from the demands of "essential domestic reform." Nasser understandably denied any aspiration for "empire over the Arab states" and asserted Egyptian involvement in the affairs of other Arab states to be reactive in character and aimed solely at the "avoidance [of] outside domination" of the Arab world.

Nasser's protestations of regional innocence made to a foreign diplomat cannot alone be taken as sufficient evidence of his position. But this conversation receives considerable corroboration in a memo of April 1957 by Muhammad Hasanayn Haykal summarizing his own conversations with Nasser.[85] Like Hare, Haykal recalls Nasser according the internal struggle for economic progress the highest priority in his plans in 1957. In regard to Egyptian policy in the Arab world Nasser articulated a policy of regional caution and reserve: while he did wish to extend Egyptian contact with "progressive Arab forces," nonetheless he was leery of undertaking initiatives that would involve Egypt in unwanted crises. Despite the fact that Nasser anticipated that the crucial arena for Egypt in the immediate future was the Arab one ("as for the battle which will soon impose itself on us, it is the battle for the heart of the Arab world"), he expected regional turmoil to emerge as a result of Western efforts to counter Egyptian prestige and influence rather than because of Egyptian initiatives.

Egypt had neither the aspiration nor the expectation of achieving Arab unity after Suez. When Prime Minister Sabri al-`Asali of Syria raised the subject of unity with Nasser early in 1957, Nasser's response was that the Egyptian public had yet to be prepared for such a drastic step; in his view the realization of unity would take "at least five years."[86] Well into 1957 Nasser was publicly disavowing any Egyptian intention to establish an Arab "empire,"[87] stating that "I am not thinking of in terms of [Arab] federation or confederation for the present,"[88] and predicting that, due to current inter-Arab political rivalries, "Arab unity will take a long time to accomplish."[89] Even in early January 1958 only a few days before the inauguration of the negotiations that were to lead to Egyptian-Syrian unity later that month, Nasser told a Lebanese newspaper that Arab unification was unlikely to be realized in the immediate future.[90]

Nasser's predictions were wrong. On January 12 1958, a delegation of Syrian Army officers reflecting the views of a recently-formed Military Council (but not the position of the civilian government of Syria) went to Egypt to plead for immediate Syrian-Egyptian unity as the only way to avoid political chaos in Syria.

Few Egyptian leaders were enthused about the idea of Egyptian unity with Syria in late 1957-early 1958. In Syria Ambassador Riyad had attempted to dissuade the Syrian military delegation from travelling to Egypt to seek unity.[91] When the delegation arrived, the Egyptian *Mukhabarat* cautioned about the practical obstacles of uniting two different Arab countries.[92] With the possible exception of `Abd al-Hakim `Amr, most of Nasser's associates appear to have either opposed or had strong reservations about union with Syria in January 1958.[93] Fathi Radwan's comment to Nasser on the eve of union captures the obvious and major problem that unity with Syria posed for Nasser and Egypt: "tomorrow you will become President of the Syrian state. Yet you have never set foot in it [Syria], and you don't know much about it."[94]

Ultimately Nasser's position was the one that mattered. His initial reluctance about integral Egyptian-Syrian union is well-documented. He told Sayyid Mar`i at the time that "unity would be a large financial burden on the Egyptian budget" and simultaneously would draw Egypt into conflict with the Great Powers.[95] According to `Abd al-Latif al-Baghdadi, Nasser's preference was still for a federal union for five years, after which the possibility of integral unity could be reconsidered.[96]

When Nasser met with the Syrian delegation on January 15, he countered Syrian arguments in favor of unity with stating his own view that unity would be a burden for Egypt; eventually he stalled for time by telling the Syrians that he would respond only to an official request for unity made by the Syrian government rather than by a self-appointed military group.[97] Only when Foreign Minister Salah al-Din Bitar came to Egypt and belatedly endorsed the officers' call for unity on behalf of the Syrian government did Nasser make the decision to accede to the Syrian request for union.

Why did Nasser accept Egyptian-Syrian union in January 1958? Over the course of 1957, as Syria stumbled from one political crisis to another, Nasser appears to have become genuinely worried over the possibility of political disorder, civil strife, and possibly eventual Communist ascendancy within Syria.[98] The Syrian initiative itself created a new situation that Nasser could not evade: in view of the position of Arab leadership he had assumed over the past few years, Nasser realized that "circumstances compelled him to accept some sort of union."[99] 'Ali Sabri summarized the situation neatly; "they've placed us in a bind."[100] When both the Syrian military and Syrian politicians agreed to Nasser's stringent conditions for unity (the withdrawal of the Syrian Army from politics; the abolition of political parties in Syria; and a popular plebescite to ratify union) Nasser overcame his reservations and agreed to the integral union of Syria and Egypt.[101] Even then apprehension persisted: Nasser told Fathi Radwan that Syrian pressure had forced him to to accede to union even though he shared Radwan's own skepticism,[102] and he explained the union to his Cabinet as something forced upon him by circumstances.[103] He was equally apprehensive with US Ambassador Raymond Hare, telling him that "it's going to be a big headache, because we're not set for it. We have to do it but it'll be a big headache."[104] Such were the expectations with which the most important effort to realize the integral Arab unity of different Arab states, the United Arab Republic, was created.

In their early years in power, the leadership of the Egyptian revolutionary regime viewed Egyptian involvement in Arab nationalism through an Egyptian prism. The perceived needs of Egypt were the primary reasons offered as the basis for the effort to assert Egyptian leadership of the Arab nationalist movement. At least until 1958 the form of Arab nationalism manifested by Nasser and his colleagues retained a sharp sense of Egyptian separateness within the body of the Arab nation and perceived Egyptian involvement in Arab politics largely in terms of the furtherance of Egyptian purposes.

This policy of instrumental Arabism did not represent a radical departure from the positions taken by Egyptian governments on regional politics before the Revolution of 1952. When Egyptian policy-makers began to involve Egypt in regional issues such as the Palestine issue in the later 1930s, or when in the 1940s they took the lead in the creation of the League of Arab States and later went as far as to involve Egypt in war in the (unsuccessful) defense of Arab Palestine, the main considerations impelling Egyptian politicians toward regional involvement had been a similar concern for the defense of what were perceived to be Egyptian national interests and the assertion of Egyptian hegemony within an emerging regional state system.[105]

To be sure, the revolutionary regime pursued a policy of Egyptian leadership of Arab nationalism with greater vigor and persistence than its predecessors. It also had greater success in asserting Egyptian leadership of Arab nationalism than prerevolutionary regimes. But the thrust of the preceding analysis is that, at least until the creation of the United Arab Republic in 1958, the major difference between the new military regime and its civilian forerunners lay in the circumstances that permitted it to assume a position of Arab leadership (the recession of imperial control over regional politics after World War II; the Cold War and the leverage it offered smaller states; Nasser's own personal prestige acquired in his anti-imperialist successes of 1955–1956) than in the nationalist outlook of its leaders. It was calculations of opportunity and options that differed from earlier Egyptian regimes; motivating drives by and large did not.

The manner in which the new revolutionary regime in Egypt adopted an Arab nationalist position raises some interesting questions about interpreting nationalist politics. The "modernist" view of nationalism as the inexorable consequence of the massive transformations wrought by industrialism and print capitalism is of unquestioned value in understanding the social and intellectual aspects of nationalism. But it is of limited relevance when we seek to analyze the involved and shifting political positions taken by nationalist leaders. In terms of politics, the insights of John Breuilly, Sami Zubaida, and Roger Owen are more useful. For Breuilly nationalism is "best understood as an especially appropriate form of political behavior in the context of the modern state and the modern state system;"[106] nationalist behavior can thus best be understood within the context of the control of the state, the needs of the state, and the competition among states operating in the same environment. Zubaida has emphasized the central importance of the "modern political field," that "complex of political models, vocabularies, organizations and techniques [that comprise] a *political field* of organization, mobilization, agitation, and struggle" for understanding Middle Eastern politics.[107] It is this political field that sets the parameters within which political behavior unfolds, and in which "the *conception* of the nation becomes the field and the model in terms of which to think of . . . other commitments and loyalties."[108] For his part Roger Owen has emphasized the importance of the colonial state in establishing new territorial units that, whatever their original historical reality or artificiality, once created provide the framework for subsequent political activity: "methods of political organization and styles of political rhetoric are largely defined by the context. . . . From the colonial period on, this context was created by the territorial state."[109]

I would suggest that it was a combination of the political field defined largely by the existence of an Egyptian territorial state, as well as the realities and imperatives of Egyptian state power, which were most important in determining the nationalist policies of the Egyptian government in the 1950s. It seems to have been the constraints imposed by the modern state—maintaining both domestic control versus serious rivals and relative position versus external rivals for regional influence—that bulked largest in shaping the "Arabist" policies of the Nasserist regime. Similarly, the regime's pursuit of Arab leadership as the best possible sphere for Egyptian national assertion and the enhancement of Egypt's international stature (what Nasser in 1955 phrased as the need for "an independent personality" and "an influence on what goes on around us") is inconceivable without the particular regional political field found in the Middle East in the postwar era, when several newly independent Arab states shared the common concerns of how to deal with the old problem of European imperialism as well as the new issues of the Cold War and Israel.

These considerations of state power, both domestic and international, were the primary factors generating the Arab nationalist policies pursued by the Egyptian regime in the 1950s. The assertion that "Pan-Arabism is little more than an ideology of interstate manouevre"[110] may be too strong for the Fertile Crescent, where the beginnings of a sense of Arab nationalism antedate the modern state system and where the foundations of individual states were shallow. But it comes closer to the mark for Egypt, where the option of involvement in the Arab nationalist movement developed well after the formation of the Egyptian state and where the existing territorial state was the dominant element in the political field.

PART IV

―――

Polycentrism

9

The Formation of Palestinian Identity:
The Critical Years, 1917–1923

Rashid Khalidi

When did a significant proportion of the Arab inhabitants of Palestine begin to think of themselves as Palestinians? What are the constituents of this sense of identification with Palestine, and how does it relate to other forms of identity, whether national, religious, or otherwise? These and other basic questions related to Palestinian identity have engendered extensive polemics[1] and some valuable scholarship.[2] They are the focus of this essay.

As with the identity of the peoples of several other Arab countries in the modern period, the case of Palestinian identity is complicated by the difficulty of explaining how it relates to broad, powerful, transnational foci of identity, in particular Arabism and Islam, and to other regional and local loyalties. The fact that in the perception of people in the Arab world throughout most of this century, these and other elements simultaneously constituted the identity of a Palestinian Arab is difficult to explain to those accustomed to thinking of national identity in simple, unidimensional terms, with reference to models derived from an idealized version of the Western European experience. Thus it would be normal for a Palestinian to identify *primarily* as a Arab in one context, as a Muslim or Christian in another, as a Nabulsi or Jaffan in yet another, and as a Palestinian in a fourth. The same pattern of multiple foci of identity applies to the populations of many Arab countries in the modern era.

However, unlike that of the other Arab peoples—indeed, perhaps uniquely—the Palestinian case is further complicated by the intimate intertwining of the Palestinian narrative with that of Israel and the Jewish people over the past century. In view of the truism that self-definition takes place with reference to an "other" (as Stuart Hall puts it, "only when there is an Other can you know who you are"[3]), it is understandable that discussions of contentious questions of national identity tend to gravitate in the direction of such polarizations.

It goes without saying that this overlap of the two narratives has primarily affected that of the Palestinians, as Palestinian identity has since its beginnings struggled in the outside world for acceptance and legitimacy,[4] and even for recognition of its very existence as a category of being. Golda Meir's famous dismissive remark that "There was no such thing as Palestinians. . . . They did not exist" was significant not only for its broad impact on public discourse but also as expressing a view that came to be widely held among Westerners in general.[5]

All of this has complicated what might otherwise have been a relatively straightforward story. In the case of the national identities of the peoples of other Arab countries that came into being in their modern form in the wake of World War I, similar processes of the construction of new identities using elements of old ones as part of a new synthesis has occasioned little attention, and limited controversy, whether within these countries or elsewhere. The main exception is Lebanon. And in the instance of Lebanon, the resulting debate has been primarily an internal one among Lebanese, for whom the definition of Lebanese identity proved to be a bitterly disputed subject throughout this century, contributing to the civil strife that afflicted the country in 1958, and again from 1975 until the early 1990s.[6] While the question of Lebanese identity has occasioned some scholarly attention outside of Lebanon, this was restrained and unpolemical by comparison with that devoted to the Palestinian case.

With this background in mind, this essay attempts to reconstruct the formative period in the genesis of Palestinian national identity, specifically the years immediately after World War I. It builds on the assumption that many of the constituents of this identity—patriotic feeling, local loyalties, Arabism, religious sentiment—were already widespread before World War I, without yet coalescing into a sense of community as Palestinians that constituted the primary focus of identification for most Palestinians. Its main thesis is that under the impact of rapid, momentous, and unsettling changes during the period from the outset of World War I to the beginning of the British Mandate for Palestine in 1922, the sense of political and national identification of most politically conscious, literate, and urban Palestinians underwent a sequence of major transformations. The end result was a strong and growing national identification with Palestine, as the Arab residents of the country increasingly came to "imagine" themselves as part of a single community. This identification was certainly not exclusive—for Arabism, religion, and local loyalties still remained extremely important, and continued to make it possible for Arabs in Palestine to also see themselves as part of other communities.

In succeeding decades this identification with Palestine was to be developed and refined significantly, as Palestinian nationalism grew and developed during the Mandatory period and after 1948. Equally important, it spread beyond the relatively narrow elite that was initially affected by these ideas to broader sectors of the population—outside the upper classes in the cities, and in the countryside. Ongoing social and economic trends that can be traced back to the years before World War I, such as the growth in the urban population and of wage labor, the expansion of the press and of the educational system, and the spread of literacy, all played major roles in this process. This profound transformation of the sense of self of the Arab population of Palestine, which began during the years immediately after World War I, resulted in the emergence of a Palestinian national identity where before no such thing had existed.

Among the elements that caused the Arab population of the country to identify with Palestine before World War I, several stand out. First among them was a religious attachment to Palestine as a holy land on the part of Muslims and Christians. This attachment was felt by followers of both faiths everywhere, but was particularly strong for those who lived in Palestine. Although Muslims and Christians had somewhat different conceptions of what made Palestine a holy land, and of its boundaries and extent, they shared a similar general idea of the country as a unit and as being special. In the Christian case, as Alexander Schölch has pointed out most clearly,[7] this conception was based on the biblical definition of the country as running from "Dan to Beersheba," and was reinforced by the boundaries of the jurisdiction of the Greek Orthodox and Latin Patriarchates and the Protestant Episcopate of Jerusalem, all of which included the entirety of Palestine.

Both Schölch and Yehoshua Porath have described how the Muslim perception of Palestine as a holy land—it is called *"al-ard al-muqaddasa"* (meaning "the holy land") in the *Qur'an* (5:21)—developed over time.[8] This took place notably through such genres as the "Fada'il al-Quds" literature, which praised Jerusalem, Hebron, and other parts of Palestine and was widespread before, and even more so after, the Crusades.[9] Also important in this regard were annual seasonal pilgrimages to local holy sites, notably the Nabi Musa celebration, which traditionally attracted thousands of Muslim pilgrims from all over the country to the site where Moses is traditionally believed by Muslims to be buried, at a twelfth/thirteenth-century shrine located half-way between Jerusalem and Jericho.[10]

Various authors have also described how Ottoman administrative boundaries, and European ambitions and aspirations in Palestine, helped to shape the local inhabitants' conception of the country. From 1874 onwards, the *sanjaq* of Jerusalem, including the districts of Jerusalem, Bethlehem, Hebron, Beersheeba, Gaza, and Jaffa, was administered independently from any other Ottoman province, and as such was under the direct authority of Istanbul. In earlier times Jerusalem had briefly been capital of a larger province with the name "*Filastin*," which encompassed all of what is now Palestine, including Nablus, Haifa, and the Galilee. More frequently, the Jerusalem *sanjaq* was included with other regions within the province of Damascus.[11]

The way in which these administrative arrangements affected local conceptions of the country can be seen in recommendations for action by the new Ottoman Parliament published in the Turkish and Arabic press by a former official of the Jerusalem *sanjaq*, the Lebanese Najib ʿAzuri, in 1908. Among these recommendations was expanding the *sanjaq* of Jerusalem, and raising it to the rank of a *vilayet*, which ʿAzuri argued was necessary "since the progress of the land of Palestine depends on it."[12] ʿAzuri had earlier aroused the ire of Sultan Abdul Hamid for his outspoken opposition to government policies, notably regarding Zionism. He had been sentenced to death for treason in absentia after his flight to France, where in 1905 he wrote the prophetic book *Reveil de la Nation Arabe*, which predicted a momentous conflict between Zionism and Arab nationalism. His opposition to Zionism was undoubtedly one of the bases for his argument that Palestine should be a separate province, but it was clearly predicated on the assumption that there was such a thing as a "land of Palestine," an idea that must have been shared by the readers of *Sabah* and *Thamarat al-Funun*.

This bears out Schölch's statement that "the administrative experiments and facts mentioned here, especially the elevated position of the *sanjaq* of Jerusalem (which lasted for almost half a century), doubtless contributed to the emergence of the concept of Palestine as an administrative entity."[13] Porath goes further: "at the end of the Ottoman period the concept of *Filastin* was already widespread among the educated Arab public, denoting either the whole of Palestine or the Jerusalem *sanjaq* alone."[14] This resulting local consciousness of Palestine as a discrete entity, based on religious tradition and long-standing administrative practice, was only enhanced by the fact that foreigners also saw it as such.

It was natural that the covetousness of the European powers regarding Palestine, and in particular their constant efforts to expand their influence and standing there throughout the nineteenth century,[15] would affect the self-view of the inhabitants of the country. The inhabitants of Palestine had long perceived that control of Palestine was a prize of value to Western powers, and such a consciousness did much to cement a sense of community and belonging, and to spur patriotic feeling regarding Palestine. Such a feeling was originally particularly strong among Muslims and had been widespread among them at least since the Crusades.[16] In the nineteenth century many Palestinian and other Arab Christians came to share this fear of European imperialism, while at the same time many Christians were among the first local inhabitants to be affected by Western notions of nationalism and patriotism obtained in missionary schools and through other contacts with Europeans.

As was the case in other Islamic cities, there was a strong tradition of what might be called urban patriotism in the cities of Palestine. Jerusalemites, Nabulsis, Gazans, and Khalilis (inhabitants of Hebron—*al-Khalil* in Arabic) all took pride in their cities, as can be seen from the profusion of local histories devoted to cities and regions of Palestine, and from the frequency of the use of the name of a city—al-Maqdisi, al-Nabulsi, al-Ghazzawi, al-Khalili, and so on—as either a family name or as an identifier in addition to a family name. Outside the cities there was also a deep attachment to place, including pride in the village as special and better than others, and a related pride in family and lineage. With the spread of a broader notion of patriotism as modern education reached wider circles of the population, and with the increased ease and speed of travel in the late nineteenth and early twentieth centuries as roads and railways were constructed, these local loyalties were gradually supplemented by a sense of belonging to a larger entity than a city, town, or village and its immediate environs. These loyalties were never superseded, however, and they still retain their vitality in the cities and villages of Palestine.[17]

The reaction of the Palestinian Arabs to modern political Zionism drew upon all these preexisting elements: religious attachment to what both Muslim and Christians believed was a holy land, the conception of Palestine as an administrative entity, the fear of external encroachment, and local patriotism. Before going into details of this reaction, it is worth stressing that these elements of attachment to Palestine all antedated the encounter with Zionism. It is necessary to point this out because of the common assertion that Palestinian identity was no more than a reaction to Zionism, and the attachment of Palestinian Arabs to the country no more than a response to the attachment to it of those inspired by Zionism. There is a kernel of truth in these assertions: in some measure, as we have already seen, identity develops in response to the encounter with another. But as we shall see, there were other "others" besides Zionism: the British and other Arabs among them. And in any case, as I have shown, the attachment of the population of the country to it—albeit in prenationalist terms—was strong long before the arrival of modern political Zionism on the scene in the last years of the nineteenth century.

As has been analyzed by Neville Mandel and others, there was a widespread and sophisticated opposition to Zionism among educated, urban, and politically active Palestinians from a very early stage in the implantation of the Zionist movement in Palestine.[18] There was, in addition, a strong current of opposition to Zionism among the peasantry in areas where Zionist colonization led to the displacement of *fallahin* from their lands.[19] All of this was reflected in the press, where the issue had a broad impact on public opinion, and helped to shape both Arab views of Zionism, and the conception of Palestine as a land under threat.[20] At the same time the issue of Zionism was a defining one for many Palestinian papers, notably *al-Karmil*, founded in Haifa in 1908 by Najib Nassar, and *Filastin*, established in Jaffa in 1911 by the cousins 'Isa and Yusuf al-'Isa. The very titles of these papers—in Arabic, *Filastin* means Palestine, while *al-Karmil* means Mount Carmel, overlooking Haifa Bay—are indicative of the local patriotism that inspired their establishment. For several decades thereafter, these remained among the most important newspapers in Palestine and were unwavering in their opposition to Zionism.

One of the clearest and earliest prewar examples of this conception of Palestine as a land under threat from the Zionist movement, and of the Palestinians as an entity, can be seen from the opening words of a special issue of the Jaffa newspaper *Filastin* entitled "An Open Letter to Subscribers." In it, the editors commented sarcastically on a failed attempt by the Ottoman authorities to close down the newspaper in May 1914 in response to their published attacks on the Zionist movement: "Dear readers, it seems we have done something serious in the view of the central government in warning *the Palestinian nation* [*al-umma al-filastiniyya*] [my italics] of the danger which threatens it from the Zionist current."[21] As significant as the sentiment that Palestine was endangered by Zionism, was the use of the term "Palestinian nation" in this context. Perhaps equally significant, Yusuf and 'Isa al-'Isa fought the government closure in local court, won, and were carried from the courtroom on the shoulders of a delirious throng of well-wishers.[22]

It can therefore be understood why, although other foci of loyalty were still more powerful for most of the Arab inhabitants of Palestine before World War I, the idea of Palestine as a source of identity and as a community with shared interests had already taken root. It competed with and complemented loyalty to the Ottoman state and to the Muslim and Christian religious communities, the growing sense of Arabism fostered by the spread of education and the expansion of the influence of the press, and other more local loyalties—to regions, cities, villages, and families. In this context the growing problem of dealing with Zionism provided Palestinians with the occasion to feel part of a larger whole, whether Ottoman or Arab, which they hoped might help them to deal with an opponent that they already began to fear they could not resist alone. The extent to which the question of Zionism was addressed in Ottoman politics, in parliament and in the press, and the degree to which Arabist politicians and newspapers stressed their opposition to Zionism, encouraged this tendency. At the same time, as time went on this problem contributed to the tendency for Palestinians to feel separate and abandoned, for in the end the Ottoman authorities failed to take seriously the complaints of the Palestinians regarding Zionism, while even those Arabist politicians who seemed sympathetic proved equally ineffective.

The overlap between these various loyalties, and the way in which one developed from another can be seen from the remarks of `Isa al-`Isa, editor of *Filastin*, about the motives that led him to found his newspaper in 1911. In a speech many years later at the Arab Orthodox club in Jerusalem, he stated that at the outset his aim was to defend the Arab Orthodox cause.[23] Very soon afterward, however, he found himself in the midst of a national conflict with two fronts: one Arab-Turkish, and the other Arab-Jewish, and he joined in both, without abandoning the Orthodox cause.[24] Clearly, for an individual such as `Isa al-`Isa, all of these loyalties were compatible with one another, and notable among them was the sense of Palestinian identity that his words in the *Filastin* editorial cited above show clearly to have existed even before World War I.

World War I changed many things as far as Palestinian identity was concerned, however. Of the elements of identity for Palestinians and other Arabs whose attraction had waned by the end of the war, two stand out: they were Ottomanism and religious affiliation. The reason for the collapse of Ottomanism as a focus of identity is obvious. Beyond the defeat of the Ottoman army and the withdrawal of Ottoman authority from the Arab provinces by the end of 1918, Ottomanism as an attempt at a transnational ideological synthesis was rendered obsolete by the outcome of World War I. Among Turks and Arabs, Armenians and Kurds, its place was taken by the national principle. That principle had already asserted itself forcefully in the decades before 1914, as it dissolved many of the bonds that held together the multinational Empire, and its appeal was greatly strengthened during the war, when President Wilson made national self-determination one of his Fourteen Points. Although the Ottoman heritage was to continue to have a powerful influence on the Arab world in the years that followed (one that has been unjustly ignored and insufficiently examined), in a period of a few years, Ottomanism as an ideology went from being one of the primary sources of identification for Palestinians and other Arabs to having no apparent impact at all.

With regard to the Arab provinces, it can be argued in hindsight that even before the war the Ottoman synthesis was gravely undermined because of what many Arabs came to perceive was the rise of Turkish nationalism as the governing principle of the Ottoman state and its ruling party, the Committee of Union and Progress (CUP).[25] Similarly, the decline of religion as the governing principle of the Ottoman state in the waning years of the Empire, and what was perceived by many as the cynical exploitation of Islam by the highly secular CUP from 1908 to 1918, accelerated a decrease in the saliency of religious identification in the empire before and during the War. This complemented and enhanced a growing shift to secularism and secular nationalism on the part of some of the younger segments of the Ottoman elite, but this shift was by no means as definitive as the eclipse of Ottomanism. For many sectors of the population, and perhaps for most people in the successor states of the Ottoman Empire, religion continued well into the present century, and indeed up to the present day, to be the most important single source of identification and community feeling. This was true not only of the lower classes and the rural populace but also of many members of the upper classes and among city dwellers, particularly the older ones.

The end result was nevertheless that the two of the central pillars of identity before 1914, Ottomanism and religion, were diminished in importance by the end of the war. This left the field open for nationalism, the ideological rival of both, which had been growing rapidly in influence in the late Ottoman period. The only question, in Palestine and elsewhere, was not whether nationalism would supplant other forms of loyalty but, rather, which specific form of nationalism. And, at the outset, the answer to that question seemed to be clear: Arab nationalism appeared to be the obvious successor to Ottomanism as the hegemonic ideology throughout the former Arab provinces of the now-defunct Ottoman Empire.[26] However, in Palestine, as elsewhere in the Arab world, matters were not quite that simple.

"A nation which has long been in the depths of sleep only awakes if it is rudely shaken by events, and only arises little by little. . . . This was the situation of Palestine, which for many centuries had been in the deepest sleep, until it was shaken by the great war, shocked by the Zionist movement, and violated by the illegal policy [of the British], and it awoke, little by little."[27] These were the words used soon afterwards by the eminent Jerusalem writer and educator, Khalil Sakakini, to describe the situation in Palestine in the immediate aftermath of World War I, a period during which crucial changes in consciousness and perception among much of the population took place.

Each of the factors Sakakini listed had a major impact on Palestine, starting with the war, which initially brought with it a massive Ottoman military presence to support the campaigns across the Sinai desert against the Suez Canal launched by Jamal Pasha's Fourth Army. This was followed by the arrival of the allied army commanded by General Allenby, fighting its way north through the country in 1917 and 1918. Parts of Palestine were devastated by combat, notably the Gaza region, many trees were cut down to fuel steam locomotives, draft animals were requisitioned by both armies, famine prevailed in some areas, and virtually all the draft-age men were inducted into the Ottoman army, some never to return. Many others were arrested, executed, or exiled by the authorities on suspicion of aiding the allies.[28] The economic results of the war were debilitating, as was its demographic impact, which has been estimated in the most careful assessment of the demography of Palestine during this period as leading to a population decrease of over 6 percent in little more than four years.[29]

However serious was the material impact of the war on Palestine, its political and psychological consequences were even greater. The effect of the collapse of the Ottoman state, within whose framework over twenty generations of Arabs had lived for four centuries in the countries of the Fertile Crescent, has already been mentioned. This event left a huge vacuum in political consciousness—particularly for the older generation—one made all the greater by the occupation of the region by the British and the French, an eventuality much anticipated and much feared by most of the population before the war.[30] As the quotation from Sakakini indicates, the issuance of the Balfour Declaration and the revelation of the Sykes-Picot accords by the Bolsheviks —both in November 1917, only weeks before Jerusalem fell to Allenby's forces—had an enormous impact in Palestine.[31] Suddenly the Palestinians found that their country was occupied by the greatest imperial power of the age, Great Britain, which had made arrangements for its disposition with France and had proclaimed its support for the national aspirations of the Zionist movement in Palestine.

These upheavals in the world around them, upheavals that impinged

directly on the structure of the lives of the entire population, made possible, and at the same time necessitated, extremely rapid changes in attitudes and consciousness on the part of the Palestinians. The speed of
these changes is striking. By way of contrast, mentalities and ideology
appear to have evolved relatively slowly in Palestine in times of peace
and stability, such as the years stretching from the late 1860s through
1914 (and in this respect Palestine appears to have been similar to other
Arab regions of the Ottoman Empire). We know that there were important changes in government, social structure, education, and ideology
over this period. But the pace of change, at least as regards attitudes,
mentalities, and self-view, appears to have been fairly sedate. However,
it is clear from the evidence for the years after 1914 that in this time of
crisis, when the population was subjected to great stress, their attitudes
and identities were transformed with extraordinary rapidity and with
only minimal apparent dislocation for those whose self-view was thus
transformed. It would appear that this propensity of peoples to reassess
fundamental attitudes and beliefs at times of major historical shifts is a
general pattern, and not one exclusive to this time and place.[32]

For primary material providing Palestinian perceptions of events for
the war years and the first year afterward, we are unfortunately restricted to memoirs, private papers, a limited number of published documents,
and the occasional pamphlet or interview in the press outside of Palestine. Both British and Zionist sources are of course available in abundance for the early years of the British occupation of Palestine, but they
are of limited utility for this purpose.

Perhaps the most crucial source for evaluating Palestinian public attitudes and perceptions for most of this century, the press, was shut down
by the Ottoman authorities on the outbreak of the war and only reappeared slowly afterwards, starting in 1919, when it operated under strict
British military censorship. The postwar delay can be explained in part
by the fact that the country was under military rule—under the rubric
Occupied Enemy Territory Administration (South)—until 1920, and
indeed was an active scene of combat for most of 1917 and 1918, until
the armistice in November of the latter year. During much of the hard
winter and spring of 1917–1918, moreover, a near-famine reigned in
many parts of Palestine.[33] The British military regime was only superseded by a civilian one in July 1920, which itself maintained tight control over newspapers and other publications.[34]

Many established prewar publications, such as `Isa al-`Isa's Jaffa newspaper *Filastin*, only resumed publication well after the war ended, following many delays in reopening. In al-`Isa's case, this did not take place
until March 1921 because of his exile from the country by the Ottoman

authorities during the war, his service with Faysal's government in Damascus for two years thereafter, and what appears to have been a British ban on his reentry into Palestine for several months after that.[35] Najib Nassar's *al-Karmil*, another important prewar Palestinian paper, resumed publication in Haifa only in February 1920, while Elie Zakka's less influential *al-Nafir* reappeared in the same city in September 1919.[36]

In the years immediately after the war, the first new newspaper to be established in Palestine was *Suriyya al-Janubiyya*, published in Jerusalem beginning in September 1919 by the lawyer Muhammad Hasan al-Budayri, and edited by `Arif al-`Arif.[37] This paper was important in several respects: it appears to have been the most influential organ of opinion during its short lifetime; it was highly political and intensely nationalist; and its articles were extremely vividly written—for many years indeed only *Filastin* among Palestinian papers could approach *Suriyya al-Janubiyya* for the pungency and power of its prose, and as we have seen, it was two more years before *Filastin* reopened. That this new newspaper should have attracted such talented writers is not surprising, given that it was affiliated with the Arab nationalist club *al-Nadi al-`Arabi* in Jerusalem, that the Arabist movement had been a magnet for talented journalists since well before the war,[38] and that during this period Arabism benefited from the prestige that attached to the new Arab state in Damascus.[39]

The newspaper was certainly taken seriously by the British authorities, as was evidenced by their closing it for a month after the first ten issues and then shutting it down permanently following the disturbances of April 1920, after it had published for less than a year. The first issue after the first closure in November 1919 reports the paper's reopening after a month of enforced silence, while insisting staunchly that it will not change its "Arab principles." This issue shows a slight softening of its normally militant nationalist tone by comparison with earlier numbers, a softening that does not continue in the later issues of the paper that are extant.[40]

The newspaper's title, meaning "Southern Syria," was indicative of the political temper of the times: at this stage many in Palestine were were motivated by the hope that all of Syria (here meaning greater Syria, including modern Syria, Lebanon, Jordan, and Palestine/Israel) would remain united under the state established by Faysal as a first stage towards a larger Arab unity, a hope that was to wane in succeeding years, although it remained alive. The salience of this hope, and its diminution over time, can be traced from the varying frequency of the employment of terms reflecting it in the slogans that were found at the top of the pages of nationalist newspapers like *Suriyya al-Janubiyya* and its nationalist successor, *al-Sabah*;[41] the names chosen for conferences, meetings, and political parties and clubs in Palestine; the wording used in communiqués and statements; and the letters and papers of Palestinians during the first few years after the war.

The background and import of the commitment to southern Syria at this time in Palestine requires some explanation and is illustrative for this exploration of the emergence of Palestinian identity. The Arab state in Syria was seen quite differently by different constituencies. For the British, the entity headquartered in Damascus was not a state; it was no more than a temporary military administration of one area of a region where Britain had multiple commitments and interests. Great Britain in fact never recognized this state, or Amir Faysal in his capacity as ruler of Syria: when in London and at the Paris Peace Conference, he was received as the representative of his father, whom the British recognized as King of the Hijaz. Ultimately, of course, in July 1920 the British gave in to insistent French demands that they honor their commitments to France embodied in the Sykes-Picot agreements of 1916 and allowed French forces to take over Syria, expel Faysal, and dismantle the Arab state.[42]

In contrast for many Arabs, this state was a harbinger of a new era of Arab independence and unity, the first stage in the reconstruction of an Arab polity whose roots were seen as going back to the earliest era of Islam and, fittingly, to the great Umayyad state, whose capital was Damascus.[43] The boundaries of this new Syrian state were always problematic, however. While the linguistic lines separating mainly Arabic-speaking areas of Syria from mainly Turkish-speaking areas of Anatolia served as rough boundaries, the separation of Syria from Egypt and the Hijaz was generally recognized, and the relation of Syria to Iraq was settled by the Iraqis holding a congress in Damascus which called for a separate state, the precise status of Lebanon and Palestine was less clear. These coastal areas of greater Syria, or *bilad al-Sham*, were the ones that the European powers coveted the most, where they had the most extensive interests, and which these powers had agreed in the Sykes-Picot accords during the war to keep under their direct control. The Arab state in Damascus nevertheless claimed sovereignty over the littoral, and although Arab troops were expelled from Beirut by the French in 1918, and the British never allowed this state to extend its authority to Palestine, both Lebanese and Palestinians sat in the Syrian Parliament and many of them served as ministers in the Syrian government.[44]

For the Palestinian elite, therefore, a commitment to seeing their country as southern Syria was in large measure an indication of devotion to Arabism and to its incarnation, the first modern Arab state of

Syria with its capital in Damascus. As with Palestinian identity, there is little in the prewar period to indicate an intense commitment to Syria as a focus of identity on the part of Syrians, while, as in the Palestinian case, there is much to show a general consciousness of Syria as an entity. The encroachments and ambitions of foreign powers, in particular France, whose government explicitly and publicly declared its desire to control Syria from 1912 onwards had had an impact in Syria; until World War I, however, the response to this external challenge more often took an Ottomanist or Arabist cast than a Syrian one.[45] Southern Syria as a focus of identity was therefore new, its emergence as rapid as that of Palestine as a focus of identity, and like Palestinian identity, it overlapped with Arabism, albeit to an even greater degree during the two brief years when Syria was the location of the Arab state that seemed the incarnation of Arab nationalist aspirations. With the crushing of this Syrian experiment by the French in 1920, Syria was to fade as a focus of identity for Palestinians, although it remained important for many Lebanese.[46]

We can see the centrality of Syria for Palestinians soon after the war in the earliest extant issue of *Suriyya al-Janubiyya*, dated 2 October 1919, where the focus is clearly on Syria, and in particular on news about developments relating to the country at the Paris Peace Conference. Already at this early date, a note of alarm creeps in as to the possibility that Syria will be partitioned: an article by `Arif al-`Arif reports rumors that the Paris conference was going to confirm the separation of both Lebanon and Palestine from the rest of Syria and the right of the Zionists to immigrate to the latter.[47] Another article in the same issue, reprinted from the newspaper *al-Istiqlal al-`Arabi* in Damascus, gloomily concludes that after Iraq has been forgotten by the Arabs and abandoned to the British (who at this stage were intent on imposing direct rule there on the Indian model) now it is the turn of Palestine, which will be separated from the rest of the Arab lands, and abandoned to the "shadow of Zionism."[48]

The same notes of defiance are struck even after the paper's closure by the British. In the first issue after it was reopened, in November 1919, one article commented on news from Paris regarding the likely partition of Syria, arguing that "we are residents of Southern Syria, we do not want partition, we want an independent Syria, and we are against Zionist immigration."[49] A second article, reporting a public speech by Sir Herbert Samuel at the London Opera House on the second anniversary of the Balfour Declaration, categorically stated that the Arab nation had awakened from its sleep, and that "our country is Arab, Palestine is Arab, and Palestine must remain Arab."[50] This passage is interesting in that it combines local patriotism, focused on Palestine as "our country," with a strong commitment to Arabism—a combination that was to become characteristic. Such an assertive response can be understood in light of the content of Samuel's speech, in which he said that while the Zionist movement did not intend to turn Palestine into a "purely Jewish state" immediately, its aim was to create as soon as possible "a purely self-governing Commonwealth under the auspices of an established Jewish majority."[51] Not entirely surprisingly, this moderation on Samuel's part failed to reassure Palestinians suddenly faced with the specter of becoming a minority in a country that they naturally assumed was their own. The focus on Syria continued through 1919 and into early 1920 in *Suriyya al-Janubiyya*, which by this time had established itself as the most influential newspaper in Palestine.[52] A December 1919 article entitled "Warning, Warning!" cautioned against meetings between Arab leaders and the Zionists at which deals were made at the expense of Palestine: it stressed that any agreement that harms "the Arab grouping (*al-jami`a al-`arabiyya*) and Syrian unity" would be opposed by the people.[53] Similar language is used in a March 1920 article that stated that Amir Faysal knew better than to make an agreement with the Zionists at the expense of Arab rights, for the Arabs, especially "the people of Southern Syria," knew their history and their rights.[54] Such a stress on Arabism and on the unity of Syria is to be expected at a time when the elected First Syrian General Congress, including representatives from Syria, Palestine, Lebanon, and Jordan, had just concluded its meetings in Damascus in early March 1920 with radical resolutions proclaiming Faysal King of a united Syria, rejecting a French mandatory, as well as both the Sykes-Picot agreements and the Balfour Declaration, and stressing the unity of Syria as a part of the Arab homeland.

In fact, as Muhammad Muslih and other historians have shown, by this time many Palestinians, including the most devoted Arabists among them who were in Damascus serving the new Sharifian state, had grown disillusioned with Faysal's willingness to compromise with the Zionists, and with the lack of concern shown by many Syrian leaders regarding the issue of Zionism.[55] This disillusionment can indeed be read without difficulty between the lines of the articles just cited. It became clear to these Arabist Palestinian intellectuals and politicians in Damascus that for some Damascene politicians, the survival of an independent Arab state in Syria in the face of French imperialist ambitions would require great sacrifices, including perhaps a sacrifice of Palestine to Britain and the Zionists, who might then support Syrian independence against the incessant pressures from the French.

This can now be seen to have been a short-sighted calculation, for neither the British nor the Zionists had the ability to deter France from its drive to control Syria, even had they the desire to do so. In any case, within a few months these questions were rendered moot, as the entry of French troops into Damascus ended Syrian independence and delivered a crushing blow to Arab and pan-Syrian aspirations. The effects of these momentous events were naturally felt strongly in Palestine: just as the destruction of the Ottoman Empire forced a fundamental rethinking of questions of identity on Palestinians, so did the destruction of Faysal's much shorter-lived kingdom in Damascus.

Even before this, however, and before *Suriyya al-Janubiyya* was shut down for good by the British in the wake of the Nabi Musa riots of April 1920, the paper had begun to reflect other ideological trends. Side by side with a continuing commitment to Arabism, and with it to a unified Syria, this important organ of opinion showed a growing concentration on purely Palestinian matters. A remarkable article by Hajj Amin al-Husayni (later to become Mufti of Jerusalem) argued that the Arabs should take heart from the experience of a people (*"qawm"*) long dispersed and despised, and who had no homeland but did not despair and were getting together after their dispersion to regain their glory after twenty centuries of oppression (nowhere are the Jews or Zionism mentioned by name, although the meaning is unmistakable). While ostensibly addressed to the Arab people as a whole, the fact that this exhortation was directed primarily at a Palestinian audience is indicated by comments such as: "you can see others with far less then yourselves trying to build their house on the ruins of yours," an unmistakable reference to Zionism and Palestine.[56]

More blatant than the subtle argument of Hajj Amin was a piece published in January 1920 over the signature "Ibn al-Jazira," a pseudonym perhaps for `Arif al-`Arif, entitled "Manajat Filastin" (meaning a confidential talk or spiritual communion with Palestine) that began with the fulsome peroration:

> Palestine, oh stage of the Prophets and source of great men; Palestine, oh sister of the gardens of paradise; Palestine, oh Ka`ba of hopes and source of fulfilment; Palestine, oh beloved of millions of people; Palestine, oh lord of lands and pride of worshippers; Palestine, oh source of happiness and spring of purity; Palestine, my country and the country of my forefathers and ancestors; Palestine, only in you do I have pride, and only for you am I ashamed; Palestine, oh maiden of nations and desired of peoples; Palestine, my honor, my glory, my life and my pride.

This remarkable paean was followed by a lengthy series of further declarations of loyalty to Palestine and love for it, stressing in particular the "patriotic bonds and national rights" that tie the people of Palestine to their country. Noting that these were the sorts of expressions of the love of Palestinians for their country, by which they proved to all how attached they are to it, the piece concludes with the words "Long live dear Palestine and its honest, sincere sons."[57] This is classical nationalist rhetoric, notable for the fact that it is solely Palestine, and not the whole of the Arab lands, and solely the people of Palestine, not all the Arabs, which are referred to.

Even more striking than this example of overripe romantic nationalism in terms of the terminology employed are news articles in *Suriyya al-Janubiyya* like the March 1920 article that discussed the new-found unity between Christians and Muslims in Gaza "after all old sensitivities and frictions had been removed from spirits and hearts." This unity, the author of the article noted in conclusion, was demonstrated by the establishment of a Muslim-Christian Society in Gaza aimed at building a united front against Zionism and against attempts by the British and the Zionists to divide the Arabs on religious lines. The Gaza branch was one of a series of such societies established in cities all over Palestine at this time and representing a new form of organization of Palestinian Arab politics in response to the British occupation and the boost it gave to the fortunes of the Zionist movement.[58] The article concludes that, God willing, this Society would have a positive effect in terms of "*al-wataniyya al-Filastiniyya khususan wa al-`Arabiyya `umuman*" (Palestinian nationalism/patriotism in particular, and Arab nationalism/patriotism in general).[59]

This crucial distinction between Palestinian and Arab patriotism, while ostensibly putting the two forms of patriotism on the same level, in fact privileged the former, for it was this form that was operative in the day-to-day political activities of Palestinians in this period and onward. This distinction formed the practical basis of nation-state nationalism in Palestine and other countries of the Arab *Mashriq* in the years that were to follow, as commitment to Arab nationalism continued but eventually over the decades declined into little more than lip-service. It was only a matter of time before this change could be seen in small but significant shifts in terminology, visible in the daily press. While Damascus was described as "the capital" in the same March 1920 issue of *Suriyya al-Janubiyya*,[60] its successor as the leading nationalist organ in Jerusalem after its closure, *al-Sabah*, published in the following year by Muhammad Hasan al-Budayri's cousin Muhammad Kamil Budayri in the same offices and with the same political line, mentioned in its first issue in October 1921 that it was being published in Jerusalem "the capital of Palestine."[61] Minor though this difference in wording may seem, it bespoke a subtle but important change in focus in little over a year and a half for many Palestinians, who now saw that Jerusalem was the center, not Damascus.[62]

This "South Syrian" interlude has been examined by a number of historians, notably Muhammad Muslih and Yehoshua Porath, although both tend to focus on broad trends of political history, and neither seems to have closely examined the press closely.[63] This interlude marked a crucial hiatus between pre-1917 political attitudes of the Palestinians, and those that were to last for the rest of the Mandate period. As we have seen, the Southern Syrian idea was linked to and mainly espoused by fervent Arab nationalists. In the immediate aftermath of the war, as the idea of independence for the Arabs, via the creation of a federation of three large states—Syria, Iraq, and the Hijaz—linked together by a Hashimite dynastic connection, seemed to be on the brink of realization, the initial optimism among Arabs that allied policy would allow such an outcome was encouraged by a combination of factors. These included what was known of the British promises to Sharif Husayn in 1915 and 1916, combined with public declarations by the allies such as the Anglo-French statement of 7 November 1918, promising the Arabs of Syria and Iraq liberation from Turkish rule and freely chosen governments;[64] the reassuring confidential counsels of British advisors and officials to various leading Arab figures such as Faysal;[65] and a strong dose of wishful thinking.

While these hopes animated many Arabs, in Palestine from the very outset of the post-Ottoman period the specter of the Balfour Declaration clouded these bright expectations. During Allenby's ceremonial entry into Jerusalem in December 1917, which was attended by a host of French and Italian military and political representatives and contingents of their armed forces, the British had excluded Arab forces, Arab military flags, and representatives of the Arab army.[66] This was in striking contrast to the situation elsewhere in Syria, where Arab forces were often given pride of place, as for example in the capture of Damascus and the entry of allied troops into the city. And in violation of the principle of strict maintenance of the status quo ante bellum as regards the holy places and the rights and privileges of the various communities, which Allenby proclaimed as the basis of the military government soon after the occupation of Jerusalem, important changes were soon made in favor of the Jewish community, such as the use of Hebrew as an official language.[67] Not surprisingly, this important change, which concerned language, so important where issues of identity and nationalism are salient, deeply disturbed the Palestinians. The behavior of representatives of the Zionist movement, who assumed that the Balfour Declaration meant that they would rapidly become the rulers of the country, and who soon began to arrive in Palestine in large numbers, only increased these initial concerns.[68] Within a short time, many Palestinians came to believe that the British intended to carry out their pledge to facilitate the establishment of a Jewish national home in Palestine, although others continued to hope that this was not the case.

Against the background of a growing understanding between Britain and France regarding the partition of the Arab lands, their disregard for Arab claims in Palestine, the unwillingness or inability of Faysal and other Syrian leaders to act against Zionism, and the failure of both the Arab and the Syrian ideas as practical vehicles either for the organization of political life or for obtaining support against the British and the Zionists, the Palestinians found themselves all alone and confronted by a Zionist movement that seemed to move from strength to strength. In this precarious situation, the Palestinians were obliged to find a satisfactory basis for their resistance to a multiplicity of external threats. In view of developments in Palestine before World War I and the experiences of the other Arab countries in similar situations—such as Syria, Iraq, Lebanon, and Jordan[69]—it seems most likely that a Palestinian particularist response would have emerged eventually, irrespective of the goad of Zionism, and would have ultimately developed into Palestinian identity and eventually a territorially based nationalism. Certainly that is the logic of every other entity in the eastern Arab world within the frontiers drawn by the imperial powers. But in the event Palestinian identity crystallized much more rapidly than it might otherwise have done due to the urgency of the threat that the Zionist movement posed, and the already existing high level of Palestinian entity-consciousness. Indeed, it is apparent that within a few years of the end of the war, a well-developed sense of Palestinian identity had already emerged, at least among certain sectors and strata of society.

This can be seen in a variety of places, notably in the pages of the press, which both shaped opinion and reflected it. Thus the nationalist successor of *Suriyya al-Janubiyya* in Jerusalem, *al-Sabah*, explained in its first issue in October 1921 that while one of its purposes was to defend the Arab cause, its main aim was "to serve the cause of the Fourth Palestinian Arab Congress, and to support the objectives of the delegation of the nation which is defending the Palestinian Arab cause in Europe, as part of the general Arab cause."[70] This delegation represented a coalition between various Palestinian political forces with a view to putting their collective critical position regarding the Balfour Declaration and other aspects of British policy before British policymakers in London. Through the various qualifications and caveats about the Arab cause in the passage quoted, it is apparent that the practical focus of this news paper, and of the broad political trend in Palestinian politics represented by the delegation that it supported, had narrowed to Palestine itself.

In *al-Sabah* and other nationalist papers, and in general Palestinian political discourse in the years that followed, the "general Arab cause" would continue to be mentioned, but this was increasingly lip service: what really mattered was the "Palestinian Arab cause." If this was the line of the Arabist *al-Sabah*, it should not be surprising that *Filastin*, which even before the war had stressed Palestinian particularism, should be even more emphatic in stressing a separate Palestinian identity after its reappearance. Its lead editorial in its first issue in March 1921, after a hiatus of six years, explicitly talks of "Palestine and its sister Syria," thereby making clear that each is a separate country.[71] This terminology—"sister Syria"—represents the mature discourse of Arab nation-state nationalism. This is the discourse in which for over half a century now, independent Arab states have been referred to as brothers and sisters, implying that they are members of one family out of respect for the myth of the existence of one Arab nation, even while it is perfectly clear to all concerned that they act completely independently of one another.

And beyond the press, beyond political discourse, this separate nature of Palestine was being emphasized and established in myriad ways. Among the most important was education, for my discussion so far of the growth of Palestinian national consciousness applies mainly to the urban, literate upper- and middle-class and highly politicized segments of the population, which were a minority in the early 1920s. Contrary to the condescending views of most British colonial officials[72] and Zionist leaders, however, some degree of politicization had already affected other strata, notably parts of the rural population, as could be seen from clashes between peasants and Jewish settlers in the countryside even before 1914.[73] The growth of the educational system in Palestine, and the attendant spread of nationalist concepts through this system, greatly facilitated the politicization of the countryside and provided a sort of conveyor belt whereby the ideas we have been examining rapidly became widespread beyond the cities and the literate population in the years that followed.

In the educational system in Mandatory Palestine, the salience of Arab nationalism has already been noted by many authors: the Peel Commission Report, in somewhat exaggerated fashion, claimed that Arab teachers had turned the government schools into "seminaries of Arab nationalism."[74] What has been less noticed is the degree to which the system fostered a specifically Palestinian national consciousness.

One example will suffice to illustrate this point. As early as 1923 Sabri Sharif `Abd al-Hadi, who taught geography in the Nablus secondary school, had published a book entitled *Jughrafiyyat Suriyya wa Filastin al-Tabi`iyya* (The Natural Geography of Syria and Palestine).[75] The book is an otherwise unremarkable text, which discusses the natural features, agriculture, communications routes, demography, and administrative divisions of Syria and Palestine. Its importance lies in the fact that all over Palestine students were already in 1923 learning that Palestine was a separate entity, a unit whose geography required separate treatment. Clearly, no one who disputes the widespread existence of Palestinian identity, and the beginnings of a Palestinian national consciousness during the Mandate period can have examined the country's educational system in even a cursory manner.

What this essay has attempted to show is that even before the Mandate for Palestine had been formally confirmed on Britain by the League of Nations in July 1922, important elements of the country's Arab population had already come to identify primarily with Palestine. This Palestinian identity was to remain strongly tinged and to overlap with elements of Arabism (it will be recalled that the delegation to London described itself as a Palestinian *Arab* body, and the most common self-description of political groupings during the Mandate was as Palestinian Arab) and religious sentiment, which had been among its precursors. It was to spread significantly in succeeding years to broader segments of the population outside the cities, primarily via the press and the educational system. Nevertheless, this early period saw the emergence in a relatively complete form of the basic self-identification of Palestinians as Palestinians that has characterized them until the present.

Note: Chapter 9 is an earlier version of a chapter in Rashid Khalidi, *Palestinian Identity: The Construction of Modern National Consciousness* (Columbia University Press, 1997).

10

The Palestinians
Tensions Between Nationalist and Religious Identities

Musa Budeiri

ISLAM AND POLITICS

The disintegration of the Ottoman Empire and the advent of the secular-izing Turkish Republic as its successor state signalled the end of what to the Muslim inhabitants of the empire was the Caliphate state, *Dawlat al-Khilafa*. Its Arab territories, now occupied and partitioned by Britain and France, were no longer administered according to the Islamic *shari`a*. A process was under way that relegated Islamic practice to the private sphere. This process remained uninterrupted in the postcolonial era. Independence and statehood did not halt or even slow down the pace of secularization, which while not as radical and abrupt as that undertaken by Kemalist Turkey, nevertheless seemed to indicate that the social role of Islam would "continue to shrink until it became at most a matter of private observance."[1]

This has not taken place. A vibrant and often violent Islamic move-ment is challenging the legitimacy of nearly every existing Arab regime. The radical activism of Islamic movements is not usually viewed in terms of a newfound belief, or as a manifestation of heightened or pro-found religiosity. Rather, this is perceived as the outward expression of the denial of a reality that is held to be corrupt and in need of transfor-mation. The return to Islam is not the outcome of a religious conversion but the outward manifestation of the rejection of the status quo. Islam here assumes the role of "a last line of defense."[2] On the material level, radical Islamic movements are the legitimate offspring of the slums and working-class districts of metropolitan centers that house an underclass of poor workers and new immigrants from the countryside. These are the end product of a two-pronged process: the secular state educational system established in the post-World War II period, and the massive rural-urban migration called forth by the economic policies pursued by the state under the slogan of industrialization and development.

On another level it is recognized that the retreat of existing ideologies, whether nationalist or socialist, has created a vacuum.[3] In their search for a source of power and a source of unity in order to accomplish what secular ideologies have failed to deliver, people turn to religion. The ruling regimes are viewed as a blocking force threatening any kind of action that would subvert the political, economic, cultural, and military hegemony exercised by the West and that is seen as posing a threat to Arab national identity. The Arab nation is deemed to be under siege both physically and morally. Sheltering within Islam, it is hoped, will arrest this process of disintegration. If nothing else, Islam serves to define a distinct identity for the people, while at the same time providing a sense of psychological compensation for the prevailing bad times, *al-zaman al-radi'*.

Not everyone subscribes to an explanation that tends to search and find answers in the secular sphere. To many observers the visible part of the Islamic effort in the emphasis it pays to ritual, separation of the sexes, clothes, prayer, etc., does not indicate a preoccupation with core problems in the economic and social realm. Indeed, no program of significant economic transformation appears to be on offer. Thus the existence of these movements must be accounted for in other ways. We have to look to the realm of politics. They are in fact radical nationalist in import and "only marginally Islamic." It is the political role that Islam itself is wont to perform that is the real issue.[4] Drawing legitimacy from religious rhetoric, Islamic movements bring together the politically disaffected, the socioeconomically disadvantaged, and the spiritually frustrated. The very essence of these movements' activities is the attempt to "recenter society and politics around Islamic values"[5] in the belief that only Islam is capable of preserving Muslim identity from being submerged by the tidal waves of Western culture circling the globe.

A number of Islamic thinkers reject as artificial the separation between religious and nationalist discourse. Taking Kawakibi as an example, they argue that the intellectual and political movement that gave birth to Arab nationalism came out from "under the Islamic robes . . . from the pit of Islamic society,"[6] and was only secularized later on. The intellectual origins of Arab nationalism we are told, arose from within *al-halla al-Islamiyya* (the Islamic condition). Kawakibi spoke as an Arab and a Muslim; he "did not have to choose between his Arabism and his Islam."[7]

The insistence on a separation of Islam from Arabism is the work of nationalist ideologues, and it is they who have created this false dichotomy in people's minds.[8] Now with the defeat of the nationalist project, people have turned to the Islamic trend. At the core of this misunderstanding is the conflict between Nasser as the symbol of Arab nationalism in the 1950s and 1960s and the Egyptian Muslim Brothers movement. This was simply a moment in an otherwise symbiotic relationship with nothing inevitable or everlasting about it. Current attempts at bridging the gap between nationalists and Islamists highlight the areas of common ground.[9]

There is no denying that Islamic radicalism "feeds on the same slogans as far as content is concerned as radical nationalism did in a previous era."[10] Thus nationalists are able to accommodate themselves to a political Islam that is merely an extension of Arab radicalism, while Islamists viewing Arabism in Islamic terms, treat Arab identity as being subservient to and as an appendix of Islam. Secularists on the other hand, critical of the extravagant claims increasingly being put forward by neo-Islamist ideology, stress the absurd practice of using sacred texts to arrive at an identification with what is essentially a modernist ideological stance,[11] namely "nationalism in its fascist manifestation."[12]

THE OTTOMAN EMPIRE'S LAST DAYS: A NATIONALIST AWAKENING?

The Arab inhabitants of the Empire seem to have been the last of the Sultan's subjects to experience an awareness of selfhood that went beyond religious affiliation. It is possible that they entertained overlapping self views or identities without feeling that this involved a contradiction at all. For the most part, they were Muslims, Arabs, and Ottomans. To the end of World War I, that is, the destruction of the empire at the hands of its external foes, the majority of the Arab political class, the a`yan (notables), remained loyal Ottomanists, and Arab nationalism as an organized political movement remained a minority strand.[13]

The situation was transformed as a consequence of the 1908 Revolution. This resulted in the loss of legitimacy as the Committee of Union and Progress (CUP) pursued a path of Turkification, which eventually detracted from the Islamic character of the empire and led to the withdrawal of support. Two Islamic trends are discernable as a consequence of these transformations. The first continued to support the state primarily because it was Islamic and thus had to be defended against foreign powers. This support did not diminish as a result of Jamal Pasha's draconian policies. Supporters of the Anglo-French alliance were regarded as self-serving and ambitious, and at times even as agents of imperialist powers. It was only when Faysal was ensconced in Damascus or well on his way there that they threw in their lot with the nationalist cause. The other trend was likewise averse to severing ties with the Ottomans but declared for the nationalist side as a result of disillusionment with CUP policies that were increasingly difficult to defend. With the passage of the war years, nationalist demands were becoming legitimate among the a`yan class and no longer a bid`a (innovation). But there is no evidence to suggest that nationalist sentiment, much less activity, was evenly spread throughout the various parts of Suriyya al-Tabi`iyya.

The existing territorial states that today occupy the space of geographic Syria, with the notable and problematic exception of Israel, did not come about as a result of the triumph of national movements aspiring to nationhood and self determination. With the exception of Egypt, the Arab Mashriq does not seem to possess a state formation with an ancient and well-defined structure. There were no significant political movements in Iraq, Syria, or Palestine calling for the establishment of an Iraqi or Palestinian nation-state at the turn of the century. In the words of a prominent Egyptian diplomat, existing Arab states were established "by mistake."[14] Consequently, the existing territorial states of today are of recent parentage, and nation-building was the consequence of the "Mandated Nationhood"[15] imposed on a colonially dominated Syria, Lebanon, Jordan, and Iraq.[16] The absence of a Palestinian nation-state would render the task of nation-building in that particular case a more daunting endeavor. It is not clear however that Lebanon, with its continuing confessional tensions, or Iraq, with its dissenting Kurdish and Shi`ite populations, have proved successful in this enterprise.

The Arab national movement that took center stage in the aftermath of Ottoman defeat and disintegration allied itself with the Hashimites who, eager to fulfill their dynastic ambitions, had in turn attached themselves to the British. Previous to its occupation by British and Australian troops, the area defined as Palestine was made up of two administrative districts. The north, encompassing Nablus and Tiberias, was centered on Beirut. The southern parts made up the Mutasarrifiyya of Jerusalem, whereas those parts that lay to the east of the river Jordan were part of the Wilaya of Damascus. When Faysal was crowned King of Syria in Damascus it was self-evident that his domains would include the southern part of Syria currently under control of the British. Palestinian delegates represented the inhabitants of Southern Syria in the First General Syrian Congress held in Damascus in 1919. This is not to deny that participation of Palestinians in the narrow elite that constituted the Arab national movement was demonstrably weak. There was no counterpart to the Iraqi or Syrian class of notables making their own bid for power and statehood. Even after it became clear that Britain was not going to relinquish its control and that Faysal himself was not going to risk a clash with the British, the inhabitants of Southern Syria continued to look to Damascus. Not only were there no local contenders for separate statehood in Palestine, an indication that the local elite was well integrated into the wider Syrian class of a`yan, but it was only after Faysal's defeat and expulsion from Damascus that the realization dawned that they had to assume responsibility for their own fate separate from other Syrians who were now preoccupied with their own narrow territorial agendas.

WHAT PALESTINIAN IDENTITY?

Forced to fend for themselves, the inhabitants of Mandated Palestine were ill-equipped for the task at hand. It is indeed possible to argue that they did not succeed, throughout the Mandate years, in establishing a strong and unified national movement. Furthermore, they demonstrated an inability to overcome factionalism, to marshall their resources, and to mount an effective defense of their very existence. There is no evidence to support the contention that there already existed among them a strand "supportive of a distinctly Palestinian nationalism," stressing local Palestinian independence and cooperation with the British. If as the author asserts "the pull of Palestinian nationalism ultimately prevailed,"[17] this was the result of an externally enforced partition of Syria that left no viable option other than giving priority to the organization of a local nationalist movement. In point of fact, and despite the British occupation, there was initially an insistence on the attachment to Syria, and this continued to manifest itself, both orally and organizationally.[18] Palestine was not a distinct geographic historic entity whose people had had a separate historical existence since time immemorial. Prior to the British occupation, the country was made up, as mentioned earlier, of various administrative districts whose borders bore little resemblance to the Victorian imagination of Biblical Palestine.

The key to an understanding of the future development of Palestinian identity lies in the recognition that it was the establishment of territorial states in the region that played a pivotal role in the shaping of their peoples' identities. Unlike other Islamists who are currently challenging the legitimacy of the national state, the Islamic movement in Palestine was instrumental from the very beginning of the British Mandate in assimilating a nationalist discourse. It is indeed difficult to establish a demarcation line separating Islamists from their "nationalist enemies" when reviewing the activities of the national movement in the years of the Mandate. The first *nationalist* response to the British occupation was the establishment of Muslim/Christian societies in the summer of 1918. Branches were established throughout Palestine, and they held their first Congress in January 1919 as a demonstration of national unity. The Islamic idea was not central to these organizations' activities, and they have been characterized by an Islamic writer as "secular and nationalist," though they were usually headed by prominent religious figures.[19] The weakness of a nationally grounded identity and the narrower focus of loyalty based on smaller reference groups was evident from the very start. Despite the existence of two enemies, the British and the Zionist movement, the Husayni/Nashashibi rivalry exhibited itself at an early date, in the form of the establishment of competing organizational structures; the rival National Muslim Societies. Founded in 1922 and expressing support for the British proposed Legislative Council, they declared their acceptance of the Mandate in direct opposition to the stand taken by the Mufti as the most prominent spokesperson of the national movement. The announcement of their foundation was couched in Islamic language, as was the *fatwa* of the Mufti of Jerusalem against land sales to Jews.[20] The overt articulation of goals and policies was expressed in terms of Islam. Indeed it could not have been otherwise. No other ideological idiom would have been familiar or comprehensible to the rural inhabitants of the country, who constituted a majority and to whom the idea of nation and national interest was totally alien.[21]

Throughout the Mandate period Islam served to shape an ideology of resistance to an other, who not only belonged to a different faith but was also an outsider and openly proclaimed that the realization of his aims involved emptying the country of its original inhabitants. The tools for this campaign were the *Imams* and *Khatibs* of village and town mosques who used the Friday sermon to convey the necessity of resistance as a religious duty. Islamic concepts and historical parallels were utilized to mobilize the people en masse to social action. Religion was the medium not the message. The language and the symbols were cultural categories familiar to a society that through the long years of Ottoman rule had grown accustomed to viewing itself in religious terms. Concepts such as *Jihad, Shahid, Fida'i, al-Buraq, al-Ard al-Muqaddasa* were the terms commonly and frequently employed in the nationalist discourse of the period. The Crusades were repeatedly conjured up to give historical depth and to inculcate a sense of historical continuity to peoples' sense of identity. It is not that the Palestinians betrayed an early fundamentalist bias or possessed a doctrinal bent, but their struggle against Jewish colonization was perceived in religious terms and this was their only recognizable *Weltanschauung*.

During the thirty-odd years of British rule, the Palestinians produced two heroes. Both were religious figures, though their invented histories are more firmly embedded in the realm of nationalist mythology and martyrdom than in their strictly religious roles as `ulama. These were Amin al-Husayni, the Mufti of Jerusalem, and `Izz al-Din al-Qassam, a lowly religious functionary and political exile from Syria.[22] For both, their political activism was unquestionably part and parcel of their religious beliefs, yet neither established or laid the foundations for an Islamic grounded organization.

Islam was a mobilizing force that the Mufti utilized to highlight the threat to Muslim hegemony in Palestine. The historical narrative concerning al-Qassam is rather sparse. Very little factual evidence exists regarding what the man actually said or did during his sojourn in Palestine.[23] Moreover he was killed on his first encounter with British troops in 1935. Despite the fact that very few people were acquainted with his activities before his death, this in no way diminished the growing perception of the importance of his role in the ensuing struggle for Palestinian independence[24] since he was first rediscovered in the late 1960s and early 1970s. He has since been rediscovered on numerous occasions, both by academics,[25] and eventually by Islamic propagandists.[26] His deeds and personality have been highly extolled by the most radical leftist and secular groups within the Palestine Liberation Organization (PLO),[27] while Israelis have credited him with having founded "the first Arab terrorist movement in Palestine."[28]

Al-Qassam is lionized by both nationalist and Islamic sources for having initiated the most heroic period of contemporary Palestinian history, the 1936 rebellion. His movement is deemed to have constituted the organized backbone of the three-year armed struggle against the British that ensued.[29] Irrespective of the historical validity of such a claim, it is undeniable that the al-Qassam legacy has been utilized in a way that is conducive to heightening the popular conception of armed struggle "as a religious and therefore a moral and ethical duty." From the little we know about him, it would appear reasonable to assume that Islam was the "dominant organising idiom and motivation" for al-Qassam's movement. Posthumously his martyrdom served to transform Islam from being a part of a`yan politics to becoming a means of mobilizing popular participation in the struggle for independence. Al-Qassam's current place in the Islamic movement's grand narrative is indicative of its attempt to appropriate Palestinian history. He has been appropriated not merely as a symbol but also as the visible part of an organized movement, which moreover was "ten years in the making," and with it the whole history of armed struggle in Palestine. This makes the armed struggle an intrinsic part of the history of the Islamic trend itself, serving to endow it with enhanced national legitimacy.

In the period stretching from the end of Ottoman rule to defeat and dispersal in 1948, the confrontation with Zionism and British imperialism did not permit the crystallization of a clearly defined sense of national identity. Various strands coexisted together. Grafted on top of a continuing narrow attachment to kin, faction, village, region, was added Islam and a more widely held consciousness of Arab national *qawmi* feeling. Palestinian patriotic *watani* feeling was probably the weakest among all the overlapping senses of identity. The determining factor in the shaping of this identity was not only the historical baggage bequeathed by the long span of Ottoman rule but also the necessity of existing in and having to come to terms with a newly structured entity severed from its natural environment. The perceived aim of the Zionist movement, Jewish hegemony, presented a constant challenge that could only be met by appeal to a vocabulary of identity that, to make itself comprehensible, had to express itself in recognizable cultural categories embedded in a familiar historical narrative. This could only be provided by Islam. Simultaneously, the political class acquired a Pan-Arab outlook that was not diminished as a result of the failure to realize Arab unity. It continued, despite the reality of foreign domination, to look for support to other Arab states, so much so that from the mid-1930s onward, it was the neighboring Arab states who had the deciding say in the affairs of Palestine's Arab inhabitants.

POST-1948 IDENTITIES

Unlike in neighboring Arab states, the Mandate years in Palestine did not prove to be a transitional stage to independence and nation-building, but culminated in a process of expulsion, dispersal, and dissolution. The dispersal resulted in the assumption of different identities depending, among other things, on the attitude of the host countries. The small minority of those who remained on their lands and villages became `Arab Isra'il (the Arabs of Israel), and when two decades later they attempted to stress their Palestinian identity, this was viewed as treasonable intent. The largest concentration, in terms of number, congregated in what is currently the West Bank and was made up of the original inhabitants of the region in addition to the refugees expelled from Israeli-controlled territory. This area was to fall under Jordanian control and its inhabitants were accorded full Jordanian citizenship,[30] enabling them to enjoy legal and political equality with native Jordanians, inclusive of the right to passports and the ability to travel and seek employment opportunities abroad.[31]

The second largest congregation was in the Gaza Strip, the only part of Mandate Palestine that continued to exist as such and that was administered by the Egyptian army up to 1967. Large numbers of refugees also made their way to Syria and the Lebanon where they were housed in camps and treated as foreign residents.[32] Conditions and developments in these three areas of concentration were by no means similar. Within the Gaza Strip, run by an Egyptian military administration that was extremely repressive, any kind of political activity was regarded as subversive and little distinction was made between various political groups whether nationalist, communist, or Islamic. The most active were the Muslim Brothers, who functioned as an extension of the central office in Cairo and who succeeded in establishing a strong and permanent base for themselves.[33] Jordanian rule in the West Bank was welcomed right from the beginning by a large section of the *a'yan* class who already during the Mandate years had expressed support for Prince/King `Abdullah. There was little opposition from the remnants of a shattered national movement, as the advantages that accompanied Jordanian rule and the imposition of Jordanian citizenship were much too attractive to reject.

On the whole the Palestinian diaspora adopted an Arab nationalist stance and was an enthusiastic supporter of Nasser and his policies. Palestinians were active and prominent in all political organizations, the Ba`th, the Arab Nationalists, the Syrian Nationalists (PPS), and the Communists, but the mid-1950s and early 1960s witnessed the dominance of Arab nationalist discourse and they were its most ardent proponents. Bereft of alternatives, they chose to put their faith in Arab unity as the necessary prerequisite for the battle of liberation and return. The only place that the religious trend was allowed institutional expression was in Jordan. After a brief interlude of liberal experimentation in the mid-1950s, the King suppressed all political activity. The only group to be exempted from that ban, which remained in place until the mid-1980s, was the Muslim Brothers movement.[34]

It was only in 1964 with the establishment of the PLO that a distinct Palestinian identity was actively fostered and accorded official Arab sanction. This signalled the beginning of a nation-building process that greatly gathered momentum after 1967.[35] It is significant that this took place outside the borders of the state that had the largest numbers of Palestinians living within it, Jordan, and that took active steps to weaken its own citizens' identification with this development. In pursuit of this aim, it made common cause with its natural allies, the Muslim Brotherhood movement, who were pursuing their own feud with Nasser and who regarded the PLO as his creation and Shuqayri, its appointed head, as his creature.

Yet this process was facilitated in many instances by the rejection of the host society of any sort of identification with the Palestinians living in their midst, such as in Lebanon and the Persian Gulf states. Consequently, Palestinian identity was forged in the refugee camps of the Arab world and among the Palestinian communities of the Gulf states, not in what remained of Palestinian territory. It continued to be weakest in Jordan and the West Bank where the process was delayed until the replacement of Jordanian by Israeli rule. The latter, in a move that complemented Jordanian policies, continued to insist on the legal fiction that the inhabitants of the West Bank were Jordanian. The only Palestinian body that the Israeli occupation authorities allowed to operate in the immediate aftermath of June 1967 was the Higher Islamic Council.[36] This was made up of religious dignitaries and ex-Jordanian civil servants, and was to serve for a short time as the focus of anti-occupation activities.

TRANSFORMATIONS UNDER OCCUPATION

The growth and development of the Islamic movement in the West Bank and Gaza Strip cannot be understood outside the framework of the struggle between the PLO and the Jordanian regime for legitimacy and representation. Official Islam remained under the control of the Jordanian Ministry of *Awqaf*, a situation that the Israeli authorities were more than happy to countenance. The leadership of the Islamic movement, particularly in the West Bank (and this provides an explanation for the greater degree of activism and militancy in the Gaza Strip) was part and parcel of the Jordanian religious hierarchy. This was conservative by nature, having been nurtured in the Jordanian Islamic alliance spanning the nineteen-year period of Jordanian rule. It was largely made up of Jordanian civil servants employed in the various offices of the *Waqf* departments in the West Bank, who continued to draw their salaries from the Jordanian treasury. From 1970–1971, when the armed Palestinian organizations were ejected from Jordan, until the Jordanian-Palestinian rapprochement in the 1980s after the PLO's expulsion from Lebanon, the two parties were in conflict over the hearts and minds of the residents of the Occupied Territories. Although the Arab summit in Rabat in 1974 recognized the PLO as the sole legitimate representative, and the King gave his public assent to the summit's resolutions, the battle continued to be joined in the Occupied Territories themselves. Throughout this period, the Islamic movement did not place resistance to the occupation high on its order of priorities, and for this reason (in addition to forming part of the pro-Jordanian camp) tended to be tolerated by the Israeli authorities.[37]

The transformations that took place were slow and part of a process linked to the growth of a generation of West Bankers who had no experience of Jordanian rule. They were also the outcome of the increased involvement of the PLO constituent groups in the Occupied Territories, especially, after 1982, in an attempt to create a political presence for themselves at the grass-roots level. The crystallization of a secular Palestinian identity was hampered by the fact that the political discourse of the dominant political faction within the PLO, FATAH, which attracted the largest number of Palestinians to its ranks, was markedly Islamic.[38] It was seen, and rightly so, by the more radical Palestinian groups to possess a conservative social and political agenda. Arguably it was this that enabled it to draw support from every sector of the community,[39] and it continued to engage in a popular discourse that was heavily laced with religious imagery and well-entrenched within the framework of an Islamic-oriented value system.

The slogans and rallying cries of the anti-occupation movement have shown an increasing tendency since the 1980s to couch themselves in an Islamic mode. The most important potent symbol and rallying cry of the occupation, Jerusalem, is put forward in religious terms. The depiction of Jews is a reflection of old Islamic attitudes arising out of the conflicts in Arabia between the early community of believers and neighboring Jewish tribes. The practice of holding demonstrations after Friday prayers when people are congregating at mosques, the use of mosques as social support networks, their use as relatively safe havens and to carry out teaching when schools are closed and later as centers for the distribution of food and money, all tended to reinforce the view that political commitment is an extension of religious belief and that a central component of civil society is the religious identity of its most active participants. Indeed, the aim was to appeal to the more traditional among the Occupied Territories' inhabitants, and it has been argued that the highly ambiguous nature of Islamic idioms, which are open to all sorts of possible interpretations, has enabled FATAH to broaden its base of support.

Despite the removal of visible physical barriers between Palestinian and Israeli society in the pre-Intifada period, the secular nature of Israeli society has had very little impact on Palestinian life.[40] The two societies have remained essentially separate and have very little to do with each other outside the sphere of the sale and purchase of labor power (there is of course a confrontational relationship acted out daily and in multitudinous forms between occupied and occupier). Thus the secular experience has not been part of the life cycle of the overwhelming majority of Palestinians because their lives have not been acted out in Israel but in the seclusion of their dormitory-type villages and camps. It is also important here to keep in mind the hundreds of thousands of Palestinians who, having become enabled as a result of acquiring marketable skills, made their way to the labor-hungry societies of the Gulf where a generation has spent its life in traditional societies that continue to pay lip service and maintain the outward appearances of attachment to Islam.

For these very reasons, the actual tensions that coexist in Palestinian identity have to be seen as the outcome of the course of Palestinian history since the conquest of the territory by Britain and the consequent unfolding of events. They have to be explained in terms different from the absence of legitimacy or otherwise and the failures that characterize the policies of secular and traditional elites elsewhere in the region.

ARMED STRUGGLE AND ISLAMIC AWAKENING

The absence of ideology on the part of FATAH, which has been the dominant political force in Palestinian politics since 1968, and its resort to religious symbols and ideology to mobilize and enlist support, cast doubt on the often repeated assertion that FATAH, and by implication the Palestinian movement, is a secular force. Islam was and continues to be one of the paramount elements of Palestinian national identity, more so among Palestinians inside the Occupied Territories. This in itself serves to explain the ease with which support for a seemingly secular PLO was transformed into sympathy, and in many cases even allegiance, to the Islamic movement. If we are to discount a sudden outbreak of religiosity as the cause of this phenomenon, it becomes necessary to look elsewhere to try and explain the shift of support from the traditional forces of the PLO to those new and radical forces, which, it must constantly be remembered, are active and have their origin in the Occupied Territories themselves.

The years following the expulsion of the PLO from Beirut in 1982 saw a gradual decline in the standing of the PLO despite the increased level of action and involvement of its constituent groups in the Occupied Territories. While continuing to express commitment to the strategy of armed struggle, actual practice increasingly revolved around political action and institution-building. This sought to make use of the relatively large space made possible by tolerance for protest and civil rights activities, which the Israeli authorities believed would somehow contribute to a state of normalization. To all intents and purposes the PLO was well on its way to being transformed into a vehicle whose primary task was the pursuit of diplomatic activity.

Simultaneous with the unfolding of this process, the Islamic movement was undergoing its own transformation. A younger generation of members and sympathizers of the Muslim Brothers movement were questioning the organization's passivity and lack of involvement in the ongoing anti-occupation struggle. There were new role models. The electronic media had brought the news of a worldwide Islamic revival into the refugee camps of Gaza and the villages of the West Bank. They were fully cognisant of the triumph of the Islamic Revolution in Iran, of the exploits of the Islamic Resistance in Southern Lebanon, of the victories of the *mujahidin* in Afghanistan, of the militancy of the various Islamic groups in Egypt engaged in violent conflict with the Sadat regime and its successor, and of the brutal suppression of the Islamic movement in Syria. All this stood in sharp contrast to the quietism and inner withdrawal preached by the traditional leadership of the movement. This resulted in a politically inspired split that led to the birth of the Islamic *Jihad* movement. Its establishment was the signal for the beginning of a new campaign of violent attacks on Israeli civilians, settlers, and army personnel. Thus no sooner had the PLO abandoned the banner of armed struggle than it was raised again by the Islamic forces.

The period leading up to the outbreak of the Intifada in December 1987 saw the political fortunes of the PLO at their lowest ebb. The Camp David accords between Egypt and Israel had divided the Arab states. While the war unleashed by Iraq against Iran, with the former's loud protestations of defending the Arab world against the Farsi threat, seemed to provide a suitable diversion enabling a weary Arab political order to place the Palestine issue on a back burner.

The view from within the Occupied Territories was despondent. The PLO was becoming irrelevant as a regional player, marginalized and increasingly unable to influence the diplomatic game. The abandonment of the armed struggle, which represented the essence of its appeal to large numbers of young people looking for means to express their anger and rejection of the occupation, meant that little was now demanded of them except to perform the role of spectators. They were superfluous to the process of institution-building. Yet this period saw an intensification in the number of violent attacks directed against Israelis, mostly carried out by members or sympathizers of the Islamic *Jihad*. Many of these operations were spectacular, characterized by acts of daring and courage and serving to restore confidence in a period of declining prospects. They undoubtedly served to endow the Islamic movement as a whole with a credibility it had hitherto lacked. It appeared as if a new avenue was opening up. There now existed a framework that welcomed those desirous of engaging in violent confrontation with the enemy. The banners under which these actions were undertaken were Islamic, but the nature of the activities was the same as those carried out by nationalist groups in a not so distant past.

In the event, Israeli repression was more or less successful in containing the activities of the Islamic *Jihad*. Its members were arrested, killed, or deported and there was a marked decrease in its level of activity. This however could not check the spread of its example. The propaganda of the deed proved a success.[41] But the Islamic *Jihad* was primarily a conspiracy. It carried out no political activity and concentrated solely on violent actions. Thus it could not acquire a mass base. Its political success was in the pressure it exerted on the mainstream Islamic movement, the Muslim Brothers, to abandon their passiveness and involve themselves in the nationalist struggle for self-determination and statehood.

ISLAM AND INTIFADA

It is not necessary to grant any credence to the claims made by the Islamic movement of having organized and planned the outbreak of the Intifada to recognize the significance of this event in providing the framework for the participation of the Islamicists in the anti-occupation struggle and in promoting their fortunes. The movement did not have to undergo an ideological transformation in order to participate in the mass upheaval taking place. This did not initially appear to amount to more than another phase in the cycle of resistance and repression that had come to characterize the workings of the occupation. The Muslim Brothers were already under pressure to assume an activist stance even prior to December 1987 as a result of the widely publicized activities of the Islamic *Jihad*. The outbreak of the Intifada merely intensified the pressure from among the ranks of their own supporters and from society at large. This was accommodated by the adoption of a public stance, throughout the Occupied Territories, calling for active resistance to the occupation. Leaflets were published and circulated right at the start of the outbreak of strikes and confrontations, calling for an intensification of anti-occupation activities. The name under which they chose to advertise their entry, the Islamic Resistance Movement (HAMAS), represented a notable departure from past historical practice. The same can be said of the contents of the movement's program,[42] *al-Mithaq*, which has been recognized as expressing a "most innovative and unorthodox theoretical move."[43] The main innovation is in the emphasis on the concept of homeland and the support extended to the idea of the nation-state. The historical narrative the document maps out is totally Palestinian, stressing the role of al-Qassam as the most significant moment in the Islamic movement's long struggle to liberate Palestine, while making clear its understanding that patriotism is an intrinsic part of religious belief.[44] The attitude to Israel manifests itself primarily in ahistorical and religious terms. The Jews were the enemies of the Prophet right from the very beginning and have incurred the wrath of God by straying from his revealed message.[45] Fighting them is a divinely ordained task. Thus there is an added religious endorsement for the nationalist imperative of striving for independent statehood in Palestine.

The independence exhibited by HAMAS in refusing to join the Unified National Leadership as yet another grouping under the umbrella of an overarching PLO served to enhance its status. The movement persisted adamantly to project itself as a potential alternative to the PLO and thus a legitimate spokesperson for all Palestinians. Its active participation in the Intifada served to strengthen its nationalist credentials, and its resort to armed actions at a time when the mainstream PLO leadership was seen to be increasingly involved in diplomatic maneuverings struck a receptive chord among a public that was growing frustrated and despondent as a result of the failure of the Intifada to yield any positive results.

The recovery of the Islamic movement has been remarkable. In the space of a few years, and as a result of involvement in the Intifada, it has been able to compensate for its long absence from the political arena. The regaining of legitimacy can only be explained in terms of loss of faith in the ability, perhaps even the willingness, of the PLO to pursue the dream of independent statehood. This is what HAMAS now has on offer. It is not preoccupied with theological disputations and other sacred concerns.

In a previous era the failure of Arab states to establish unity and to mobilize their resources to face Israel led to the dissipation of Arab nationalist illusions and the rise of a specific Palestinian nationalism. The current disillusionment with a peace process which does not satisfy even the minimalist aspirations outlined in the program for independent statehood in the West Bank and the Gaza Strip has catapulted HAMAS into becoming the mouthpiece of Palestinian opposition to the current settlement, overshadowing organizations such as the Popular and Democratic Fronts that have a much longer track record. Its hard-line position, enshrined in the legend now abandoned by the PLO—liberation from the river to the sea, *min al-nahr ila al-bahr*—has gained it the support of people who are not necessarily observant, yet who feel betrayed by the unfolding political process and see it as "a forum offering them some hope which they badly need in order to keep their psyche intact."

THE CONTENT OF IDENTITY

Over the last ninety years the inhabitants of Palestine have undergone numerous transformations as a result of domination by a succession of various foreign rulers. The changes have mainly affected their public identity. They started out as Ottomans; currently they are Palestinians. Throughout there were two fixed components to their make-up, the Arab and the Islamic. Some would argue that it is possible to have two or three identities side by side, or even superimposed on each other. It is my contention that the absence of statehood, and thus the nation-building project, has thwarted the growth of a specifically territorial Palestinian identity similar to what arguably exists in neighboring Iraq or Syria and that accounts for the existence of a narrowly based Syrian or Iraqi nationalism. The demise of the Ottoman Empire, followed by a period of British rule and the subsequent collapse of all the structures of Palestinian society, social, economic and political, drove the Palestinians to assert the primacy and centrality of their Arabness. The Arab states, however, remained preoccupied within their own narrow territorialism. In Palestinian eyes this translated into the negative attributes of disunity and abandonment and drove them in turn to emphasize their own particularism and separateness. They have not been able, however, to implement their own territorial nationalist program. This has led to disillusionment with the leadership believed to be responsible for this failure. A large section from among those strata that have traditionally provided the reservoir for the active militants and street fighters that made up the cadres of FATAH as the largest constituent group within the PLO have now turned to the Islamic movement. This did not require any change in their perception of what and who they are. They have not and are not undergoing an identity problem and there has been no accompanying existential upheaval. The explanation lies in the nature of the Islamic movement itself. It has always preoccupied itself with the political sphere. Right from the start it endowed the nationalist struggle with its language and imagery, making it possible for people who were neither religious nor devout to enter its ranks and shelter under its banner while continuing to pursue an agenda firmly rooted in the nationalist struggles of a postreligious age.

11

Arab Nationalism in the Age of the Islamic Resurgence

Emmanuel Sivan

These are not easy times for pan-Arab nationalism. Three of its major myths have withered in the harsh winds of the last quarter century.

The first to be hit was the myth of "Arab Piedmont and Prussia." As an ethnic-cultural nationalist movement, Arabism got much of its inspiration from nineteenth-century European nationalism, especially from the Italian and German experiences. Sati` al-Husri drew already in 1940 a pivotal lesson from that experience, namely, that it is not enough to build from below, through education and the organizing of civil society. Given the deep chasms within the Arab world, it is incumbent to have a solid territorial basis, i.e., a state strongly committed to Arab unification and headed by a powerful leader. Such a state should be ready and capable of serving as magnet for those ludicrous fragments of Arab political entities; of appealing directly to the masses; and, if need be, of imposing itself, with their help, upon these statelets. The only Arab candidate to fulfill this role, played in Italy by Piedmont and in Germany by Prussia, was Egypt. Husri had no doubt about that, impressed as he was by her demographic and cultural weight, her geopolitical location, and her military potential.

Nasser inherited this vision and tried to implement it. The 1967 war was evidently a severe blow for the dream of Egyptian leadership, yet the quest for an "Arab Prussia" remained alive. As Sadat's Egypt followed a separatist path, believers in Arabism had to look elsewhere. Qadhafi attempted in vain to cloak himself with the leader's mantle, but it was apparent that his resources were too paltry. Syria could have assumed the leadership, but Asad, always the paragon of realpolitik, has drawn the lesson of Nasser's failure and circumscribed the horizon of his ambitions; since 1974, the Ba`thist regime turned to the path of al-Sham or "Greater Syria"—a revised version of Antun Sa`ada's concept (minus Cyprus). And then, to the pan-Arabists' sigh of relief, Saddam Husayn rose in the late 1970s and took up in Iraq's name the scepter of the supreme commander of the struggle for unity.

Like his role model, Nasser, Saddam tried to exploit the confrontation with an external enemy, so as to generate solidarity and promote his hegemony. The confrontation led to a war that ended in defeat and ignominy. In accordance with Karl Marx's dictum, history repeated itself twice: once as a tragedy (1967), and once as a farce (1991). A patent truth was exposed: Iraq and its ruler were a giant with feet of clay. When that giant crumbled down, there was no pretender to the title of "Arab Prussia."

The second myth to be dissipated was that of "artificial borders." This is how Pan-Arabists dubbed the demarcation lines separating political entities created in the Middle East upon the ruins of the Ottoman Empire. Artificial—for they were nothing but the product of Imperialism and its native henchmen, the reactionary Arab regimes. The pressure of the Arab masses from down below, and Arab Piedmont and Prussia from above, were supposed to erase these borders and reunite the Arab-speaking lands.

It is indeed in the name of this myth that Saddam Husayn justified his invasion into Kuwait and its subsequent annexation in August 1990. For could one imagine a better example of an utterly artificial British creation than this despicable emirate, which Iraq had always considered part and parcel of its historical territory. Arab public opinion, including most intellectuals, applauded the annexation. And no wonder. The myth's hold was still powerful. Other territorial entities in the Middle East have acquired some legitimacy over the past half century, but Kuwait and the other Gulf emirates (and to some extent Jordan and Lebanon as well) remained suspect: a memento for an era of weakness and subservience, a reminder for a "divide and rule" policy imposed by colonial powers.

The Kuwait annexation laid bare an astounding state of affairs: despite the reactionary regime, the local population adamantly refused to collaborate with Saddam. The Iraqi ruler could not even establish a puppet regime. Kuwaiti society, however lacking in a tradition of voluntaristic association, organized civil disobedience, even armed resistance, and that in the face of ruthless Iraqi repression. It became strikingly evident that even entities founded artificially—such as Kuwait—may, as has so often happened in Africa, develop a community predicated upon a common attachment to territory, upon a collective memory and upon a cultural variant of the Arab-Islamic civilization. Such a community is most likely to seek for itself, according to the self-determination norms of our century, a political expression. Otherwise put, it seeks to become a nation-state; such a state the citizens are ready to die for. If this was the case in Kuwait, all the more so in Jordan, whose inhabitants withstood the crucial loyalty test of "Black September" (1970), and entities with deep historical roots such as Syria, Algeria, and Sudan.

Last but not least, came the turn of the third Pan-Arab myth, "the common interests." Following the 1967 debacle and the rise of Arab territorial states in the 1970s, an alternative path for unity was proposed. No more the laying bare, from under the debris of history, of an eternal Arab reality but the cumulative building up of such a united entity, through the education of the masses and especially by a growing cooperation between states. The 1973 war and oil boycott seemed to augur success for such a scenario: military plus political-economic coordination produced impressive Arab achievements.

The following decade proved, however, that the oil-rich states do not subscribe to the vision of the "alliance between Saudi capital, Egyptian brains and Yemeni muscle" (according to one telling formula). These vulnerable states preferred to recycle petro-dollars in Western financial institutions in order to insure their value for the day when oil and gas run out. To the extent they invested in their poor Arab neighbors, this was almost solely in real estate in metropolitan areas. The upshot was a spiraling inflation in housing prices, which hit in particular the lower-middle class and young university graduates.

It is true that the manpower needs of the oil-rich states created for the first time a substantial movement of working population across Arab borders. More Arabs than in any time past came to other Arab lands and stayed there for long periods, getting to know fellow Arabs. Yet intimacy bred contempt and animosity. Most temporary Arab migrants were laborers who moved from poor to rich states, employed there in exploitative conditions, treated with suspicion and condescension.

The *schadenfreude* toward Kuwait's fate in summer and fall of 1990 fed upon the experiences of these guest laborers, as well as upon the jealousy elicited by the conspicuous consumption of the Gulf nouveaux riches, flagrantly indulged in during their hedonistic visits to Cairo, Beirut, and Amman. "Our daughters prostitute themselves in the Mercedes of filthy rich Saudis," wailed an audiocassette of a popular Egyptian singer.

The belief in the myth of Arab interest-based cooperation was faltering by the late 1980s, yet some effort continued, at elite levels, to create institutions for strategic and economic coordination. There was still room for optimism: a common Arab market in communications was being fleshed out, owing to the rapid development of a "median Arabic," combining literary (but simplified) grammar with a common, modern vocabulary. The gap between the written language and the local dialects—which was a sore spot of Arabism in the past—was in the process of being bridged. Increased communications, it could be hoped, may help create a common consciousness. Yet common interests between Arab economies failed to materialize, for these economies are not complementary but rather competitive (in oil, tourism, textile exports). The path pioneered by Sadat—an American orientation plus peace with Israel—further poisoned the Arab debate over strategic interests. The Iran-Iraq war complicated the clash of strategies, putting Egypt, Saudi Arabia, and Syria in the anti-Saddam camp.

All these contradictions were laid bare in a most virulent fashion in 1990–1991 when Saudi, Egyptian, and Syrian forces were positioned in battle formation, flanked by Western forces, against Iraq and its Arab allies. And subsequent to the war, the mass expulsion of Palestinian residents from Kuwait and of Yemeni workers from Saudi Arabia has provided yet another refutation of the "common interests" myth. Such commonality was bluntly sacrificed for the sake of territorial-state homogeneity and internal security. The third major pan-Arab myth expired in the sands of the Peninsula.[1]

Given the decline of Pan-Arabism, one could barely expect it to loom large in radical Islamic thought and propaganda. After all, we are far removed from the heyday of Nasserism when pathbreakers such as Sayyid Qutb had to gather all their courage in order to denounce Arabism as an ersatz religion. It was a quantum jump in the 1950s to argue that the nexus between Arab nationalism and secularism is inherent and inevitable, both being Western imports. But one could ask: Have not such arguments gone stale, lost their poignancy by dint of repetition and given the collapse of the then victorious pan-Arabism?

Thus it comes as a surprise to find Arabism as a frightful bogey in Islamic audiotapes today. These taped sermons are the major vehicle through which the radical message is relayed from Afghanistan to Morocco. Cheap to produce and to copy, accessible to the illiterate half of the population as well as to the rest, often diverting due to their mix of recurrent, formulaic psalmody and uplifting moral admonition and satire, audiotapes are increasingly popular. Their very orality, even though it is electronic, relies upon the existence of listeners (in most cases the tape is recorded during a live performance). It is these listeners the preacher must be attuned to, and they often take an active part in the sermon through interjections and/or questions. This opens to us a tiny window to peer through into that big unknown, the mood and preoccupations of the rank and file of Islamic movements who attend such gatherings. The interaction with the audience is greater (and informality higher) in the lesson (*dars*) forum, usually delivered by the preacher, in the mosque, just before the Friday prayer or on a weekday evening and revolving around a Qur'anic verse or a Hadith. Here the audience may pose many questions and may even challenge the `alim's interpretation. The preacher resorts to a homely style, often in colloquial Arabic, picking examples from recent events or daily life. One can hear the audience laugh, jeer, and talk back.

Moreover, the use of voice as major vehicle and the open structure it produces give a premium to the affective rather than to the analytic, which is highlighted by closure-bound written texts. The spoken word, with its acoustic quality, moves from interior (the mouth cavity) to interior (the outer ear) and thus creates a direct encounter of man to man. It is possible, then, to uncover emotional layers—the performer's as well as the listeners'—layers that underlie the readily accessible, rationally constructed arguments. Because orality joins people together, predicated as it is upon a sense of presence-cum-participation, communally generated and shared, it is perhaps the most apt tool for inquiring into questions of identity, in our densely socialized world of vocal-electronic communication.[2]

I have chosen to discuss only popular audiocassettes, dating from the 1980s and 1990s, which have passed a market test of impact. (Videotapes, as a rule, were not included, being costlier and enjoying a lesser share of the communications interaction.) Yet these audiotapes must be interpreted in the framework of the still more prestigious form, written texts, designed for the cadres of the movement, not for rank and file or for sympathizers. For I am dealing here with what specialists call the age of secondary orality: literacy is hegemonic (unlike the situation in the pre-Gutenberg age of orality), yet electronic orality is on the rise, shaped by but also expanding, modifying—at times subverting—the written message.

Pan-Arabism cannot be said to be an obsession for the electronic preachers, the way it was for the fathers of radicalism in the 1950s and 1960s, but it is no doubt an oft-beaten drum. "Arab nationalism was conceived in sin and born in corruption and dissolution," says `Abdallah `Azzam, a Palestinian-Jordanian preacher and activist of Afghanistan guerrilla warfare. It is a modern progeny of the age-old Crusading idea, part and parcel of the West's ongoing onslaught upon Islam, intended to pervert the latter's mindset.[3]

Yusuf al-`Azm, the leader of the Jordanian Muslim Brethren, and the Egyptian *Shaykh* Salah Abu Isma`il concur that Arabism was concocted by European Orientalists such as Margoliouth and Brockelmann who built upon the ideas of the French Revolution in order to separate Arabs and Turks, thereby weakening Islam and facilitating Western takeover. To that very end they also helped create the Pan-Turanian idea. These twin ideas, and the movements they spawned, indeed contributed to the demise of the Ottoman Empire, helped as they were by local Christians, notably the graduates of missionary schools and of the University of Beirut, that hotbed of subversive infidel ideas both then and now. Prominent among the Syro-Lebanese agents of doom, profoundly hostile to Islam, and hell-bent upon the destruction of the Caliphate and the creation of a substi-tute, secular, religion, were people such as Jurji Zaydan, George Antonius, Edward Atiyah. They spread their gospel all the more avidly upon the ruins of the Caliphate, and they found successors of the same ilk in Michel `Aflaq and George Habash. ("No wonder" remarks al-`Azm acid-ly, "that the Ba`th regime was an easy prey for Jewish spies like Elie Cohen.") The Christian agents were aided and abetted by other agents of dubious origin, e.g., Sati` al-Husri, said to be a Donmeh Jewish convert (an accusation usually hurled at Ataturk who had snatched from the Arabs the province of Alexandretta, availing himself of their weakness following the abolition of the Caliphate).[4]

This brew of conspiratorial explanations, guilt by association, and sus-picion toward non-Muslims is obviously designed with vituperation in mind. Nor does the deleterious impact of Arabism stop at the confines of the Middle East, where the "so-called Arab revolt" did as much as the Young Turks to bring down the Caliphate. In North Africa this "poiso-nous" ideology is supposed, for example, to have greatly helped the French colonial plan to drive a wedge between Arabs and Berbers (at the time of the Berber *Dahir* of 1930). A tool of European colonialism, Arab-ism turned after World War II into a tool of American imperialism. In a manner common to modern Islamic (and Arab) historiography, the re-corded sermons advance this argument not merely in the "objective" sense (i.e., which foreign powers did Arabism profit?) but also in a "sub-jective" one (what were the actual intentions of the pan-Arabists?). Nas-ser, they argue, was an actual ally/collaborator of the CIA, this being based upon his contacts with Miles Copeland; moreover, his secularism and vision of Egypt as leader of the Arabs had been originally shaped by Taha Husayn, "that agent of the French Deuxième Bureau" (which had even found Husayn a French wife). Arabism informed Nasser's concept (borrowed, again, from Taha Husayn) that "Islam is the sole major ob-stacle impeding the progress of our civilization." Outside Islam salvation would come. A pipedream which led straight into the 1967 debacle, much as the Arab League, creature of pan-Arabism and its British masters—

and not the Palestinians—which was responsible for the 1948 defeat and the loss of Palestine, argues *Shaykh* Tamimi (of the Islamic *Jihad*).[5]

`Ali Belhadj of the Algerian Front Islamique du Salut (FIS) uses the 1967 defeat as proof that Arabism, being a form of racism, cannot elicit a sense of community, pride, and readiness for sacrifice. Echoing Mawdudi's famous diatribe against Muhammad `Ali Jinnah's Muslim nationalism in pre-partition India, Belhadj stresses that on top of it all, this is fake racism: there is no "Arab race" in actual fact, due to centuries of intermarriage promoted by Islam's own ethos that disregards all indicators but faith. "Religious belief," cries the eloquent young *shaykh*, "is superior to the blood nexus." Only it can create the fraternal solidarity that Muslims seek today in their fight against Israel. The most conclusive proof is the Jewish-Israeli case itself: a nationalism based upon religion is viable, cohesive, and combative and can withstand many a trial.[6] In the same manner Tamimi uses post-1948 wars with Israel (up to and including the Lebanon invasion) as ample proof of the bankruptcy of "those in the Palestinian movement who set pan-Arab nationalism instead of Islam, and socialism instead of the *Qur'an*."[7]

Despite all this well-earned divine punishment, the preachers still have cause for alarm: Arabism—especially in its Ba`thi or Qawmiyyun guise—has retained some of its capacity to woo innocent youth with its self-depiction as Faith and Prophecy (*al-`uruba din wa nubuwwa*). This subversive work has dismal consequences, claims the Jordanian Ahmad Nawfal: it perpetuates division between states in the Middle East, bolsters dependence upon the United States, promotes a spirit lacking in self-reliance and readiness for struggle. Such a spirit can be generated by religion alone. During the last decade nationalism has contributed in particular to "divide the Arab-speaking countries from Iran, which, whatever its mistakes, is involved in a revolutionary endeavor to enhance the cause of Islam and certainly humiliated the arrogant U.S. in the hostage affair."[8]

Why do these speakers breathe so much fire and brimstone? Most of them are old enough to remember Nasser's persecution of the Muslim Brethren, that defining moment of contemporary Islamic radicalism. The equation Arabism = police state, is for them, albeit not necessarily for their audience, experiential and affective.[9] This is particularly true for those who suffered directly from ill-treatment during the 1965–66 wave of arrests (like the Egyptian popular preacher, *Shaykh* Kishk). But persecutions and `*uruba* are mentioned in tandem even by younger preachers (such as the Egyptian Dr. `Issam al-`Iryan, Bassam Jarrar of the HAMAS, or `Ali Belhadj). Here this identification is an integral part

of the formation myth of Sunni radicalism—a soaring drama of martyrdom, where the real-life workings of the hegemonic power structure
are laid bare, through the discourse and acts of the nation-state. It is virtually an article of faith, learned by rote, exemplified by horror stories.
Some such stories are assured prominence by the role they play in the
movement's training of cadres (including many of today's young
preachers): by reading prison memoirs of Egyptian and Syrian founding
fathers, but also by hearing many of the older generation, who came to
maturity during the heyday of Nasserism and of the Ba`th; people such
as Sa`id Hawwa who grew up in the traditional town of Hama, influ-
enced by the Naqshbandi Sufi order and by local `ulama, marginalized
by the Ba`th rise to dominance; or Rashid Ghannushi, a Tunisian student
at the University of Damascus, a fervent adept of Arabism and of the
Ba`th almost until the Six Day War.[10] This is even truer of the large
number of former inmates of Nasser's gaols (for example, `Umar al-
Tilimsani, Salah `Ashmawi) who were still around in the 1970s and in
the 1980s to tell of their horrible ordeal.[11]

But is the audience as immersed in that identification as the preachers?
This is difficult to judge. In any case the latter must assume that such
invocations are useful as a sort of long-term "inoculation" against Pan-
Arabism, which appears now in new guises and calls for "dialogue" with
radical Muslims. The new-fangled pan-Arabists tend to reassert the Islamic dimension of Pan-Arabism, the close alliance between pan-Islamist and
Arab nationalists in the 1930s and 1940s; they also take care to apologize
for the "violent deviations" of the Arab "progressive" regimes during the
1960s.[12] This is particularly relevant in Egypt, Syria, Jordan, Lebanon, and
among the Palestinians. Diatribes on the horrors of the past, usually end
up by targeting the new-style Ba`th or Nasserist circle and take frequent
gibes at the Popular Front for the Liberation of Palestine (PFLP) and the
Democratic Front for the Liberation of Palestine (DFLP), successors of the
Qawmiyyun al-`Arab.
   One has the impression the anti-Arabist tirades touch a raw nerve
among the listeners, as evidenced by the shocked cries or loud, derisive
laughter, recorded on the tapes. But such reactions recur all the more often
when the vagaries of pan-Arabism are interlaced in another context—the
behavior of oil-rich states toward their poor Middle-Eastern neighbors,
presented as proof of the delusion of the idea of Arab solidarity. This topic
gets at least as much attention as historical arguments, if not more. And
no wonder. For here we deal with an experience common to many listeners (either directly or through members of their family and social circle).
The objects of all this sound and fury are the "rich Arab" or "Arab bil-

lionaires"—terms borrowed from the language of the media and denoting either the regimes or the citizens of the Gulf emirates, Saudi Arabia (and sometimes also Libya). The adjective "Arab," in this context, is double-edged: Arab signifying desert—i.e. primitive—origin, in premodern usage and from the viewpoint of the civilized urban areas, as well as identification with the notion of an Arab *umma*. This second meaning embodies claims of solidarity with fellow ethnic group members that were dashed by Gulf greedy employers, suspicious police, stingy states, and profligate tourists who came to the poorer countries for fun and games.

"Our compatriots working in the Gulf suffer insults as Egyptians, and that despite Egypt's generous help to these countries in the field of education," recounts *Shaykh* Salah Abu Isma`il. *Shaykh* `Abd al-Hamid Kishk tells vivid stories about the way prosperous Arab visitors behave in Cairo's Pyramids Street, indulging in wine, betting, and the pursuit of easy women from amongst "our daughters." And, of course, he adds with sarcasm, these super-rich Arabs never bother to give aid to Egypt.[13] In the same vein *Shaykh* Kishk addresses the `ulama of Hijaz: "Why don't you rebuke your rulers for failing to share [Saudi] wealth with the poor lands of Dar al-Islam; with Egypt for instance, whose inhabitants live on lentils and beans alone. Why don't those rulers take the camels and sheep slaughtered during the pilgrimage, process them, and send them in cans to poor Muslims all over the world? We in Egypt had to buy a whole ship loaded with English meat cans, which was discovered upon arrival at Port Said to be rotten, because it had been slaughtered years ago. And all this in order to enable Arab [sic] merchants and middlemen to draw a hefty profit!"[14]

Ahmad al-Qattan, a Kuwaiti preacher whose cassettes are popular in Jordan and in the Occupied Territories, confirms such arguments by tales of his own about the loose manners of Gulf people in Cairo nightclubs. His series on child-rearing, though designed for a Kuwaiti audience, is widely distributed in the Middle East and can merely bolster the low esteem in which Gulf Arabs are held. He takes to task parents in Kuwait who indulge their offspring's every whim (including consumer goods that are beyond the reach of common mortals in the Middle East), who send their sons to private schools where foreign nationals, "usually atheists," teach and where they are introduced to rock music and drugs. They send their daughters to finishing schools abroad and let male members of the household have access to pornographic magazines and/or Marxist books. Smaller children are raised by Christians, usually by Philippine nannies. In another of Qattan's sermons, consecrated to corruption in Kuwait, these nannies figure as objects of licentious exploitation by their employers. This is indeed one of the major sins that account for God's wrath and retribution, namely, the Iraqi occupation of 1990–1991.[15] The present writer has seen many a Palestinian listener nod in acquiescence upon hearing these stories and make remarks that denote finding in them the justification for the listener's own lack of sympathy for Kuwait at the time of her misfortune. Qattan rebuked his own countrymen as well as the Saudis (whom he dubs "rich Arabs") for not caring at all about the fate of the Palestinians in the Occupied Territories, the Intifada itself never inspiring them into action.[16]

It is small wonder, then, that the Palestinian *Shaykh* As`ad Bayyumi al-Tamimi sniggers at the "empty-headed *a`rab* (bedouins)"—a term of opprobrium directed at the Gulf Arabs—addicted as they are to mundane pleasures and sublimely indifferent to Palestinian suffering. The discovery of oil in the Arabian Peninsula and the absorption of modern technology by the "statelets" were an omen of Allah's solicitude for His believers, yet the locals have chosen to squander the riches He had bestowed and do not deign to share them with their less fortunate neighbors.[17] During the Gulf crisis, add Bassam Jarrar and `Ali Belhadj, the Saudis and the Kuwaitis heaped humiliation upon sin by calling upon the United States, which was headed by that arch-enemy of Islam, "George Ibn Bosh," to station her troops upon the hallowed soil of Arabia and by providing the latter with logistic support.[18]

Moral dissolution and lack of solidarity alike could be expected to be given a purely Islamic spin. What could be more apt in sermons? One could, for instance, lament the fact that a kingdom created by puritan Wahhabis is now immersed in sin, or how Muslims in these wealthy lands are oblivious of the misery of Egypt, that age-old fulcrum of Dar al-Islam as well as of the occupation by Infidels of the "blessed land of Palestine," where the third most holy shrine of Islam is located. And yet, it is an *Arab* sin that virtually all preachers choose to speak of: super-rich Arabs disdain and exploit fellow Arabs; due to the indifference of Arab haves to the fate of Arab have-nots, Arab solidarity has been proven to be a chimera.

For the preachers, indeed for many a listener, the experience was lived as an encounter between fellow Arabs, not between fellow Muslims; an encounter all the more disappointing as the discourse of the 1950s and 1960s, as well as the hype of the post-1973 decade, led them to hope that Arab solidarity is a spiritual reality that just needs to be fleshed out; for instance, through preferential treatment to Arab migrant workers (in comparison to Pakistanis, let alone to non-Muslims such as Indians and Koreans). That dream has gone sour, leaving a bitter taste.

Still, the "Arab world," the "Arab *umma*," the "Arab peoples," are terms common to most taped sermons; the frontiers of Arabhood extend there,

according to the sacred formula "from the Gulf to the [Atlantic] Ocean."
Even an older generation preacher such as the octogenarian Syrian
Nasir al-Din al-Albani views Dar al-Islam as divided between an Arab
sphere and an *a`jami* (Persian, non-Arab) one; though, as could be
expected, neither he nor *Shaykh* Kishk accept this antinomy as a justification for the Iran-Iraq war, deplored as *fitna* (internecine war between
fellow Muslims).[19] The tyrannical Arab regimes are the incarnation of
all evil (a "rudderless ship," says Ahmad Nawfal). The peoples, exploited and oppressed as they are, constitute a glimmer of hope, for their religiosity is on the rise.[20]

Is this a contradiction in terms? Do the preachers, usually so attuned
to the sensibilities of the audience, fail to gauge its mood? This does not
seem to be the case. Let us note that usage of the term "`*arabi*" is limit-
ed to adjective form, it is never substantive or adverbial. The function is
merely descriptive. "Arab" signifies a cultural attribute, it does not generate solidarity or fraternity (as the term "`*arabiyyan*" could, for in-
stance). It is certainly not embedded in an integral, historical-familial
web of relationships. The solidarity claims staked out by Arab nationalism are never alluded to. They are, as some militant `*ulama* spell out,
nothing but an artificial and secular construct. The leader of the Islamic
Jihad, Fathi Shqaqi, tells—in a story the listeners confirm by assenting
interjections—of his own disillusionment when he came as a young student from Gaza to Egypt, full of admiration for "Egypt the throbbing
heart of Arabism." In Zaqaziq University he discovered that in the eyes
of his fellow students he was just a foreigner, a Palestinian. The plight of
his people was of no interest. It was only among the few Islamic-mind-
ed students that he found any real compassion. From the rest he encountered the same indifference that Egyptian preachers bemoan with regard
to the treatment of their countrymen in the Gulf states.[21]

Yet use of the term "Arab" is neither necessarily pejorative nor even
just neutral. After all, the Islamic activists, whose voices we hear in the
tapes, are people who excel in articulating the Arab language (classical
but also dialectal and, in some cases, median-journalistic); people whose
life trajectory has almost never (with rare exceptions such as `Abdallah
`Azzam) taken them to non-Arabic-speaking lands. And in that they are
no different from the bulk of their listeners. Yusuf al-`Azm is, in this
respect, quite typical: born in Ma'an (Jordan), he attended high school in
Iraq (under the monarchy) and graduated from `Ayn Shams University
in Egypt. The cassette on Arabic culture (entitled "Pens Writing in Arabic Letters but Subservient to Foreigners") records a lecture he delivered
in Yemen. During the question and answer portion of that tape, he gives
a limpid formulation of the notions discussed above: "My Arabness

refers to my linguistic identity; I'm Islamic in heart, in civilization and consciousness. It follows that I reject both the age-old barbarian-*jahili* Arabism and the secular Arabism of today."[22] Note the emotion-laden, derogatory term "*jahili*," a key concept of Sayyid Qutb, which is still very much in vogue. Arabism in the ethnic sense is, hence, anti-Islamic: this was true of the bedouin version of pre-Islamic (and early Arab conquest) times; it is likewise valid for the modern incarnation of this state of mind.

Listening to the tapes, it is important to note that the speakers are engaging in a half-improvised exercise in popularization. One could hardly expect the preachers to have the systematic and theoretical sophistication of major writers such as Anwar al-Jundi[23] in the 1970s or Rashid Ghannushi and others of his ilk today. The Tunisian Ghannushi distinguishes between two connotations of the term "Arabness": one, which he endorses, is that of a "historical-cultural reality"; the other, which he considers presumptuous, even false, is that of an ideology, a totalistic, all-embracing vision, a sort of civil religion. The former version of `uruba had created "an existential entity," anchored in culture and in politics, which served as a powerful vehicle for Islam and helped it absorb many peoples and communities living outside the Arab Peninsula by dissolving the bonds of ethnicity and race. By virtue of the inextricable relationship between the Arab language and Islam it is vain to attempt to transform Arabness artificially in to a non- (maybe anti-) religious ideology or belief system—a source of identity pretending to exclude non-Arab-speaking minorities (e.g., Kurds and Berbers). The historical-experiential sense of Arabness is a historical given that no true-blue Muslim can deny. By the same token that Muslim cannot accept the latter-day version. That version borrowed Western notions of nationalism and/or Communist ones in the manner of "Arab Socialism," and reduced (or eliminated) the role of Islam as the linchpin of identity and way of life. It manipulated Islam as a tool for mobilizing the masses or for legitimating certain policies, whether in a Western (nationalist) or Communist guise. Arabism thus served to intensify the dependency upon non-Muslim powers and cultures.[24] Even when he agreed to publish his most recent book under the auspices of the Research Center on Arab Unity (Beirut), Ghannushi did not budge one inch from these views. He extols in it Islamic solidarity as the only one available.[25] It is perhaps a sign of the times that the center, a bastion of Arab nationalism, sought out the exiled Tunisian writer to add prestige to its booklist, rather than the other way round.

The Moroccan thinker `Abd al-Salam Yasin states succinctly: "Both

the allegiance to Allah and the allegiance between His believers are dia-
metrically opposed to racial or nationalist (*qawmi*) allegiance. Nationalism is our scourge and plague, for it sows divisiveness among Muslims,
based upon a presumed ethnic affiliation. It further leads to political,
internecine fights initiated by the nationalist statelets. . . . The Prophet
himself has declared solidarities predicated upon blood and ethnicity to
be *jahili*, dregs of the past, which must be combatted and erased."[26]
Yasin's book is written in a lucid Arabic style, and the reading list for the
movement's cadres comprises a special section on Arabic language and
grammar (the entire list is made of books originally written in Arabic
with the exception of translations of Mawdudi and Nadwi).[27]

The same tune can be heard, perhaps more clearly, from that growing
breed, the former Arab nationalists and Marxists who converted to radical Islam from the late 1970s on. The Egyptian `Adil Husayn says that
his personal transformation began when he perceived how inextricably
the national identity was associated with religious affiliation. He discovered that society was made of institutions, themselves divided into sub-
units, and that the only cement holding together this intricate structure
was religion. He was particularly struck by the role Sufism played in the
lower classes, in blending the individual into minisocieties and the latter
into larger wholes. Yet instead of building upon and improving this
socioreligious structure, the state demolished it and atomized individuals, eliminating all intermediary forces between them and the state.
Bereft of civil society, the state could have no real hold over individuals—hence the 1967 debacle. After a long search for a panacea to rehabilitate civil society, hesitating between Arab and Egyptian formulas, it
dawned upon Husayn that only the glue that had held traditional civil
society together, namely, Islam, could serve to reconstruct it. The impact
of that discovery upon him was profound; at that moment (ca. 1980), all
the pieces fell into place.[28]

The Palestinian thinker Munir Shafiq came like Husayn from the
Marxist wing of Arab nationalism, but as he was a non-Muslim (Greek
Orthodox), his conversion was even more radical. He finally converted
to Islam out of admiration for Fundamentalism. Shafiq began his militant life by adopting a positive yet instrumental view of the Islamic
component of pan-Arabism, given the fact that while the Arab nationalist elite are secularist the masses are profoundly permeated by Islam; a
stance typical of other thinkers as well (e.g., Manh al-Sulh, Anwar `Abd
al-Malik) who reacted to the Iranian revolution and to the resurgence of
Islam in the Arab world. Yet Shafiq did not stop there. In the course of
the 1980s he perceived that even among the elites only Islam can actually touch human beings at the affective level and generate an authentic

solidarity. He recounts a key experience: "I once came to visit a physician friend and stayed the night at his home. I woke up at dawn and found him reciting the Qur'an, moaning, weeping loudly, his tears moistening the Holy Book. I wished I could experience such a profound belief, such humility before the transcendental." The hybrid alliance between Arab nationalism and militant Islam—which he had been preaching recently—now seemed to him illusory.[29]

Against this background it is not surprising that for these thinkers there was no return to the 1950s concepts of Arab unity as a milestone on the road to Islamic unity and Arab identity as part of an Islamic one. Arabism was laid bare: a Western import, an artificially concocted idea, an abstraction with no grounding in social reality and in collective sentiment. The divorce consummated at the time of Sayyid Qutb remained valid: *Qawmiyya* infused with Muslim values is an oxymoron.

When writers such as Shafiq use terms like "Arab-Islamic world (or community)," they do it with a hyphen between the two adjectives, namely, to denote the Arab-speaking part of an Islamic social network of believers. In that they are no different from old-timers such as *Shaykh* Muhammad al-Ghazali who used to believe, in the manner of Hasan al-Banna, in "allying Arabism and Islam" under certain conditions, but discovered their incompatibility during Nasser's brazen attempt to make Arabism into a civil religion. Today Shafiq never tires of stressing that this attempt was no accident: it brought onto the surface what had been an ever-lurking potentiality and one intimately linked with the deep seated nature of Arabism.[30]

Among major Islamic thinkers today perhaps only the Sudanese Hasan al-Turabi still advocates the cause of "concentric circles of identity," but in an attenuated version. He views Arab unity (as distinct from unity between any two Arab countries that have an Islamic regime, which Shafiq and his disciples also cherish) as a valuable stage on the road toward restoring the unity of Dar al-Islam. In that he is, in a way, no different from the Syrian Muslim Brethren in exile (perhaps also the Yemeni *Tajammu` al-Islah* militants) who speak of the "Arab arena" or "Arab countries" as virtually identical with the geopolitical term "the Middle East," with a salient linguistic-cultural factor as common denominator. Arabhood is never spelt out as a national identity.

Turabi uses a softer, less confrontational language toward Arab nationalism, both in his own writings and in the resolutions of the Arab and Islamic Popular Congress, of which he is the founder (1991) and secretary-general. The motivation seems to be to woo former or present believers in Arabism (or Arab Socialism) into the Islamic orbit. Yet when Turabi gets to marshaling solidarity for the Palestinian cause, he relies—

much like HAMAS spokesmen—upon the Islamic quality of that cause (the Blessed Land, the Third Most Holy Shrine, Muhammad's Night Journey and Ascension), not upon the Arabhood of the land. In the final analysis, only religion can generate solidarity.

In effect, in those of his writings directed at a readership from inside the Islamic resurgence, Turabi presents essentially the same concept as Ghannushi:

> The Arab-Islamic reality today consists of separate territorial states with fixed, rigid borders, governed by self-centered regimes which rely upon intermeshing special interests and local-tribal allegiances. Beyond that, there is an Arab framework, predicated upon culture, history, territorial proximity, interests and interaction. And well beyond, there is an Islamic framework, made of peoples who appertain to the community of the believers and share with the Arabs creed, beliefs, and heritage. They are animated like them with a feeling of solidarity as well as by common interests.[31]

Turabi is explicitly opposed to Arab nationalism as a secular Western import, for nationalism in Europe has developed in the era of Christianity's decline, aspiring to fill in the vacuum created by that process. Still, Turabi differs from Ghannushi in thinking that this is not an inevitable dichotomy but the product of specific circumstances of the first third of the twentieth century. One could, he assumes, win over certain circles of Arab nationalism, particularly as this movement as a whole has lost its self-confidence and many an activist has returned, in various guises and to different degrees, to the True Faith. While Turabi hopes that Arab unification may be a step toward Islamic unity, he knows that both are long-term aims, given the current state of affairs where resurgent Islam is mostly in opposition. And even when Islam takes power in an Arab country, that Muslim regime may not easily export the revolution to neighboring Arab countries and ultimately establish a union with them, as a sort of stepping-stone toward Arab-Islamic unity. For it could very well be that a neighboring non-Arab country may be a more opportune target (is he thinking of the Horn of Africa or even West Africa?). In proximate Arab states there may further be complicating factors such as the existence of non-Muslim minorities, suspicious of Islam despite the resurgence moment's protestations of commitment to tolerance.[32]

That belief in Islamic solidarity as *the* major authentic and reliable bond can be heard on the audiotapes as well. Listen to `Ali Belhadj speak, his voice choking with tears, the audience loudly crying, about the shooting by Israeli police at the esplanade of al-Aqsa. Belhadj bemoans the neglect by *Muslims* of the question of Palestine. It is the 17th Sura of the *Qur'an (al-Isra')* that he quotes in order to legitimate the obligation to succor "our persecuted brethren." In the same breath he links Jewish attacks upon Palestinian Muslims to Fundamentalist Indian massacres of Islamic believers. When Bassam Jarrar deals with the same question he praises the aid Indian Muslims gave in the 1930s and Pakistan extends today to "our cause." And he adds acidly that the "Arab rulers" wash their hands completely of any responsibility for the Palestinians' fate.[33] When Belhadj mobilized the Algerian public for Iraq during the 1990–1991 crisis he made sure to distance himself from Saddam and called "for help to Iraq as a Muslim people," whereas "the homeland we must defend is an Islamic homeland; not as a soil but as part and parcel of Dar al-Islam which is permeated by the same creed, the same Divine Law." Another Palestinian *Shaykh*, Hamid al-Bitawi, responds in kind: the same "anti-Islamic, Crusading onslaught" perpetrated in the Occupied Territories goes on in Algeria where the electoral process has been suspended, the FIS outlawed, its militants persecuted.[34] The Kuwaiti Ahmad al-Qattan, who preaches in favor of "support for the peoples of Lebanon and Palestine," refers in the case of the former country to help for isolated Muslim communities, while with regard to the latter he mocks the attempts to garner aid and solidarity "in the name of *Qawmiyya* and its hollow slogans;" it is Islamic solidarity with the people of the "land of *al-Aqsa'*" to which one should appeal; and it will inevitably elicit Islamic virtues such as forbearance (*sabr*) in times of defeat, etc.[35]

Needless to say, it is the fate of the Muslims of Bosnia that today occupies pride of place when the taped speakers harp on the theme of solidarity. Indeed Bosnia serves to illustrate, in the manner Afghanistan used to more than a decade ago, the state of an Islam besieged by the evil forces of modernity. But the tone today is shriller, perhaps due, among other reasons, to the recurrent images of Sarajevo on TV screens in the Islamic global village. Other Muslims in danger (in Burma or the Philippines) may be mentioned, but none can compete today with Bosnia, with its role as producer of a sense of a worldwide Islamic community fighting for its survival. To judge by the sermons, the listeners know what happened there in ample and vivid detail.[36]

In comparison, Arab solidarity may be pooh-poohed as an insignificant sociopsychological force, having proven (in the words of al-Qattan) "its utter futility and impotence in the face of our enemies,"[37] as was evident during the Kuwait crisis. This is not to say that the Islamic militants are complacent vis-à-vis the Arab cultural dimension. They may, on the one hand, call for the further extension of the reach of Arabic, for instance as a teaching language in the exact sciences and medicine, or in institutions of higher learning (instead of English or French).[38]

On the other hand, they worry that the growing Arab "communications common market," pushed by technological and marketing progress and facilitated by the rapid evolution of the median language, has created a powerful tool for the spread of modern, Western-infatuated, hedonistic, individualistic modes of thought. These attitudes are easily accessible by the masses through films, TV, soap operas, songs (diffused by radio and audio/video tapes), popular magazines etc. "Muslims the world over are indifferent to the death of thousands of Jihad fighters while the whole of the land of Arabism [*ard al-ʿuruba*] is in deep mourning over the death of one songstar," scoffs a Palestinian preacher.[39] Marketing Arab-language artifacts is easier now and becoming more so every day, but the contents of these products is almost to a fault un-Islamic, nay even anti-Islamic. They represent "an artistic rot" (the title of a popular audiotape series).[40] The very term *"butula,"* conferred upon so-called heroes of movies, TV series, and plays, makes them into icons that in a subliminal fashion attract tepid and none-too-sophisticated believers into the orbit of secularism and profanation. Lifestyles of rich-and-famous artists are paraded as a sort of vicarious gratification for underemployed, unemployed, badly housed youth— not merely in Egypt where this ʿafan fanni is produced—but in any other Arab country where the masses devour these artifacts (vehiculated in median Arabic). The loose mores of Egyptian and Algerian stars (sex, alcohol, drugs, family violence) are laid bare in the media for all to hear and see. And it is typical of militant Islamic spokesmen's frame of mind that they detect the hand of the regimes' security services in the performance (or marketing) of licentious songs, designed to lull disgruntled youth and lead them astray. By the same token activists see the fingerprints of a Hollywood-based, "Judeo-Masonic" conspiracy to de-Islamize the *umma* in the production of movies, soap operas, shampoo ads, based on foreign artistic themes and techniques but adapted to the cultural norms of an Arab-language public.

If in the past dangers lurking with regard to Arabic concerned literary attempts to infuse it with colloquialism and use diglossia so as to divide the Arabs, now it is the median language that constitutes the threat. As for consumption by a more educated public, Yusuf al-ʿAzm waxes nostalgic about "problematic" writers such as ʿAqqad and Taha Husayn. Whatever their faults, notably the "ivory tower syndrome," they at least wrote in a pure classical style immersed in the Islamic heritage and did not decry classical Arabic as incapable of adapting to the modern age. Now people tend to write in a debased journalistic style with few traditional

resonances. Modern Arabic poetry is even worse, for it endeavors to subvert the classical norms and ape the latest Western fashions.[41]

What is at stake is not just the peril of contamination of Muslims
through the very language that had been the vehicle of Islam. Muhammad Husayn Fadlallah and Yusuf al-`Azm concur that the Islamic resur-
gence movement has greatly contributed to this state of affairs. Preoccupied as the movement was by political and organizational tasks it never
developed a meaningful activity in the cultural sphere, in the manner
that Arab and Iranian Marxists, or Arab nationalists had done (quite successfully) for a while. With the collapse of pan-Arabism and Marxism,
the Islamic resurgence did not attempt to fill in the cultural void, by providing products such as Ahmad Sadiq al-Rafi`i's in the interwar years.
The void is being filled by market-oriented popular entertainment and,
at an upper level, by modernist (implicitly or explicitly secular) poets
and writers such as Nizar Qabbani. The battle for the hearts and minds
is on. Arabic, a dimension of that potential `uruba, which is decried by
Jarrar, is a major weapon in the hands of the secularists. Islam should be
on the alert and strike back.[42]

The dangerous world that Islamic militants live in is, however, not that
of Arabism but of nation-states; a fact becoming all the more entrenched
in the post-1989 New World Order, which preoccupies many a preacher.[43] The watani (territorial state nationalism) dimension of identity
does not seem to them alarming as such. "The notion of an Arab or Persian is illegitimate," but the watan, says `Ali Belhadj, "is legitimate, sig-
nifying as it does respect for the fatherland and its traditions and culture." Any so-called watani who does not hold his religion in awe, respects nothing else. "Look at France and England, they have a sort of
wataniyya which is irreligious and this is why they apply human rights
merely to their own nationals and within their own borders, as we Al-
gerians have learned during the years of French colonial rule. Islam, on
the contrary respects Man everywhere."[44] And it is as an Algerian and a
Muslim that one must support Afghanistan.

Belhadj is steeped in Algerian history: talking about the War of
Liberation (and its "Islamic spirit which assured us of victory"), of prewar French atrocities, the role of the Reformist Ulama Association in
preserving collective identity and paving the way for the Front de Libé-
ration Nationale (FLN). Yet the order of precedence is crystal clear. He
retorts sharply to the declaration by an Algerian Minister of the Interior, according to whom "we do not want an imported religion, we
want an Algerian Islam," implying that the neo-Hanbalite bent of the
FIS has no basis in Algerian religious tradition that accepts only the

Malikite school of Law; the FIS is alleged to hark back to Wahhabi puritanism and Saudi influence (the latter epithet being particularly derogatory). "There is no Algerian Islam," thunders Belhadj in rebuke; there may be local (*watani*) variations, and certainly attachments to one's place of birth, but Muslim cultural tradition is built upon a constant exchange of persons and ideas, intermeshing to create one whole. Neo-Hanbalism is no cause for shame: it was founded by Ibn Taymiyya and Ibn Kathir, who are respected everywhere in Dar al-Islam. Neither should one be ashamed of the connection with the Arabian Peninsula. The founders of the Ulama Association (al-`Uqbi, Brahimi, al-Milli), whom the FLN itself claims to cherish, had studied there; and as for the major figure of the Association, *Shaykh* Ben Badis, he studied not in Algeria but in the Zaytuniyya in Tunis. Claims that one should be at least Maghribi, not Middle East (*Mashriq*)-oriented are likewise scoffed at. Although Belhadj who is very learned is amply aware of the political theory of Ibn Hazm of Cordova, which goes much further than Ibn Taymiyya (for example, on the right of revolt), he relies almost exclusively on the latter medieval thinker, a Syrian.[45]

The same note can be heard among the Palestinians, another well-defined *wataniyya*. After quoting, as is the norm, Qur'anic verses on the Night Journey to Jerusalem, a *Shaykh* harangues his audience: "The land [of Palestine] that we should fight for is a mosque, neither a soil nor an orange tree."[46] And another *Shaykh* remarks that surely Palestine is a positive value, but when the battle for Palestine is not enjoined in the name of Islam, no wonder it ends up in "*khiyana wataniyya*" (national treason) at the time of the Madrid Conference. For not everything can be justified in the name of the *watan* as the present Palestinian leadership, erratic and secular, loves to do.[47]

Major Islamic thinkers draw further conclusions from these premises, which they share with the preachers. The nation-state is a fact of life, the standard unit of world politics, but one should beware, warns Turabi, of accepting its self-representation as a sort of eternal entity, coming to self-awareness in our times through the awakening of a primordial collectivity. The nation-states are after all a product of history, of the millennium of dissolution of Islamic unity and of the introduction of Western ideas. Or, as Yasin puts it, "there is one Islamic *umma* across the borders created by the *fitna* (internecine wars)."[48] One should strive to make this cultural and affective unity into a political reality first by greater coordination between militant Muslim movements, and second by avoiding the ritualization of the political unity slogan as a mere long-term goal. For this may lead to unity being discarded to oblivion, warns `Adil Husayn (a former adept of another supranational creed, Arabism).

Whenever a movement comes to power it should strive to form a union with a neighboring state (not necessarily Arab, remarks Turabi in a similar context; for it may be black African and the supranational creed may be Pan-Africanism).[49]

Still, not everyone is convinced of the feasibility of the second goal. Jamal al-Banna wonders whether the restoration of the Caliphate has not been the wrong path to follow in this century. Given its size, the Ottoman Caliphate could have survived solely through decentralization; it may be that to this extent the early paragons of Arab nationalism (*ahrar al-ʿarab*), among whom he places al-Kawakibi and Rashid Rida, were right. Their campaign was aborted when Pan-Turanian concepts prevailed with the help of the Young Turks. (The slide of Arab nationalism toward secularism thus begins only on the eve of World War I and is a reaction to external stimuli.) Given the climate of the New World Order, which is hostile to Islamic unity, the lessons of the Caliphate's fall are more poignant today than ever before. The Islamic Resurgence movement may survive only if it is deliberately organized in a pluralistic, decentralized mold; no one group (or regime, if one comes to power) may be allowed a position of hegemony—flexible collaboration and solidarity based on mutual interests should be the watchword.[50]

The challenge that Resurgent Islam presents to nation-state identity may seem less direct than the manner in which it defies pan-Arabism. Yet it remains a challenge. This is particularly true regarding the criteria for inclusion in the community. For if the sole legitimate case for *wataniyya* is Islam, local Christians may not become fully fledged members of the nation, both as *dhimmis* and as twentieth-century advocates of Western ideas. Needless to say, such a concept constitutes a head-on attack on the standards of inclusiveness, or norms of citizenship, of Arab nationalism.

Major Islamic writers proclaim adherence to notions of equality before the law and of human rights and are constructively ambiguous on the problem of making such notions compatible with the *dhimma*.[51] This is not what one hears from the preachers. Listen, for instance, to the popular Egyptian *Shaykh* Ahmad al-Mahalawi: "Before this Friday sermon, an official of the Religious Endowments Ministry came and gave me a paper containing instructions to preach on Islamic tolerance towards Ahl al-Dhimma. I protested against such dictates but I'll readily tackle the subject. Verily Islam is and has always been tolerant with regard to Dhimmis, yet on the condition that they know their place." In Egypt the Copts do not fulfill this condition and the state gives them free reign. If Egypt has anti-Coptic riots, Mahalawi goes on to say, which I do not condone but understand, this is in part due to the government's criminal negligence; has it not permitted them to build new churches, though there are more than enough of them in a country where over ninety percent of the inhabitants are Muslims; has the regime not let them parade their religious affiliation in public (e.g., crosses on car stickers and dresses), which is a sheer provocation to Muslims, nay even to store arms in churches and set up summer training camps?

The paragon of this Christian arrogance [*ghatrasa*] is Butrus Butrus Ghali, among whose other sins are the Camp David Accords and the Bosnian tragedy.[52]

For *Shaykh* Kishk such arrogance is personified by Pope Shenouda III, that "American agent," and his assertive politics. Like other preachers, Kishk delves into the past: there were no Christians among the political prisoners in 1955, 1965, 1974, and 1977, only true believers (namely the Muslim Brotherhood and its radical offshoots). Yet there were many Copts on the staff of the military prisons. When Kishk was arrested in 1965, a Coptic prison doctor mocked him: "How come you have pains in your joints if you pray?" Earlier crimes soon come to the preacher's mind: Coptic (and Syrian Christian) collaboration with imperialism, subversion of the Ottoman Empire (inter alia through Arab nationalism and missionary work), their aid to the Crusades in the twelfth and thirteenth centuries, and so on.[53]

Ultimately the Egyptian, Palestinian and Kuwaiti *Shaykhs* reach back to the original discord: Muhammad's disputation with fellow monotheists, where it is evident, according to al-Qattan, that the "Christians are in a pretty bad way, though not as bad as the Jews." To prove this point both he and the Egyptian Muhammad Hasan sort out the Qur'anic polemics against Christianity: the spuriousness of the Trinity, the Resurrection, the Second Coming. The Crucifixion is claimed to be a punishment meted out to Jesus because his disciples attributed divinity to him.[54] Hasan hastens to draw what for him is the logical conclusion: as nonbelievers but monotheists Christians are entitled to our forbearance, but should live on sufferance and pay the polltax as a sign of their second-rate position. In that he is joined by the Palestinian Tamimi: "We are not against the Christians; they will have their rights and duties according to the Pact of `Umar." The Maronites who have transgressed the pact get their retribution at the hands of Hizbullah.[55]

Or listen to another popular cassette (and TV) star, who occupies the gray zone between dyed-in-the-wool Fundamentalists and conservatives, *Shaykh* `Umar `Abd al-Kafi. In a lesson delivered in his Cairo mosque he gives a detailed *fatwa* in response to a question about when and how one should salute Coptic neighbors and fellow workers. "Never be the first to salute," he advises, "and when you do salute, just use the perfunctory *sabah al-khayr/sabah al-nur*, and not a more effusive salutation. And above all, never, never go out of your way and give them your good wishes on their holidays, especially not those related to false beliefs such as Resurrection Day." Sociability should be kept to strict minimum. In a meeting with women, he anwers in the negative a question by a student who shares a room in a dorm with a Coptic girl as to whether she can undress before her at night. Says `Abd al-Kafi: "This is *haram*, for it would be tantamount to male gaze being set upon you; it is an affront to your chastity."[56] Such pieces of advice obviously fly in face of the *wahda wataniyya* so dear to the regime's heart.

That the *wahda* is often called into question is evident in the popularity, as attested to by Cairo shopkeepers, of audios that claim to expose the "secrets of the Coptic church" (moral turpitude, conspiracies with foreign agents and missionaries), coming from the mouths of recent converts to Islam (like that Sam`an al-Sisi who has become Fu'ad al-Mahdi). And on a more strident note, the extremist *Shaykh* `Umar `Abd al-Rahman seems to have rendered licit, in a *fatwa*, the robbing of Coptic jewelers in Upper Egypt in order to finance Islamicist operations (it is a moot point whether he also legitimated the killing of "Coptic zealots"). The Fatwa Commission of HAMAS is given to like-minded preoccupation with regard to boundary setting. In spring 1994 it ruled, for instance, the Christian militants (PFLP/DFLP) killed during the Intifada may by no means be deemed *shuhada*. Their sacrifice for Palestinian nationalism is devoid of religious significance.[57]

In the everyday Islamic market of audiotapes, these theological disputes and responsa circulate widely in Sudan, Egypt, Jordan, the Occupied Territories, the Gulf, Muslim communities in Western Europe, and perhaps elsewhere. They are harbingers of the battle for cultural hegemony being waged today in the matter of collective identity—its nature, standards, history, and practical applications.

PART V

Nationalist Diffusion from the Bottom Up

Other Voices

12

The Other Arab Nationalism

Syrian/Arab Populism in Its Historical and International Contexts

James L. Gelvin

On 20 July 1920, six days after the initial French ultimatum to the Arab government of Amir Faysal and four days before French troops entered Damascus to begin their quarter-century occupation, insurrection erupted in the Syrian capital. Throughout the city, petit-bourgeois merchants, neighborhood toughs, unemployed youths, refugees from the Biqa` Valley, and recently demobilized soldiers from the regular Arab army took to the streets, while former members of the prorogued Syrian General Congress, `ulama, and political agitators denounced the government which had acceded to French demands from minbars and street corners. Popular leaders raised *sanjaqs*, distributed leaflets that warned of the conspiracies threatening the nation, and broadcast reports of atrocities committed by French soldiers stationed to the west. In the quarters of Shaghur and the Maydan, where less than two weeks before residents had disarmed and beaten military policemen who had attempted to enforce the government's despised conscription policy, the same residents now attacked a contingent of troops loyal to the "traitorous" (*kha'in*) amir who was believed to be collaborating with the enemies of the nation.[1]

When the Arab government tried to retake the streets, fighting broke out between regular army units loyal to the amir and the population. One group of insurrectionists, shouting anti-Faysal slogans, attacked the royal palace (on the roof of which the amir, anticipating rebellion, had placed machine guns) and the Damascus Citadel where arms and ammunition were stored and where, the rebels assumed, the government had interned political prisoners. According to British estimates, over one hundred Damascenes died in the clashes; Faysal himself later estimated one hundred and twenty killed and two hundred injured. During a similar revolt that broke out a day later in Aleppo, an explosion at an arms depot claimed between five and six hundred casualties.[2]

On the afternoon of 21 July, popular leaders toured the quarters of Damascus encouraging residents to assemble at Baramki Station to await transportation west to Khan Maysalun, where General Yusuf al-'Azma was organizing a stand against the invading French. At Baramki, Shaykh Kamal al-Khatib led evening prayers and, in anticipation of the coming battle, prayers for the dead. Of the seventeen hundred volunteers from one Damascus neighborhood, only seven hundred carried weapons. Many of the volunteers who had earlier resisted conscription into the army of the Arab government now departed for the front, anticipating heroic death in *"al-jihad al-watani."*[3]

Just five months after the events described above, Stephen P. Duggan of the Institute of International Education delivered an address to the American Historical Association in which he outlined the evolution of nationalism in Syria from the late nineteenth century through the first months of French occupation.[4] Duggan's lecture was structured in the form of what Hayden White and Northrop Frye have described as the "pre-generic plot-structure" of tragedy.[5] He thus began by tracing the auspicious origins and early promise of Arab nationalism (the nineteenth-century Arab literary renaissance, the appeal of "the principles of liberty, equality and fraternity under a national and representative government"), pursued his narrative through false hopes (the Syrian-Arab Congress of 1913, the Arab Revolt, the Anglo-French Declaration of November 1918, the King-Crane Commission) and trials (repression by the Committee of Union and Progress, the defensive politicization of the movement through secret societies, the *seferberlik* [the suffering endured by Syrians during the Balkan Wars] and World War I famine, the passion of the Syrian martyrs), and concluded by recounting betrayal and, ultimately, disaster (the wartime agreements, Zionism and the Balfour Declaration, British abandonment and French occupation). Duggan failed to mention the July insurrections in his remarks: since every plot-structure circumscribes and defines the array of options available to the historian—from the questions to be investigated to the selection and organization of data—Duggan could only regard the July events, if he regarded them at all, as irrelevant or anomalous. Insurrectionists who had claimed the title *"thuwwar"* (revolutionaries) subsequently became "extremists," or "the mob" to the infrequent historian who did include them in his account.

The significance of Duggan's address does not lie in its originality;

indeed, it is noteworthy precisely because it is one of the earliest examples of the predominant strategy that has been used to emplot the story of Arab nationalism from the *nahda* through the mandate period. Not only did Duggan's colleagues—historians and advocates of "the Arab cause" such as T. E. Lawrence, John de Vere Loder, Hans Kohn, Richard Coke, Elizabeth P. MacCallum, and George Antonius—also situate their accounts within the selfsame narrative structure, but after more than seventy years many contemporary historians of Arab nationalism continue to do so as well. As a result the various assumptions and inferences derived from the application of this structure—including the tendency for historians to treat the history of Arab nationalism as "intellectual" history and to look to indigenous elites as the sole originators, carriers, and disseminators of nationalism—are shared by several generations of historians.

Although the findings of intellectual historians, when applied with circumspection, have contributed to the understanding of Arab nationalist ideologies, the attempt to place Arab nationalism solely within the domain of elite politics is essentially ill-conceived. While the role played by elites in the nationalist movement cannot be dismissed, it was, notwithstanding the formidable powers attributed to "charisma" and to the efficacy of vertical mobilization, far from comprehensive. Because the capacity of nationalist elites to define and dominate the political field was ultimately circumscribed by the ability of their ideas to articulate the aspirations of the nonelite majority, histories that place nationalist politics solely within the domain of elites fail because they present only one moment of the nationalist dialectic. They omit the other moment, the domain of popular politics, the manifold attributes of which cannot entirely be ascribed to elite designs. The political movements that took place within this domain, such as those represented by the July insurrectionists, their predecessors and successors, are the subject of this essay.

THE ORIGINS AND CHARACTERISTICS OF ELITE NATIONALISM

During the nineteenth century, two interconnected phenomena induced far-reaching economic, political, and social changes within the Ottoman Empire. First, the accelerating rate of integration of the region into the periphery of the capitalist world system hastened, albeit unevenly, the integration of local marketplace economies into a broader market-economy.[6] The salience of capitalist relations and concomitant institutions thus increased for many inhabitants of the empire who now produced crops destined for regional and international markets, competed with workers overseas, sold their labor, loaned or borrowed money at usurious rates, and participated as middlemen and factors in foreign trade.[7] The expansion of capitalist relations was facilitated by the second phenomenon, the attempts made by the Ottoman government throughout the century to strengthen and rationalize central control. While the regulations promulgated in Istanbul often had desultory and even antithetic results when applied in the provinces, over the course of the late nineteenth and early twentieth centuries they enabled government on all levels to expand substantially its role in society and its control over the citizenry. Furthermore, because government policies prompted the construction of institutions that were congruent with those of Europe, they abetted the further penetration of European capital and thus the diffusion of capitalist relations throughout the empire.

The transformation of Ottoman society, particularly in the second half of the nineteenth century, affected both the role and composition of local economic and political elites. In coastal cities such as Beirut, for example, the size and economic power of the so-called Christian bourgeoisie swelled as European governments extorted favorable terms for trade and special privileges for their clients from the Ottoman government. In Damascus, Aleppo, and other cities of Syria, the status and prerogatives of those families that both derived their wealth from landed investment and fostered good relations with the central Ottoman administration in Istanbul—the so-called land-owning, bureaucratic elite—also expanded, eclipsing in status and prerogatives those families that lacked one asset or the other. Concurrently, a new social category, a "middle strata," emerged, comprised of the skilled professionals, belletrists, civil servants, and trained military officers whose skills were both made possible by and were necessary for the continued expansion of market relations and administrative apparatus.[8]

According to most historical accounts, one or more of the above categories of elites, inspired by the appeal of "the principles of liberty, equality and fraternity," by elective ties of affinity derived from common religious affiliation, education, or experience that bonded them to their European counterparts, or by an instinctive aversion to alien (Turkish, European) control, acted as the progenitor(s) of Arab nationalism, the literary/cultural revival that preceded it, or both. However, while it is unarguable that many from these social categories did align themselves with varieties of nationalism, explanations based solely on willful choice or instinctive anti-imperialism do not provide sufficient grounds for understanding why this should be so. These accounts fail to appreciate that nationalism is not fare to be selected or rejected from an ideological menu; rather, nationalism represents, in the words of Benedict Anderson, a comprehensive "cultural system," a specific framework for the organization of social relations and social reproduction, and for the diffusion and allocation of power.[9]

Because each of the above-cited elite groupings originated as the result of the expansion of peripheral capitalism and the attempt to introduce uniform institutions of governance throughout the Ottoman Empire, the specific categories and constellation of categories used by individuals within these groupings to organize their world and order their society naturally cohered with or duplicated those enjoined by the dominant culture within the métropole. These categories "sanctioned" a multiplicity of analogous ideologies—Ottomanism, Arabism, Phoenicianism, etc.—the survival and propagation of which depended on factors external to the ideologies themselves (the degree to which the ideology was institutionalized, the resources available to those who promoted the ideology, and the political environment in which competing ideologies were situated). As a result, the fundamental ideological divide within Middle Eastern society during the late nineteenth and early twentieth centuries did not separate Ottomanists from Arabists; rather, the fundamental ideological divide separated Ottomanists, Arabists, and their ilk from the remainder of society, whose transformation and integration had been less thoroughly accomplished or whose encounter with the transformation was less agreeable.

Many of the nationalist elites that were affiliated with the Arab government of Amir Faysal during the immediate post-Ottoman period themselves recognized the centrality of this cleavage. Not only did they, through discourse and ritual activity,[10] divide the Syrian population between those fit to rule (a select group of notables and a self-identified grouping drawn from the middle strata, the so-called "men of culture" [*mutanawwirun*]) and the vast majority of the population that was fit only to be ruled, but the descriptions of the Syrian future that they proffered reflected their Comteanism and technocratic pragmatism:

> [Looking into the future,] I saw . . . the people now turning their attention to the founding of schools and colleges until no village remained without an excellent primary school. I saw prosperity spreading throughout the country and railroads connecting populous villages and farms. I saw farmers using the most modern agricultural techniques, extensive trade, and flourishing industry. Damascus appeared to me to be the most advanced of cities in terms of its construction. Its streets and lanes were paved with asphalt and the Barada River was like the Seine, traversing the city from east to west. On its banks was a corniche on which towering buildings stood. I saw Aleppo: its water, brought by canals from the Euphrates, sus-

tained its gardens and parks and anointed its waterless desert. . . . Factories were founded throughout the kingdom so that the country had no need for manufactured goods from the West, but instead exported its products to China, India, and Africa. Its people grew rich, its power increased, and it moved to the forefront of advanced nations.[11]

In a similar vein, during the same period al-'Asima, the official journal of the Faysali government, and al-Kawkab, a publication initially financed by the British government to support the Arab Revolt by identifying it with Islamic reformist ideals, ran articles urging Syrian women to study and emulate their more liberated counterparts in the West. "Today, women of the East must immerse themselves in the physical and moral sciences so that they might traverse the field of life through which the pageant of enlightened nations, guided by the light of knowledge, have paraded."[12] But beneath the calls for Syrian women to devote themselves to culture and the arts, to undertake acts of charity, and to renounce frivolity and frippery in order to devote themselves to the nation ("Damascene women possess gold jewelry whose value exceeds a million lira. . . . If all this money were collected and placed in a savings account, it could be used to establish an academy"[13]) was the attempt to create a perfect facsimile of the two spheres—a public sphere dominated by men and the sphere of cultured domestic femininity—that defined idealized gender roles among the nonfeminist European bourgeoisie of the nineteenth century:

> If woman is not held back, she would be a treasure-house of knowledge and a depository of the humanities and art. Only she does not want the divine aptitude that would prepare her to be an engineer or lawyer or khatiba or journalist, but she wishes that it make her a mother and mistress of the house and nursemaid to her infants and children. Those who attempt to fill her head with various sciences and arts on the contrary fill the void in her thoughts with matters which separate her from what was created for her sake and drive her away from the execution of her natural functions.[14]

The attitudes cited above cohere with a host of others, including an advocacy of free market economics, the celebration of "self-made men" ('isamiyyun), denunciations of worker indolence and amusements ("if a city had no coffeehouses, then the idle would focus their attention on finding work"[15]) pronounced daily in speeches and disseminated through print by those nationalist elites allied with the Arab government of Amir Faysal. Because they infused their discourse with appeals to such recondite concepts as "progress" and "secularism" ("Religion belongs to God, the nation to all"), and because of the narrow range of interests their discourse represented, their ideology appeared not only to be "alien" and imitative, it also lacked resonance for nonelites more attuned to the discourse emanating from their more "authentic" adversaries within the nationalist tendency. Thus, for example, while for the *mutanawwirun* Europeanized women represented an image of a "civilized" Syria, for much of the remainder of the population they represented imported ideas, hauteur, and sycophancy to the very European powers that planned to subject Syria to division and foreign rule. As a result, women in Western dress were so frequently attacked on the streets of Damascus that authorities had to issue public statements expressly condemning the assaults. Likewise, when the Syrian General Congress attempted to extend the franchise to women and schooling to girls, the protests of popular leaders effectively immobilized the congress up until a week before the French occupation of inland Syria. Thus for much of the population of Syria, the adoption and reification of European categories of gender by nationalist intellectuals symbolically placed these intellectuals on a par with those French soldiers who were the tangible representatives of imperialism's violation of the unity and integrity of the *umma*.[16]

THE ORIGINS AND CHARACTERISTICS OF POPULAR NATIONALISM

The elites were not, of course, the only strata to be affected by the transformation of Ottoman society. Over the course of the nineteenth century, particularly after the onset of the Great Depression of 1873, nonelites within the empire who increasingly found themselves at the mercy of market and state vented their rage by undertaking acts of resistance that ranged from draft evasion and emigration to open rebellion. Strikes for higher wages were common among Damascene journeymen weavers who were threatened not only by a decline in real wages but also by the weakening of guilds and guild-sponsored welfare programs, proletarianization, and unemployment or employment in sweatshops. In the Hawran, the grain-producing region of Syria south of Damascus, the decade of the 1890s brought increased taxation and more efficient tax collection, a severely depressed international market for wheat, and the restructuring of land tenure and the renegotiation of cultivation rights. As a result peasants abandoned their harvests, withheld taxes, and even fought pitched battles with Ottoman troops that had been deployed into the region to quell the disturbances—in one case inflicting more than six hundred casualties.[17]

Strikes, tax revolts, and the wholesale abandonment of villages are examples of what Charles Tilly calls "reactive collective actions." Undertaken to defend a traditional social order or moral economy, these acts of resistance lack both the political program and organizational structure that would enable participants to maintain large-scale, long-term mobilization.[18] But the very factors that provoked the reactive collective actions in Syria also presaged the appearance of conditions necessary for programmatic and complex mobilization. The expanding influence of the "merchants and statemakers" and the incipient diffusion of the policies with which they were associated contributed to the breakdown of the parochialism and verticality that, according to most historians, had previously characterized the predominant pattern of political and social relations in the Middle East. Simultaneously, the weakening and/or dissolution of customary bonds of patronage and consanguinity, brought about by, for example, increased physical mobility and the aforementioned status revolution, facilitated the emergence among Syrians of horizontal and associational ties that, particularly during periods of crisis, came to rival, subsume, and even replace the narrower vertical ties that were incompatible with the transformed social and economic landscape.[19]

Urban areas in which vertical ties of patronage were particularly weak or absent as a result of immigration and/or rapid growth often served as epicenters for sustained political mobilization. For example, because the Maydan quarter of Damascus increasingly assumed the role of entrepôt for grain and immigrants from the Hawran during the late nineteenth and early twentieth centuries, the quarter contained a large population of newcomers and transients whose connections with the rural hinterland from which they came frequently superseded those within their new urban environment. As a result, during the months preceding the French invasion of inland Syria, Maydanis provided reliable, and often enthusiastic, support for organizations that pioneered unmediated and horizontal forms of political mobilization. In addition, Maydani volunteers, trained and equipped in Damascus, joined guerrilla bands, such as the Druze-led units operating in the areas of Rashaya and Hasbaya and a squadron of cavalry led by Mahmud Fa'ur in the Golan, raised to harass the French army occupying the Syrian littoral.[20] The Maydan, designated a "faubourg révolutionnaire" by French diplomats, continued its anti-French resistance after most other quarters of Damascus had been "pacified," and residents of the quarter also played a prominent role in the 1925 Great Revolt.[21]

The Maydan was not unique: the demographic expansion and economic development of Palestinian cities during the interwar period generated similar political effects. The increased demand for wage labor fostered by, for example, British-directed infrastructural projects such as the enlargement of the port of Haifa, acting in conjunction with an international agricultural depression and local factors (peasant indebtedness, Zionist land purchases, policies of regressive taxation), encouraged both the seasonal and permanent migration of peasants into cities and broadened the interdependence between rural and urban economies. As the needs and concerns of migrants transcended and/or overtaxed the capabilities of the local notable-dominated economy, the newcomers forged new bonds through labor and political associations, the structure and function of which corresponded more closely to the contemporary urban milieu than could the politics of notables. The combination of these associations with the porous boundaries linking city and countryside ensured the existence of conditions requisite to promote and support the 1936–1939 Palestine Great Revolt.[22]

Thus by the first decades of the twentieth century a social and economic framework that would permit sustained and proactive political mobilization was in place throughout much of Syria. During the nine months that preceded the July insurrection described above, for example—a period of economic chaos and political uncertainty—the Arab government increasingly lost control of the streets of urban Syria and much of the countryside to popularly elected councils, such as the Higher National Committee and its quarter-based branches and on local committees of national defense dispersed throughout Syria.[23] These committees, comprised of a variety of social classes ranging from wealthy but disempowered grain factors to lower- and middle-class merchants, `ulama, and artisans, organized their constituents to challenge both imperialist designs and the policies and institutions of the Arab government. Furthermore, by linking local, regional, and national councils together within a comprehensive structure, these organizations were able to assume primary responsibility for a variety of tasks that had previously been entrusted to the state or state-connected notables: they mustered volunteer militias to provide internal security and national defense, ran guns, collected taxes, licensed monopolies, dispensed poor relief and refugee assistance, guaranteed a "fair price" for grain, and so on. An analogous mobilization took place in Palestine almost two decades later when, during the aforementioned Palestine Great Revolt, locally based "national committees," "nourishment and supply committees," and peasant bands wrested control of similar functions from the hands of the state and the traditional notability.[24]

The new structural realities that Syrians encountered, mediated through the affective horizontal bonds that united them into a political community, not only catalyzed the entrance of previously passive or

excluded nonelites into public life but also informed the content of popular ideology. In the immediate post-Ottoman period, for example, the
attempt made by the Arab government and its extragovernmental allies
to disseminate slogans that included the call for "complete Arab independence"—a phrase derived from the 1915 Damascus Protocol drawn
up by members of secret nationalist societies—fell flat; it was soon supplanted in leaflets, graffiti, and chants in planned and spontaneous demonstrations by slogans advocating the more popular "complete independence for Syria within its natural boundaries." While the Syrian/Hijazi/
Iraqi confederation promoted by pro-Arab government nationalist elites
appeared artificial and abstract to most Syrians, "Syria within its natural boundaries" connoted the community whose borders coincided with
and lent meaning to the furthest extent of regional market relations and
informal migratory circuits.[25]

Popular ideology was not just a byproduct of social transformation,
however. By affirming and articulating the horizontal bonds that linked
otherwise uprooted or anomic individuals with a wider community—
what anthropologist Victor Turner calls the "undifferentiated, equalitar-
ian, direct, nonrational" bond of "communitas"[26]—the ideology disseminated through popular committees in 1919–1920 was integral to the
process of communal reconstruction.

Within popular nationalist discourse Syria was not merely the sum
total of semiautonomous communities and vertically organized fief-
doms situated within internationally agreed-upon borders; Syria was an
historically determined and integrated entity rooted in the soil that "has
soaked up the blood of our grandfathers and fathers." Syrians were family, and just as a family is composed of interdependent members united
by ties of kinship, Syria was composed of interdependent individuals and
associations united by ties of mutual obligation. "Thus," wrote one activist, "I encourage people of good will of every quarter to form associations whose purpose is the collection of tithes from the rich to transfer
to the poor, and for all endeavors aimed at creating harmony among the
individuals of the nation."[27]

The organic notion of Syria held by popular leaders and their constituents governed their attitude toward the nature of state and its proper relation with civil society. While in the eyes of many the Arab government lacked legitimacy for a number of reasons—the prominent role
played by "foreigners," particularly "barbaric" Hijazis;[28] the incompe-
tence of its economic policies that failed to curtail a devastating inflation;
its seemingly sycophantic and overly conciliatory foreign policy—the
"language of dissociation"[29] used by many affiliated with the government to divide the ruling elite from their charges, a language that re-

flected the dominance of an imperious state over civil society, affirmed a cleavage that appeared particularly unnatural and provocative.

Because for these Syrians the state was but "a shadow of the nation,"[30] the state could not be the engine of national reconstruction but would, instead, be the product of national reconstruction. As described in the charter of the Higher National Committee,

> Public action for the nation cannot succeed if the individuals of the nation are not prepared for it. The requirement [for public action] is mutual assistance, which is necessary to foster it. These were the circumstances underlying the creation of patriotic formations in the capital of Syria. The need for them was felt in homes of every neighborhood and in the heart of every individual. Thus, the people rushed to realize this undertaking on every front, and the people of [each] district did their part independently, compelled by patriotic duty. This glorious creation, which was given the name the Higher National Committee and its branches, arose from the totality of their labors.

In return, the committees would effect "the transformation of the entire nation into a single powerful bloc which feels one feeling and strives for one powerful interest."[31]

Thus, it is apparent that, although fueled in part by sentiments of anti-imperialism and anti-Zionism, the mobilization of Syrians in 1919–1920 and of Palestinians during the 1936–1939 Great Revolt were not merely reactive or oppositional. Rather, both movements served as moments in a process through which a significant portion of the population of the Fertile Crescent, facing a crisis the seriousness of which rendered conventional structures of authority ill-suited or ill-prepared, both reconceptualized their community and undertook its reconstitution.

Interestingly, these movements were, to borrow a phrase from Angus Stewart, strangely "Janus-faced."[32] On the one hand, participants selectively repudiated Eurogenic and modernist conceits that often underlay the nationalism of their social betters: they reaffirmed their commitment to "traditional" values, rejected market-based relations in favor of a return to economic paternalism, and drew their inspiration for their egalitarian future from a mythologized past. On the other hand, the traditionalizing discourse used in both movements masked, as it commonly does in modern social movements, their truly innovative character. Although the discourse that accompanied both movements extracted symbols from popular religion and folklore ("Muhammad the Arab calls you to sacrifice your lives and money to save your country. . . . Follow the examples of Ibn al-Walid, Tariq, `Uqba, Ibn al-`As and Ibn al-Khattab"[33]), radically different circumstances imbued them with new meaning and, in the process, transformed them into nationalist symbols. At the same time unprecedented consensual political and social institutions temporarily dominated and redefined public life, impressed into service those who had previously been disenfranchised, and reconstituted these political neophytes as the subjects of political action and the architects of "popular will." While the combination of traditional and nontraditional elements within a social/political movement is hardly exceptional, their presence provides the clue for rethinking popular nationalism in the Middle East and for resituating popular movements in their historical and international contexts.

THE NATURE OF POPULISM

Although in the past historians of the Middle East have commonly presented Arab nationalism as a phenomenon sui generis that reflects, for example, presumptive cultural or historical processes unique to the region, it is difficult not to be struck by the similarity between the popular movements described above and the "populism" generated in other regions of the world that experienced comparable rapid and unsettling transformation as a result of the spread of capitalist relations and the consolidation of modern state institutions. For example, Paul W. Drake describes the circumstances that preceded the emergence of populism in Chile and Argentina in the following familiar manner:

> It appears that the failure and dislocations of tardy and dependent capitalist development, rather than its absence, tended to produce populism. Stimulated by the growth of the export economy in the latter decades of the nineteenth century, urban modernization began gathering the necessary mobilizable mass and socioeconomic issues for populism to take hold in the opening decades of the twentieth century. Urbanization outstripped industrialization. Fluctuations in the international economy caused disruptions in local production and state finances which helped spawn populist movements. When raw material-producing economies were jolted by market forces beyond local control, openings appeared for mass mobilization against traditional upper-class, laissez-faire policies. . . . In this sense, populism constituted a reaction against expanding and unstable capitalism.[34]

Similarly, Ernesto Laclau's explanation for the ideological content and discursive form of populist ideology in Latin America parallels the arguments made above. According to Laclau, the popular movement in Argentina rejected the alien ideology of liberalism common among the local landowning oligarchy and instead adopted a discourse that was distinctively "populist" in both form and content for four reasons. First, because liberalism advanced the interests of the dominant classes at the expense of the majority of the population, and because implementation of liberal policies was thus impossible without repression, liberalism was incompatible with popular democratic aspirations. Second, liberalism presented "economic development" as a positive value even though this clashed with the experience of most Argentineans. Third, liberalism was associated with "Europeanism" and a correlated distinction between the "civilization" of Europe with the "backwardness, obscurantism and stagnation" of indigenous culture. Finally, those who advocated political liberalism—which, in this context, connoted political contestation among elites who backed their claims by mobilizing their dependents—treated the new stratum of national leadership whose expanding base of power resided in nonclientalist forms of political organization as pariahs. Laclau sums up his findings in the following manner:

> These four ideological elements, of which liberalism was the articulating principle, constituted the system of coordinates defining the ideological domain of oligarchic hegemony. Positivism was the philosophical influence which systematised these distinct elements into a homogeneous whole. Popular ideologies . . . exhibited the opposite features. It was therefore natural for popular resistance to be expressed in anti-liberal ideologies; for it to be nationalist and anti-European; for it to defend popular traditions against the corrosive effects of capitalist expansion; for it to be, therefore, *personalist* and to lend support to popular leaders who represented a politics hostile to the status quo.[35]

While the term "populism" has begun to appear with increasing frequency in the works of Middle Eastern specialists to describe movements that range from nineteenth-century peasant revolts in Syria to the 1979 Iranian Revolution, authors who have used it have tended to regard its meaning as self-evident. This lack of rigor reflects the ambiguity and contentiousness attached to the term as it has been applied in the broader literature. Although "populism" has been part of the standard social science vocabulary since the mid-1950s (historians had previously used the term to denote two specific phenomenological referents—the Populist movement of the 1890s in the United States and the *Narodniki* in Russia)[36]—social scientists have yet to reach a consensus on a number of fundamental issues, such as whether populism refers to a movement or an ideology; whether it is imposed from the top down as the result of elite manipulation or emerges naturally as the logical consequence of social disruption; whether it is multiclass or fundamentally anti-class; whether its place of origin is urban or rural; and even whether the term is a useful construct or whether, in the words of one critic, "It is, to adapt Thurber, a naive little concept, but we ought not to be too amused by its presumption."[37]

That which renders the formulation of an ideal-typical populism difficult is the extraordinary diversity of phenomena—ranging from the previously cited *Narodniki* to H. Ross Perot's presidential campaign—commonly labeled "populist" by participants and outside observers. Nevertheless the literature is replete with attempts to construct a comprehensive definition. For example, both Ernesto Laclau and Margaret Canovan, among others, suggest that the only thread uniting populist phenomena is a commonality of rhetorical themes.[38] Thus, borrowing the notion of "interpellation"—the means by which an individual or group becomes both subject and object of an ideology—from Louis Althusser, Laclau maintains that populism "consists in the presentation of popular-democratic interpellations as a synthetic-antagonistic complex with respect to the dominant ideology." To put it more simply, for Laclau populist discourse differs from, for example, Marxist discourse in that it not only declaims from the standpoint and in the name of "the people," but that, instead of class conflict it presents (or as Laclau would describe it, it "mystifies") the struggle between "the people" and the "ruling bloc" as the fundamental objective contradiction that divides society.

Using the work of Laclau and others as a starting point, it is possible to obtain an even more practicable and precise definition by regarding populism not merely as a type of discourse but rather as a type of community of discourse. Participants in this community not only share a common discursive field—the "space" that encompasses, arranges, integrates, and thereby shapes the meanings to be derived from the community's preeminent and collectively held symbols (such as the "people"/"ruling bloc" antinomy, correctly described by Laclau as the distinguishing polarity within populist discourse)—they also share institutions that, because they are imbued with socially constitutive meaning by the discursive field, both validate and make substantial the proper ordering of society as apprehended by community members. The institutionalization of the discursive field also assures the autonomy of the community of discourse.[39] Thus populism combines attributes associated with both an ideology and a politico-social movement. The fact that the institutions that support populist mobilizations—labor unions, agricultural cooperatives, political parties, popular committees, etc., acting singly or in combination—vary widely, depending on the specific political and social environment in which each movement arises, is, undoubtedly, the reason why observers such as Laclau and Canovan have dismissed their importance and have, as a result, formulated an idealized version of populism.

It is therefore not merely a coincidence of rhetorical flourishes that unites the Peronist *"descamisados"* (shirtless ones) of Argentina with the *"mankubun"* (wretched ones) and *"mushaghibun"* (agitators) of Faysali Syria in their common struggle against the *"vendepatria"*/*"al-dassasun alladhina ba`u watanahum kal-bida`a"* ("traitors who sell their nation like merchandise"). The populist insurgency in Argentina and Syria, along with American populism of the late-nineteenth century and the Palestine Great Revolt, all might be seen as a process by which a population or a segment of a population that has undergone or perceives itself as having undergone economic, social, and/or political peripheralization not only re-conceptualizes itself but also reconstitutes itself as "the nation" in opposition to the politically dominant "anti-nation."

In other words, populism arises as a political response to a societal disjuncture, such as that prompted by the rapid and uneven spread of capitalist relations described by Drake. Not only does the variable scope and timing of social transformation cleave society into dissimilar and competing segments, it generates a new political bloc from among the disaffected and excluded. Typically, this bloc includes so-called "declining elites" (such as those `ulama who, increasingly excluded from power in late Ottoman and post-Ottoman society, played a particularly important role in Syrian populism) who experience what T. S. di Tella calls "status incongruence" as the result of the divergence between their expectations for and the reality of their position in society,[40] as well as nonelites who are commonly mobilized for, but not integrated into national political life. Although these groups have not been at the vanguard or the chief beneficiaries of social change—they have, in the words of one observer, been *"exposed to* but not necessarily *part of* social change"[41]—they are able to take advantage of modern forms of mobilization in their attempt to recover an (imagined) *gemeinschaftlich* political community in which class differences are temporarily subsumed to a single unifying principle—the demand for a "just" (i.e., inclusive) and harmonious social order.

THE SIGNIFICANCE OF A POPULIST FRAMEWORK FOR THE MIDDLE EAST

Almost ninety years ago Rosa Luxemburg polemicized against the leadership of the German trade union movement that, having watched the Russian Revolution of 1905 from the sidelines, concluded that mass strikes were like a pocketknife "which can be kept in the pocket clasped 'ready for any emergency,' and according to decision, can be unclasped and used."[42] For Luxemburg the mass strike was not a tactic that could be employed or deferred at will; instead, the mass strike was an "historical phenomenon" that both resulted from and catalyzed further the specific form of social relations realized under capitalism. Thus, Luxemburg predicted, regardless of the activity of union leaders, mass strikes would not only continue to erupt in Russia, but would erupt at an accelerating rate.

While, in the light of subsequent history, many of the assumptions contained in Luxemburg's pamphlet can easily be dismissed, she does provide a paradigm and raise questions that might be usefully adapted and employed in the study of populism. In particular, her understanding that mass strikes serve as a catalyst for social transformation, and her underlying assumption that, during periods in which "traditional" patterns of social relations devolve, a wide and seemingly contradictory variety of such relations coexist, may explain not only the continued importance of elites within the nationalist movement even in the aftermath of populist insurrection, but their ultimate displacement as well.

One of the reasons it has been easy for historians to overlook populism in Syria in 1919–1920 and in Palestine during the 1936–1939 Great Revolt was the continued existence of vertical ties side-by-side with the newly emergent horizontal political and associational ties. For example, although in the former mobilization populist committees pioneered new forms of political organization, they simultaneously took advantage of preestablished family and patron/client ties where those bonds were still effectual and when the use of such ties proved practical, such as for the induction of tribal and village-based contingents into service of the Higher National Committee and the committees of national defense.

Even in the aftermath of populist uprisings, nationalist elites were able to reassert their authority within the nationalist tendency for a variety of reasons. First, French and British authorities violently suppressed any movement that displayed the characteristics of populist nationalism in their respective mandated territories. Immediately after the French army entered Damascus in July 1920, for example, French authorities forcibly disbanded the populist organizations and sentenced the most important populist leaders to death. Similarly, the British deployed twenty thousand troops to Palestine during the Great Revolt, imposed collective punishments on villages suspected of harboring "terrorists," and organized commando-style Special Night Squads and "peace bands" from among their Zionist and Arab allies.[43] Second, nationalist elites not only continued to enjoy sufficient social prestige to attract the spontaneous consent of nonelites but, because of their control of the machinery of local governance and networks of communication, for example, they often possessed formidable powers for the inculcation of values, mobilization, and/or coercion. Finally, nationalist elites possessed unique capabilities that made them indispensable for the success of any nationalist under-taking. While populist leaders assumed uncompromising, nonnegotiable positions that, while congruent with their fundamentally apocalyptic view of politics, were invariably doomed to failure when pitted against the superior resources of the imperialist powers, the position of the na-tionalist elites atop society, combined with their Westernized *Weltan-schauung*, afforded them the opportunity to mediate between the stric-tures imposed by the international community and the indigenous pop-ulation. In other words, only nationalist elites, not populist leaders, were capable of translating the established principles of a world divided into nation-states into local vernaculars.

Nevertheless the position of the nationalist elites within the nation-alist tendency was not without its ironies. Although the local notables who provided a significant segment of the nonpopulist nationalist lead-ership in Syria, Lebanon, and Palestine frequently participated in and/or guided the nationalist movement for a variety of reasons, including a desire to retain their status among the increasingly politicized nonelites and to ensure the dominance of a nationalist program that promoted anti-imperialism while frustrating radical forms of interest representa-tion, the horizontal nature of the national bonds they were obliged to promote ultimately served to undermine their privileged social and po-litical positions. This contradiction inexorably led to the shackling or eradication of this stratum by a new generation of nationalist leaders in the decades following World War II.

While the domain of nonelites was thus not the only, or even, at times, the predominant moment in the nationalist dialectic, situating the 1919–1920 popular mobilization in Syria, the 1936–1939 Great Revolt in Pales-tine, and, perhaps, other post–World War I Middle Eastern politicosocial movements that, at least cursorily, display similar characteristics within the populist framework remains significant for a number of reasons: To begin with, the existence of populist movements in the initial decades of the twentieth century not only demonstrates the early emergence and resiliency of the expansive horizontal bonds upon which popular Arab nationalism was built, it also calls into question the assumption, common in elite historiography, that maintains that nationalism, the product of a small clique of military officers, professional agitators, and salon habi-tués, was thrust on a recumbent population with "revolutionary abrupt-ness"[44] sometime during the Mandate period. Furthermore, both the fac-tors responsible for the populist movements cited above—uneven devel-opment, rapid urbanization, mobilization without integration—and the attributes that defined these movements—the focus on economic justice and political inclusion, the problem of communal reconstruction—were

responsible for and defined other seemingly disparate political phenomena that have occurred since the early twentieth century, such as the
nationalism-cum-etatism of midcentury military regimes and contemporary Islamicist movements. Although commonly dissociated from each
other on the basis of their distinct symbolic languages—a practice that
has rendered the population of the Middle East capricious, to say the
least—their coherence becomes apparent when they are incorporated
within the common framework of populism. Finally, the reemplotment
of Arab nationalism serves both to contextualize and recenter the study
of nationalism in the region by providing a paradigm for comparative
studies and by endowing nonelites with the capability of acting as subjects of their own history.

13

Arab Workers and Arab Nationalism in Palestine

A View from Below

Zachary Lockman

On a hot July day in 1932, the one hundred and fifty construction workers employed by the contractor `Aziz Khayyat on the northern outskirts
of Haifa, in British-ruled Palestine, decided that they had had enough.
These workers, nearly all of them Palestinian Arabs, were part of the
large workforce engaged in developing the Iraq Petroleum Company's
oil dock, storage facilities, and related structures in Haifa's burgeoning
industrial zone, where crude petroleum from the oilfields of northern
Iraq was to be pumped onto tankers, and in building the Customs Office
nearby, intended to service Haifa's new deep-water harbor, which would
open the following year. British administrators regarded the petroleum
installation and the new harbor as central to their plans for the economic
development of Palestine, which Britain had controlled since the end of
the First World War under a "Mandate" from the League of Nations—
in fact a thinly veiled form of colonial rule.

Khayyat's workers spent twelve and a half hours a day on the job,
including an hour off for lunch, and they were no longer willing to put
up with such a long working day, especially onerous in the hot summer.
Not a few of these workers had some familiarity with, or even direct
experience of, trade unionism. For example, some of the forty stonecutters employed by Khayyat were members or former members of the
Palestinian Arab Workers' Society (PAWS), Palestine's oldest and largest
organization of Arab workers, and so their first move was to turn to it for
advice and support. PAWS had been founded in 1925 by a group of Arab
railway workers, some of whom had briefly joined the (until then exclu-

sively Jewish) Union of Railway, Postal and Telegraph Workers, only to quit a few months later after reaching the conclusion that their Jewish colleagues put their Zionist commitments ahead of their commitment to a joint union that would encompass all the railway workers, Arabs and Jews.[1] The leaders of the PAWS aspired to build an influential country-wide organization, an Arab counterpart to the Histadrut, the "General Organization of Hebrew Workers in the Land of Israel," which had been founded in 1920 and had become a powerful force in the Jewish community in Palestine and the Zionist movement. But they had so far been unable to realize their vision, so that in the early 1930s the core of the PAWS' membership still consisted of Haifa-area railway workers, around whom a fluctuating periphery of workers drawn from a variety of trades gravitated, including some of the stonecutters employed by Khayyat.

On the advice of the PAWS, the stonecutters' leaders told Khayyat that they would henceforth work no more than eight hours a day. Khayyat replied that he had no work for anyone unwilling to accept a twelve and a half hour working day, to which the stonecutters responded by declaring a strike and walking off their jobs. They did not, however, post pickets and try to stop work at the site; instead they simply found new jobs elsewhere. Khayyat was easily able to replace the stonecutters who quit, leaving the issue unresolved and the rest of Khayyat's employees still dissatisfied. The PAWS, whose leadership tended to be cautious, failed to take any further action, suggesting only that the remaining workers at the site hand over membership dues and join up.

The scaffold erectors now took up the demand first raised by the stonecutters. They organized a meeting at which they announced that they too wanted an eight-hour day and elected one of their number, a man named Jurji, as their representative. But when Khayyat fired Jurji and threatened the rest of them with dismissal, they backed down. It was at this point that the scaffold workers accepted the advice of the one Jew among them, a Histadrut member, to seek the help of the Haifa Workers' Council, the local organ of the Histadrut.

Abba Hushi, the abrasive and dictatorial but energetic Council secretary who envisioned himself as the labor boss of Haifa, a city that was well on its way to becoming Palestine's main industrial center and seaport, had for years been pressing the Histadrut leadership in Tel Aviv to devote greater resources to developing contacts with Arab workers and organizing them under its tutelage. Hushi was convinced that this would serve the goals of Zionism, by "insulating" Arab workers from Palestinian Arab nationalism and facilitating the Histadrut's struggle to secure more jobs for Jews, often through displacement of Arab workers. Earlier in 1932 Hushi and his colleagues had organized a union of Arab port workers in Haifa, which became the first component of the Histadrut's new organization for Arab workers, known in English as the Palestine Labor League (PLL), in Hebrew as *Brit Po `alei Eretz Yisra'el,* and in Arabic as *Ittihad `Ummal Filastin.* Now Hushi hoped to bring `Aziz Khayyat's employees into the Histadrut's embrace as well.

Hushi told the Arab workers who came to see him that the stonecutters, the PAWS, and the scaffold workers had gone about things all wrong: one could not go on strike without proper preparations, and if one did launch a strike one didn't just find another job somewhere else. After this scolding—quite characteristic of both the man and his movement—Hushi offered to instruct their one Jewish coworker to approach Khayyat and threaten a strike if Jurji was not rehired. Hushi also asked the workers to contact the PAWS and convey the Haifa Workers' Council's desire for cooperation. Three days later the Arab workers' delegation returned and told Hushi that the PAWS leaders had rejected cooperation with the Histadrut, because the latter was a "Zionist organization which wants a strike so that it can remove the Arab workers from this workplace in order to replace them with Jews, just as [according to the secretary of the PAWS] the Histadrut had done after the lightermen's strike at the port of Haifa." (The lightermen handled the boats—"lighters"—which carried cargo between the quays of the old port of Haifa and the ocean-going vessels anchored offshore.)

This accusation was not ungrounded: the Histadrut was indeed a Zionist organization and was moreover strongly committed to achieving what it termed "Hebrew labor," i.e, exclusively Jewish employment in all Jewish-owned enterprises in Palestine as well as maximal Jewish employment in every sector of the country's economy, a goal that certainly entailed displacing Arab workers. But Hushi brought an Arab lighterman who belonged to the PLL to a meeting with `Aziz Khayyat's workers in order to refute the PAWS' accusation, and the refusal of the PAWS to cooperate with the Histadrut made the latter look reasonable.

However, the Histadrut was unable to take advantage of these circumstances in order to develop its relations with these Arab construction workers and try to recruit them into the PLL. For just as these workers had contacted both the PAWS and the Histadrut to achieve their ends, they had also appealed for help to the District Commissioner, the British colonial official responsible for overseeing local administration. The District Commissioner rejected the workers' demand for an eight-hour day, insisting that Palestine was not like England or other European countries where such a demand might be plausible, but he did secure the agreement of Khayyat and other contractors to reduce the working day by one hour, to eleven and a half hours. Some of the building workers favored accepting this proposal, while others rejected it as inadequate. We do not know for sure how things ultimately turned out, but because there is no further evidence of unrest among this particular group of workers it seems likely that most if not all of them ultimately accepted Khayyat's offer or quietly found jobs elsewhere.[2]

For my purposes here the actual outcome of this episode is in any case not crucial. I tell this story in order to introduce several arguments about how historians and others have portrayed the origins and development of Palestinian Arab nationalism during the Mandate period. First, most studies of this particular nationalism have approached it from above, by examining what various members of the educated Arab upper and middle classes in late Ottoman and then Mandatory Palestine wrote, said, and did. This is true not only of most Palestinian and other Arab scholars but also of Israeli scholars such as Yehoshua Porath, as well as of most foreign scholars. In contrast, the ways in which members of the great peasant majority of the Arab population of Palestine, and of the growing urban working class (many of them dispossessed peasants who had migrated from the countryside), gradually came to see themselves as belonging to a distinct people that was both Arab and Palestinian (and other things besides); how this (always complex) new form of identity was related to older conceptions of kinship, village and regional ties, religion, and links with regions now outside the boundaries of Palestine; the contention over the meaning(s) of nationalism and over the symbols through which it would be expressed—these dimensions of the development of this nationalism have received relatively little attention.[3]

Second, I would suggest that this focus on elites is partially rooted in, and has tended to reinforce, a view of Palestinian Arab nationalism (and Arab nationalism in general) as monolithic, as a single and distinct object with an essential meaning. This is true not just of Palestinian and other Arab nationalist ideologists and activists themselves who, like all nationalists, have an obvious interest in portraying their nationhood as an essential identity with ancient roots that was "recovered" in the modern era, rather than something that was constructed relatively recently out of materials old and new. It is also unfortunately true of many scholars of Palestinian nationalism, and of other forms and offshoots of Arab nationalism in general. The elitist, idealist, and essentialist assumptions that inform much of the literature on Arab nationalism have served (as James Gelvin has nicely put it) to give that nationalism "a homogeneity and coherence in retrospect that it never achieved in actuality."[4]

The episode I have just related may serve to illustrate how (various conceptions of) Palestinian Arab identity, and the actions that flowed from embrace of those conceptions, have been construed in ways that tend to make complexity, contestation, and constructedness disappear. There is little room in conventional narratives of Palestinian Arab nationalism for such an episode, not only because it concerns impoverished and nonliterate workers rather than educated middle- or upper-class people but also because it shows them doing something that seems a departure from the official nationalist line, i.e., seeking assistance from an obviously Zionist labor organization in the hope of improving their lives. Yet when we take a close look at the historical record, and especially at segments of it that involve the lower classes and have largely been ignored, we often find that things are more complicated, messier, and more contradictory than one might think from most of the scholarship, and especially that portion of it embedded (consciously or not) within a nationalist paradigm.

We find, for example, that it was possible for Arab workers who were certainly not unaware of the Histadrut's Zionist priorities to nonetheless deem it expedient to seek its help in their unequal struggle with their Arab employer, just as they also sought the assistance of colonial officials as well as the PAWS, a wholly Arab labor organization openly aligned with the national movement. From within an Arab nationalist framework, such actions could only be understood as the outcome of these workers' ignorance—they were "duped" into cooperation with Zionists because they lacked an adequate grasp of their authentic national identity and proper knowledge of the truth about the Zionist threat—or of bribery, or (at worst) of perfidy, of willful, traitorous collaboration. Similarly, from within a Zionist framework, Jews in Palestine or elsewhere who expressed sympathy with Palestinian Arab grievances and support for Palestinian Arab rights were defined as either sadly ignorant of the self-evident correctness of Zionism or as pathological "self-haters" who had betrayed their own "authentic" (i.e., nationalist) Jewish selves. This is not to suggest moral or any other kind of symmetry between Zionism and Palestinian nationalism; it is simply to point to a certain paradigm, a certain system of categorization, that is characteristic of nationalist discourse.

It is certainly true that some Arab workers in Palestine did not immediately grasp the full import of the Zionist project for the fate of the country's Arab majority, and, as I have documented elsewhere, left-wing Zionists had self-interested (if also complex and even contradictory) motives in their dealings with Arab workers and were not above misleading them about their true aims and affiliations.[5] Yet it will not do to accept uncritically the (bourgeois nationalist) portrayal of the actions of these workers as deviant—meaning deviant in relation to some (bourgeois nationalist) norm—or to attribute that purported deviance to ignorance, manipulation, individual pathology, or "collaboration," none of which are unproblematic categories. These ways of posing the problem implicitly deny lower-class Palestinians any capacity for agency, for making their own sense of complex circumstances and acting to further their interests as they defined them. They also take for granted, and operate from within, nationalism's conception of itself as a unitary and internally unconflicted ideal that represents the authentic core of personhood in all circumstances, superior to or even excluding all other identities, sentiments, interests, loyalties, and aspirations. And they reinforce the elitist assumptions and perspective of most discussions of Arab nationalism in Palestine.

We need, I think, to try to imagine other ways of approaching this particular nationalism, but also nationalism in general, by starting from the premise that like religious faith, gender, race, class, etc., nationalism (or national identity) is not a thing but a set of relations and forces that in each particular case unfolds and takes shape within a specific historical conjuncture, social context, and discursive arena. It is moreover always the object of struggles among various sociopolitical forces over its meaning and over what is to be "done" with it. Thus it *always* means different things to different people in different contexts, it is *always* "used" in a variety of ways, and it therefore cannot be treated as a unitary or self-evidently coherent ideal object. Efforts to grasp what it means to real people living in specific historical conjunctures must therefore also presume their perspectives and actions to be contingent, complex, and sometimes even contradictory. We must start, in other words, from what various segments of an inevitably heterogeneous "people" actually think, say, and do, instead of gauging their conformity to or deviation from what a nationalist ideology formulated by members of the middling and elite strata defines as their proper identity and mode of behavior.

In the hope of contributing to this volume's collective effort to rethink Arab nationalism, I would like to illustrate and expand upon some of these arguments by relating and discussing several episodes from the Mandate period that involve Palestinian Arab workers. By offering at least glimpses of how the national question impinged on various groups of workers in Haifa and Jaffa, and how they "handled" that question in the context of their working lives, I hope to do several related things.

For one, I would like to show that although conventional accounts of Palestinian Arab nationalism tend to focus on "high" culture, politics, and diplomacy (i.e., what the upper and middle classes were saying and doing) and thereby largely ignore the lower classes, the diverse segments of the lower classes were nonetheless always present and by their agency compelled the nationalist movement to take them into account and at least go through the motions of addressing their concerns. It is fairly well-known that a vigorous Palestinian Arab labor movement (one wing of which was led by communists) emerged in the 1940s and sought to assert itself within the Arab community, but I will argue that one can trace the presence and agency of Arab workers, and their importance for nationalism, back to the 1920s.

Second, I will argue that the willingness of Arab workers in Palestine to cooperate with Zionists under certain circumstances is not fully, or even usefully, explained as a product of ignorance, manipulation, deception, or collaboration, at least not in any simple sense of those terms. Rather, it requires us to adopt a more complex and flexible conception of national identity, one that treats it not as a unitary thing or a fixed model, but as a complex of ideas, symbols, sentiments, and practices that people from various sociopolitical groups appropriate selectively and contingently.

Toward that end I will, last of all, discuss a largely unknown episode from the run-up to the popular revolt against British rule and Zionism that erupted in the spring of 1936, in the hope of suggesting one route by which Arab workers came to embrace a radical nationalism and exercise agency in its behalf. By presenting episodes centered on largely illiterate working people who are unlikely to have ever read a nationalist tract, I hope to at least complicate the conventional nationalist narrative and point to flaws in its underlying premises. In the conclusion I will address some of the broader implications of what I have tried to do here.[6]

CARPENTERS AND TAILORS IN HAIFA, 1925

In the fall of 1925, seven years before the Haifa construction workers employed by `Aziz Khayyat sought allies wherever they could find them to escape their onerously long working day, one hundred or so Arab carpenters employed in some twelve small Arab-owned workshops in Haifa, along with about thirty Arab tailors also employed in small enterprises, went on strike to demand an increase in their meager wages, a shorter working day, and an end to abuse by their employers. The carpenters and tailors had been discontented for a long time, but their grievances were transformed into organization and then action through the medium of a "General Workers' Club," which the Histadrut had established for Arab workers the previous July in a busy, largely Christian, Arab section of the "old city" of Haifa.

As I have already noted, Arab and Jewish railway workers in Haifa had been involved in efforts to form a joint union for some years, and it was the collapse of the recently formed joint union a few months earlier that led to the establishment of Palestine's first Arab labor organization, the

PAWS, in the summer of 1925. It was in large measure to counter the PAWS, which hoped to expand its membership beyond the railwaymen, that the Histadrut made its first foray into organizing Arab workers by opening this club. The club's secretary was a young Arab tailor named Philip Hassun, but he worked under the supervision of Avraham Khalfon, a Jew from a family long established in Palestine who had been hired as the Histadrut's chief organizer of Arab workers in Haifa.

The club seems to have met a need among Haifa's Arab working class, for it quickly attracted the attention and interest of a substantial number of skilled craftsmen, mainly tailors and carpenters. It offered evening classes in the Hebrew language and in Arabic literacy, lectures by members of various left-wing Zionist parties, and Arabic newspapers from Palestine and elsewhere. Through the club a number of Haifa workers also gained access to a special vocational training course at the Technion, the Jewish technical institute that had been founded in Haifa shortly before the war. But the club's main activity was organizing, which it pursued through the creation of new unions for tailors and carpenters.

The initiative for strike action came for the workers themselves, who pressed Hassun and Khalfon to help them organize a strike if their employers would not agree to raise wages and institute the eight-hour day. Khalfon at first resisted this pressure because he did not think the workers were ready for a strike, but in October, with the approval of the Histadrut executive committee, he agreed to take action. On behalf of the General Workers' Club he sent letters to the owners of the workshops in which the unionized carpenters were employed, setting forth the workers' demands and requesting a response within ten days. It should come as no surprise that it was Khalfon who signed the letters; because he was not himself an employee he was safe from the kind of reprisals which the workers would have faced had they spoken up for themselves. However, the employers, never before faced with this kind of organized action on the part of their workers, simply ignored the letters. The carpenters and tailors responded by launching a strike, under the leadership of Khalfon and Hassun and with the backing of the Histadrut.

The strike was peaceful at first, but clashes ensued when the employers tried to bring in strikebreakers from the nearby town of Acre. The police intervened and arrested a number of the strikers, but the well-connected Khalfon was able to free them, by posting bail for them and by sending the alcoholic English police inspector in charge a case of his favorite brand of whiskey. Nonetheless, as the strike went on, it became increasingly clear that the clashes and arrests were exhausting the meager resources at the workers' disposal, despite financial support from the Histadrut and the (Jewish-led) railway workers' union. There was also growing pressure on the workers from the local Arab press and local church officials. Haifa's oldest Arabic newspaper, *al-Karmil*, was strongly anti-Zionist, and while expressing sympathy for the workers' demands it also expressed fear that the strike would serve Zionist rather than Arab nationalist interests. "We fear," *al-Karmil* declared,

> that the purpose of inducing the Arab workers to strike is (1) to incite them to rebellion; (2) to cause a disturbance in the business activity of Arab enterprises; (3) to raise prices so that it will be easier for Jewish goods to combat and compete with the Arabs and take jobs from them. We warn the leaders of this movement against falling into a trap, even as we acclaim the workers' awakening, for we are disgusted that someone should enrich themself from the sweat of the worker's brow.[7]

Local Christian clerics echoed *al-Karmil* and other Arab newspapers. The spiritual leader of Haifa's Maronite community, Father Francis, called in twenty of the strikers to warn them against cooperating with the Jews, whom he said were spreading Bolshevism in Palestine, and he called on them to form their own Muslim-Christian union, which would be free of Jewish influence.

According to the Histadrut's account of the meeting, the Arab workers replied that the Socialist International had delegated the task of organizing workers in the Near East to the Histadrut and they must therefore affiliate with it.[8] The Socialist International had of course done no such thing, but the claim does convey the sense of proletarian *mission civilatrice* with which socialist Zionists in Palestine were often imbued. The strikers were also said to have told Father Francis that there was nothing to fear from the Jewish workers because the latter would not accept the meager wages paid to Arab workers. This may have been true in tailoring and carpentry, but of course one of the Histadrut's chief goals was to secure more jobs for Jews, regardless of whether Arab workers would be displaced in the process.

After meeting with a delegation of strikers, Najib Nassar, the editor of *al-Karmil*, invited the two sides to meet at his newspaper's offices and resolve their conflict. The strikers insisted that Khalfon and Hassun accompany them to the meeting. Nassar was unhappy that the two officials of what his newspaper referred to as the "Zionist workers' association" had come, but they were ultimately allowed to remain as observers. After several hours of negotiations an agreement was reached by which, after two weeks, the strike was brought to an end. The workers achieved gains that, given the miserable conditions that had prevailed until then, were not insubstantial: a nine-hour work day, a half-hour lunch break and seven paid sick days a year.[9]

How are we to make sense of this episode? It can be interpreted sim-ply as an instance of Zionist manipulation: these guileless Arab carpen-ters and tailors were duped into joining unions controlled by the Hista-drut and striking against their employers, fellow Arabs, thereby serving the aims of Zionism. These craftsmen may not in fact have had a very clear or complete understanding of the aims of the Histadrut or of the Zionist project of which it was becoming a key institution. Moreover, in certain ways the unions and the strike probably did serve Zionist inter-ests—or more precisely, the interests of the "labor-Zionist" camp with-in the Zionist movement. The Histadrut's relationship with these Haifa workers allowed it to portray itself, to its exclusively Jewish membership as well as to the international labor and social-democratic movements whose support and sympathy it sought, as the true champion and defender of the Arab masses in Palestine. It hoped thereby to bolster its campaign to delegitimize Arab nationalism, which left-wing Zionists insisted was inauthentic, a fraudulent tool of wealthy and grasping Arab landowners and obscurantist clerics that lacked any real social base. Histadrut leaders also certainly hoped that if they helped organize Arab workers they could keep them out of the "clutches" of Arab nationalists. Moreover, in the 1920s not a few left-wing Zionists believed that an effort to help Arab workers to organize and win higher wages and bet-ter working conditions would aid the Zionist cause by reducing the "threat" that cheap, unorganized Arab labor posed to Jewish immi-grants' ability to compete for decently paid jobs in Palestine.

But there is more that needs to be said about this; we need to try to see things from the perspective of these impoverished and exploited carpen-ters and tailors, instead of treating them as mere pawns manipulated by others. It is important to remember that their grievances predated their contacts with the Histadrut and its organizers. Though the General Workers' Club was certainly a Zionist-controlled "front organization," these workers responded positively to its establishment because it seemed to them to meet a genuine need. It provided social and educa-tional services of a kind to which they had had no previous access, and it addressed itself to them specifically as workers. Moreover, the club ini-tially had no competitors, for the PAWS was at this early stage very small and weak and had little presence beyond the railway workshops. There is also no evidence that by joining Histadrut-sponsored unions these car-penters and tailors in any sense embraced Zionism; rather, one can see that move as a tactic, one that certainly had broader implications and con-sequences but that was very much rooted in a particular set of circum-stances, including a lack of any good alternatives.

So instead of portraying these craftsmen as either mere dupes or collaborators, we must try to see them as responding to the conditions in which they found themselves, including ruthless exploitation by their employers and the Arab (nationalist) elite's profound lack of interest in the plight of the lower classes, as well as its antipathy to class conflict. It is also important to remember that it was in large measure the initiative and militancy of these and other workers that compelled other segments of their community, in particular middle-class nationalists, to begin to take the workers' concerns more seriously. In its account of the strike's settlement *al-Karmil* expressed hope that in every trade a "guild" of employers and workers could be established to deal with the workers' grievances and thereby "block the involvement of Zionists in the affairs of Arab workers."[10] Nassar, and the Palestinian Arab bourgeoisie as a whole, were with few exceptions quite conservative on social issues and did not initially have much interest in the needs or interests of the emerging Arab working class. But events like the October 1925 strike pushed them toward greater awareness of, and interest in, workers' grievances, demands, and efforts to organize.[11]

As it happened, the October 1925 strike marked the Histadrut-backed club's greatest success. A barrage of nationalist criticism dissuaded most Arab workers from coming anywhere near it, while an economic downturn in many trades and an influx of migrants from Syria, many of them refugees from the anticolonial uprising there, weakened the capacity of local craftsmen and workers to organize and wage successful struggles for higher wages and better working conditions. The unions of carpenters and tailors soon disintegrated and the Histadrut found it impossible to win footholds in other trades. By 1927 the club was moribund, though the Histadrut had by no means given up on its project of organizing Arab workers under its tutelage.

ON THE JAFFA WATERFRONT, 1934–1936

Until this point I have been discussing workers in Haifa, but henceforth I will focus on Jaffa. Though Haifa's deep-water harbor opened in 1933, Jaffa's port remained important, especially as an outlet for Palestine's booming citrus exports. The Arab stevedores and lightermen who worked there, employed through Arab labor contractors, had accumulated grievances that made them receptive to the idea of organization. Though paid a fixed daily wage, in the busy citrus export season the stevedores might be compelled to work up to eighteen hours a day; they were therefore interested not only in a higher daily wage but also in compensation for overtime. Rather than a daily wage, the lightermen received a share of the receipts of the boat on which they worked, which gave the boat owner or contractor for whom they worked control over their income and plenty of opportunity to shortchange them. They wanted some reform of this system to make their income more predictable and enhance their control over how much they worked and earned. Both lightermen and stevedores were engaged in dangerous work and suffered numerous accidents for which they were only rarely compensated by their employers.

At the same time these workers (who were mostly Palestinians from Jaffa itself or from the towns and villages of its hinterland on the coastal plain) had enjoyed some job security (though employment at the port fluctuated seasonally). They now saw their jobs and wages threatened by migrant workers coming from the Hawran region in Syria (and to a lesser extent Egypt) who were attracted to Palestine by the country's relative prosperity and were taking over jobs at the port. The stevedores and lightermen hoped that by forming a union they could protect their wages from the downward pressure threatened by the presence of these low-wage competitors and secure their jobs through enforcement of the principle of local preference in the allocation of work.[12]

Though nominally a countrywide organization the main base of the PAWS remained in Haifa, so that before 1934 there was no effective Arab trade union presence in Jaffa. This left the field open for the Histadrut to try to organize the discontented port workers there through its Palestine Labor League. Early in 1934 Eliyahu Agassi, a Jew of Iraqi origin who was the Histadrut's chief organizer of Arab workers, began to develop ties with a group of Jaffa stevedores and support their efforts to organize a trade union. PLL opened a club near the port, which offered these workers medical services, a loan fund, and legal assistance. The latter was particularly important, because although the government of Palestine had promulgated legislation requiring employers to compensate workers for work-related injuries, few Arab workers knew about the law or possessed the means to take advantage of it. The first cases in which Histadrut lawyers sued Arab employers on behalf of injured Arab stevedores made a strong impression on Arab workers in Jaffa and enhanced the reputation of the PLL and the Histadrut there. Histadrut leader Dov Hoz also intervened on these workers' behalf with the British officials who ran the port and sought support from dockworkers' unions in Britain.

By the fall of 1934 the PLL was claiming about one hundred Jaffa stevedores as members of an affiliated union, and after lengthy negotiations some of the lightermen were also beginning to join. The fact that many port workers left Jaffa and returned to their home villages during slack seasons made it difficult to sustain the Jaffa stevedores' union: it had in effect to be reestablished when the citrus export season began in the late fall. But for Histadrut officials the PLL's apparent success in organizing these workers during 1934 made it possible for them to envision a situation in which, as one of them put it, "*we* will be the rulers in the port of Jaffa and will be able to do great things there, both politically and economically." Among other things they hoped to use their base among the Arab workers there to get Jews hired on as port workers.[13]

THE EMERGENCE OF THE ARAB WORKERS' SOCIETY

The PLL's successes in organizing Arab workers in Jaffa during 1934, especially the dockworkers, alarmed Arab trade unionists and their nonworker nationalist allies and stimulated much more vigorous and effective efforts to counter the Histadrut. The summer of 1934 witnessed the emergence, initially under the patronage of a prominent politician from an elite family, of a new Arab labor organization, which became quite active in Jaffa. The politician was Fakhri al-Nashashibi, nephew and devoted assistant of Raghib al-Nashashibi who had been mayor of Jerusalem since 1920 and led the opposition to the Husaynis and their allies within the Palestinian Arab elite. Despite occasional tactical resorts to ultranationalist rhetoric, the Nashashibis led the more pro-British and pro-Hashemite segment of that elite, while the Husaynis and their allies, led by Hajj Amin al-Husayni, the Mufti of Jerusalem, took a stronger anti-British, anti-Zionist, and distinctly Palestinian stance. Both factions still believed, however, that they could block the Zionist project and achieve Palestine's independence through negotiations with the British.

Relations between the two camps deteriorated sharply in the early 1930s. The Arab Executive, on which all the major factions and leading elite families had been represented, was formally dissolved in August 1934, opening the way for the creation of rival political parties, each linked to a particular family or faction. As the Nashashibis and their allies moved toward the creation of their own political organization, Fakhri al-Nashashibi came to see in Arab workers a potential constituency that could be organized for the benefit of his faction. He therefore proclaimed the establishment in Jerusalem of an "Arab Workers' Society" (AWS), with himself as president. In October 1934 an AWS branch was established in Jaffa, under the leadership of Michel Mitri, a young Palestinian engineer who had grown up in Latin America and received his education there. The AWS was strongly supported in its efforts by the pro-Nashashibi *Filastin*, which hailed Fakhri al-Nashashibi as "protector of the workers" and began to devote unprecedented attention to labor affairs.[14]

To build support, the AWS quickly seized on an issue of concern to many Arab workers: the Histadrut's campaign for Hebrew labor and the complementary effort to induce Jewish consumers to boycott Arab products (especially agricultural produce) and "buy Jewish." In the spring of 1934 the Histadrut had launched a largely unsuccessful campaign to compel Jewish citrus farmers to dismiss their largely Arab work force and hire Jews instead, in keeping with its principle that Jewish-owned enterprises should employ only Jews. When that effort in the countryside yielded only meager results, the Histadrut decided to shift the campaign to the cities, deploying mobile bands of pickets who moved from one construction site to another, in Tel Aviv and other towns, and sometimes went beyond picketing by trying to forcibly expel Arab workers from their jobs. These tactics led to clashes between Jews attempting to keep out or drive out Arab workers, and Arab workers trying to get to or stay at their jobs. Employers would frequently call in the police to restore order and protect their Arab workers; this in turn led to fights between Jewish pickets and the police, and arrests of Jews for disturbing the peace.[15]

This campaign in the cities achieved only limited success. This was a period of prosperity and low unemployment for the Jewish community in Palestine, and in the absence of a large mass of unemployed Jews desperate for jobs the Histadrut found it almost as difficult to enforce the hiring of Hebrew labor in the cities as it had in the countryside. But its campaign did succeed in inflaming Arab-Jewish relations and heightening the anxiety and resentment with which many Arabs regarded Zionism and the Jewish community in Palestine, especially in a period when Jewish immigration was surging dramatically owing to the Nazi seizure of power in Germany and increasingly virulent anti-Semitism elsewhere in Europe. To alert the public to what was going on, the Arab press, along with the Palestine Communist Party's clandestine or front publications, were quick to translate and publish the Histadrut calls for the imposition of "Hebrew labor" and the boycotting of Arab produce, manufacturers, and shops, and news of clashes at urban building sites spread quickly.

Fakhri al-Nashashibi and his new AWS sought to capitalize on growing concern about this issue by publicly demanding that the British authorities take forceful action against the Hebrew labor pickets. The AWS also called on Arab workers to adopt weapons from Histadrut's arsenal by setting up their own picket lines and boycotting Jewish products and produce. In December 1934 Fakhri al-Nashashibi set up in Jerusalem what *Filastin*, his biggest booster, described as "the first Arab picket." This was in reality not so much a picket line as a march by al-Nashashibi and some of his followers through the streets of Jerusalem,

in the course of which buildings being put up by Arab contractors were
visited and the employment of Jews at those sites (generally as skilled
workers) was protested.[16] The AWS does not in fact seem to have carried
out any sustained picketing in this period, though as we will see Michel
Mitri would use this tactic to great effect in the spring of 1936.

JAFFA PORT WORKERS AND THE HEBREW LABOR ISSUE

The Jaffa port workers whom Eliyahu Agassi (assisted by his colleague
Reuven Zaslani, who under the name Reuven Shilo'ah would later become a founding father of Israel's intelligence and security apparatus)
had helped organize were quite aware of, and concerned about, the issue
of Hebrew labor. Agassi and Zaslani were compelled to recognize that
these workers were quite uneasy about their links with the Histadrut,
which was increasingly perceived as an organization devoted to taking
jobs away from Arab workers. In November 1934, in an effort to seize
the initiative from their opponents in the struggle for the support of the
Jaffa dockworkers, the two Histadrut organizers went so far as to invite
the secretary of the Jaffa branch of the PAWS to a meeting of some fifty
Arab workers, most of them stevedores, at the PLL's club, for a direct
confrontation over the issue.

According to Zaslani and Agassi, who submitted a report on the
meeting to the Histadrut and to the Jewish Agency's Political Department, the PAWS leader denounced Histadrut for stealing Arab jobs,
reminded the stevedores of the "disaster" that had occurred at Haifa
harbor (i.e., the introduction of Jewish workers after the organization of
the PLL-sponsored port workers' union there), and asked if they wanted to allow the Histadrut to bring about the same outcome in Jaffa as
well. In their response, Zaslani and Agassi did not directly address the
substance of their opponent's charges but instead sought to put him on
the defensive and undermine his credibility by demanding that he provide proof of his allegations.

The Jewish unionists felt they had made their case successfully, but
they had not counted on the rank and file workers speaking up for themselves. After the PAWS secretary left, the stevedores reiterated his alle-
gation that the Histadrut was seeking to bring Jewish workers into the
port, take it over, and deprive the Arabs of their livelihood. They pressed
Agassi and Zaslani for an explicit promise that the Histadrut would not
seek to bring Jewish workers into Jaffa harbor. Zaslani and Agassi could
not of course make such a promise, since the Histadrut did in fact hope to
secure more jobs for Jews at Jaffa's port as elsewhere; indeed, one of the
PLL's raisons d'être was to facilitate that effort. In the end the stevedores

had to settle for a much vaguer promise that no Histadrut member would take a job from any permanently employed Arab port worker. Zaslani also had to promise that the stevedores' union would remain independent even after it affiliated with the PLL.[17]

Agassi and Zaslani concluded their report by stating that "one may say with confidence that as a result of this meeting our organization in Jaffa has been strengthened and *innoculated*" (emphasis in the original). This statement soon proved to be rather overconfident. The PLL's Jaffa branch remained under constant pressure from Arab labor organizations: a few days after this debate, Zaslani reported to Agassi that both Fakhri al-Nashashibi's AWS and the newly active Jaffa branch of the PAWS were leafleting the stevedores affiliated with the PLL and that this activity had led at least one member of the union's leadership to resign. Ibrahim al-Sawi, who was receiving money from the PLL and acting as its main agent among the stevedores, was said to be displaying dictatorial behavior and angering union members. Moreover, the port workers were now insisting on keeping some distance between their union and the PLL: they had refused to sign their names to the application of the PLL Jaffa branch for registration as an officially recognized organization. For the same reason, the letter the Jaffa stevedores' union sent to the various labor contractors at Jaffa's port in January 1935 contained no mention whatsoever of the PLL or the Histadrut, though it was Zaslani who forwarded a translation of the letter directly to L. K. Pope, the port manager at Jaffa.[18]

The stevedores' tough questions at the meeting and their insistence on independence from the PLL indicate that they were not quite as unaware, guileless, and docile as labor-Zionist leaders (but also, it should be said, bourgeois Arab nationalists) tended to depict them. Agassi would later speak of his effort to instill "proletarian consciousness" (*hakara po`alit*) in these workers, by which he meant labor Zionism's conception of how Arab workers should think and behave, including rejection of nationalism and sympathy for Zionism.[19] In fact the stevedores, and other groups of Arab workers elsewhere, seem to have had their own sense of who they were and what they wanted, a sense that did not necessarily fully coincide with what either the Histadrut or Arab nationalist activists proposed. The stevedores understood that several rival labor organizations were seeking to win their support and sought to turn that rivalry to their advantage; they also knew that identifiable union members were subject to threats and harassment from the labor contractors through whom they were employed, hostility from the British officials who administered the port, and even permanent deprivation of their livelihood. They were obviously well aware of the Histadrut's commitment to Hebrew labor and that policy's implications for their own livelihood. As a result, though they were not in principle unwilling to cooperate with the Histadrut, whose clout and resources they knew to be considerably greater than those available to any Arab labor organization, they sought as much as as possible to do so on their own terms, despite extremely adverse conditions.

British officials at Jaffa's port hoped to avoid any labor trouble and preserve the status quo until the end of the citrus export season, but growing tensions eventually erupted into open conflict. At the end of February 1935 some sixty Arab workers employed at the port expansion project went on strike, originally to protest the dismissal of a comrade who had been fired after a dispute with his foreman and then to demand an eight-hour day, a six-day work week, and higher wages. AWS leader Michel Mitri quickly appeared on the scene and sought to negotiate on the workers' behalf. Though the strike ended in failure after a week, it was a clear manifestation of growing discontent. The contractors' efforts early in 1935 to break the stevedores' union by harassment and, for a time, by refusing to employ union members led to persistent friction and sometimes violent conflict on the docks. To restore order and deflect questions being raised by Labor Party members of parliament, the British authorities in Palestine appointed a committee to investigate labor conditions at the port of Jaffa. Because the committee was chaired by the British port manager, its report predictably declared that the stevedores had no serious grievances and that no immediate government action was called for—and in fact no further official action was taken before the outbreak of the 1936 general strike.[20]

During the latter part of 1935, the PLL's base of support at the port of Jaffa largely disappeared. This was in part the result of stepped-up repression: with the support or acquiescence of British port officials, the contractors sought to break the dockworkers' union by various means, including the denial of work to union members and other "troublemakers." Poignant evidence of the use of this tactic has survived in the form of a petition bearing the signatures or thumbprints of fourteen Jaffa dockworkers who had been dismissed by their boss, Mahmud al-Qumbarji (or al-Onbarji), at the very end of June 1935. But as we have seen, the stevedores and lightermen themselves grew increasingly wary of the PLL and the Histadrut, as competition from the Arab unions and rising political tensions exacerbated by the Histadrut's Hebrew labor campaign helped increase the costs of cooperation with it well beyond any actual or potential benefits to Arab workers. Then in October 1935 a barrel purportedly containing a shipment of cement accidentally broke open while being unloaded at Jaffa and was found to contain arms and ammunition being smuggled into Palestine for the Hagana, the largest of the semiclandestine Zionist military organizations. The discovery created an uproar in the Arab community and went a long way toward destroying what was left of the PLL's base among the Jaffa dockworkers. By the end of the year most of the stevedores and lightermen had severed their links with the PLL, or simply allowed them to lapse, and gravitated into the orbit of Arab trade unions. When the general strike (about whose antecedents I will have more to say later on) erupted in April 1936, the Jaffa port workers immediately joined in, shutting the port down for many months. During the years of the revolt the port workers were generally seen as staunch nationalists.[21]

A nationalist reading of this episode might portray the Jaffa port workers as originally having been duped (or, in a few individual cases, bribed) into collaboration by the Histadrut organizers with whom they were in contact, and then later having "woken up" to reality and become good nationalists. But this portrayal does not fully account for what went on. The stevedores and lightermen seem to have been aware of Agassi and Zaslani's Zionist affiliations and loyalties virtually from the start; yet they were ready to avail themselves of what the Histadrut had to offer even as they sought to maintain their independence. And they were willing to maintain relations with the Histadrut and endure harsh repression, including loss of livelihood, out of loyalty to their union, though in nationalist eyes that union was tainted by its links with the Histadrut. They seem to have been able to regard themselves as authentically Arab (and as their attitude toward Hawrani and Egyptian migrant labor suggests, authentically Palestinian) even as they accepted certain kinds of support from Zionists. So rather than trying to pigeonhole these Jaffa port workers as either victims of ignorance and manipulation or loyal nationalists, we should perhaps try to understand their actions and sentiments contingently, so as to allow room for complexity and even contradiction. In the right circumstances the Jaffa stevedores and lightermen would display excellent nationalist "credentials," suggesting that it makes little sense to classify them as mere "dupes" or "collaborators" earlier on. Such crude dichotomizations make it difficult to adequately account for the complexities of people's beliefs and actions or for transformations in what they believe and do.

ANTECEDENTS OF REVOLT: THE AWS AND HEBREW LABOR

As the political climate in Palestine grew increasingly tense during the latter part of 1935, broad segments of the Arab community became increasingly receptive to a more radically anti-British and anti-Zionist stance than the old-line elite politicians were initially prepared to embrace. In this shift Arab workers played a significant though little-known part, a part I discuss in order to extend and complicate the conventional narrative of the run-up to the outbreak in the spring of 1936 of the Arab general strike, which soon became a popular anticolonial insurrection.

As I have already noted, the years since 1932 had seen a surge in Jewish immigration and a dramatic increase in the size of the Jewish community in Palestine, heightening Arab fears: for the first time, a Jewish majority and Jewish statehood appeared feasible, perhaps even imminent. Reports of large-scale Zionist land purchases made the threat of dispossession ever more palpable. The discovery that arms and ammunition were being smuggled into Palestine for the Hagana seemed to confirm longstanding Arab fears that the Zionists were preparing to seize the country by force. Government policies, which Arab public opinion perceived as pro-Zionist, also exacerbated Arab resentment and anger. At the same time the Italian conquest of Ethiopia and Germany's reoccupation of the Rhineland made war among the European powers seem imminent and underscored Britain's apparent weakness.

Moreover, the years of prosperity had come to an end in 1935, leading to rising unemployment and social discontent. Shantytowns sprang up around Haifa and Jaffa, inhabited by thousands of destitute migrants from the countryside. The residents of these shantytowns provided a constituency for radical nationalists, notably Shaykh `Izz al-Din al-Qassam of Haifa, who called for moral renovation and denounced the factionalism and ineffectiveness of the elite politicians. Al-Qassam, a popular preacher, eventually organized a small guerrilla band that in 1935 took to the hills in the hope of sparking an armed revolt against British rule and Zionism. In November 1935 al-Qassam was killed in a gun battle with police near Jenin, but his death and funeral aroused strong nationalist and religious sentiments and dramatically increased pressure on the politicians to put aside their debilitating factional squabbles and take a much more aggressive stance toward Palestine's British overlords. Palestinian Arabs were also well aware of, and inspired by, nationalist upsurges in neighboring Egypt and Syria.

The supercharged political climate and high unemployment among Arab workers at the end of 1935 notwithstanding, the Histadrut leadership came to the conclusion that the end of the construction boom and rising unemployment among Jews justified another escalation of the Hebrew labor campaign. Given the circumstances, this escalation not surprisingly provoked an unprecedentedly vigorous and militant Arab response. Once again the AWS in Jaffa took the initiative, under the creative and effective leadership of its young president, Michel Mitri. Mitri had taken over the organization after Fakhri al-Nashashibi lost interest in labor affairs during 1935, and had built it into a strong local force that claimed some 4,700 members. In some respects Mitri was a forerunner of the new kind of Arab labor leader who would emerge during and after the Second World War. An educated man with knowledge and experience of the wider world, he was a capable organizer who knew how to seize on an issue and use it effectively to build his movement. He also understood the importance to the labor movement of building broad-based alliances with other forces. For example, he was quite willing to cooperate with radical nationalist and leftist forces in the Arab community, including members of the left wing of the pan-Arab nationalist *Istiqlal* (Independence) party and even with Arab communists.

In December 1935 Mitri sent a letter to the District Commissioner of Jaffa claiming that more than a thousand of his organization's members were unemployed and requesting permission to hold a protest march through the streets of Jaffa. Mitri's explanation of the purposes of the demonstration suggests that Arab unionists clearly perceived a connection between Arab unemployment, Hebrew labor, and Zionism: "to ask for the relief of unemployment, to protest against Jewish picketing, the Judaization of the Port and the policy of immigration according to the absorptive capacity of the country." The District Commissioner prohibited the march, but Mitri and his colleagues proceeded to escalate their campaign against Hebrew labor. Mitri sought to build support for that campaign by convening a national conference of Arab trade unionists in Jaffa.

In February 1936, using the same arguments that the Histadrut advanced in defense of Hebrew labor, Mitri protested the awarding of a contract for three schools in Jaffa to the Histadrut's contracting office, which generally employed only Jews. He pointed out that the buildings were located in a predominantly Arab city, that Arabs were never given contracts for construction in Jewish areas, that the Histadrut had forcibly driven Arab workers away from Jewish building sites, and that unemployment among Arab workers was very high. When no relief was forthcoming, AWS members adopted the Histadrut's own tactics: unemployed Arab workers began picketing building sites where Hebrew labor prevailed, in particular the three schools under construction. This led to clashes in which Arab workers were arrested by the police.

The pickets seem to have been well aware of what was at stake. One of those arrested told the judge before whom he was brought that "we Arab workers are unemployed. We asked the government to remove Jewish workers from Arab enterprises but it took no interest in our just demand. So we went to the site and tried to expel the Jewish workers from jobs to which we have more right than anyone else, and the police arrested us." The strategy seems to have produced results: the government eventually agreed to require that 50 percent of the jobs at the school construction sites be given to Arab workers, though it rejected the demand that Arabs also be guaranteed 50 percent of the total wage bill. But Mitri was not satisfied and, emulating the Histadrut leadership, demanded 100 percent Arab labor. A leaflet issued by the AWS in the spring of 1936 conveys the pitch of militancy its campaign had attained: it called for mass picketing of construction sites "until the jails are full of [Arab] workers" and designated alternative leaders for the AWS in the event that Mitri and his colleagues were arrested.[22]

On 10 April 1936, with tensions rising and Arab public opinion demanding that the nationalist politicians set aside their differences and close ranks, representatives of the various segments of the Arab labor movement in Palestine gathered again, this time in Haifa, to lay the foundations of an all-Palestine Arab labor federation. Among those attending were `Abd al-Hamid Haymur, the veteran Haifa railway worker who was secretary of the PAWS; Sami Taha, who would later emerge as that organization's preeminent leader; Michel Mitri and George Mansur, leaders of the AWS in Jaffa; Khalil Shanir, one of the Palestine Communist Party's top Arab leaders; Hamdi al-Husayni of Gaza, a radical young journalist who belonged to the *Istiqlal* party and had links with clandestine Arab nationalist groups preparing for armed revolt; and Akram Zu`aytir of Nablus, another radical Istiqlalist in contact with members of al-Qassam's guerrilla band holed up in the hills around Nablus.[23] This gathering manifested the convergence of the fledgling Arab trade union movement with the most radical segment of the nationalist movement and with the Arab communists, signalling not just a desire for labor unity but also a sense that the Arab labor movement must play an important role in the more militant phase of the national struggle that seemed about to begin.

In fact the storm broke sooner than expected, and the vision of a vigorous and united Arab workers' movement was swept aside in the tide of popular energy that engulfed the Palestinian Arab community when the general strike erupted in the second half of April 1936. Yet the Haifa conference, and the convergence of sociopolitical forces that it manifested, suggest that accounts that depict the outbreak of the general strike and revolt as entirely spontaneous and unexpected are inadequate, since they fail to take into account the kinds of grievances, struggles, and developments discussed here that prepared the ground for that explosion. The revolt had antecedents, for example, in the rising tide of worker militancy which the AWS campaign against "Hebrew labor" both built on and stimulated. At the same time, that campaign strengthened the links between worker grievances and militancy on the one hand and the national question on the other, links that were further reinforced by the labor movement's new ties with radical nationalists anxious to mobilize the populace at large. These dynamics were in turn energized by the example of al-Qassam's resort to arms the previous fall and the popular sentiments it unleashed, and more generally by the poverty and despair in the shantytowns and working-class neighborhoods of Haifa and Jaffa that had nourished al-Qassam's movement.

Nationalism and Identity

That this episode of worker mobilization in the streets of Jaffa around the Hebrew labor issue, its rapid evolution into something much broader, and the way it fed into the outbreak of the revolt have received little scholarly attention tells us something.[24] It underscores the elitism that has characterized much of the published research on Palestinian Arab nationalism and its narrow focus on the actions, pronouncements, and writings of a small number of politicians and intellectuals. It also points up the literature's implicit reliance on an understanding of nationalism as a unitary form of identity, which was first formulated by intellectuals and politicians and crystallized in certain key nationalist texts, and was then disseminated to, and passively absorbed by, the lower classes.

It is of course not at all surprising that nationalist discourse strives to make diversity, complexity, and internal conflicts disappear, or that it represents the nation as an ancient entity imbued with a singular essential identity, vision, and goal—rather than as a relatively recent construct comprising heterogeneous elements that triumphs by absorbing, subordinating, or suppressing other forms of identity, to the disproportionate benefit of particular sociopolitical forces. By obliterating potentially complicating differences, or at least by subsuming them in the larger category of the nation and insisting that that category supersedes all others, nationalist movements increase their prospects of winning mass support and mobilizing it to achieve their goals. It is equally unsurprising that nationalist movements feel compelled to struggle against, and if possible extirpate, forms of behavior they define as "collaboration."

But if we cannot reasonably expect nationalist ideologists and activists to be very critical (or even aware) of the essentialism and elitism that inform their vision of the world, or to recognize (much less celebrate) the irreducible heterogeneity of "the nation," we certainly can and should expect historians not to see the world as nationalists do, at least in terms of the paradigms of historical analysis they deploy. As I argued earlier, we need to pay greater attention to the ways in which nationalisms are historically constructed, initially by certain sociopolitical forces with their own agenda(s), by means of selective appropriations of elements and interpretations of the past within a specific historical conjuncture and in relation to (and competition with) many other discourses and practices of identity. To accomplish this, however, we also need to extend our analysis beyond local elites to encompass the rest of the population, in order to explore how various subordinate social groups accept or reject, in whole or in part, the forms of identity their social superiors seek to disseminate, forms that are, moreover, always contested. This in turn implies that we cannot treat "ignorance," or "collaboration," or even "resistance" for that matter, as simple, transparent, uncomplicated categories, which is just what nationalist ideologies do as a matter of course.

This is not to suggest, as have the late Elie Kedourie and others, that Arab nationalism was little more than a fraud perpetrated by a handful of confused and frustrated intellectuals, aided and abetted by British colonial officials. For this school of thought, non-Western nationalisms were "invented" in the most negative sense of the term, i.e., deliberately made up out of whole cloth. I am arguing, however, that it is more helpful to think of them (as of all nationalisms) as having been assembled in diverse and complex ways from elements old and new in specific historical and social contexts, and genuinely embraced by various sociopolitical forces. This implies further that we need to rethink (and, I would argue, reject) the sharp distinction that many students of nationalism have drawn between purportedly liberal, territorial, and individualistic (i.e., "good") western European (and by extension United States) nationalisms and the illiberal, organicist, and statist (i.e., "bad") kind of nationalism allegedly typified by nineteenth-century Germany, which is presumed to have served as the model for Arab and most other Asian and African nationalisms. This dichotomy is rooted in a dubious interpretation of modern European history, focuses on the writings and speeches of small groups of intellectuals and politicians while neglecting who the rest of the population thought they were and what they did about it, and thus offers little help in understanding nationalism as an historical phenomenon, in Europe or anywhere else.

With regard to Palestine, my basic argument is that historians need to unpack Arab nationalism in that land much more thoroughly than has hitherto been done. This involves, among other things, exploring in greater depth the ways in which all segments of the indigenous Arab population, and not just its literate minority, did not merely absorb but actively *appropriated* this new form of identity and the practices that went with it, combining them with other elements drawn from other discourses of identity and other practices. This will in turn require abandonment of certain premises that have informed much nationalist but also much scholarly writing on this particular nationalism (but on most if not all other nationalisms as well, including of course Zionism), especially the assumption that this specific national identity had a singular meaning that was primordial, uniform, and dominant. By presenting a number of vignettes involving Arab workers in Palestine, I have tried to show that it is more helpful to understand that identity as complex, contingent, and variable, expressing not some authentic self awaiting discovery but a set of sentiments, symbols, and practices that could and did mean different things to different people, and could and did lead to different (even sometimes apparently "antinationalist") kinds of actions in certain circumstances.

In part, this is a plea for much more attention to the social and cultural history of modern Palestine and to "history from below," all of which have been sorely neglected in favor of elite-focused political and diplomatic history. But it also seems to me that we need to explore new ways of looking at, and writing about, modern history, and perhaps particularly the histories of colonized peoples in the colonial and postcolonial periods—ways that at least try to step outside not only the colonialist and Orientalist paradigms but also the conventional nationalist framework of historical understanding. This is not to invalidate the importance to people of their national identities, which are often (not least for Palestinians) crucial to their sense of themselves and that still give definition to struggles to end alien and oppressive rule and achieve a greater measure of freedom and a better life. The point is rather to attain a fuller understanding of the complex meanings that the nation, national identity, and nationalism have had for diverse groups of people in actual historical contexts, as well as the different uses to which people have put that assemblage of ideas, sentiments, symbols, and practices.

14

The Paradoxical in Arab Nationalism
Interwar Syria Revisited[*]

Philip S. Khoury

The study of Arab nationalism, as an ideology and as a system of political and social mobilization, has until recently concentrated on grand narratives constructed by and about elites. The narratives begin with an idea, or rather ideas, emerging in the late nineteenth century and bursting forth, when the time is right, into the organizing and mobilizing principles of a political movement. The ideas that laid the basis for an ideology of Arab nationalism set forth by Arab intellectuals have to do with a language constructed in a particular way, a history also constructed in a particular way, and the supposed "natural rights" that accrue to those who not only recognize their own "peoplehood" but who get others to recognize it as well. The right time was provided by the dismemberment of the Ottoman Empire after World War I and the imposition of direct European control on most of the Arabic-speaking provinces.

It is a measure of the dominance of an Arab intellectual and political elite that the history of the Arab world since, say, 1880 has largely been written around the idea of nationalism: When did it emerge? Amongst whom? Why? What was it? Who were nationalists? Who were not? These questions have mostly been posed and answered in reference to the political and intellectual elites of the Arab world. Recently, however, historians under the influence of post-structuralist theory and method have begun to offer alternative readings of the history of Arab nationalism. They are concentrating on those groups that have been treated as

[*]I wish to thank Mary Christina Wilson for the constructive ideas she contributed to this article.

historically marginal or passive in the grand narrative: peasants, workers, minorities, tribes, and women. They are elevating these neglected groups to a position of equal importance with elites in the scholarly discourse. In place of a single metanarrative, they are introducing micro- or local narratives to explain how Arab nationalism entered the consciousness of diverse groups in Arab society and, in particular, of marginal or neglected groups. In so doing, they are rejecting the more common totalizing history that assumes the validity of its own truth claims in favor of stories that do not make any truth claims. They are also nonetheless validating the centrality of nationalism as established by the elites. Being nationalist, or not, is still the measure of agency.

The new historians of Arab nationalism depend considerably less on standard literary texts and documents written by elites for elites than on a range of popular texts and oral traditions. Their histories posit that Arab nationalism has never had a single, agreed-upon meaning but, rather, multiple meanings based on how different groups constructed their identities and needs. They argue that although nationalist elites may have superimposed a national identity on all other identities—family, town and village, religion, class, or profession—Arabs formed a multiplicity of societies or groupings each with its own set of identities and interests. Undoubtedly, under the circumstances of European colonialism a number of groups or communities began to construct national identities, but the meanings and strength of these identities likely differed from one group to the next according to their particular usefulness. Moreover these meanings and identities were always shifting; for those trying to follow these shifts, no one meaning or identity is more privileged than the next.

The dilemma for those of us trying to rethink Arab nationalism is that while we are trying to broaden our view as to the groups who participated in shaping Arab nationalism, participate they must. In trying to include the many groups who make up Arab society we may become guilty of overdetermining their behavior, of calling their behavior nationalist because of our needs rather than their realities. This I believe has to do with the present context in which the history of Arab nationalism is being rethought. Just as George Antonius's *The Arab Awakening* (1938) was written at a historical moment and can be explained in light of that moment, so our rethinking is taking place at a time when the Arab nationalist agenda, whatever it is, is still far from complete. Nationalism in our time provides the only framework to consider the still-pressing questions about sovereignty, about who belongs to the national community, about state structure, and about proper relations with the rest of the world that continue to bedevil the Arab world.

In light of the effort to rethink Arab nationalism, it is particularly important to recognize that the study of interwar Arab nationalism has long faced a fundamental paradox. The nationalist elite was remarkably small at the beginning of the period and not much bigger at its end. It was a very small group to carry the vast weight of national metahistory. To obviate the paradox, some historians assumed that nationalist thinkers and leaders were simply dipping into a great well of unspoken patriotic feeling and national attachment that characterized the population at large. Others assumed passivity or ignorance, meaning unimportance, on the part of non-elites. Still others recognized the paradox but minimized it by assuming an expanding nationalist elite, expanding in terms of number and in terms of social provenance, through the ranks of national education and under the influence of new media.

If we recognize that the expansion was very small indeed, and that other groups hitherto considered marginal or not considered at all in the metahistory of Arab nationalism may have had equal importance in shaping national consciousness, why not just forget about the elite, expanding or not? Well, at the risk of being obvious, because an elite is by definition small, and because it is also by definition (its own, as well as historians') disproportionately influential in shaping events and in shaping how we understand events. In order better to understand how non-elites shaped and were shaped by nationalism in relation to elites, I would like to look at a moment in the development of nationalism amongst the political elite in Syria when that elite expanded in however slight a manner to incorporate new elements with new ideas and new interests. The point is that the nationalist elite was aware of nationalist feelings and constructs different from their own. When they were not able to ignore them or reinterpret them, they tried to co-opt them. The process of doing so tells us something about the nationalist elite, about ideological hegemony, and about available alternatives.

The moment to which I refer lasted from 1933 to 1937. In 1933 young nationalists from all the countries still under British and French Mandate and from Iraq secretly gathered in the Lebanese mountain village of Qarna'il to chart a course of Arab unity. Among those at Qarna'il were recent graduates of the law faculty of Damascus and the expanding secondary schools of Damascus and the other towns of Syria. Their new ideas were associated with what has commonly been referred to in the literature as radical pan-Arabism. Their interests were those of the emerging modern middle classes in Syria and other Arab countries in the interwar period. These ideas and interests were embodied in the League of National Action, the political organization that emerged at Qarna'il.[1] While the league was formed to express dissatisfaction with the current nationalist elite and to challenge its leadership, by 1937 its ideology and, to a considerable extent, the leaguers themselves had been co-opted into the mainstream of the national independence movement led by the older generation of urban politicians in the National Bloc.

The leaguers were a product of an expanding educational system. The number of primary and secondary school students in government institutions nearly doubled during the first half of the Mandate.[2] The boys who went to these schools, though of some means, were generally not the social equals of the elite that provided the leaders of the National Bloc. By 1933 tuition in all government primary schools was free while secondary schools, which charged a yearly fee, also provided some assistance.[3] The provision of scholarships enabled the children of the professional middle classes in the towns, and an increasing number of children from the petty bourgeoisie, most notably the sons of small shopowners and traders, to attend.[4] During the Mandate enrollment in the government school system grew at a quicker pace than it did in private and foreign schools, reaching 50 percent of the total school population in 1933. Nevertheless the growth of public education was hardly dramatic. It was still restricted and almost exclusively available to boys.[5]

In late Ottoman times, there had been only one government secondary school in Damascus, Maktab `Anbar, located on the inner edge of the Jewish quarter in the old city. Conceived of as a national school, Maktab `Anbar produced the vanguard of the national independence movement during the Mandate. In 1918 it became known officially as the *tajhiz* (preparatory school). It remained on the grounds of the `Anbar Palace and maintained its status as the elite secondary school of Damascus. In 1932, long after it had exhausted its limited space, it was relocated to new spacious quarters with modern laboratories and other facilities in the Europeanized Salhiyya district, not far from the new Parliament building. At this time, the school's enrollment increased by nearly 40 percent to nearly seven hundred teenage boys.[6]

The Damascus *tajhiz* accepted boarders from as far away as Hama and Homs. Because students paid only a nominal tuition, the *tajhiz* was not as prohibitive as Maktab `Anbar had been. Twenty percent of the students in 1933, for example, were exempted from all fees. Nevertheless education during the Mandate retained its elitist status; in the early thirties the Syrian literacy rate was still only 28 percent and only 4 percent of the population had a secondary school education.[7]

The schools were organized on a French model in preparation for the baccalaureate examination. Each government school had one director of French studies and French occupied a prominent place in the curriculum, although the language of instruction was Arabic. The majority of the *tajhiz's* full-time faculty of twenty-six were trained in Paris; they offered their students excellent instruction in literature, history, mathematics, and sciences, all in the medium of Arabic.

The *tajhiz*, despite its Frenchified form, became one of the principal centers of nationalist activity during the 1930s. In addition to the study of modern sciences and Western philosophy and literature, students were encouraged to commit to memory the nationalist verse of well-known Arab poets such as the Egyptian Ahmad Shawqi. The history of the Arabs and their fundamental contributions to the progress of world civilization was taught in the most exacting national terms. Because Syria did not enter the interwar years with a host of local intellectuals to whom this young generation could turn, it looked to Egypt and elsewhere in the Arab world for intellectual nourishment. This reinforced a national identity stretching beyond Syria's newly imposed frontiers. As this generation reached maturity in the early 1930s, pan-Arabism appeared to undergo a revival.

The National Bloc had recognized the need to harness the energy of teenage boys, usefully concentrated in city schools, in the late 1920s when it formed the Nationalist Youth (*al-Shabab al-Watani*), the first significant political organization for educated youth in the towns during the Mandate.[8]

The day-to-day politicization and organization of the rising generation of educated youth was the responsibility of a group of lawyers and teachers, men not much older than their young followers. This marked the beginning of a shift on the part of the National Bloc from the old stalwarts of the urban notables, the traditionally educated and attired merchants and religious leaders and the unlettered *qabadayat* (local bosses) of the popular quarters, to a new set of clients.

Some National Bloc leaders strongly believed that the independence movement required its own militia and looked to the burgeoning Syrian Boy Scout movement as a prototype for the future Syrian army. In 1929 the bloc established its own Boy Scout troop, the Umayyad Troop, and attached it to the newly created Nationalist Youth. Over the next two years the highly politicized Umayyad Troop competed fiercely with the non-affiliated Ghuta Troop, which had been established in 1927.[9] But when Umayyad scoutmasters, through the mechanism of the Nationalist Youth, were obliged to defend publicly the bloc's policy of "honorable cooperation" with the French, which had not visibly advanced the struggle for Syrian independence, scouts in the Umayyad Troop began to defect to the Ghuta Troop. Eventually the Umayyad Troop collapsed. In the meantime the Ghuta Troop led the effort to federate all scouting in

Syria, both to acquire a higher level of organization and to become affiliated on international scouting councils. By 1933 Syrian Boy Scouts were grouped into several troops in most Syrian towns and numbered 3,000. Scouts were inculcated with pan-Arabist ideas by their scoutmasters, while the Scouting organization's directors were among those plotting the establishment of the League of National Action.[10]

The Syrian University also expanded in this period, and opportunities opened for the brightest high school and university graduates to go to French universities on scholarship in a wide variety of fields, including law, medicine, and teacher training. A significant number of *tajhiz* graduates went on to study law at the Damascus Law Faculty or in Paris.[11] Some ended up as teachers at the *tajhiz* of Damascus and Syria's other major cities, while others became teachers in smaller towns and villages. Closely associated with the *tajhiz* was the Damascus Law Faculty, established in 1919, where many *tajhiz* graduates went on to study. Not surprisingly, law graduates and school teachers became deeply involved in politicizing the younger *tajhiz* students.

These opportunities in education and in extracurricular organizations certainly played a role in broadening the horizons of some urban youth and in shifting the focus of their activities out of the medieval town quarters into modern, "nationwide" institutions and organizations. As their focus shifted, so did their expectations. But although modern education paved the way for social mobility and afforded middle-class status, middle-class incomes were not guaranteed. The rising but unfulfilled expectations of the newly educated created a reservoir of frustration and antagonism, which only grew during the depression.

The depression did not significantly loosen France's economic hold over Syria. As long as the Syrian-Lebanese lira was pegged to the French franc, the Syrian economy had little room to engage in its own development free of French controls. The devaluation of the franc at this time may have encouraged some Syrian exports, but it also drove up the costs of Western imports valued by the emerging modern middle classes.[12]

Syria in 1933 was also in the throes of the most devastating drought since World War I (some said "in living memory"). Famine began to reach alarming proportions as wheat production fell in 1933, on average 16 percent from the previous year, and even more sharply in the breadbasket known as Hawran. In Damascus and other towns, where the general economic crisis had created a large glut on the labor market, the influx of peasants fleeing the deteriorating conditions in the countryside meant banditry in the agricultural areas around the towns and larceny within them. A member of the Jewish National Fund reported that in the spring of 1933 between 25,000 and 30,000 Hawranis fled their lands, 90 percent to Palestine and the remainder to Damascus and Beirut. In Palestine these refugees were absorbed into the Jewish-controlled sector of the labor market, though by the autumn 30 percent had returned home. The same source claimed to have saved peasants from starvation and Syria from massive upheaval.[13] In the absence of local measures to address the problems of loss of agricultural production and unemployment, some Syrians migrated to neighboring Arab countries, expressing by migration a pan-Arabist solution to local economic problems.

The spirit of pan-Arabism implicit in the migrations of peasants was articulated by *tajhiz* graduates. The issue of pan-Arabism gave ideological shape to the amorphous disillusionment with the National Bloc's policy of "honorable cooperation" and its failure to achieve anything tangible in the way of political autonomy or economic independence. The growing disaffection of some Nationalist Youth members with their leaders and with National Bloc policies in general produced a schism in the Damascus student movement. There were several ways this schism was made manifest. More and more *tajhiz* students began to boycott the National Bloc leadership's favorite café, the Globe, in favor of the Ghazi café. They gravitated toward a new bookstore, Maktabat al-`Umumiyya, which had been opened by a wealthy merchant and well-known pan-Arabist, forsaking the novelties shop and bookstore on the Rue Rami owned by the principal leader of the Nationalist Youth. And in traditional Middle Eastern manner, headgear distinguished rival youth groups: the increasingly radicalized group of lawyers, doctors, and other professionals who were involved with the Ghuta troop and with the dissenting student movement at the *tajhiz* began to sport the Iraqi *sidara*, the army headgear invented by King Faysal and a symbol for pan-Arabist youth, instead of the familiar fez, worn by National Bloc leaders and their followers in the Nationalist Youth. At the most important student congress of the Mandate, held in Hama in February 1932, none of the various resolutions made reference to the National Bloc or Nationalist Youth; they did, however, include the general principles associated with pan-Arabism at this time.[14]

By 1933 the bloc's policy of "honorable cooperation," which had governed its strategy vis à vis the French ever since the end of the Great Revolt in 1927 and was focused narrowly on Syrian goals, had achieved nothing. Negotiations for a treaty of independence, not unlike the one Iraq secured from the British in 1930, had collapsed; the French were unwilling to loosen their grip on the country. At the same time the first generation of young men educated in government schools in terms of the glorious history of the Arabs and attuned to intellectual currents outside of their immediate environs came of age. Defections from the

Nationalist Youth and the crucial institutions in which it had influence resulted.[15] These defections were particularly visible in the Boy Scouts and the *tajhiz*. Law students and young lawyers constituted the most vital component of the League of National Action's leadership; students at the *tajhiz* provided the numbers at the protests, strikes, and boycotts that occurred so frequently in the 1930s in Damascus and the other urban centers of nationalist activity.

Gathered at Qarna'il in August 1933 was a group of nearly fifty radical pan-Arabists from Syria, Lebanon, Transjordan, Palestine, and Iraq, many of whom were activist lawyers and youth leaders in their respective countries. These men were motivated by one goal: to set the national independence movements in the Arab territories on a firmer footing by systematically coordinating their activities.[16] To achieve this goal they founded the League of National Action.

The league was based in Syria but connected to similar parties in the neighboring Arab territories. The new organization embodied the beliefs and ambitions of a new generation of angry young men that had begun to emerge throughout the Arab East. The preference for the term *qawmi* in its name (`Usbat al-`Amal al-Qawmi*) was indicative of the league's orientation; pan-Arabists frequently used *qawmiyya* to mark a "feeling of loyalty to the whole Arab nation," thus distinguishing it from the term *wataniyya*—the preference of the National Bloc and the Nationalist Youth— which denoted an attachment to the specific country of one's birth.[17]

The league's goals were Arab sovereignty, independence, and comprehensive Arab unity. Unlike the bloc, it emphasized the need for economic development and integration in order to wage a successful struggle against the exploitation of foreign powers and against feudal landlords. With specific reference to Syria, its program demanded the rejection of the policy of "honorable cooperation" and of all attempts to get the people to accept the fraudulently elected parliament and the French-appointed government in Damascus. Its program makes clear that the league was neither socialist nor Marxist-Leninist. For class struggle it substituted national struggle.[18] It was radical in its reformism but its populist tendencies were superficial. The league's program also revealed a strong inclination toward authoritarianism. In this way it was similar to other groups or parties that had recently cropped up in the Arab territories under Mandate, in particular the Ahali group in Iraq and the Istiqlal Party in Palestine. Both also had populist pretensions, stressed economic and political reformism, rejected "class struggle" for "national unity," and had a pronounced authoritarian streak.[19]

One of the specific goals of the Qarna'il conference was to mastermind the infiltration of all pan-Arabist groupings so as to coordinate their activities and ultimately to lead the drive for Arab independence and unity from Baghdad to Casablanca. With the League of National Action in Syria as the main frontal organization, its members would coordinate the activities of the Istiqlal Party in Palestine, the Ahali group in Iraq, and similar radical nationalist organizations.

The league's first secretary-general was also chairman of the committee that organized the secret Qarna'il conference. `Abd al-Razzaq al-Dandashi belonged to the Al Dandash clan of Tall Kalakh but grew up in Tripoli, where he was born in 1905. He had studied law in Brussels and been active there in Arab student politics. Upon his return to Syria, he settled in Damascus to practice law in a firm that included another league leader, `Adnan al-Atasi, son of Hashim, the President of the National Bloc. By the early 1930s Dandashi had already won a reputation as a courageous and uncompromising champion of the Arab nationalist cause. He was an impassioned orator and extremely popular with high school and law students, young journalists, and café intellectuals.

In its leadership, the league came from the same social milieu as the bloc. The vast majority of its members, however, were either from the poorer branches of these landed and bureaucratic families or were unpropertied, which differentiated them from bloc leaders, of whom more than 60 percent belonged to the urban absentee landlord class. In fact league leaders were almost completely dependent on their salaries in the liberal professions for their livelihood. Seventy percent were either practicing lawyers or instructors of law; the remainder was divided among the other professions. The league incorporated a generation which was, on average, twenty years younger than the bloc leadership. In 1933 their average age was thirty.[20]

From the outset the league attempted to organize along the lines of a modern political party. It had a central political council, which provided for the division and distribution of power and the allocation of responsibilities. It had a core of regular dues-paying members, governed by a set of party rules. It also had a political program and its own political mouthpiece, a weekly newspaper called *al-`Amal al-Qawmi*. And it had several chapters, in Homs, Hama, Dayr al-Zur, and Antioch, which were linked to its Central Council in Damascus. The chapter in Antioch led the struggle against Turkey's ultimately successful efforts to pry away the Sanjaq of Alexandretta from Syria in the late 1930s.[21]

The league, however, proved to be anything but a mass-based party. Nor did it ever encourage anything of the sort. Rather, despite its provenance in a slightly broader social milieu than the National Bloc's, or maybe because of it, the league was fiercely elitist. While it actively campaigned for pan-Arab economic integration, it failed to build relations with merchants in the suqs and it neglected the artisans and the unemployed or casually employed in the popular quarters, with whom the bloc maintained ties. The league also made no systematic efforts to build bridges to the Syrian officer corps.[22] This was in part because its young, gifted leaders were often aloof, unwilling to broaden their efforts beyond the institutions from which they themselves had emerged—the *tajhiz* and the Faculty of Law in Damascus for the most part. In fact, the league adopted a cliquish demeanor, characterized by the young man in a sports jacket sitting at the league's favorite café, proudly displaying the latest edition of the prestigious Cairo newspaper *al-Muqattam*, or maybe the literary and scientific journals *al-Hilal* and *al-Muqtataf*. There, he and his companions spent countless hours sipping strong coffee and plotting courses of action against the most recent French decrees. The average leaguer, in short, lived in a world quite foreign to the one most Damascenes inhabited.

Like the National Bloc, the league pictured political life in its own image. The schools and other modern institutions were the province of leaguers; it was there that their political life took shape and there that their politics were enacted. While Syrian urban politics had begun to move out of the quarters by 1933, the move was by no means complete. Thus the leaguers were even more narrow in their political appeal and outlook than the National Bloc. The older and more experienced bloc leaders, whose own styles were a mix of traditional city patron and modern party man, preserved their links with the popular quarters and their leaders: religious *shaykhs*, merchants, and *qabadayat*. Thus instead of toppling the bloc, the crises of the early 1930s, and the League of National Action to which they gave rise, merely provided more grist for the bloc's perpetual factionalism.[23]

National Bloc leaders belonged to two urban-based and intertwined groups—absentee landlord and the (non-comprador) commercial bourgeoisie—and included a growing number from the professional middle classes who steered the Nationalist Youth. As men of capital, bloc leaders were among those who had been denied access to foreign capital. Some couched their opposition to the Mandate in terms of a struggle to assert what they believed was their rightful claim to adequate economic consideration from the French. Others believed that their interests were intrinsically incompatible with French and other foreign commercial and financial interests and wanted to break the dominant local alliance of compradors and French capital by laying the foundations of a national economy whose markets would stretch across the Arab world.

These latter represented the pan-Arab wing of the bloc and had the strongest ties to like-minded nationalists in other Arab countries.[24] They were known as the Istiqlalis and owed their name to a post-World War I party that had been active in Syria and Palestine during Amir Faysal's reign in Damascus and later during the Syrian Revolt of 1925.

It was the Istiqlalis led by Shukri al-Quwatli who worked most assiduously to co-opt the league between 1933 and 1937. Their aim was twofold: to contain radical pan-Arabism by absorbing into the bloc some aspects of the league's ideology and some of its most important personnel; and to use the league to gain leverage over bloc moderates who controlled bloc policy and strategy.

Quwatli's own political career established a model for the way the league would be co-opted.[25] He was a latecomer to the bloc leadership, having only been amnestied by the French in 1930 owing to his pan-Arab activities during the Syrian Revolt of the mid-1920s. By that time the National Bloc was unrivalled in its influence over the Syrian independence movement. Although he did not favor the moderate stance adopted by Damascus bloc leaders, which gave them, among all nationalists, nearly exclusive access to French Mandate authorities, he also realized that by remaining locked outside in direct opposition to the Damascus bloc he would always be a marginal political actor. By joining the bloc he hoped to set it on a less compromising course. To gain leverage, Quwatli widened his political base. He had strong followings in a number of popular quarters and among merchants and especially nascent industrialists, but his bloc rivals controlled the Nationalist Youth. Therefore he and other Istiqlalis quietly encouraged defections from the ranks of the Nationalist Youth in the early 1930s. Some defectors eventually became leaders in the League of National Action.

Quwatli knew of the secret gathering of young radical pan-Arabists at Qarna'il in the summer of 1933, and he moved quickly to put the league squarely in his own political orbit, something he pursued quietly for the next three years. Because league leaders were able to ride the wave of pan-Arabist sentiment in this period, they saw no reason to break their sacred principle of refusing to collaborate with the National Bloc; they preferred to work outside the established framework of politics, expanding their organization and promoting Arab unity as the best way of achieving independence. Quwatli managed to advance the co-optation process only slightly before 1936, by helping to bankroll the league's first serious financial enterprise, a national land development company designed to save indebted Syrian landowners from selling their properties on the borders of Syria and Palestine to the Jewish National Fund. When this failed, he placed some league leaders on the board of directors of his own National Conserves Company, one of a number of modern Syrian industries that National Bloc leaders and wealthy merchants had started up after the Syrian Revolt. Because the Istiqlali wing of the bloc made efforts to undermine the dominant alliance of French capital and the comprador bourgeoisie through the vehicle of economic nationalism, league leaders saw a reason to join Quwatli's company board. What they did not at first understand was that claims to economic nationalism also served the bloc and the classes it represented because it kept attention riveted on the French occupation and away from the internal competition and conflicts between classes arising from the uneven spread of capitalist relations in Syria. As long as the French remained in Syria, national struggle took priority over class struggle.[26]

New opportunities eventually arose for the co-optation of the league. The first was the sudden death of `Abd al-Razzaq al-Dandashi in August 1935 in a tramway accident in Damascus.[27] The ensuing competition for the post of secretary-general revealed a previously undetected schism in the leadership between those who wanted the league to stay out of daily government-level politics and those who argued that the league could never have a lasting impact on nationalist politics unless it entered the arena of daily politics. A compromise candidate, Sabri al-`Asali, became the new secretary-general.

As the league's leadership question was being sorted out, Syrians launched in January 1936 a general strike that contributed to the revival of treaty negotiations, this time between the bloc and France. Quwatli was not appointed to the bloc negotiating team in Paris, but he was made vice president in charge of the bloc's internal affairs. In the period between the Syrian delegation's departure for Paris in March 1936 and its return in the fall, he dedicated himself to the task of unifying nationalist ranks by bringing the league under the bloc's wing. Ultimately, he would have liked to form a single national party, but he realized that many of the league's younger and more militant members were still unprepared to join ranks with the bloc. An intensification of the rivalry between the league and the Nationalist Youth did not help matters; after the strike both had established paramilitary branches that battled in the streets of Damascus and other towns.[28]

Sabri al-`Asali and Shukri al-Quwatli were a generation apart in age but they had much in common. Both came from notable families in two of the most popular and politically active quarters of Damascus (al-Maydan and Shaghur) and both moved comfortably between the upper level of politics and the urban masses. Moreover, they had worked closely after the Syrian Revolt in the cause of pan-Arabism and especially to enlist the support of the Saudis as a check on Hashimite designs in

Syria.[29] Therefore, `Asali was already sympathetic to the older genera-
tion of Istiqlalis headed by Quwatli by the time he was tapped as the
league's next secretary-general.

While National Bloc moderates were still in Paris, Quwatli moved
quickly to infuse the bloc with more radical elements. He invited `Asali
and two other league stalwarts to join the National Bloc Council in the
summer of 1936. His aim was to keep these young militants informed of
the treaty negotiations in order to convince them that the delegation in
Paris was not compromising Syria's national and territorial integrity.
`Asali accepted the invitation, precipitating a crisis within the league.
When league efforts to woo him back to the fold failed, he was expelled
from the Secretariat and soon thereafter from the organization itself. In
November he ran successfully on the National Bloc's electoral list in
Damascus, winning a seat in Parliament.

The league leadership, socially close to the National Bloc leadership,
were prime candidates for co-option. Soon Quwatli used the bait of government posts to lure other young radicals into the bloc. More and more
league leaders began to break their organization's cardinal principle and
serve in the new National Bloc government.

Not only had Shukri al-Quwatli managed to weaken the League of
National Action, thus making the National Bloc's ascendancy that much
more complete, he had also managed to strengthen his own position at the
expense of Jamil Mardam, his main nationalist rival in Damascus. As for
the league, it remained active in pan-Arabist politics and especially in
organizing Syrian support for the revolt in Palestine, but it no longer
posed a serious challenge to the National Bloc's paramount position within the independence movement. What had once been a challenge to bloc
leadership from the outside now became part of the factional infighting
of the bloc with the Istiqlalis and a younger generation of pan-Arabist ex-
leaguers around Shukri al-Quwatli. In fact, the bloc outlived the league,
which suffered another major setback when the French outlawed it on the
eve of World War Two. It would rear its head time and again during the
war years, but by then some of its former leaders from more peripheral
Syrian regions had already joined together with other claimants to the
mantle of pan-Arabism to form a new political organization, which became known as the Ba`th Party. In the Ba`th, some of the league's personnel and ideas lived on, and it continued to pose a challenge to the National Bloc long after its wartime leader, Shukri al-Quwatli, had become
the first President of an independent Syria.

What can we learn from this effort to narrate a brief moment in the life
of the politics of Arab nationalism? First, our understanding of interwar

Syria has been formed to a large extent by our focus on Arab nationalism, whether we have concentrated on its history from above or from
below or from somewhere in the middle. Whether we like it or not, nationalism has defined the period. As nationalist elites defined everything
in terms of nationalism, so historians have tended to measure all groups
by the extent to which they constructed their identities as "national"
identities. This is what I mean by ideological hegemony.[30]

What is especially trenchant in the case of the League of National Action is that it is best remembered not for its economic programs, which
expressed a degree of difference with the interests and programs of the
National Bloc, but for its pan Arabism. Pan-Arabism in the interwar
period, as in later periods, was a subset of Arab nationalism: many of its
defining characteristics were (and in some ways still are) common to
Arab nationalism, although it had its own orientation conditioned by
the historical realities of the era. Interwar pan-Arabism was stronger in
societies that had significant religious and ethnic minorities (Syria, Iraq,
Palestine) than in societies that were religiously and ethnically homogeneous (Egypt, Saudi Arabia).[31] It was also more an effect of the difficulties of state formation in the interwar years than it was a cause of
those difficulties.[32] It received greatest emphasis and attention in those
periods when country-specific independence movements were unable to
make progress against the European occupying powers. It called for the
political coordination and, ultimately, the unification of all country-specific independence movements as the most effective means of liberating
the Arab world from European imperial rule. It offered specific economic and social reform programs that were often absent in the platforms of
country-specific independence movements and that were intended to
challenge the legitimacy of these other movements and, in particular,
the elites that led them. It was almost exclusively an urban phenomenon, one that especially benefited from the improvement in modern
transportation and communication links between towns in the Arab
East. Its direct appeal was to modern educated individuals and groups. It
was fundamentally a secular movement intimately associated in the
interwar years with the ongoing Arab cultural revival. It was also intimately associated with the radicalization of interwar Arab politics.[33]

In the end, however, pan-Arabism's inattentiveness to the cultural
and social needs and traditions of the nonliterate urban and rural masses gave it insufficient strength to wrest control from any of the country-
specific independence movements that dominated nationalist politics in
the interwar years. Despite the inclusion of ideas of economic reform in
pan-Arabism, its attention was focused on distant horizons. It put off effective consideration of immediate and specific local problems for the

deferred gratification of a pan-Arabist future. Differences of social provenance that might have given rise to a more broadly conceived nationalist movement in terms of class were left behind in favor of a nationalist movement broadly conceived in terms of territory.

Second, we should rethink factionalism within the framework of the
politics of Arab nationalism. In *Syria and the French Mandate* and elsewhere, I have portrayed factionalism in negative terms, arguing that it
rendered nationalist elites ineffective in the face of colonial powers and,
after their departure, as rulers.[34] Factionalism was possible, I thought,
only because there was such a huge gulf between the nationalist political
elite and everyone else. Factionalism was, in short, a luxury conveyed by
class and ultimately injurious to class position. Now I am beginning to
see that factionalism was a very useful tool with which to incorporate
challengers. Factionalism conveys many-sidedness. As long as the bloc
was an aggregation of different opinions, interests, and tendencies, it
could use its different facets to appeal to rival ideas and groups and incorporate them into the mainstream of the national independence movement. What has often been interpreted to be a congenital weakness in the
nature or character of nationalist elites—their being prone to intensive
factionalism—may, in fact, have been an asset in the politics of Arab nationalism. This, rather than absolute social and political dominance, may
be why the class from which the National Bloc leadership arose felt no
compulsion to act as a class during the interwar years.

Our present goal is to rethink nationalisms. We are doing so by attempting to "decenter" the nationalist elite. Nationalism was many things
to many people. We know that when different groups demonstrated in the
streets or boycotted foreign goods and foreign-owned concessions, the nationalist elites always constructed these events exclusively as expressions
of nationalism in support of their own leadership. Those who marched and
boycotted, however, may have been motivated by other considerations.
What the historically marginal groups that participated in such manifestations actually understood by their acts and aimed at is the secret historians are now trying to unlock. Looking beyond "rethinking nationalisms," we may be able to decenter Arab nationalism itself. This is a sword
that cuts two ways. On the one hand, we may be able to recognize more
clearly the self-interestedness of the nationalist elites. On the other, we
may find that advancing national ideals is not the sole measure of historical agency in the twentieth-century Arab world.

Notes

Introduction

1. Ernest Renan, *Qu'est que c'est une nation?* (Paris, 1882), 26–29.
2. Arnold Toynbee, *Nationality and the War* (London, 1915), 13.
3. Hans Kohn, *The Idea of Nationalism* (New York, 1944), 10.
4. Karl W. Deutsch, *Nationalism and Social Communication* (Cambridge, MA, 1953).
5. Benedict Anderson, *Imagined Communities: Reflections on the Origins and Spread of Nationalism* (2d. ed.; New York, 1991), 6.
6. Max Weber, *Vorhandlungen des Zweitens Deutschen Soziologentages* (Tübingen, 1913), 50.
7. Elie Kedourie, *Nationalism* (2d. ed.; New York, 1961), 9, 18, 49.
8. Ernest Gellner, *Nations and Nationalism* (Ithaca, 1983), 1.
9. John Breuilly, *Nationalism and the State* (2d. ed.; Chicago, 1994), 14.
10. Anthony D. Smith, "Gastronomy or Archeology? The Role of Nationalism in the Construction of Nations," paper delivered at the seminar on "Rethinking Nationalisms," Weiner Library, Tel Aviv University, 23 March 1993; see also his "The Myth of the 'Modern Nation' and the Myths of Nations," *Ethnic and Racial Studies* 11:1 (January 1988), 1–26.
11. Gellner, *Nations and Nationalism.*
12. Anderson, *Imagined Communities.*
13. For an example of the biologically based approach, see Pierre Van den Berghe, *The Ethnic Phenomenon* (New York, 1979).
14. John Armstrong, *Nations before Nationalism* (Chapel Hill, 1982); Anthony D. Smith, *The Ethnic Origins of Nations* (New York, 1986).
15. Breuilly, *Nationalism and the State.*
16. Eric Hobsbawm and Terence Ranger (eds.), *The Invention of Tradition* (Cambridge, 1983).
17. Eric Hobsbawm, *Nations and Nationalism Since 1780* (Cambridge, 1990).

18. Liah Greenfeld, *Nationalism: Five Roads to Modernity* (Cambridge, MA, 1992).

19. Partha Chatterjee, *Nationalist Thought and the Colonial World: A Derivative Discourse?* (London, 1986); idem, *The Nation and Its Fragments: Colonial and Postcolonial Histories* (Princeton, 1993).

20. Homi K. Bhabha (ed.), *The Nation and Narration* (London, 1990), 1–2.

21. Ibid., 2. For other examples of this approach, see Hayden White, *Metahistory* (2d. ed.; Baltimore, 1993); *Tropics of Discourse: Essays in Cultural Criticism* (Baltimore, 1978); idem, *The Content of the Form* (Baltimore, 1987); Scott Lash and Jonathan Friedman (eds.), *Modernity and Identity* (Oxford, 1992); Itamar Even-Zohar, "Polysystem Studies," *Poetics Today* 11:1 (Spring 1990).

22. The following are leading examples of the primarily ideological approach to Arab nationalism: William L. Cleveland, *The Making of an Arab Nationalist: Ottomanism and Arabism in the Life and Thought of Sati` al-Husri* (Princeton, 1971); idem, *Islam Against the West: Shakib Arslan and the Campaign for Islamic Nationalism* (Austin, 1985); C. Ernest Dawn, *From Ottomanism to Arabism: Essays on the Origins of Arab Nationalism* (Urbana, 1973); idem, "The Formation of Pan-Arab Ideology in the Interwar Years," *International Journal of Middle East Studies* 20 (1988): 67–91; Sylvia G. Haim, *Arab Nationalism: An Anthology* (Berkeley, 1962); Albert Hourani, *Arabic Thought in the Liberal Age, 1798–1939* (Oxford, 1962); Majid Khadduri, *Political Trends in the Arab World: The Role of Ideas and Ideals in Politics* (Baltimore, 1970); Hazem Zaki Nuseibeh, *The Ideas of Arab Nationalism* (Ithaca, 1956); Fayez A. Sayegh, *Arab Unity: Hope and Fulfillment* (New York, 1958); Bassam Tibi, *Arab Nationalism: A Critical Enquiry*, trans. Marion Farouq-Sluglett and Peter Sluglett (New York, 1981).

23. Important examples include Amatzia Baram, *Culture, History, and Ideology in the Formation of Ba`thist Iraq, 1968–1989* (London, 1991); Joel Beinin and Zachary Lockman, *Workers on the Nile: Nationalism, Communism, Islam, and the Egyptian Working Class, 1882–1954* (Princeton, 1987); Ralph M. Coury, "Who 'Invented' Egyptian Arab Nationalism?" *International Journal of Middle East Studies* 14 (1982): 249–281 and 459–479; Israel Gershoni, *The Emergence of Pan-Arabism in Egypt* (Tel Aviv, 1981); Israel Gershoni and James P. Jankowski, *Egypt, Islam, and the Arabs: The Search for Egyptian Nationhood, 1900–1930* (New York, 1986), and *Redefining the Egyptian Nation, 1930–1945* (Cambridge, 1995); Nels Johnson, *Islam and the Politics of Meaning in Palestinian Nationalism* (New York, 1982); Philip S. Khoury, *Syria and the French Mandate: The Politics of Arab Nationalism, 1920–1945* (Princeton, 1987); Muhammad Y. Muslih, *The Origins of Palestinian Nationalism* (New York, 1988); Yehoshua Porath, *The Emergence of the Palestinian-Arab National Movement, 1918–1929* (London, 1974); idem, *The Palestinian Arab National Movement, 1929–1939: From Riots to Rebellion* (London, 1977); Reeva S. Simon, *Iraq Between the Two World Wars: The Creation and Implementation of a Nationalist Ideology* (New York, 1986).

24. Rashid Khalidi, Lisa Anderson, Muhammad Muslih, and Reeva S. Simon (eds.), *The Origins of Arab Nationalism* (New York, 1991).

25. Jean-François Lyotard, *The Postmodern Condition: A Report on Knowledge* (Minneapolis, 1984), 9–23.

26. Michel Foucault, *The Order of Things: An Archeology of the Human Sciences* (New York, 1970), 71–76.

1. Rethinking the Formation of Arab Nationalism in the Middle East, 1920–1945: Old and New Narratives

1. Anderson, *Imagined Communities*, 6.

2. For recent discussions of competing national allegiances in the modern Middle East, see Rashid Khalidi, "Arab Nationalism: Historical Problems in the Literature," *American Historical Review* 96 (1991): 1363–1373; Roger Owen, *State, Power, and Politics in the Making of the Modern Middle East* (London, 1992), 81–107; James Piscatori, *Islam in a World of Nation-States* (Cambridge, 1986); Amatzia Baram, "Territorial Nationalism in the Middle East," *Middle Eastern Studies* 26 (1990): 425–448.

3. Fouad Ajami, "The End of Pan-Arabism," *Foreign Affairs* 57 (Winter 1978–79): 355–373; Tawfic E. Farah (ed.), *Pan-Arabism and Arab Nationalism: The Continuing Debate* (Boulder, 1987).

4. For representative literature on this, see Fouad Ajami, *The Arab Predicament* (Cambridge, MA, 1981); Tawfic E. Farah (ed.), *Political Behavior in the Arab States* (Boulder, 1983); B. Korany and A. E. Hilal Dessouki (eds.), *The Foreign Policies of Arab States: The Challenge of Change* (2d. ed.; Boulder, 1991), in particular the article by Paul C. Noble, "The Arab System: Pressures, Constraints, Opportunities," 49–102; Martin Kramer, "Arab Nationalism: Mistaken Identity," *Daedalus* 122 (Summer 1993): 171–206; Emmanuel Sivan, "The Arab Nation-State: In Search of a Usable Past," *Middle East Review* (Spring 1987): 21–30; Menahem Klein, "Arab Unity: A Nonexistent Entity," *The Jerusalem Journal of International Relations* 12 (1990): 28–44; Issa J. Boullata, *Trends and Issues in Contemporary Arab Thought* (New York, 1990); Asad Abukhalil, "A New Arab Ideology? The Rejuvenation of Arab Nationalism," *Middle East Journal* 46 (1992): 22–36.

5. On early Arab nationalism see the collection of articles in Rashid Khalidi et al., *Origins*, and Frank Clements, *The Emergence of Arab Nationalism From the Nineteenth Century to 1921, A Bibliography* (Wilmington, 1976).

6. Dawn, "Formation," 67.

7. See, for example, Robert G. Woolbert, "Pan-Arabism and the Palestine Problem," *Foreign Affairs* 16 (January 1938): 309–322; H. A. R. Gibb, "Toward Arab Unity," *Foreign Affairs* 24 (1945–1946): 119–129; Costi K. Zurayk, "The Essence of Arab Civilization," *Middle East Journal* 3 (1949): 125–139; Nicola A. Ziadeh, "Recent Arab Literature on Arabism," ibid. 6 (1952): 468–473.

8. This paper deals only with works and studies on Arab nationalism written in Western languages, mainly English. Studies written in Arabic by Arab historians and scholars constitute a topic for further discussion.

9. White, *Metahistory*, 430.

10. Nuseibeh, *Ideas*; Sayegh, *Arab Unity*.

11. Kedourie's articles on the subject of the 1950s and 1960s were later published in his *The Chatham House Version and Other Middle-Eastern Studies* (London, 1970); Hourani, *Arabic Thought*; Haim, *Arab Nationalism*.

12. Khadduri, *Political Trends*; Hans E. Tütsch, *Facets of Arab Nationalism* (Detroit, 1965); Leonard Binder, *The Ideological Revolution in the Middle East* (New York, 1964); Anwar G. Chejne, "Egyptian Attitudes Toward Pan-Arabism," *Middle East Journal* 11 (1957): 253–268; idem, "The Use of History by Modern Arab Writers," ibid. 14 (1960): 387–398; Bernard Lewis, *The Middle East and the West* (New York, 1964); W. C. Smith, *Islam in Modern History* (Princeton, 1957); Patrick Seale, *The Struggle for Syria* (Oxford, 1965); Nissim Rejwan, "Arab Nationalism: In Search of an Ideology," in Walter Z. Laqueur (ed.), *The Middle East in Transition* (New York, 1958), 145–165; Hisham B. Sharabi, *Nationalism and Revolution in the Arab World* (Toronto, 1966); Eliezer Be'eri, *Army Officers in Arab Politics and Society* (London, 1970).

13. Haim, *Arab Nationalism*, 35.

14. Hourani, *Arabic Thought*, 307.

15. For approaches to intellectual history, see Arthur O. Lovejoy, *The Great Chain of Being* (Cambridge, 1936); John Higham, "American Intellectual History: A Critical Appraisal," in Robert Merideth (ed.), *American Studies: Essays on Theory and Method* (Columbus, Ohio, 1968), 218–235; Rush Welter, "The History of Ideas in America: An Essay in Redefinition," ibid., 236–253; John Higham and Paul K. Conkin (eds.), *New Directions in American Intellectual History* (Baltimore, 1979); Preston King (ed.) *The History of Ideas: An Introduction to Method* (London, 1983); and the special issue of the *Journal of the History of Ideas* devoted to "The History of Ideas," no. 48 (April/June 1987). Many classic analyses of nationalism such as those of Carlton Hayes, Hans Kohn, and Jacob Talmon also approach the topic primarily as *Ideengeschichte*. The intellectual perspective prevalent in early studies of nationalism unquestionably influenced the old narrative on Arab nationalism.

16. Higham, "American Intellectual History," 220.

17. Kedourie, *Nationalism*. Kedourie acknowledges the influence of Lovejoy in his preface.

18. We refer mainly to their scholarly works published in the late 1940s and the 1950s.

19. Nuseibeh, *Ideas*, v.

20. Hourani, *Arabic Thought* (paperback ed., 1983), viii.

21. Haim, *Arab Nationalism*, 3–72.

22. Sayegh, *Arab Unity*, 63, 97.

23. Ibid., 63–94.

24. Nuseibeh, *Ideas*, 57–97.

25. Haim, *Arab Nationalism*, 35–61.

26. Hourani, *Arabic Thought*, 308–316.

27. Khadduri, *Political Trends*, 177–205.

28. Hourani, *Arabic Thought*, 313.

29. Haim, *Arab Nationalism*, 40–55; Nuseibeh, *Ideas*, 68–77; Khadduri, *Political Trends*, 179–205; Sayegh, *Arab Unity*, 74–75.

30. Smith, *Ethnic Origins*, 191.

31. For the Arab nationalist approach to history see Chejne, "History;" Nuseibeh, *Ideas*, 77–88; Haim, *Arab Nationalism*, 35–61; Hourani, *Arabic Thought*, 308–315.

32. Nuseibeh, *Ideas*, 65–97; Haim, *Arab Nationalism*, 35–61; Hourani, *Arabic Thought*, 308–316; Khadduri, *Political Trends*, 179–205.

33. Nuseibeh, *Ideas*, 88–97; Haim, *Arab Nationalism*, 35–49, 52–61.

34. Ibid., 39.

35. Ibid., 39–40.

36. Ibid., 39. See also Nuseibeh, *Ideas*, 65–97; Hourani, *Arabic Thought*, 308–313.

37. Ibid., 308. For other interpretations of the Arab nationalist treatment of Islam, see Haim, *Arab Nationalism*, 43–45, 53–56; Khadduri, *Political Trends*, 199–205; Smith, *Islam*, 93–160; Anwar G. Chejne, "Some Aspects of Islamic Nationalism," *Islamic Literature* 8 (1956): 434–445; Sylvia G. Haim, "Islam and the Theory of Arab Nationalism," in Laqueur, *Transition*, 280–307; G. E. von Grunebaum, *Modern Islam: The Search for Cultural Identity* (New York, 1964), 276–334; E. I. J. Rosenthal, *Islam in the Modern National State* (Cambridge, 1965), 103–124.

38. Haim, *Arab Nationalism*, 43–45.

39. Khadduri, *Political Trends*, 177–209.

40. Sayegh, *Arab Unity*, 85.

41. Nuseibeh, *Ideas*, 77–84.

42. Ibid., 42–97; Sayegh, *Arab Unity*, 44–141; Haim, *Arab Nationalism*, 35–61; Hourani, *Arabic Thought*, 291–323; Khadduri, *Political Trends*, 176–211; Elie Kedourie, "Pan-Arabism and British Policy," in Laqueur, *Transition*, 100–128, and later republished in his *Chatham House Version*, 213–235; Tütsch, *Facets*, 77–90.

43. Haim, *Arab Nationalism*, 39–55; Kedourie, *Chatham House Version*, 213–219; Nuseibeh, *Ideas*, 52–97.

44. Sayegh, *Arab Unity*, 44–80; Hourani, *Arabic Thought*, 307–316; Smith, *Islam*, 73–85, 113–122.

45. Hourani, *Arabic Thought*, 308.

46. Kedourie, *Chatham House Version*, 213–214.

47. Kedourie, "The Kingdom of Iraq: Retrospect," in his *Chatham House Version*, 236–285.

48. Ibid., 273–275.

49. Kedourie, "Pan-Arabism," in his *Chatham House Version*, 213–215; Haim, *Arab Nationalism*, 51–52; Nuseibeh, *Ideas*, 45–50.

50. See Khadduri, *Political Trends*, 264; Kedourie, *Chatham House Version*, 227–228; Haim, *Arab Nationalism*, 51.

51. Sayegh, *Arab Unity*, 111, 115–116.

52. See Kedourie, *Chatham House Version*, 215; Haim, *Arab Nationalism*, 52; Chejne, "Egyptian Attitudes;" 253; Binder, *Ideological Revolution*, 90; Be'eri, *Army Officers*, 375–379.

53. Be'eri, *Army Officers*, 373–387; Haim, *Arab Nationalism*, 51–53.

54. For example, see Dawn, "Formation," 68–80; Simon, *Iraq*, 75–114; Phebe Marr, "The Development of a Nationalist Ideology in Iraq, 1920–1941," *Muslim World* 75 (April 1985): 85–101.

55. Khoury, *Syria*, 535–562. See also Philip S. Khoury, "Divided Loyalties: Syria and the Question of Palestine, 1919–1939," *Middle Eastern Studies* 21 (1985): 324–348.

56. Porath, *1918–1929*; Muslih, *Origins*, 131–210.

57. Gershoni and Jankowski, *Egypt.*

58. See Simon, *Iraq*, 67–73, 107–165; Marr, "Development," 92–101; Michael Eppel, "The Hikmat Sulayman-Bakir Sidqi Government in Iraq, 1936–1937, and the Palestine Question," *Middle Eastern Studies* 24 (1988): 25–41.

59. Khoury, *Syria*, 539–566, 626–630.

60. Porath, *1929–1939*, 109–139, 274–303; Ann Mosely Lesch, *Arab Politics in Palestine, 1917–1939: The Frustration of a National Movement* (Ithaca, 1979), 102–154.

61. Gershoni, *Emergence*, 35–88; James Jankowski, "Egyptian Responses to the Palestine Problem in the Interwar Period," *International Journal of Middle East Studies* 12 (1980): 1–38.

62. Albert Hourani, "How Should We Write the History of the Middle East?" *International Journal of Middle East Studies* 23 (1991): 135.

63. For a discussion of these influences see Israel Gershoni, "Egyptian Intellectual History and Egyptian Intellectuals in the Interwar Period," *Asian and African Studies* 19 (1985): 333–364.

64. Cleveland, *Making.*

65. Tibi, *Arab Nationalism.*

66. Cleveland, *Making*, ix-xiii.

67. Ibid., 59–77.

68. Tibi, *Arab Nationalism*, x.

69. Ibid., xi–xii.

70. Dawn, "Formation," 68.

71. Simon, *Iraq*, 75–114. See also Reeva S. Simon, "The Teaching of History in Iraq Before the Rashid Ali Coup of 1941," *Middle Eastern Studies* 22 (1986): 37–51; Nimrod Hurvitz, "Muhibb al-Din al-Khatib's Semitic Wave Theory and the Emergence of Pan-Arab Ideology in the Interwar Period," ibid. 29 (1993): 118–134.

72. Itamar Rabinovich, "Inter-Arab Relations Foreshadowed: The Question of the Syrian Throne in the 1920s and 1930s," in *Festschrift in Honor of Dr. George S. Wise* (Tel Aviv, 1981), 237.

73. Ahmed M. Gomaa, *The Foundation of the League of Arab States: War-time Diplomacy and Inter-Arab Politics, 1941 to 1945* (London, 1977), 3–56; Yehoshua Porath, *In Search of Arab Unity, 1930–1945* (London, 1986), 1–57; Rabinovich, "Inter-Arab Relations," 237–250; Khaldun S. Husry, "King Faysal I and Arab Unity, 1930–1933," *Journal of Contemporary History*, 10 (1975): 323–340.

74. See Dawn, "Formation," 67–80; Simon, *Iraq*, 1–73; Porath, *Arab Unity*, 1–57, 149–196; Gomaa, *Foundation*, 1–97; Khoury, *Syria*, 27–70, 397–433, 535–562, 619–630; Albert Hourani, *A History of the Arab Peoples* (Cambridge, MA, 1991), 315–400.

75. The concept of a "professional intelligentsia" is developed in Anthony D. Smith, *The Ethnic Revival in the Modern World* (Cambridge, 1981), 108–133. The concept of a "new class" of professionals is mainly taken from Alvin Gouldner, *The Future of Intellectuals and the Rise of the New Class* (New York, 1979). For examples of the use of the latter in the study of the Middle East, see Vernon Egger, *A Fabian in Egypt: Salamah Musa and the Rise of the Professional Classes in*

Egypt, 1909–1939 (New York, 1986), especially ix–xvi, and David Commins, "Religious Reformers and Arabists in Damascus, 1885–1914," *International Journal of Middle East Studies* 18 (1986): 405–425.

76. Hourani, *Arab Peoples*, 338.

77. Smith, *Ethnic Revival*, 116.

78. Ibid., 116–133; see also Smith, *Ethnic Origins*, 153–173.

79. Smith, *Ethnic Revival*, 117–119.

80. Ibid., 119–122.

81. See Simon, *Iraq*, 75–169; Eppel, "Hikmat Sulayman," 25–38; Porath, *Arab Unity*, 159–161.

82. Dawn, "Formation," 67–85; Cleveland, *Making*, 59–77; Marr, "Development," 89–101; Simon, *Iraq*, 75–169.

83. Simon, *Iraq*, 75–114; Porath, *Arab Unity*, 161–164, 169, 176.

84. Simon, *Iraq*, 110.

85. Ibid., 15–165; Cleveland, *Making*, 74–77; Porath, *Arab Unity*, 192–193.

86. Khoury, *Syria*, 397–433, 622–630; quotation from 626.

87. Ibid., 627.

88. Ibid., 626–627.

89. Ibid., 400–433.

90. Ibid., 627.

91. Porath, *1929–1939*, 109–139 (quotation from 118); Lesch, 105–115.

92. Porath, *1929–1939*, 118–119.

93. Ibid., 118–139; Lesch, *Arab Politics*, 102–121.

94. Porath, *1929–1939*, 125.

95. Lesch, *Arab Politics*, 105–106.

96. Ibid., 102–141, 198–238; Porath, *1929–1939*, 109–199.

97. Gershoni and Jankowski, *Egyptian Nation*, 1–31.

98. Richard P. Mitchell, *The Society of the Muslim Brothers* (New York, 1969), 1–34, 209–294, 328–331; James P. Jankowski, *Egypt's Young Rebels: "Young Egypt," 1933–1952* (Stanford, 1975); Gershoni, *Emergence*; Israel Gershoni, "The Evolution of National Culture in Modern Egypt: Intellectual Formation and Social Diffusion, 1892–1945," *Poetics Today* 13 (1992): 325–350.

99. Mitchell, *Muslim Brothers*, 5–19; Jankowski, *Young Egypt*, 1–21; Gershoni, *Emergence*, 29–45; P. J. Vatikiotis, *Nasser and His Generation* (London, 1978), 67–97.

100. Israel Gershoni, "Arabization of Islam: The Egyptian Salafiyya and the Rise of Arabism in Pre-Revolutionary Egypt," *Asian and African Studies* 13 (1979): 22–57; idem, "The Emergence of Pan-Nationalism in Egypt: Pan-Islamism and Pan-Arabism in the 1930s," ibid. 16 (1982): 59–94; idem, "Evolution," 329–341; Gershoni and Jankowski, *Egyptian Nation*, 35–142.

101. Porath, *Arab Unity*, 149–196; Gershoni, *Emergence*, 35–83; Hourani, *Arab Peoples*, 333–349; Coury, "Who 'Invented'," 249–281, 459–479.

102. Khoury, "Divided Loyalties," 324.

103. Simon, *Iraq*, 65–73; Michael Eppel, *The Palestine Conflict in the History of Modern Iraq: The Dynamics of Involvement* (London, 1994).

104. Khoury, *Syria*, 444–456, 535–566, and "Divided Loyalties," 324–345.

105. Ralph M. Coury, "Egyptians in Jerusalem: Their Role in the General Islamic Conference of 1931," *Muslim World* 82 (1992): 37–54; Thomas Mayer,

Egypt and the Palestine Question 1936–1945 (Berlin, 1983); idem, "Egypt and the General Islamic Conference in Jerusalem in 1931," *Middle Eastern Studies* 18 (1982): 311–322; idem, "Egypt and the 1936 Arab Revolt in Palestine," *Journal of Contemporary History* 19 (1984): 275–287; Gershoni, *Emergence*, 35–83; idem, "The Muslim Brothers and the Arab Revolt in Palestine, 1936–1939," *Middle Eastern Studies* 22 (1986): 367–397; Gomaa, *Foundation*, 30–66; Jankowski, "Egyptian Responses," 1–38; idem, "The Government of Egypt and the Palestine Question, 1936–1939," *Middle Eastern Studies* 17 (1981): 427–453; Gershoni and Jankowski, *Egyptian Nation*, 167–191.

106. Porath, *Arab Unity*, 162–175 (quotation from 162); idem, *1929–1939*, 274–294; Gomaa, *Foundation*, 45–56; Jankowski, "Government of Egypt," 427–453; Khoury, *Syria*, 535–562.

107. This is the thrust of both Gomaa, *Foundation*, and Porath, *Arab Unity*.

108. Porath, *Arab Unity*, 312.

109. Quotations from ibid., 303.

110. Gomaa, *Foundation*, 30–66, 153–271; Porath, *Arab Unity*, 149–159; Mayer, *Egypt*, 41–308; Jankowski, "Egyptian Responses," 1–38; idem, "Government of Egypt," 427–453; Gershoni and Jankowski, *Egyptian Nation*, 35–142.

111. Porath, *Arab Unity*, 257–319; Gershoni and Jankowski, *Egyptian Nation*, 195–211.

112. For the term "history of meaning," see William J. Bouswma, "From History of Ideas to History of Meaning," *Journal of Interdisciplinary History* 12 (1981): 279–291.

113. John E. Toews, "Intellectual History After the Linguistic Turn: The Autonomy of Meaning and the Irreducibility of Experience," *American Historical Review*, 92 (1987): 879–907.

114. Ibid., 907.

2. The Formation of Yemeni Nationalism: Initial Reflections

1. For the North, see J. Leigh Douglas, *The Free Yemeni Movement, 1935–1962* (Beirut, 1987); Sultan Naji, "The Genesis of the Call for Yemeni Unity," in B. R. Pridham (ed.), *Contemporary Yemen: Politics and Historical Background* (Beckenham, Kent, 1984); for the South, T. Bernier, "Naissance d'un nationalisme arabe à Aden," *L'Afrique et l'Asie* no. 44 (1958); M. S. al-Habashi, *Aden* (Algiers, 1964); Ahmad Jabir `Afif, *al-Haraka al-Wataniyya fi al-Yaman* (Damascus, 1982); Joseph Kostiner, *The Struggle for South Yemen* (Beckenham, Kent, 1984). My own *Arabia without Sultans* (Harmondsworth, 1974) provides an early account of the nationalist movement in the South. The special issue of *Revue du Monde Musulman et de la Mediterrannée*, "Yemen, passé et présent de l'unité," no. 67 (1993) has several relevant articles, notably those by Paul Dresch, Jacques Coland, and Abu Bakr al-Saqqaf.

2. In Sami Zubaida (ed.), *Race and Racism* (London, 1978).

3. Anthony Smith, *Theories of Nationalism* (2d. ed.; London, 1983), 21, gives a clear account of the "core" doctrines.

4. I am grateful to Anthony Smith for the term "perennialist," the alternative, in his analysis, to "modernism" as in the work of Gellner and Anderson.

Smith categorises himself as an "ethno-symbolist." For the development of his critique of "modernism" see *National Identity* (London, 1991).

5. The term "identity" is, in its current political usage, another recent, contingent term with the implicit normative claim that an individual must conform to this set of given characteristics. In strict philosophic terms, an individual can only be identical with him/herself.

6. Gellner, *Nations and Nationalism*; Anderson, *Imagined Communities*.

7. Hobsbawm, *Nations and Nationalism Since 1780*; Ephraim Nimni, *Marxism and Nationalism* (London, 1991); Fred Halliday, "Bringing the 'Economic' Back In: the Case of Nationalism," *Economy and Society* 21:4 (November 1992).

8. I.e., the espousal of the core doctrines identified above, note 3.

9. For standard Yemeni accounts see Afif Jabir and Said el-Attar *Le Sous-Développement économique et sociale du Yemen* (Algiers, 1964).

10. Robert Stookey, *Yemen: The Politics of the Yemen Arab Republic* (Boulder, 1978), chapter 1.

11.`Abd al-Muhsin Mad`aj al-Mad`aj, *The Yemen in Early Islam: A Political History* (London, 1988).

12. As in other cases, the attempt to identify a "historic" territory lends itself to maximalist claims. The Yemeni geographer al-Hamdani (born 280/893) and other Arab writers delineate a Yemeni land from somewhere south of Mecca that often stretches well into contemporary Oman. The largest claims are, however, based on earlier delimitations: Ptolemy's *Arabia Felix*, often equated with Yemen, stretched from south of Aqaba and over to the Persian Gulf. Some Muslim writers derive the name "Yemen" from the story according to which the prophet Muhammad, atop a hill near Tabuk, delimited all to the north as *al-sham*, and all to the south (i.e., to his right) as *al-yaman* (see the interesting survey in *Encyclopaedia of Islam*, 4, 1155–1158). Paul Dresch reports that in northern discourse *yaman* was often synonymous with south of wherever one is standing, the opposite being *qibli*, i.e., toward Mecca. (Paul Dresch, *Tribes, Government, and History in Yemen*, Oxford, 1989).

13. Douglas, "Free Yemeni Movement," 50–68.

14. See al-Habashi, *Aden*.

15. Douglas, "Free Yemeni Movement," 216.

16. I have gone into this in detail in *Revolution and Foreign Policy: The Case of South Yemen 1967–1987* (Cambridge, 1990), chapter 4, "The Enigmas of Yemeni 'Unity.' "

17. On the 1994 conflict see Sheila Carapico, "From Ballot Box to Battlefield: The War of the Two `Alis," *Middle East Report*, no. 190 (September/October 1994): 24–27; Fred Halliday, "The Third Inter-Yemeni War," *Asian Affairs* 26:2 (June 1995): 131–140; Jamal al-Suwaidi (ed.), *The Yemeni War of 1994* (London, 1995).

18. Comparison may be made with a modernizing nationalism in other third world states that avoided colonial rule—Nepal, Afghanistan, Ethiopia.

19. On the role of the Arab Nationalists Movement in Yemen see Sultan Ahmad `Umar, *Nazra fi Tatawwur al-Mujtama` al-Yamani* (Beirut, 1970); Kostiner, *Struggle*; Walid Kazziha, *Revolutionary Transformation in the Arab World* (London, 1975).

20. See `Umar, *Nazra*; Kostiner, *Struggle*; and my *Arabia without Sultans*.

21. At times of confrontation, real or imagined, with Saudi Arabia, official speeches appeal to "the sons of Saba and Himyar." The queen of Saba (or Sheba), Bilqis, is an important, often invoked, figure in Yemeni myths and history: the emblem of the (pre-1990) North Yemeni State and ruling party consisted of "the pillars of Bilqis."

22. *Revolution and Foreign Policy*, 105–107.

23. I am grateful to the distinguished Yemeni historian, the late Sultan Naji, for verbal elucidation on this point.

24. Thus in the founding document of the National Liberation Front, the 1965 Charter, the southern area is referred to as both "South Yemen" and "the Yemeni south" so that the very name of the organization is rendered alternatively as *al-Jabha al-Qawmiyya li-Tahrir Junub al-Yaman al-Muhtall* (64) and as *al-Jabha al-Qawmiyya li-Tahrir al-Junub al-Yamani al-Muhtall* (109): *al-Mithaq al-Watani*, text agreed at first congress of the NLF, 22–25 June 1964, Aden, n.d.

25. In the aftermath of the 1994 inter-Yemeni war some people in the South began to reject the term "Yemeni" and to describe themselves again as "South Arabian." A southern term of abuse for northern administrative practices was "Turkish."

26. Paul Dresch, "A Daily Plebiscite: Nation and State in Yemen," in *Revue du Monde Musulman et de la Mediterrannée* no. 67 (1993): 68.

27. On the Jewish community in Yemen see the chapters in Joseph Chelhod and others, *L'Arabie du Sud: Histoire et civilisation*, 3 vols. (Paris, 1984).

28. Dresch, "Daily Plebiscite," 73, alludes to the possibility of the tribal areas of the east and north, known as Hamdan, forming a separate nation.

29. In the immediate aftermath of Southern independence, in 1967, some Yemenis did assert this claim, but it was never sustained. A related dispute over the Kuria Muria Islands was also shelved (*Revolution and Foreign Policy*, 13, 21).

30. Among the ways in which Hadramaut does not conform is the failure of its inhabitants to chew the narcotic leaf *qat*.

31. Dresch, *Tribes*, 389–391.

32. Summary of World Broadcast, ME/2994/A/9, 7 February 1969.

33. Associates of former President `Ali Nasir Muhammad, ousted in an interregime clash in 1986 (*al-Hayat*, 21 July 1994).

34. See Dresch, *Tribes*, especially chapter 9, on the meanings of "tribe" and shifting "tribal" identities.

35. In the South, the revolutionary regime in 1967 banned the use of "tribal" names to denote regions and instead, on the Algerian model of the *wilaya*, divided the country up into six *muhafazat* or governorates. This did not prevent people from continuing to use the tribal/regional names, and in the 1980s, as part of an attempt to reduce the distance between regime and population the anterior names were restored.

36. Robert Burrowes, *The Yemen Arab Republic: The Politics of Development 1962–1986* (Boulder, 1987), chapter 5.

37. *Hizb al-Wahda al-Sha`biyya al-Yamaniyya*, "al-Barnamij al-Siyasi," 1979. *Hizb al-Wahda* was the core party around which the larger National

Democratic Front, set up in 1976, organized. In 1990, following the unification of North and South, it merged with the Yemeni Socialist Party in the South.

38. For one other attempt to do this, in the case of Eritrean nationalism, see Fred Halliday and Maxine Molyneux, *The Ethiopian Revolution* (London, 1981), chapter 5.

3. The Tropes of Stagnation and Awakening in Nationalist Historical Consciousness: The Egyptian Case

1. In general, my understanding of Orientalism as a discourse and the practices derived from it follow Edward Said's *Orientalism* (New York, 1978). For a neatly crafted exposition of academic Orientalism see Fred Halliday, " 'Orientalism' and its Critics," *British Journal of Middle Eastern Studies* 20:2 (1993): 145–163.

2. For a parallel analysis of the morphology and function of Orientalism in Zionist/Israeli historiography, see my "Domestic Orientalism: The Representation of 'Oriental' Jews in Zionist/Israeli Historiography," *British Journal of Middle Eastern Studies* 23:2 (December 1996).

3. Hayden White, *Metahistory*; idem, "History, Historicism, and the Figurative Imagination," *History and Theory* 14 (1975), 48–67; idem, "The Fictions of Factual Representation," in Angus Fletcher (ed.), *The Literature of Fact* (New York, 1976), 21–44; idem, "The Question of Narrative in Contemporary Historical Theory," in his *Content of the Form*, 27–57; idem, "Narrativity in the Representation of Reality," ibid., 1–26. Anderson, *Imagined Communities*.

4. Though I lay emphasis on the analogy between the approaches of White and Anderson, an important difference should also be noted. Anderson's understanding of historical reality, in a subtle and sophisticated way, is basically material and empirical. Although he undermines the dichotomy between "invented" and "real" communities, his explanation is ultimately material: technological changes bring about changes in the conception of time and space; only within the latter is modern consciousness conceivable. Hayden White's approach consists of a combination between Russian Formalism and French Poststructuralism. From his perspective, past reality as it occurred is chaotic and meaningless. What shapes and endows it with meaning is the consciousness of the present, which unfolds through language and, in the particular case of modern historiography, through a variety of narrative emplotments.

5. Peter Novick, *That Noble Dream: The "Objectivity Question" and the American Historical Profession* (Cambridge, 1989).

6. Timothy Mitchell, "The Limit of the State: Beyond Statist Approaches and Their Critics," *American Political Science Review* 85:1 (1991): 77–96.

7. White, "Fictions," 22–29.

8. White, "Question," 27.

9. Ibid.

10. This is a recurring and fundamental argument in White's work as a whole. Most indicative is the title White gave to his 1987 collection of essays, *The Content of the Form*.

11. White, "Question," 42–43.

12. White, "Fictions," 23–26.

13. I am aware of Partha Chatterjee's critique of Anderson. Chatterjee himself, however, notices the transformative potential of the concept of imagined community, and he criticizes other facets in Anderson's work. See his *Nationalist Thought and the Colonial World*, 19–22, and *The Nation and Its Fragments*, 13–14.

14. Alon Confino, "The Nation as a Local Metaphor: Heimat, National Memory, and the German Empire, 1871–1918," *History and Memory* 5:1 (Spring/ Summer 1993): 42–86.

15. These are "Census, Map, Museum" and "Memory and Forgetting" (chapters 10 and 11 respectively).

16. Smith, *Ethnic Origins*, 7–13.

17. Ibid, 10.

18. Anderson, *Imagined Communities*, xii.

19. Ibid., 6 and 6n.

20. Ibid., 4–5, and chapter 2 ("Cultural Roots").

21. Clifford Geertz, "Ideology as Cultural System," in his *The Interpretation of Cultures* (New York, 1973). For a stimulating evaluation of Geertz's theory and its relevance to historians see Dominick LaCapra, "Culture and Ideology," *Poetics Today* 9:2 (1988): 377–394.

22. Among the works I have hitherto seen there are two serious and fruitful attempts to apply Anderson's approach: one, cited above, is Alon Confino's study of the German Heimat; the other, fascinating because it takes Anderson beyond the realm of the nation, is Zachary Lockman's examination of the Egyptian working class ("Imagining the Working Class: Representations of Society and Class in Egypt Before 1914," *Poetics Today* 15 [1994]).

23. An important qualification should be registered. Owing to the way in which my study has hitherto evolved, I have not yet dealt properly with the work of `Abd al-Rahman al-Rafi`i, which doubtless played a major role in shaping the territorial Egyptian narrative. Rafi`i's work will be thoroughly examined in the next stage of my study.

24. Gershoni and Jankowski, *Egypt*; idem, *Egyptian Nation*; a concise exposition of their thesis is formulated in Gershoni, "Evolution."

25. Ursula Wokoeck, "State, Islam, and Nation in Egypt," Wiener Seminar on "Rethinking Nationalism," Tel Aviv University, 1993 (unpublished). I thank the author for permitting me to cite her paper.

26. Gershoni, "Evolution."

27. Sami Zubaida, "The Nation-State in the Middle East" in idem, *Islam: The People and the State* (London, 1989), 121–182; Owen, *State, Power, and Politics.*

28. Edward Said, "Identity, Negation, and Violence," in idem, *The Politics of Dispossession* (London, 1992), 353. As acknowledged by him, Said stimulatingly borrows this term from Martin Jay's interpretation of Adorno.

29. Shafik Ghorbal [Shafiq Ghurbal], *The Beginning of the Egyptian Question and the Rise of Mehmet Ali* (London, 1928), xiii–xiv and 1–2. I am not unaware of Youssef Choueiri's thorough examination of Ghurbal's historiography in his book *Arab History and the Nation-State* (London, 1989), 65–104. As the space and topic of this particular essay are ill-suited for a lengthy discussion of

a single rationalist historian, I do not deal here with Choueiri's interesting interpretation.

30. Ghorbal, x–xi.

31. The use of *rukud* in this particular context appears frequently in the introductions to the two following books by al-Shayyal: *Ta'rikh al-Tarjama fi Misr fi 'Ahd al-Hamla al-Faransiyya* (Cairo, 1950); *al-Ta'rikh wa al-Mu'arrikhun fi Misr fi al-Qarn al-Tasi' 'Ashr* (Alexandria, 1958).

32. Al-Shayyal, *Tarjama*, 3–6, and *Ta'rikh*, 7–10. The thesis recurs in his later publications in English.

33. Al-Shayyal, *Tarjama*, 196–197.

34. In al-Shayyal's *Ta'rikh*, Lam (Arabic).

35. See for instance the following classifications: Shimon Shamir, "Self-View in Modern Egyptian Historiography," in idem (ed.), *Self-Views in Historical Perspective in Egypt and Israel* (Tel Aviv, 1981), 47–49; Rifaat Ali Abou El-Haj, "Social Uses of the Past: Recent Arab Historiography of Ottoman Rule," *International Journal of Middle East Studies* 14 (1982): 187–195.

36. Muhammad Anis, *Madrasat al-Ta'rikh al-Misri fi al-'Asr al-'Uthmani* (Cairo, 1962).

37. Muhammad Anis, *al-Dawla al-'Uthmaniyya wa al-Sharq al-'Arabi* (Cairo, n.d.), 140.

38. Al-Shayyal, *Tarjama*, 11.

39. Anis, *Madrasa*, 14 and, in another formulation, *Dawla*, 141.

40. Abdul Rahman Abdul Rahim, "The Ottoman Rule and its Effects on Egyptian Society," *Journal of Asian and African Studies* [Japan], 13 (1977): 57–76.

41. Ibid, 76.

42. For a concise exposition of this discourse see again Gershoni, "Evolution," 326–329.

43. Anderson, *Imagined Communities*, 9–36.

44. The passage that discusses this classification is based on Shamir, "Self-View," 37–51.

45. Ibid, 41–42.

46. Al-Shayyal, *Tarjama*, 8.

47. Ernest Renan, "What Is a Nation?"; trans. and ann. Martin Thom, in Bhabha, *Nation and Narration*, 19.

48. Anis, *Madrasa*, 27.

49. For example Abdul Rahim, "Ottoman Rule," 74.

50. Ibid, 76.

51. Al-Shayyal, *Tarjama*, 10–12.

52. Ibid, 10.

53. Ibid, 11.

54. Ibid, 12–14.

55. Ibid, 14.

56. It would not be unexpected to discover that Rafi'i's work had a formative influence on the narrative constructed in these textbooks.

57. *Al-Tarbiyya al-Wataniyya*, published in Cairo by: Tawfiq al-Mar'ashli, 1928; 'Abd al-'Aziz al-Bishri, 1929; Muhammad Rif'at and 'Abd al-'Aziz al-Bishri, 1943.

58. Al-Bishri, 175–176; al-Mar`ashli, 134–135; Rif`at and al-Bishri, 130–131 and 172–173.

59. For the accounts on the Ottoman period see ibid. Cf. the French invasion and Muhammad `Ali's rule in al-Bishri, 175–176 and 176–183; al-Mar`ashli, 135–136 and 136–139; Rif`at and al-Bishri, 132–133 and 173–174 (the French), 134–139 and 174–175 (Muhammad `Ali).

60. Rif`at and al-Bishri, contents and 172–173.

61. In the foreword to Ghorbal, *Beginning.*

62. Rif`at and al-Bishri, 174 and, in a slightly different formulation, 134; see also al-Bishri, 176 and al-Mar`ashli, 136.

63. Rif`at and al-Bishri, 132.

64. Ibid, 174.

4. The Arab Nationalism of George Antonius Reconsidered

1. *The Arab Awakening* was originally published in 1938 by the London firm of Hamish Hamilton. The references in this paper are to the Capricorn Books edition of 1965 published by G. P. Putnam's Sons. All subsequent citations of the book have been placed in the body of the text.

2. For an appreciation of both dimensions of Antonius the historian, see Albert Hourani, "*The Arab Awakening* Forty Years After," in his *The Emergence of the Modern Middle East* (London, 1981).

3. Fouad Ajami, "The End of Arab Nationalism," *The New Republic* 23 (August 12, 1991): 23.

4. Edward Said, *The Times Literary Supplement*, June 19, 1992, 19. Emphasis in the original.

5. This phrase offered Antonius's readers a mixture of Elizabethan and classical references. Euphues was the central character in John Lyly's *Euphues, The Anatomy of Wit* (1578) and *Euphues and His England* (1580). The prose of both Lyly and his title figure is verbose and somewhat pretentious.

6. Smith, *Ethnic Origins*, 58–68.

7. Anderson, *Imagined Communities*, 67; Hobsbawm, *Nations and Nationalism Since 1870*, 61.

8. Edward Said, *Culture and Imperialism* (New York, 1994), 251.

9. *Palestine Royal Commission: Minutes of Evidence Heard at Public Sessions*. Colonial, no. 134 (London, 1937), 365.

10. Antonius accepts Egypt's separation from the eastern Arab movement on the grounds that it had generated its own nationalist movement against the British occupation. See *Awakening*, 100.

11. *Palestine Royal Commission*, 365.

12. Ibid., 359.

13. Anderson, *Imagined Communities*, 156–157.

14. Ibid., 170–178.

15. Elizabeth MacCallum, *The Canadian Forum*, (June 19, 1939): 94.

16. See Anderson, *Imagined Communities*, 144–145.

17. MacCallum, 94.

18. Knabenshue (Baghdad) to Secretary of State, January 5, 1939, National Archives, Washington, D.C. RG 59/867n.01/1409.

19. Robert D. Kaplan, *The Arabists: The Romance of an American Elite* (New York, 1993), 165.

20. The *Nation*, (February 25, 1939): 239.

21. Gibb's review appeared in *The Spectator*, vol. 161 (November 25, 1938): 912; Stark's in *The New Statesman and Nation* (December 31, 1938): 1130. The review in *The Times* (London) also stresses Antonius's account of Anglo-Arab diplomacy.

22. *The American Historical Review*, vol. 44 (1938–39): 908–909. Similar views are expressed by George Rentz in *Moslem World*, vol. 29 (1939): 292–295.

23. *Political Science Quarterly*, vol. 54 (1939): 463.

24. *American Political Science Review*, vol. 33 (1939): 710.

25. *Foreign Affairs*, vol. 17 (1939): 642.

26. Khalidi et al., *Origins*. See in particular the chapters by Khalidi and C. Ernest Dawn.

5. The Imposition of Nationalism on a Non-Nation State: The Case of Iraq during the Interwar Period, 1921–1941

1. A. Schölch, "Britain in Palestine 1838–1882: The Roots of the Balfour Policy," *Journal of Palestine Studies* 22 (1992): 39–56; Mayir Vereté, "The Balfour Declaration and Its Makers," in Norman Rose (ed.), *From Palmerston to Balfour: Collected Essays of Mayir Vereté* (London, 1992).

2. Mosul was later incorporated to ensure Iraqi/British control of its petroleum.

3. Yitzhak Nakash, *The Shi`is of Iraq* (Princeton, 1994), 13.

4. Elie Kedourie, "The Iraqi Shi`is and Their Fate," in Martin Kramer (ed.), *Shi`ism, Resistance, and Revolution*, (Boulder, 1987), 135–158.

5. Anderson, *Imagined Communities*; Smith, *Ethnic Origins*.

6. Simon, *Iraq*, 101; see Dawn, "Formation," on the influence of James Breasted on the formation of an Arab nationalist ideology.

7. Tibi, *Arab Nationalism*, 122. The quote is from Husri.

8. Cleveland, *Making*, 123–126.

9. Briton Busch, *Britain, India, and the Arabs 1914–1921* (Berkeley, 1971), 175–176.

10. Samira Haj, "The Problems of Tribalism: The Case of Nineteenth-Century Iraqi History," *Social History* 16 (1991): 45–58.

11. Nakash, *Shi`is*, 89.

12. For example, the *Law Governing the Rights and Duties of Cultivators* of 1933 made the peasant "responsible for almost every disaster that might befall a crop" and kept them on the land as long as they were in debt. Marion Farouq-Sluglett and Peter Sluglett, "Labor and National Liberation: The Trade Union Movement in Iraq, 1920–1958," *Arab Studies Quarterly* 5 (1983): 139–154.

13. Nakash, *Shi`is*, 83–96.

14. Great Britain, Colonial Office, *Report by His Britannic Majesty's Government to the Council of the League of Nations on the Administration of 'Iraq for the Year 1927* (London, 1928), 19.

15. C. J. Edmonds, *Kurds, Turks, and Arabs: Politics, Travel, and Research in*

North-Eastern Iraq, 1919–1925 (London, 1957); Edmund Ghareeb, *The Kurdish Question in Iraq* (Syracuse, 1981).

16. US Dept of State, 890g.00 General Conditions/5, Knabenshue to Secretary of State, Baghdad, May 3, 1933; 890g.00 General Conditions/6, Knabenshue to Secretary of State, Baghdad, May 24, 1933.

17. Cleveland, *Making*, 62.

18. Sati` al-Husri, "al-Khidma al-`Askariyyah wa-al-Tarbiyya al-`Amma," *al-Mu`allim al-Jadid* 1 (1936): 273–278.

19. Phebe A. Marr, "Yasin al-Hashimi: The Rise and Fall of a Nationalist" (Ph.D. dissertation, Harvard University, 1966), 173–175.

20. Phebe Marr, *The Modern History of Iraq* (Boulder, 1985), 37. In 1936, of the eighty top officers in the Iraqi army, there were one Shi`i, two Christians, and not more than seven Kurds (Mohammad A. Tarbush, *The Role of the Military in Politics: A Case Study of Iraq to 1941* (London, 1982), 78–79.

21. Nakash, *Shi`is*, 115–116; Tarbush, *Role*, 73–79.

22. Reeva S. Simon, "The Education of an an Iraqi Ottoman Army Officer," in Khalidi, et al., *Origins*, 151–166.

23. Matta Akrawi, *Curriculum Construction in the Public Primary Schools of Iraq* (New York, 1943), 180.

24. Abdul Amir al-Rubaiy, "Nationalism and Education: A Study of Nationalistic Tendencies in Iraqi Education," (Ph.D. dissertation, Kent State University, 1972), 88.

25. Akrawi, *Curriculum Construction*, 165–169.

26. For an analysis of the textbooks used in Iraqi schools see Simon, *Iraq*, 75–114; Marr, "Development," 96–97.

27. Shawkat, "Ta'rikhna al-Qawmi," in *Hadhihi Ahdahfuna* (Baghdad, 1939), 43. The translation is from Haim, *Arab Nationalism*, 182.

28. Iraq, Ministry of Education, *Manhaj al-Dirasa al-Ibtida'iyya* (Baghdad, Government Press, 1940), 65–66.

29. Sati` al-Husri, *Mudhakkirati fi al-`Iraq* (Beirut, 1966–1968), 1:215.

30. Akrawi, *Curriculum Development*, 187. He does not list the names.

31. *Manhaj* (1936), 46.

32. *Manhaj* (1940), 66; Akram Zu`aytir and Darwish al-Miqdadi, *Ta'rikhuna bi Uslub Qisassi* (Baghdad, 1939), 3.

33. Nakash, *Shi`is*, 112.

34. Memo by Sami Shawkat published in *al-Zaman*, June 9, 1939. US National Archives, Record Group 84: "Notification from the Directorate General of Education to all the Native and Denominational Schools Concerning the Use of Books Prejudicial to the National Spirit."

35. The revolution of 1941 occupies a major place in the Ba`thi narrative of Iraqi pan-Arab history. In his foreword to *The Encyclopedia of Modern Iraq* (Baghdad, n.d.) Khairallah Telfah, Saddam Husayn's uncle and mentor and a participant in the Rashid `Ali movement, singles out Iraq's role in the revolution as an act by a "true Arab country."

36. Mahmud al-Durrah, *al-Harb al-`Iraqiyya al-Britaniyya 1941* (Beirut, 1969), 47–52; *Hiya `Iraqi* (Cairo, 1976), 36–41.

37. The report can be found in `Abd al-Razzaq al-Hasani, *Ta'rikh al-Wizarat al-`Iraqiyya* (Sidon, 1953–1967) 5:272–282; see also FO 624/32/292 Cornwallis

to Eden, Baghdad, 20 April 1943, for a summary of attempted reform of Iraqi education.

38. Great Britain, *Report . . . 1927*, 159.

39. FO624/24; Germany: Propaganda 448/3/41.

40. Great Britain, War Office 208/1561, Security Summary Middle East #22, 20 February 1942; see also the comment by Palestinian Jewish emissary to Iraq, Enzo Sereni, in his dispatch of 25 September 1942 (Central Zionist Archives S 6/1960).

41. Harry J. Almond, *Iraqi Statesman: A Portrait of Mohammed Fadhel Jamali* (Salem, Oregon, 1993).

42. Nakash, *Shi'is*, 110–113. This view has persisted to this day. See for example the study of Persian and Jewish education in Iraq by Fadil al-Barrak, *al-Madaris al-Yahudiyya wa al-Iraniyya fi al-'Iraq* (Baghdad, 1984) and Khairallah Talfah's infamous *Three Whom God Should Not Have Created: Persians, Jews, and Flies*. Jews and Shi'i are placed in the same category.

43. Shi'i had already begun to avail themselves of secular education as early as 1909 when the Madrasa al-Ja'fariyya opened under the authorization of a noted Shi'i *mujtahid* who understood the importance of preparing Shi'i "to assume positions and provide services hitherto fulfilled mainly by Jews" (Nakash, *Shi'is*, 52, 111).

44. Marr, "Development," 99.

45. Many followed in Jamali's footsteps and attended Teachers College, Columbia University. One of the first, Matta Akrawi, wrote his thesis in 1942 on curriculum construction in Iraqi primary schools. It is an important resource for study of Iraq in the 1920s and 1930s.

46. Marr, "Development," 99.

47. Kedourie, "Iraqi Shi'is," 135–158.

48. Yosef Me'ir, *Ha-hitpathut ha-hevratit-tarbutit shel Yehudei 'Iraq me'az 1830 ve-ad yameinu* (Jerusalem, 1989), 411–418.

49. In 1934 the Iraqi government initiated mass layoffs and firings of Jews from the Ministry of Economics. These employment terminations and later informal quotas on numbers of Jews allowed in institutions of higher education reflected not only the politicization of the regime but also evidence of the availability of Muslim candidates for these positions.

50. In the 1930s the Jewish community supported four types of schools: religious schools with elementary studies in Arabic, Alliance schools for boys and for girls, Jewish schools following the government syllabus, and the Shamash school, established in 1928 to teach the English curriculum (*Report of the Jewish Schools Committee on the Jewish Schools in Baghdad 1930*, 6).

51. Nancy E. Berg, "Israeli Writers From Iraq: Exile From Exile" (Ph.D. dissertation, University of Pennsylvania, 1991), 38.

52. Cited from Zu'aytir's memoirs in Elie Kedourie, "The Break Between Muslims and Jews in Iraq," in Mark R. Cohen and Abraham L. Udovitch (eds.), *Jews Among Arabs: Contacts and Boundaries* (Princeton, 1989), 29.

53. Hayyim J. Cohen, *Ha-Pe'ilut ha-Zionit be-'Iraq* (Jerusalem, 1969), 85–152.

54. Hebrew University, Institute for Contemporary Jewry, Oral History Division, interview by Hayyim Cohen with Murad Michael, 22 August 1963.

55. Hayyim J. Cohen, "The Anti-Jewish Farhud in Baghdad, 1941," *Middle*

Eastern Studies 3 (1966–67): 2–17; Walid M. S. Hamdi, *Rashid Ali al-Gailani and the Nationalist Movement in Iraq, 1939–1941* (London, 1987); Shulamit Binah, "The Anti-Jewish Farhud in Baghdad 1941: Jewish and Arab Perspectives" (M.A. thesis, CUNY, 1989).

56. Reeva S. Simon, "The Hashimite 'Conspiracy': Hashimite Unity Attempts, 1921–1958," *International Journal of Middle East Studies* 5 (1974): 314–327.

57. Ghareeb, *Kurdish Question.*

58. Nakash, *Shi`is*, 126–138.

59. For analyses along these lines see Kemal Karpat, "The Ottoman Ethnic and Confessional Legacy in the Middle East," in Milton J. Esman and Itamar Rabinovich (eds.), *Ethnicity, Pluralism, and the State in the Middle East* (Ithaca, 1988); and Sami Zubaida, "Community, Class, and Minorities in Iraqi Politics," in Robert A. Fernea and Roger Owen, (eds.), *The Iraqi Revolution of 1958: The Old Social Classes Revisited,* (London, 1991).

6. Nationalist Iconography: Egypt as a Woman

1. John Bull first appeared as a character representing the English nation in a 1712 satire. He is considered "a personification of the English nation; Englishmen collectively, or the typical Englishman." By the late 1890s he had come to symbolize English imperialism. From *The Oxford English Dictionary* (Oxford, 1933; rpt. 1978), 5:593.

2. Anderson, *Imagined Communities.*

3. Robin Ostle examines general motifs and themes in the iconography of Egyptian nationalism in his "Modern Egyptian Renaissance Man," *Bulletin of the School of Oriental and African Studies* 57 (1994): 184–192. Here I focus on gender in the representations of the nation.

4. See Irene L. Gendzier, *The Practical Visions of Ya`qub Sanu`* (Cambridge, MA, 1966).

5. Blanchard Jerrold, *Egypt under Ismail Pacha* (London, 1879), 218–219, 222, 107.

6. Gendzier, *Practical Visions,* 70.

7. Gendzier, *Practical Visions,* 64; Irene L. Gendzier, "James Sanua and Egyptian Nationalism," *Middle East Journal* 15 (1961): 25.

8. On readers of the Arabic press, see Beth Baron, "Readers and the Women's Press in Egypt," *Poetics Today* 15:2 (1994): 37–51; Ami Ayalon, *The Press in the Arab Middle East* (Oxford, 1995), chapter 6.

9. `Abd al-Latif Hamza claims that the paper *Abu Zayd* carried the first caricatures in the Egyptian press. I have been unable to trace or identify this paper. See his *Adab al-Maqala al-Suhufiyya fi Misr* (multivol.; Cairo, 1953–1962), 3:69.

For a brief history of the cartoon in Egypt, see Afaf Lutfi al-Sayyid Marsot, "The Cartoon in Egypt," *Comparative Studies in Society and History* 13:1 (1971): 2–15; Zahda, "al-Maistro," *Ruz al-Yusuf,* no. 2942 (29 October 1984): 34–37. For some related studies, see *Images d'Egypte: De la fresque à la bande dessinée* (Cairo, 1991); Allen Douglas and Fedwa Malti-Douglas, *Arab Comic Strips: Politics of an Emerging Mass Culture* (Bloomington, 1994). On the problems that some contemporary Middle Eastern cartoonists face, see Garry Trudeau, "Drawing, Dangerously," *The New York Times* (Sunday, 10 July 1994, Week in Review), 19.

10. See, for examples, *Abu Naddara (AN)* 5:11 (1881): 191; *al-Watani al-Misri* 1:2 (1883): 127. I have used the copies of *AN* and related journals reprinted in black and white in a multivolume issue by Dar Sadir (Beirut, n.d.)

11. *AN* 1:7 (1880): 112; *AN* 19:1 (1895): 6; and *AN* 21:3 (1897): 14; *AN* 26:4 (1902): 42; *AN* 30:10 (1906): 42.

12. *AN* 7:10 (1883): 101.

13. *AN* 7:9 (1883): 100; *AN* 8:3 (1884): 142.

14. *AN* 18:12 (1894): 50.

15. Marsot, "Cartoon."

16. On the challenges contemporary Egyptian illustrators face in reaching viewers, see Nagwa Farag, "Illustration: To Whom Is It Addressed?" in *Images d'Egypte*, 285–290.

17. Cartoons appeared in Salim Sarkis's *al-Mushir* in the mid-1890s.

18. `Ali Fahmi Kamil, *Mustafa Kamil Basha fi 34 Rabi`an*, (9 vols.; Cairo, 1908–1911), 3:70–73; `Abd al-Rahman al-Rafi`i, *Mustafa Kamil: Ba`ith al-Haraka al-Wataniyya, 1892–1908*, 5th ed. (Cairo, 1984), 61–63; Arthur Gold-schmidt, Jr., "The Egyptian Nationalist Party: 1892–1919," in P. M. Holt (ed.), *Political and Social Change in Modern Egypt*, (London, 1968), 313, n. 4.

19. Kamil, *Mustafa Kamil*, 3:71.

20. Ibid., 70; Rafi`i, *Mustafa Kamil*, 62.

21. Rafi`i, *Mustafa Kamil*, 296–298.

22. Ibid., 297.

23. Beth Baron, "Unveiling in Early Twentieth-Century Egypt: Practical and Symbolic Considerations," *Middle Eastern Studies* 25:3 (1989): 370–386.

24. Rafi`i, *Mustafa Kamil*, 298.

25. Beth Baron, "Mothers, Morality, and Nationalism in Early Twentieth-Century Egypt," in Khalidi et al., *Origins*, 271–288; see also idem, *The Women's Awakening in Egypt: Culture, Society, and the Press* (New Haven, 1994), chapter 8.

26. Liliane Karnouk, *Modern Egyptian Art: The Emergence of a National Style* (Cairo, 1988), 25–27; Iffat Naji et al., *Muhammad Naji (1888–1956)* (Cairo, n.d.), 53; Hamed Said, *Contemporary Art in Egypt* (Cairo, 1964), 120; Ostle, "Renaissance Man," 187.

27. Badr al-Din Abu Ghazi, *Maththal Mukhtar* (Cairo, 1964); Karnouk, *Modern Egyptian Art*, 14–17; Gershoni and Jankowski, *Egypt*, 186–188. The statue was later moved to the main entrance of Cairo University in Giza.

28. Karnouk, *Modern Egyptian Art*, 15.

29. Ruth Frances Woodsmall, *Moslem Women Enter a New World* (New York, 1936), 174, photo f. 168.

30. *Al-Nahda al-Nisa'iyya*, 1:1 (1339/1921), cover.

31. *Al-Kashkul (K)* no. 57 (1922):16; *K* 4:165 (1924): 10; *K* 4:185 (1924): 1; *K* 5:216 (1925): 11; *K* 6:297 (1927): 1; *K* 7:353 (1928): 11.

32. Marsot, "Cartoon," 13. See Fatima al-Yusuf, *Dhikrayat* (Cairo, 1953; rpt. 1976); Ibrahim `Abduh, *Ruz al-Yusuf* (Cairo, 1961). For Egypt as a woman, see the *Ruz al-Yusuf* cartoon reproduced in Sarah Graham-Brown, *Images of Women:*

The Portrayal of Women in Photography in the Middle East, 1860–1950 (New York, 1988), 215.

33. Sawsan el-Messiri, *Ibn al-Balad: A Concept of Egyptian Identity* (Leiden, 1978), 48.

34. P. J. Vatikiotis, *The History of Modern Egypt* (4th ed.; Baltimore, 1991), 485.

35. Ayalon, *Press*, 78. I have not seen issues of *al-Kashkul* beyond May 1932.

36. Great Britain, Public Record Office, Foreign Office (FO) 371/13880/8570, Annual Report for 1927–1928, Cairo, 26 August 1929; Ayalon, *Press*, 149.

37. FO 371/10021/5233, Allenby to MacDonald, Cairo, 8 June 1924; see *al-Kashkul* (June 1924).

38. See, e.g., *K* no. 77 (1922): 16; *K* no. 78 (1922): 16; *K* no. 86 (1923): 1; *K* no. 88 (1923): 1; *K* no. 135 (1923): 20; *K* 3:140 (1924): 11; *K* 5:233 (1925): 20; *K* 5:250 (1926): 1; *K* 6:301 (1927): 10; *K* 10:500 (1930): 32.

39. See, e.g., *K* 5:241 (1925): 1; *K* 6:265 (1926): 1; *K* 6:275 (1926): 1; *K* 6:314 (1927): 1; *K* 8:369 (1928): 1; *K* 8:371 (1928): 1.

40. See, e.g., *K* no. 34 (1922): 16; *K* 3:140 (124): 20; *K* 6:295 (1927): 1.

41. *K* no. 51 (1922): 1; *K* no. 67 (1922): 16; *K* 10:490 (1930): 1.

42. Beth Baron, "The Construction of National Honour in Egypt," *Gender and History* 5:2 (1993): 246–247.

43. Daisy Griggs Philips, "The Awakening of Egypt's Womanhood," *Moslem World* 18 (1928): 402.

44. See Maurice Agulhon, *Marianne into Battle: Republican Imagery and Symbolism in France, 1789–1880*, trans. Janet Lloyd (Cambridge, 1981).

45. Eric Hobsbawm, "Man and Woman in Socialist Iconography," *History Workshop* 6 (Autumn 1978): 124.

46. Correspondence from Zachary Lockman, 7 December 1992.

47. Gershoni and Jankowski, *Egypt*, 205.

48. From 1917 to 1927 Cairo witnessed its fastest growth until that time (Janet L. Abu-Lughod, *Cairo: 1001 Years of The City Victorious* [Princeton, 1971], 125).

7. Nationalizing the Pharaonic Past: Egyptology, Imperialism, and Egyptian Nationalism, 1922–1952

1. Quoted in translation in the *Egyptian Gazette*, February 26, 1932. Except where otherwise indicated, translations from French and Arabic are mine.

2. Having seen an Egyptian interviewee wince at the term "indigenous Egyptology," I use the more awkward "Egyptian Egyptology" here. For him, the condescending connotation of the French *indigène* (comparable to "native" in English) apparently carried over to its more neutral English cognate.

3. William Pfaff, *The Wrath of Nations: Civilization and the Furies of Nationalism* (New York, 1993), 14, 34, and Fritz Ringer, *The Decline of the German Mandarins: The German Academic Community, 1890–1933* (Cambridge, 1969), especially 109–10; F. S. L. Lyons, *Internationalism in Europe, 1815–1914* (Leiden, 1963); Joseph Ben-David, *Centers of Learning: Britain, France, Germany, United States* (New York, 1977).

4. For Antonio Gramsci's concept of cultural hegemony, see T. J. Jackson

Lears, "The Concept of Cultural Hegemony: Problems and Possibilities," *American Historical Review* 90 (1985): 567–593.

5. As quoted in Said, *Culture of Imperialism*, 162.

6. Novick, *That Noble Dream*.

7. Warren R. Dawson and Eric P. Uphill, *Who Was Who in Egyptology* (2d ed.; London, 1972), 133–34. Dawson also ignores such painful facts as that: World War I forced Borchardt and Junker out of Egypt as enemy aliens, the Nefertiti affair prevented Borchardt from ever excavating in Egypt again, Junker's replacement of Borchardt as director of the German Institute embittered the latter, Borchardt emigrated to escape the Nazis while Junker went along with them, and the British forced Junker out of his University chair at Cairo. Other well-known feuds across national lines included Salt vs. Drovetti, Brugsch vs. Maspero, Carter vs. Lacau, Budge vs. Grébaut, and Naville vs. Sethe. Intranational, or personal feuds included Champollion vs. Jomard and Breasted vs. Reisner.

8. John A. Wilson, *Thousands of Years: An Archaeologist's Search for Ancient Egypt* (New York, 1972), 123. See also his *Signs and Wonders Upon Pharaoh: A History of American Archaeology* (Chicago, 1974).

9. Smith, *Ethnic Origins*, 168; Gershoni and Jankowski, *Egypt* and *Egyptian Nation*. Gershoni and Jankowski do note the continued pride in ancient Egypt in the works of "integral nationalists" Ahmad Husayn, Fathi Radwan, and Sulayman Huzayyin.

10. Dawson and Uphill, *Egyptology*, 95–96.

11. Preliminary treatment of these national rivalries is found in Donald M. Reid, "Indigenous Egyptology: The Decolonization of a Profession?" *Journal of the American Oriental Society* 105 (1985): 233–246.

12. On Kamal, see Muhammad Jamal Mukhtar, "Salim Hasan ka-Munaqqib wa `Alim Athar," *al-Majalla al-Ta'rikhiyya al-Misriyya* 19 (1972): 73–87; Zaki Fahmi, *Safwat al-`Asr fi Ta'rikh wa Rusum Mashahir Rijal fi Misr* (Cairo, 1926) 1:331–336; Dia M. Abou-Ghazi, "Ahmed Kamal 1849–1923," *Annales du Service des Antiquités de l'Egypte* 64 (1981): 1–5; Tawfiq Habib, "Ta'rikh al-Kashf," *al-Hilal* 32 (November 1, 1923): 135–141; *al-Muqtataf*, 63 (November 1923): 273–77; Gamal El-Din El-Shayyal, *A History of Egyptian Historiography in the Nineteenth Century* (Alexandria, 1962), 60–63; Wilson, *Signs*, 193–194; Dawson and Uphill, *Egyptology*, 3.

13. On the School of Ancient Languages, see Dar al-Watha'iq al-Qawmiyya (Egyptian National Archives), Cairo (hereafter, DWQ)/Mahfuzat Majlis al-Wuzara, Nazarat al-Ashghal, Maslahat al-Athar, Alif/3/4, 1879–90; A. Rouchdy, "Note au Counseil des Ministres"; *al-Muqtataf* 63 (November 1923): 275–76; and Habib, *al-Hilal*, 32 (November 1, 1923): 139. On the second Egyptology school, see DWQ/ Mahfuzat Majlis al-Wuzara, Nazarat al-Ashghal, Maslahat al-Athar, 1/4 Matahif 1879–1914, Folder: Madrasat al-Athar, 1881–86. On the third school of 1910–12, see Jam`iyyat al-Mu`allimin, "Dirasat `Ilm al-Athar al-Misriyya bi-Madrasat al-Mu`allimin al-`Ulya," *al-Kitab al-Dhahabi li-Madrasat al-Mu`allimin al-`Ulya 1885–1935* (Cairo, 1935). Tawfiq Habib, "Dars al-Athar fi al-Jami`a al-Misriyya," *al-Muqtataf* 72 (1928): 438–443, reviews the history of all four of the Egyptology schools up to 1928.

14. Heinrich Brugsch, *Mein Leben und mein Wandern* (Berlin, 1893), 282.

15. *Ruz al-Yusuf*, March 21, 1936. My English translation from the French

translation enclosed in "Repatriated" Archives of the French Embassy in Cairo, Ministère des affaires étrangères, Nantes (hereafter, MAE)/AMB Le Caire, Enseignement égyptien, Service des antiquités, Carton 174, Dossier 53/2: "Succession M. Lacau."

16. MAE/AMB Le Caire, Enseignement Egyptienne (1892–1941), Carton 174bis, Cogordan to Delcassé, November 20, 1899.

17. DWQ/Mahfuzat Majlis al-Wuzara, Nazarat al-Ashghal, Maslahat al-Athar 1891–1907, B/3/4, Ahmad Kamal to Pres., Council of Ministers, October 28, 1892.

18. Charles Breasted, *Pioneer to the Past: The Story of James Henry Breasted, Told by His Son Charles Breasted* (New York, 1947), 368. Pp. 327–49, 358, 360–73, describe the work on the tomb through the eyes of the author's father. For Carter's view, see Howard Carter and A. C. Mace, *The Tomb of Tut.Ankh.Amen Discovered by the Late Earl of Carnarvon and Howard Carter*, vol. 1, and Carter, vols. 2 and 3 (New York, rpt. 1963). See also "The Amazing Luxor Dispute," *Egyptian Gazette*, February 16, 1924, 3, and Archives of the Foreign Office (hereafter, FO), U.K., Public Record Office, London, FO371/10055/E1407, February 1, 1924, Alan Gardiner to PM.

19. Grace Thompson Seton, *A Woman Tenderfoot in Egypt* (New York, 1923), 132, 134.

20. "The Amazing Luxor Dispute," *Egyptian Gazette*, February 16, 1924, 3.

21. As quoted in the Egyptian Gazette, "The Deadlock at Luxor," February 18, 1924, 2. *Al-Ahram, al-Akhbar*, and *al-Mahrusa* similarly opposed Carter in the dispute.

22. MAE/AMB Le Caire, Enseignement égyptien, Service des Antiquités (1892–1941), Carton 174bis, Dossier 53/3: Fouilles, September 7, 1925, Gaillard to MAE.

23. *Egyptian Gazette*, January 26, 1925, 3.

24. Wilson, *Signs*, 181–183; Breasted, *Pioneer*, 374–397; FO371/10897/J1797, June 27, 1925, Murray to Lloyd. French reactions are reflected in MAE/AMB Le Caire, Enseignement égyptien, Service des antiquités 1897–1940, Carton 174, Dossier: "Don de Rockfeller [sic]," April 6, 1926.

25. Ahmad Kamal, *al-Muqtataf*, January 1, 1923, 62, 1–5; Hasan Ahmad Kamal, *al-Muqattam*, February 20, 1924, 2, and later numbers in February and March; Selim Hassan, "Kanz," *al-Ahram*, January 1, 1923, reprinted in *al-Ahram, Shuhud al-`Asr 1876–1986* (Cairo, 1986), 80–88.

26. Wilson, *Signs*, 192–193.

27. *al-Muqtataf*, 63 (1923): 276.

28. Cairo University Archives (hereafter, CUA)/Université Egyptienne, Carton 5, Dossier 296: Missions to Europe of Princess Fatimah Hanum. July 9, 1923, Taha Husayn to Wakil of University.

29. Except where otherwise noted, information on Gabra is from his *Chez les derniers adorateurs de Trismegiste: La Nécropole d'Hermopolis Touna El Gebel* (Cairo, 1971). See also notices on him in *Bulletin de la Société d'archéologie copte* 24 (1979–82): 128–130, and *al-Kitab al-Fiddi li-Kulliyyat al-Adab, 1925–1950* (Cairo, 1951), 58–59. On Selim Hassan, see Mukhtar, *al-Majalla al-Tar'ikhiyya al-Misriyya*, 19 (1972): 73–87; Dia Abou Ghazi, "Selim Hassan: His Writings and Excavation," *ASAE* 58 (1964): 62–84; *al-Kitab al-Dhahabi,*

125–126; Dawson and Uphill, *Egyptology*, 133–134; Wilson, *Signs*, 193–194, 230. I have not found a biographical sketch of Hamza, who is mentioned in passing here and there.

30. On the first years of this fourth Egyptology school, see Habib, *Hilal*, 140–141; Habib, *Muqtataf*, 438–443; and MAE/AMB Le Caire, Enseignement égyptien, Carton 170, (52), Université 1907–1940, Dossier 4, Sousdossier "Ecole égyptienne d'archéologie," January 26, 1924, Cairo to MAE. On Golénischeff, see Dawson and Uphill, *Egyptology*, 118.

31. MAE/AMB Le Caire, Enseignement égyptien, Carton 170, (52) Université 1907–1940, Dossier 4, Sousdossier Ecole égyptienne d'archéologie, "Rapport de la commission d'archéologie," (Summer 1920): 1–4, signed Lacau, Kamal, Abdel Hamid Mostafa, G. Foucart.`Ali Bahgat, director of the Museum of Arab Art, had resigned his seat on the subcommittee for unknown reasons.

32. Labib Habachi, interview, Cairo, June 22, 1983.

33. *al-Muqtataf*, February 1, 1923, and *al-Hilal*, 32 (June 1, 1924): 912.

34. Analyzed in Paul Starkey, *From the Ivory Tower: A Critical Study of Tawfiq al-Hakim* (London, 1987), 84–87, 119, 122–125.

35. Husayn Fawzi, *Sindibad Misri* (Cairo, 1961), and Sayyid Uways, *L'Histoire que je porte sur mon dos: Memoires*, trans. Nashwa al Azhari et al. (Cairo, 1989), 86.

36. For the Zaghlul mausoleum affair, see Ralph Coury, "The Politics of the Funereal: The Tomb of Saad Zaghlul," *Journal of the American Research Center in Egypt* 39 (1992): 191–200.

37. Charles Wendell, *The Evolution of the Egyptian National Image: From Its Origins to Ahmad Lutfi al-Sayyid* (Berkeley, 1972), 272.

38. S. Somekh, "The Neo-Classical Arabic Poets," in M. M. Badawi (ed.), *Modern Arabic Literature* (Cambridge, 1993), 69–71.

39. Gabra, *Trismegiste*, 15.

40. Anderson, *Imagined Communities*, 180.

41. Gabra, *Trismegiste*, 14.

42. On Claudius Labib and his son Pahor Labib, I have relied on W. E. Crum, "Bibliography: Christian Egypt," *The Journal of Egyptian Archaeology* 5 (1918): 215; Ramzi Tadrus, *al-Aqbat fi-l-Qarn al-`Ishrin* (Cairo, n.d.), 4, 135–139; interview, Pahor Labib, Cairo, October 22, 1987; and Martin Krause (ed.), *Essays on the Nag Hammadi Texts in Honour of Pahor Labib* (Leiden, 1975), 1–3. On Sobhy, see *Bulletin de la Société d'archéologie copte*, 19 (1967–68): 315–16; 20; (1969–70): 1–3. On Mattha, see *al-Athar al-`Ilmiyya li-Ada Hayat al-Tadris bi-Jami`at al-Qahira*, (Cairo, 1958), 75–76. Statistics on Egyptology graduates are calculated from the lists in *al-Dalil al-Dhahabi lil-Asatidha wa Khariji al-Athar, Jami`at al-Qahira mundhu Sanat 1925*.

43. Quotations from Gabra, *Trismegiste*, 14–15, 150, 19.

44. Mukhtar, "Selim Hassan," 78.

45. On Newberry, see Dawson and Uphill, *Egyptology*, 216. On Junker and the German Institute, see ibid., 154–155; FO924/547/LC4763, September 1946, Egypt Exploration Society, "The Future of British Archeology in Egypt." On the Nefertiti affair, see Wilson, *Signs*, 155–157; FO 371/53375/J2263, May 20, 1946, Egyptian Ambassador (London) to FO.

46. Reisner to Hawes of Boston Museum of Fine Arts, October 9, 1924, as quoted in Nicholas Reeves and John H. Taylor, *Howard Carter before Tutankhamun* (New York, 1992), 161.

47. Wilson, *Signs*, 149.

48. MAE/AMB Le Caire, Carton 178: Personnel, Immeubles, Dossier: Personnel, September 4, 1926, Briand (MAE) to Cairo.

49. MAE/AMB Le Caire. Enseignement égyptien, Service des antiquités, Carton 174/bis, Dossier "Personnel français," October 30, 1923. Pres. du Conseil, MAE to Gaillard.

50. MAE/AMB Le Caire, Enseignement égyptien, Service des antiquités 1892–41, Carton 174bis, Dossier: Personnel français, September 24, 1925, French Minister, Alexandria to Briand; and Gaillard to MAE, November 19, 1923.

51. MAE/Service des Oeuvres françaises à l'étranger, Série D. - Levant, Carton 365: Egypte: Facultés égyptiennes, Dossier: Facultés égyptiennes, June 4, 1934, Rector of Academy, Paris, to MAE.

52. MAE/AMB Le Caire, Enseignement égyptien, Service des Antiquités 1892–1941, Carton 174bis, Dossier: Personnel français, Gaillard to MAE, February 18, 1930.

53. MAE/Service des oeuvres françaises a l'étranger, Série D - Levant, Carton 365: Egypte: Facultés égyptiennes, Dossier: Institut d'archéologie, June 6, 1935, Dir. of Education supérieure, Ministère d'éducation nationale to Marx; Service des Ouevres, Série D - Levant, Carton 178: IFAO Personnel, Immeuble, Foucart to Jouguet, 4; *al-Jihad*, March 19, 1936, translation enclosed in MAE/AMB Le Caire, Enseignement égyptien, Service des antiquités, Carton 174, Dossier 53/2: Succession M. Lacau.

54. FO371/19094/J3355, July 15, 1935, Lampson to Oliphant.

55. FO371/10897/J1411, May 6, 1925, Allenby to Chamberlain.

56. *al-Balagh*, May 26, 1936.

57. MAE/AMB Le Caire, Enseignement égyptienne, Service des antiquités 1892–1941, Carton 174, Dossier 52/3: Succession M. Lacau.

58. *Ruz al-Yusuf*, June 9, 1936, French translation in MAE/AMB Le Caire, Enseignement égyptienne, Service des Antiquités 1897–1941, Carton 174, Dossier 53/2, Succession M. Lacau.

59. MAE/AMB Le Caire, Enseignement égyptien, Service des antiquités 1897–1941, Carton 174, Dossier: Succession M. Lacau, June 1, 1937, French Minister in Egypt to Delbos, quoting *al-Balagh*.

60. MAE/AMB Le Caire, Enseignement égyptien, Service des antiquités 1897–1941, Carton 174, Dossier 53/2: Succession M. Lacau.

61. FO395/550/P2759, "Memorandum by Sir Robert Greg on the General Cultural Position in Egypt," enclosed in Lampson to Eden, June 11, 1937.

62. MAE/AMB Le Caire, Enseignement égyptien, Service des Antiquités (1897–1941), Carton 174, Nov. 17, 1937, Witasse to MAE.

63. MAE, Service des oeuvres françaises à l'étranger. Série D - Levant, Carton 266, Egypte: Facultés égyptiennes and Institut d'archéologie, Dossier: Institut d'archéologie, June 27, 1939.

64. MAE/AMB Le Caire, Enseignement égyptien, Service des antiquités, 1897–1941, Carton 174, Dossier 53/2: Succession M. Lacau, French Minister, Cairo to Debos, March 10, 1937.

65. FO371/321585/J1626, Lampson to Gaselee, March 20, 1942; F0371/ 31585/J1048, April 14, 1942, Lampson to Eden.

66. F0371/31585/J678, extract of letter, Dec. 12, 1941, Fairman to Gardiner.

67. *Akhir Sa`a*, Feb. 12, [1940?], French translation enclosed in MAE/AMB Le Caire/Enseignement égyptien, Services des antiquités, 1892–1941, Carton 174bis, Dossier: Personnel français.

68. Gershoni and Jankowski, *Egyptian Nation*, 63.

69. J. Brugman, *An Introduction to the History of Modern Arabic Literature* (Leiden, 1984), 297–98.

70. For example, Egyptian Kingdom, Presidency of Council of Ministers, *The Unity of the Nile Valley: Its Geographical Bases and Its Manifestations in History* (Cairo, 1947), with contributions by Abbas Ammar, Ibrahim Noshi, Ahmad Badawi, Mohammed Shafik Ghorbal, and Abdel Rahman Zaki; Muhammad Fu'ad Shukri, *al-Hukm al-Misri fi al-Sudan, 1820–1885* (Cairo, 1947); Pahor Labib, "Wahdat Wadi al-Nil fi al-Ta'rikh al-Qadim," in his *Lamahat min al-Dirasat al-Misriyya al-Qadima* (Cairo, 1947), 12–22.

71. Based on visits to the museum and *al-Sijill al-Thaqafi Sanat 1954*, Jumhuriyyat Misr, Wizarat al-Tarbiyya wa al-Tal`im, Idarat al-`Amm lil-Thaqafa (Cairo, 1956), 7, 594.

72. FO371/41352/J92, Jan. 6, 1944, Killearn to FO; FO371/ 41352/J1902, Glanville to Scrivener, May 23, 1944. Creswell, however, headed the Islamic Archeology section until the dismissal of all British employees of the Egyptian government in December 1951.

73. Muhammad Husayn Haykal, *Mudhakkirat fi al-Siyasa al-Misriyya* (2 vols., Cairo, 1953), 2, 121–124; MAE/Service des oeuvres françaises à l'étranger, Série D - Levant, Carton 366: Egypte: Facultés égyptiennes et Institut d'archéologie, June 27, 1939, Fr. Ambassador, Cairo to Bonnet.

74. FO371/31585/J1948, April 10 and 14, 1942, Lampson to Eden; and Dawson and Uphill, *Egyptology*, 43–44, 97–98.

75. FO371/31385/J3014, Fairman to Alan H. Gardiner, June 3, 1942, enclosed in Gardiner to Gaselee; FO371/31585/J678, December 27, 1941, Fairman to Gardiner; Fairman to Smart, April 23, 1942, enclosed in FO371/31585/J2493/ J2493, May 7, 1942, Lampson to Eden, which also includes Engelbach's assessment. On Fairman, see *Who Was Who*, 8 (1981–1990): 244.

76. *al-Dalil al-Dhahabi*. In 1970 the Department of Archeology left the Faculty of Arts to become the independent Faculty of Archeology.

77. Wilson, *Thousands*, 148.

78. M. S. Gallab, *Bulletin de la Société royale de géographie d'Egypte*, 43–44 (1970–71): 1; *Kitab al-Fiddi*, 31.

79. Mukhtar, "Selim Hassan," offers the strongest defense of Selim Hassan. `Aziz `Atiya and Kamal El Mallakh offered opposite opinions on the validity of the embezzlement charges against Hassan. Interviews with `Atiya, Salt Lake City, March 29, 1986, and El Mallakh, Cairo, October 14, 1987.

80. Gerard Coudougnan, *Nos Ancêtres les Pharaons: L'histoire pharonique et copte dans les manuels scolaires égyptiens* (Cairo, 1988).

81. Wilson, *Thousands*, 148.

82. Hassan's street is the short one in front of the Museum. Mariette street alongside the Museum is still so named on maps, although I have not seen

street signs to that effect in recent years. Champollion Street runs off Maydan al-Tahrir to the northeast, and Maspero's name survives as a stop for the Nile ferry.

83. Wilson, *Thousands*, 122.

8. Arab Nationalism in "Nasserism" and Egyptian State Policy, 1952–1958

1. Egypt, Ministry of National Guidance, *Majmu`at Khutub wa Tasrihat wa Bayanat al-Ra'is Jamal `Abd al-Nasir* (multivol; Cairo, n.d.), 1:155.
2. Ibid., 140.
3. Speech of 22 July 1955, as quoted in Keith Wheelock, *Nasser's New Egypt* (New York, 1960), 225.
4. United Arab Republic, State Information Service, *The Charter* (Cairo, n.d.), 9–10, 22.
5. Quoted in Jean Lacouture, *Nasser* (New York, 1973), 190.
6. See Georges Vaucher, *Gamal Abdel Nasser et son Equipe* (Paris, 1959), 56–67; Jean and Simonne Lacouture, *Egypt in Transition* (New York, 1958), 460; Vatikiotis, *Nasser*, 28–29.
7. Husayn Mu'nis, *Misr wa Risalatuha* (Cairo, 1956 or 1957), 3–6.
8. *Majmu`at Khutub*, 1:277–278.
9. Marlene Nasr, *al-Tasawwur al-Qawmi al-`Arabi fi Fikr Jamal `Abd al-Nasir, 1952–1970* (Beirut, 1982), 104–113.
10. *Majmu`at Khutub*, 1:564.
11. Gamal Abdel Nasser, *The Philosophy of the Revolution* (Buffalo, 1959), 62; *Majmu`at Khutub*, 1:650–654.
12. Nasser, *Philosophy*, 63.
13. Nasr, *Tasawwur*, 91–92; Muhammad Hasanayn Haykal, *Milaffat al-Suwis* (Cairo, 1986), 196–197.
14. Nasser, *Philosophy*, 63.
15. Ibid., 65.
16. See Vaucher, *Nasser*, 50–67, 96–104; Nasr, *Tasawwur*, 93–98.
17. Haykal, *Milaffat*, 284–285.
18. As cited in Fu'ad Matar, *Bi-Saraha `an `Abd al-Nasir: Hiwar ma`a Muhammad Hasanayn Haykal* (Beirut, 1975), 137.
19. For their frequency of usage, see Nasr, *Tasawwur*, 128, 214, 280.
20. Ibid., 209–212.
21. *Majmu`at Khutub*, 1:177.
22. Ibid., 548.
23. Ibid., 177.
24. See Haykal, *Milaffat*, 197; Mahmud Riyad, *Mudhakkirat Mahmud Riyad, 1948–1978* (3 vols.: Cairo, 1985–1986), 2:67; *Majmu`at Khutub*, 1:55–59, 444–445, 641–645, 650–654.
25. Ibid., 654.
26. Ibid., 666.
27. Ibid., 501; also 548.
28. Ibid., 641–643, 643–645, 645–646.
29. Ibid., 645–646, 699–700.

30. Ibid., 654, 742.

31. Ibid., 718.

32. Nasser, *Philosophy*, 59–60, 76–78.

33. Lacouture, *Egypt*, 458–459.

34. *Majmu`at Khutub*, 1:579 (italics mine).

35. Nasr, *Tasawwur*, 344–348.

36. Ibid., 349–350.

37. Marlene Nasr, "Tatawwur al-Qawmi al-`Arabi," in Sa`d al-Din Ibrahim (ed.), *Misr wa al-Qawmiyya wa Thawrat Yulyu* (2d. ed., Cairo, 1983), 53–81, especially 77–79.

38. Marlene Nasr, "al-Qawmiyya wa al-Din fi Fikr `Abd al-Nasir," in ibid., 93–101.

39. Haykal, *Milaffat*, 314–315.

40. Muhammad Hasanayn Haykal, *Li-Misr La Li-`Abd al-Nasir* (Cairo, 1987), 104–106; see also Mohamed Hassanein Heikal, *The Cairo Documents* (New York, 1973), 20–21.

41. Despatch of 12 June 1954, US/State 674.86A, 6–1254; military weekly report, 20 August 1954, US/State, 774.00(W), 8–2054.

42. Discussed in P. J. Vatikiotis, *The Egyptian Army in Politics* (Bloomington, 1961), 191–193.

43. "A General Survey of Nasser's Foreign Policy," African Department, 30 August 1957; Great Britain, Public Records Office, FO 371/125427, JE1023/24.

44. See Ghada Hashem Talhami, *Palestine and Egyptian National Identity* (New York, 1992), 70, 77, 161.

45. Speech in Aleppo, 15 October 1960; *Majmu`at Khutub*, 2:266.

46. Ibid., 1:13.

47. Discussed in depth in Joel Gordon, *Nasser's Blessed Movement: Egypt's Free Officers and the July Revolution* (New York, 1992).

48. Caffery to State, 5 September 1952, US/State, 774.00, 9–552; Caffery to State, 24 July 1953, US/State, 774.00, 7–2453.

49. For examples see `Abd al-Latif al-Baghdadi, *Mudhakkirat `Abd al-Latif al-Baghdadi* (2 vols.; Cairo, 1977), 1:195–196; Ahmad Hamrush, *Qissat Thawrat 23 Yulyu* (2d ed., 5 vols.; Cairo, 1983), 2:26; Khalid Muhyi al-Din, *Wa Al-An Atakallimu* (Cairo, 1992), 192.

50. *Majmu`at Khutub*, 1, 3, 30.

51. Nasser, *Philosophy*, 43.

52. Muhammad Najib, *Mudhakkirat Muhammad Najib: Kuntu Ra'isan Li-Misr* (Cairo, 1984), 278–290.

53. Military weekly report, 17 December 1953, US/State, 774.00(W), 12–1853.

54. Despatch of 27 January 1954, US/State, 674.00, 1–2754.

55. Military weekly report, 12 February 1954, US/State, 774.00(W), 2–1254.

56. Military weekly report, 23 April 1954, US/State, 774.00(W), 4–2354.

57. Despatch from Stevenson, 12 January 1954; FO 371/108349, JE1022/3.

58. Caffery to State, 9 January 1954, US/State, 674.0021, 1–954.

59. Haykal, *Milaffat*, 185–187; Najib, *Mudhakkirat*, 316–322.

60. US/State, 674.00, 2–2054; US/State, 5–2454; FO 371/108349, JE1022/4.

61. Despatch of 20 April 1954, US/State, 674.00, 4–2054.

62. Government sources as cited in US/State, 774.5, 5–2854.

63. *al-Jumhuriyya,* 23 May 1954, quoted in US/State, 774.00, 5–2454.

64. Interview with John Law, 5 August 1954, in despatch of 13 August 1954, US/State, 774.00, 8–1354.

65. As quoted in Seale, *Struggle for Syria,* 194.

66. US/State, *Foreign Relations of the United States, 1952–1954* (hereafter *FRUS*) (2 vols.; Washington, 1982, 1986), 2319–2322; US/State 674.00, 9–354; 774.00, 12–1754.

67. For a detailed account, see Riyad, *Mudhakkirat,* 2:101–112.

68. Byroade to State, 11 March 1955, US/State, 774.00, 3–1155.

69. Ibid.

70. Byroade to State, 4 April 1955, US/State, 774.00, 4–1455.

71. Translated in US/State, Despatch of 29 March 1955, US/State, 674.00, 4–455.

72. Despatch of 4 April 1955, US/State, 674.00, 4/1455.

73. Haykal, *Milaffat,* 185–187.

74. Ibid., 282–283.

75. Riyad, *Mudhakkirat,* 2:41–42.

76. Najib, *Mudhakkirat,* 340–341.

77. Lacouture, *Nasser,* 185–186.

78. Riyad, *Mudhakkirat,* 2:51.

79. Caffery to State, 23 February 1954, US/State, 674.00, 2–2354.

80. Despatch of 12 June 1954, US/State, 674.83, 5–2454.

81. Riyad, *Mudhakkirat,* 2:108.

82. Ibid., 121–123.

83. Moose to State, 9 August 1956, US/State, 674.83, 8–956.

84. Despatch from Hare, 16 December 1956; US/State, 674.00, 12–1656.

85. Muhammad Hasanayn Haykal, *Sanawat al-Ghalayan* (Cairo, 1988), 199–204.

86. Riyad, *Mudhakkirat,* 2:202.

87. *Majmu`at Khutub,* 1:619.

88. Interview of March 1957 as quoted in Robert Stephens, *Nasser: A Political Biography* (New York, 1971), 272.

89. Speech of July 1957 as quoted in US/State, 674.00, 7–2757.

90. *Majmu`at Khutub,* 1:771.

91. Yost to State, 14 January 1958, US/State, 674.83, 1–1458; same to same, 15 January 1958, US/State, 674.83, 1–1558.

92. Hamrush, *Qissat,* 3:49, and 4:87–88.

93. See Baghdadi, *Mudhakkirat,* 2:34–38; Sayyid Mar`i, *Awraq Siyasiyya* (3 vols.; Cairo, 1979), 2:397–399; Fathi Radwan, *72 Shahran ma`a `Abd al-Nasir* (Cairo, 1985), 99; Riyad, *Mudhakkirat,* 2:199–201; also Mahmud Fawzi, *Thuwwar Yulyu Yatahaddathun* (Cairo, 1988), 38, 55–56; Sami Jawhar, *al-Samitun Yatakalllimu* (Cairo, 1975), 50.

94. Radwan, *72 Shahran,* 104.

95. Mar`i, *Awraq,* 2:397.

96. Baghdadi, *Mudhakkirat,* 2:36.

97. Haykal, *Sanawat,* 271–277; Riyad, *Mudhakkirat,* 2:215–217.

98. For material to this effect, see US/State, 674.83, 9–657; FO 371/131328, JE1022/10; Haykal as cited in Matar, *Bi-Saraha*, 138–139; Haykal, *Sanawat*, 266–269.

99. Ibid., 277.

100. Quoted in Radwan, *72 Shahran*, 99.

101. Yost to State, 30 January 1958, US/State, 674.83, 1–3058; Baghdadi, *Mudhakkirat*, 2:36; Hamrush, *Qissat*, 3:49–50.

102. Radwan, *72 Shahran*, 103.

103. Mar`i, *Awraq*, 2:399.

104. Eisenhower Library, Raymond Hare Oral History.

105. For a discussion of Egyptian regional policies from 1936 to 1945, see Gershoni and Jankowski, *Egyptian Nation*; for the later 1940s, see Thomas Mayer, "Egypt's 1948 Invasion of Palestine," *Middle Eastern Studies*, 22 (1986): 20–36.

106. Breuilly, *Nationalism and the State*, 1.

107. Zubaida, *Islam*, 145–146.

108. Ibid., 149.

109. Owen, *State, Power, and Politics*, 20.

110. Simon Bromley, *Rethinking Middle East Politics* (Austin, 1994), 177.

9. The Formation of Palestinian Identity: The Critical Years, 1917–1923

1. Most of these polemics center on the nonexistence, or the illegitimacy, or the recent provenance, of a separate Palestinian identity. They were epitomized by Joan Peters's *From Time Immemorial: The Origins of the Arab-Jewish Conflict over Palestine* (New York, 1984). Initially praised by a number of reputable scholars, this book was shown by a devastating review by Yehoshua Porath in the *New York Review of Books* to be worthless as scholarship.

2. These include Porath, *1918–1929*; `Abd al-Wahhab Kayyali, *Ta'rikh Filastin al-Hadith*, (Beirut, 1970) (trans. as *Palestine: A Modern History*, London, 1978); Lesch, *Arab Politics*; Muslih, *Origins*; and Baruch Kimmerling and Joel Migdal, *Palestinians, The Making of a People* (New York, 1993).

3. "Ethnicity: Identity and Difference," *Radical America* 23:4 (October/December 1989): 16.

4. An early disparaging comment on the legitimacy of Palestinian aspirations came from A. J. Balfour, in a Foreign Office memo dated 11 August 1919 (cited in J. C. Hurewitz [ed.], *The Middle East and North Africa in World Politics* [New Haven, 1979], 2:189): "Zionism, be it right or wrong, good or bad, is rooted in age-long traditions, in present needs, in future hopes, of far greater import than the desires and prejudices of the 700,000 Arabs who now inhabit that ancient land."

5. *Sunday Times* (London), June 15, 1969, 12.

6. For an early example of the terms in which this debate was framed, see Marwan Buheiry, "Bulus Nujaym and the Grand Liban Ideal 1908–1919," in M. Buheiry (ed.), *Intellectual Life in the Arab East, 1860–1939* (Beirut, 1981), 62–83. Kamal Salibi, *A House of Many Mansions: The History of Lebanon Reconsidered* (Berkeley, 1988), is the best survey of the struggle over the historiography of

Lebanon. See as well Ahmad Baydun, *al-Sira`* `*ala Ta'rikh Lubnan, wa al-Ha-wiyya wa al-Zaman fi A`mal Mu'arrikhina al-Mu`asirin* (Beirut, 1989).

7. In his posthumous work, translated into English as *Palestine in Transformation, 1856–1882: Studies in Social, Economic, and Political Development* (Washington, D.C., 1993), 9–17. Schölch is concerned at the outset of his book to "ascertain the extent to which it is at all meaningful to write a history of Palestine during a certain phase in the nineteenth century when there was no administrative unit with this name and when this area's 'borders'—in other words, the area's historical-geographical identity—were contested."

8. This echoes a Hebrew term used to describe the country, "*ha-eretz ha-mikdash.*" Given the brief adoption of Jerusalem as a direction of prayer by the early Muslims, and other Jewish influences on early Islam, there is very possibly a connection.

9. See Kamil al-`Asali, *Makhtutat Fada'il Bayt al-Maqdis* (Amman, 1984).

10. Ibid., 16; Porath, *1918–1929*, 1–9.

11. Schölch, *Palestine*, 12–15; Butrus Abu Manneh, "Jerusalem in the Tanzimat Period: The New Ottoman Administration and the Notables," *Die Welt des Islams* 30 (1990): 1–44; idem, "The Rise of the Sanjak of Jerusalem in the Late 19th Century," in Gabriel Ben Dor (ed.), *The Palestinians and the Middle East Conflict* (Ramat Gan, 1978). See also `Abd al-`Aziz Muhammad `Awad, "Mutasarrifiyyat al-Quds, 1874–1914" in *al-Mu'tamar al-Dawli al-Thalith li-Ta'rikh Bilad al-Sham: Filastin* (Amman, 1983): 1, 204–223.

12. `Azuri's article, originally published in the Turkish paper *Sabah*, was reprinted in Arabic in *Thamarat al-Funun*, 23 September, 1908, 7. A copy of the article was among the papers that Ruhi al-Khalidi, the newly elected deputy from Jerusalem, was carrying with him to Istanbul from Marseilles in 1908: Ruhi al-Khalidi papers, Khalidi Library, Jerusalem.

13. Schölch, *Palestine*, 15.

14. Porath, *1918–1929*, 8–9.

15. Among monographs on the rivalries of the European powers over Palestine see A. L. Tibawi, *British Interests in Palestine* (Oxford, 1966); Rashid Khalidi, *British Policy Toward Syria and Palestine, 1906–1914* (London, 1980); Rose, *From Palmerston to Balfour*; Isaiah Friedman, *Germany, Turkey, and Zionism, 1897–1918* (Oxford, 1977).

16. See the discussion in Rashid Khalidi, "Contrasting Narratives of Palestinian Identity," in Patricia Yaeger (ed.), *The Geography of Identity* (Ann Arbor, 1996), 215–216, of a 1701 petition by notables and other inhabitants of Jerusalem to Sultan Mustafa II protesting the visit of a French Consul in Jerusalem, "since our city is the focus of attention of the infidels" and since "this holy land" could be "occupied as a result of this, as has happened repeatedly in earlier times." The meeting that produced this petition was attended by both notables and common people, testimony to the prevalence of such feelings among all sectors of urban society.

17. A recent joke shows how persistent are these local urban loyalties, and how they can still be imagined as transcending broader bonds: the scene is a street in Jerusalem, where two native Jerusalemites (currently outnumbered in the city by newcomers from Hebron) are witnessing a fight between a Pal-

estinian and an Israeli settler. The first asks the other why he doesn't intervene, and the second answers: "Why should I? It is a fight between settlers."

18. Neville Mandel, *The Arabs and Zionism before World War I* (Berkeley, 1976). See also Rashid Khalidi, "The Role of the Press in the Early Arab Reaction to Zionism," *Peuples Mediterraneans/Mediterranean Peoples* 20 (July/September 1982): 105–124.

19. Rashid Khalidi, "Palestinian Peasant Resistance to Zionism before World War I," in Edward Said and Christopher Hitchens (eds.), *Blaming the Victims: Spurious Scholarship and the Palestine Question* (New York, 1988), 207–233.

20. See Khalidi, "Role of the Press," 105–124.

21. *Filastin* special issue (described on the masthead as closed by order of the Ministry of the Interior, an order that this issue was presumably defying), 7 Nisan 1330/May 1914, 1. For details of this affair, see Khalidi, *British Policy*, 356–357.

22. Ibid.; a French consular official, commenting on this incident, remarked that it indicated widespread opposition to Zionism among the urban population of Palestine.

23. For more on the struggle of Arabic-speaking Greek Orthodox in Syria and Palestine to free their church from the control of its Greek hierarchy and to Arabize it, see Derek Hopwood, *The Russian Presence in Palestine and Syria* (Oxford, 1969).

24. The speech, delivered "at the end of the Second World War" is reported in `Ajaj Nuwayhid, *Rijal min Filastin ma bayna Bidayat al-Qarn hatta `Amm 1948* (Amman, 1981), 30.

25. They perceived this largely after the fact in the years after World War I. The rewriting of Arab history in the interwar years to fit this new version of events is a fascinating story that has yet to find its historian.

26. How Arabism supplanted Ottomanism is best treated in C. Ernest Dawn's seminal *From Ottomanism to Arabism*. See also Khalidi et al., *Origins*.

27. Khalil Sakakini, *Filastin ba`d al-Harb al-Kubra* (Jerusalem, 1925), 9. This 56-page pamphlet is a collection of articles published in the Cairo newspaper *al-Siyasa* in 1923.

28. The total number of Palestinians who were executed for nationalist activities during the war is not known. Bayan Nuwayhid al-Hut, *al-Qiyadat wa al-Mu'assasat al-Siyasiyya fi Filastin, 1917–1948* (Beirut, 1981), 46–52, discusses the cases of nine leading Palestinian personalities executed by the Ottoman authorities or who died in prison. In addition, hundreds of others were exiled to Anatolia with their families during the war on similar charges.

29. Justin McCarthy, *The Population of Palestine: Population History and Statistics of the Late Ottoman Period and the Mandate* (New York, 1990), 25–27.

30. See Khalidi, *British Policy*, for more on pre-war concerns about the occupation of Syria and Palestine by the European powers.

31. Bayan al-Hut, *al-Qidayat*, 77–78, notes that although the text of the Balfour Declaration was not officially published in Palestine until 1920, within a few days of its issuance on November 2, 1917, the Egyptian press had publishing details of it and of the jubilant reactions to it in the Egyptian Jewish

community. These provoked a strong reaction among Palestinians when the news reached them soon afterwards.

32. See Jacob Burckhardt, *Judgments on History and Historians*, trans. Harry Zohn (Boston, 1958), 221 ff.

33. Ronald Storrs, *Orientations* (London, 1937), 336–338. Storrs was the first British Military Governor of Jerusalem.

34. This can be seen from two letters from Ronald Storrs to Mustafa al-Budayri, dated August 16, 1921—one refusing permission for publication of a new newspaper entitled *al-Amal*, and the other refusing permission to open a printing press—and a third letter dated six days later requesting in a peremptory manner that Muhammad Kamil al-Budayri, publisher of the newspaper *al-Sabah*, come into the Governorate the following morning for an interview: papers from the files of *al-Sabah*, in the possession of Dr. Musa Budeiri, Jerusalem. For the Ottoman and British press laws, see Yusuf Khuri (ed.), *al-Sihafa al-'Arabiyya fi Filastin, 1876–1948* (Beirut, 1976) 147–225.

35. *Filastin*, 1–328, March 19, 1921, "Hadith qadim wa bayan jadid," 1.

36. Khuri, *al-Sihafa al-'Arabiyya*, 14–15.

37. Only a few issues of the paper exist, some in the Khalidi Library in Jerusalem, and others in the possession of Dr. Musa Budeiri. *Suriyya al-Janubiyya*, as well as *al-Sabah*, published in 1921 by Muhammad Hasan al-Budayri's cousin, Muhammad Kamil al-Budayri, was printed in a small set of rooms belonging to the al-Budayri family immediately adjacent to the Haram al-Sharif, which is now the site of *al-Maktaba al-Budayriyya*. *Suriyya al-Janubiyya* is described by Bernard Wasserstein in *The British in Palestine: The Mandatory Government and the Arab-Jewish Conflict, 1917–1929* (2d ed.; Oxford, 1991), 60, as "the nationalist newspaper."

38. See Rashid Khalidi, "'Abd al-Ghani al-'Uraysi and *al-Mufid*: The Press and Arab Nationalism before 1914," in Buheiry, *Intellectual Life*, 38–61.

39. See Muslih, *Origins*, 168, who notes that al-Budayri, al-'Arif, and Hajj Amin al-Husayni, who wrote frequently for the paper, were leading members of *al-Nadi al-'Arabi*.

40. *Suriyya al-Janubiyya*, no. 11, 11 November, 1919, 6. See also Wasserstein, *British in Palestine*, 180–182, who incorrectly ascribes to al-'Arif alone all the credit for producing the paper.

41. While *Suriyya al-Janubiyya* printed the words *"biladuna lana"* ("our country/countries are ours") across the masthead of every issue, the slogans at the top of the inside pages on issues ranging from October 1919 to March 1920 were either overtly Arabist ("we live for the Arabs and die for the Arabs") or expressed general nationalist sentiments ("there is no majesty, no glory, no honor and no life except in independence"). By contrast, *al-Sabah* employed the more general—and more ambiguous—*"bilad al-'Arab lil-'Arab"* ("the Arab countries are for the Arabs") on its masthead. An unexceptionable sentiment in Arab nationalist terms, this slogan also represented an adjustment to the new realities of 1921 with its recognition that there are many Arab countries.

42. See Malcolm B. Russell, *The First Modern Arab State: Syria under Faysal, 1918–1920* (Minneapolis, 1985) for the best account of the new Syrian state.

43. For the somewhat different attitudes of some Syrians, and especially some Damascenes to the new state, see ibid.; Muslih, *Origins*; and James L.

Gelvin, *Contesting Nationalisms and the Birth of Mass Politics in Syria* (Berkeley, 1997).

44. Among the Palestinians who served Faysal and his government were `Awni `Abd al-Hadi, `Isa al-`Isa, and Muhammad `Izzat Darwaza. See *Dhikra Istiqlal Suriyya* (Damascus, 1920).

45. See Khalidi, *British Policy*, and Khalidi et al., *Origins*, for details of these pre-war evolutions.

46. Until the 1940s many Lebanese, particularly Sunnis, refused to accept the legitimacy of Lebanon as an entity, preferring to consider the country as no more than the Syrian coastal region. See Salibi, *House of Many Mansions*.

47. "al-Anba' al-mulafaqa," *Suriyya al-Janubiyya* 8:2 October 1919, 1.

48. "Illa natadhakar Filastin?," ibid., 3–4.

49. "Zubdat al-Akhbar," ibid., no. 11, 11 November 1919, 5.

50. "Hawla al-Mas'ala al-Sihyuniyya," *Suriyya al-Janubiyya*, no. 16, 27 November 1919, 4.

51. Cited in Wasserstein, *British in Palestine*, 76. Porath, *1918–1929*, 319, n. 17, suggests that "perhaps Samuel had not precisely said what was later attributed to him," and was misunderstood by the Arabs. Samuel said exactly what the Arabs thought he had: that Zionism aimed for a Jewish majority and control of the country.

52. The only other important newspapers to publish in Palestine while *Suriyya al-Janubiyya* appeared were Bulus Shahada's *Mir'at al-Sharq*, published in Jerusalem starting in September 1919 (this became a the organ of the anti-Husayni faction in the early 1920s, and a nationalist organ later on, when Ahmad Shuqayri and Akram Zu`aytir wrote for it); and *al-Nafir* and *al-Karmil*, reopened in Haifa in September 1919 and February 1920 respectively. As mentioned earlier, *Filastin* only resumed publication in March 1921.

53. "Hidhar, Hidhar!," *Suriyya al-Janubiyya*, no. 22, 23 December 1919, 2.

54. "Hawla al-Mas'ala al-Sihyuniyya" (this had become a regular column in the paper), ibid., no. 48, 26 March 1920, 3.

55. See Muslih, *Origins*; Porath, *1918–1929*; Russell, *First Modern Arab State*.

56. "Wa la tay'asu min ruh Allah," *Suriyya al-Janubiyya*, no. 11, 11 November 1919, 3.

57. Ibid., no. 32, January 23 1920, 2.

58. See Lesch and Porath for the significance of these societies. Wasserstein claims that some British officials encouraged the establishment of these societies, presumably as a counterweight to the Zionist movement.

59. *Suriyya al-Janubiyya*, no. 48, 26 March 1920, 2. The word *"wataniyya,"* which can mean either nationalism or patriotism, is derived from *"watan,"* homeland. The article in question reported on the strong local reaction to what were described as attempts by Jewish merchants, with the connivance of the British authorities, to purchase large quantities of livestock and other food products in Gaza, and the effect of this in driving up local prices.

60. Ibid., 1.

61. *al-Sabah*, no. 1, 21 October 1921.

62. Such a shift was not necessary for the main competitor of *Suriyya al-Janubiyya*, *Mir'at al-Sharq*, whose lead editorial in its first issue, published on 17 September 1919, makes no reference to Arabism (the term *"umma,"* used

frequently, is not further specified as being the Palestinian or the Arab nation), while it stresses that it is being published *"bayna qawmina"* in Jerusalem, with the clear implication that the paper is Palestinian in focus.

63. Each devotes a chapter to this subject: Muslih, *Origins*, 131–154; Porath, *1918–1929*, 70–122. In his chapter Porath occasionally uses the press as a source, although far more frequently relying on Zionist, British, and other Arab sources.

64. For the texts of these documents, see Hurewitz, *Diplomacy*, 2:46–56, 110–112.

65. The most influential of these counselors was T. E. Lawrence.

66. Bayan al-Hut, *al-Qidayat*, 63–65.

67. Storrs, *Orientations*, 353–354. Wasserstein points out (42, n. 34) that initially Hebrew was not recognized as an official language by the military administration, but that by the end of 1919 this ruling had been overturned.

68. The speeches of Zionist leaders abroad, reported for decades in the Arabic press, had long aroused anti-Zionist sentiment in Palestine and elsewhere in the Arab world (see Khalidi, "Role of the Press"), and after the war, speeches such as that of Samuel, mentioned in n. 51, provoked a fierce reaction. But it was the speeches and actions of Zionist leaders and officials in Palestine that provoked the greatest response from Palestinians.

69. For Syria, see the recent work of James Gelvin, and for Iraq, Mahmoud Haddad, "Iraq Before World War I," in Khalidi et al., *Origins*, 120–150.

70. [Title illegible] *al-Sabah*, no. 1, 21 October 1921, 1.

71. "Sanatuna al-Khamisa," *Filastin*, no. 1, 19 March 1921, p. 1.

72. For G. S. Symes, Chief Secretary of the Mandatory government from 1925 to 1928, the Arab peasantry "obviously *couldn't* . . . manage their own affairs satisfactorily" (Wasserstein, *British in Palestine*, 134.)

73. See Khalidi, "Palestinian Peasant Resistance," for examples of this.

74. Wasserstein, *British in Palestine*, 179. See A. L. Tibawi, *Arab Education in Mandatory Palestine* (London, 1954), who notes that by 1945 nearly half the Arab school-age population was enrolled in schools. See also Ylana Miller, *Government and Society in Mandatory Palestine* (Austin, 1985), for an excellent account of the spread of education in rural areas, generally at the instigation of the rural population.

75. Cairo, 1923. The book was used widely in Palestinian schools.

10. The Palestinians: Tensions Between Nationalist and Religious Identities

1. Richard W. Bulliet, *Islam: The View From The Edge* (New York, 1994), 7.

2. I. Abrash, "Hawla Hudud Istihdar al-Muqaddas fi al-'Umur al-Dunyawiyya: Mulahazat Manhajiyya," *al-Mustaqbal al-'Arabi* 180 (February 1994): 17.

3. Olivier Roy, *The Failure of Political Islam* (Cambridge, 1994), 52.

4. Roy characterizes the FIS as an Algerian nationalist movement and considers it appropriate to speak of "Islamo-nationalism." See ibid., 130.

5. Bulliet, *Islam*, 7.

6. F. Huwaidi, contribution to the debate in A. 'Abd al-Sami', *al-Mutatarrifun: Nadwat wa Dawa'ih Hiwar* (Cairo, 1993), 133.

7. Huwaidi in ibid., 148.

8. J. Mattar in ibid., 87.

9. M. `Amara, in ibid., 71. See special issue of *al-Mustaqbal al-`Arabi,* no. 189 (November 1994).

10. S. Ibrahim in `Abd al-Sami', *al-Mutatarrifun,* 142, 184.

11. Roy, *Failure,* 50. The author suggests that Islamicists come from within the modernist sectors of society, and that Islamicism is not a reaction to modernization but a product of it.

12. A. `Azma, "Fakk al-Irtibat bayna al-`Uruba wa al-Islam," *al-Naqid* 33 (March 1991): 20.

13. C. Ernest Dawn, "The Origins of Arab Nationalism," in Khalidi et al., *Origins,* 16.

14. Tahseen Basheer. See contribution to the debate in `Abd al-Sami', *al-Mutatarrifun,* 150.

15. Johnson, *Islam,* 99.

16. See Hobsbawm, *Nations and Nationalism Since 1780,* 138.

17. Muhammad Muslih, "The Rise of Local Nationalism In The Arab East," in Khalidi et al., *Origins,* 180.

18. As late as April 1920 participants at the Nabi Musa gathering carried banners with the legend "Filastin Juz' min Surriya" (Palestine is part of Syria). See picture of demonstration with banner clearly visible in A. al-Kayyali, *Tar'ikh Filastin al-Hadith* (Beirut, 1970), 162. The first Arabic newspaper established after the British Occupation was called *Suriyya al-Junubiyya* (September 1919).

19. M. M. Salih, *al-Tayyar al-Islami fi Filastin wa Atharuhu fi Haraka al-Jihad, 1917–1948* (Kuwait, 1988), 103.

20. Johnson, *Islam,* 23–24.

21. Ibid., 57.

22. Neither of the two exhibited a marked degree of religious piety or doctrinal expertise. On the evidence of their careers both could be fairly characterized as secular Muslims.

23. For an account written prior to the spread of al-Qassam fever see S. Yasin, *Harb al-`Isabat fi Filastin* (Cairo, 1967), 60–70. The author, himself a participant in the armed struggle in the 1930s, dedicates the book to the memory of al-Qassam, "mu'assas awwal jam`iyya thawriyya fida'iyya fi Filastin."

24. Soon after its establishment in February 1969, the Democratic Front for the Liberation of Palestine brought out a large poster of al-Qassam, while one of its armed formations was actually named Quwwat al-Qassam. Initially, he was appropriated by the left who portrayed him as an early organizer of an incipient Palestinian working class, and perhaps a forerunner of another notable exile, Che Guevara.

25. The first comprehensive treatment of al-Qassam was in Porath, *1929–1939.* He was the first to propagate the myth of an organized movement, al-Qassamiyun. R. Peters, *Islam and Colonialism, The Doctrine of Jihad in Modern History* (The Hague, 1979), 97–103, provides the first scholarly attempt to situate al-Qassam within an Islamic framework.

26. S. Hammuda, *Shaykh `Izz al-Din al-Qassam: al-Wa`i wa al-Thawra* (Jerusalem, 1986). The Embassy of the Islamic Republic of Iran in Damascus held a two-day conference in Habla, al-Qassam's birthplace, in December 1992

to commemorate his memory. See *al-Shahid `Izz al-Din al-Qassam: Hayatuhu wa Jihaduhu* (Damascus, n.d.).

27. Democratic Popular Front for the Liberation of Palestine, *Malamih al-Tattawur al-Filastini: Dirasat Filastiniyya* (n.p., n.d., probably end of 1969), 9–11. Leila Khalid of hijacking fame describes him as having organized the first workers and peasants revolution in the Arab homeland. See L. Khalid, *Sha`bi Sayahya: Mudhakkirat Khatifat al-Ta'irat* (Beirut, 1973), 22.

28. See S. Lachman, "Arab Rebellion and Terrorism in Palestine, 1929–39: The Case of *Shaykh* Izz Al-Din Al-Qassam and his Movement," in Elie Kedourie and Sylvia G. Haim (eds.), *Zionism and Arabism in Palestine and Israel* (London, 1982); "Qassamite terror was particularly bloodthirsty . . . it became one of the most anarchical and destructive forces ever to arise in the Palestinian Arab community" (86–87).

29. Ghassan Kanafani, a leading spokesperson of the Popular Front For the Liberation of Palestine, writes that we must understand al-Qassam's actions in a Guevarist way, as it is certain that he was conscious of the importance of his role as the initiator of an advanced revolutionary foci. See G. Kanafani, "Thawrat 1936–39 fi Filastin: Khalfiyyat wa Tafasil wa Tahlil," *Shu'un Filastiniyya* 6 (January 1972): 62.

30. I. Sakhnini, "Damm Filastin al-Wusta ila Sharq al-Urdun, 1948–1950," *Shu'un Filastiniyya* 40 (December 1974). The Jordanian parliament passed a decree to this effect on 13 December 1948.

31. See M. Budeiri, "Tar'ikh Filastin al-Ijtima`i al-Hadith," in L. Turki (ed.), *al-Mujtama` al-Filastini fi al-Daffa al-Gharbiya wa Qita` Ghaza* (Acre, 1990), 49.

32. For the Palestinians in Lebanon see S. M. A. Ayyub, *al-Bina' al-Tabaqi lil-Filastiniyyin fi Lubnan* (Beirut, 1978), 220–228.

33. See H. Abu al-Naml, *Qita` Ghaza 1948–1967: Tatawwurat Iqtisadiyya wa Siyasiyya wa Ijtima`iyya wa `Askariyya* (Beirut, 1979), 66. According to the author, the Muslim Brothers were the strongest force in the strip until 1955, while in the post-1957 period *Harakat al-Qawmiyyin al-`Arab* became stronger (187).

34. Amnon Cohen, *Political Parties in the West Bank Under the Jordanian Regime, 1949–1967* (Ithaca, 1982), 146.

35. All sorts of groups surfaced and submerged in the post 1948 period. One such was FATAH, which originated in 1956(?) and was identified publicly in 1959 with the publication of the Beirut journal *Filastinuna* ("Our Palestine"). It is doubtful whether its particular brand of Palestinian particularism would have gained much popular support. In the event, the defeat of June 1967 and the demise of Nasser and the Arab nationalist project he symbolized catapulted it to the forefront.

36. See *Shaykh `Abd al-Hamid al-Sayih, Muzaqarat: Filastin, La Salatta Tahta al-Hirab* (Beirut, 1994), 82–83.

37. Some observers believe that it was actively promoted in order to combat the influence of the radical nationalist organizations. HAMAS itself was banned two years after the outbreak of the Intifada, in May 1989.

38. Commenting on an earlier draft, S. Tamari makes the valid criticism that this characterization "collapses all Palestinian nationalism of the pre-Intifada period into the realm of mainstream FATAH politics." I would argue that (a) secular groups within the PLO constantly shied away from any confrontation

on the terrain of religion, and (b) that despite their high degree of visibility, the constituency of the left groups was startlingly miniscule, as has been shown to be the case in the post-Oslo era.

39. On University campuses in the 1970s and 1980s, it was difficult to distinguish between students associated with FATAH and those associated with religious groups; the latter usually cast their vote for FATAH candidates in student elections.

40. A. Nüsse argues that the increased strength of Islamic movements is a reaction against the evils of modern society, and that modernity is identified with state of Israel. There is no evidence to substantiate this rather carefree assertion. See Nüsse, "The Ideology of Hamas: Palestinian Islamic Fundamentalist Thought on the Jews, Israel, and Islam," in R. Nettler (ed.), *Studies in Muslim-Jewish Relations* (Oxford, 1993), 112.

41. Most of the attacks on Israeli civilians in the period prior to the Intifada, and during the Intifada itself, were probably the work of individuals who were not necessarily members of organized groups and who carried out their activities as a result of the climate of opinion created by the Islamic *Jihad*.

42. The Charter, "al-Mithaq," was published in November 1988. It is not a programmatic document and does not go much beyond generalities. It has been criticized, not least by observers sympathetic to the movement for being too vague. See A. Rashad, *Hamas: Palestinian Politics with an Islamic Hue* (Springfield, VA, 1993), 16.

43. Nüsse, "Hamas," 108.

44. See Articles Six, Seven and Twelve of the Charter.

45. Z. Abu Ghuaima, *al-Haraka al-Islamiyya wa Qadiyyat Filastin* (Amman, 1985). The author provides two pages of Qur'anic verses as evidence of the hostility of the Jews to Arabs and Muslims (11–14).

11. Arab Nationalism in the Age of the Islamic Resurgence

1. Cf. Jalal Amin, *al-`Arab wa Nakbat al-Kuwait* (Cairo, 1991); Salah al-Din Ibrahim, *al-Khuruj min Zuqaq al-Ta'rikh* (Cairo, 1992); Burhan Ghaylun, *Mihnat al-`Aql* (Beirut, 1985); idem, *Le malaise arabe* (Paris, 1991); *al-Bahith al-`Arabi*, (London), March 1994; *al-Fikr al-`Arabi* (Libya), 57 (Winter 1994); *al-Mustaqbal al-`Arabi*, April 1994; *al-Manabir*, (Beirut), March 1994, 73; *Fi al-Mas'ala al-Qawmiyya wa al-Dimuqratiyya* (Beirut, 1993); Arab Unity Research Center (ed.), *Wahdat al-Thaqafa al-`Arabiyya*, (Beirut, 1993).

2. Cf. W. J. Ong, *The Presence of the Word* (New Haven, 1967); idem, *Orality and Literacy* (London, 1982); idem, *The Interfaces of the Word* (Ithaca, NY, 1977).

3. `A. `Azzam, *al-Ghazw al-Fikri*, audio (nos. 1, 2); idem, *Ma'sat al-Sultan `Abd al-Hamid*, audio.

4. Y. al-`Azm, *al-Ahzab al-`Arabiyya wa-Qadiyyat Filastin*, audio; idem, *Aqlam Qadiyyat `Arabiyyat al-Huruf Ajnabiyyat al-Wala'*, audio; S. Abu Isma`il, *al-Mukhatatat al-Isti`mariyya lil-Qada' `ala al-Islam*, audio. Cf. on Ba`th nationalism: *Mu`ahadat al-Khiyana*, Abu al-Qasim (Syrian Muslim Brethren), audio.

5. A. B. al-Tamimi, audio of sermon in Amman (1983).

6. `A. Belhadj, sermon audio no. 6. Cf. Mustafa Mashhuri (Egyptian Muslim Brethren), *Ummatuna wa Wahdatuna*, audio.

7. Tamimi, audio of sermon in Amman.

8. A. Nawfal, *al-Tariq ila Filastin*, audio; A. al-Qattan (Kuwaiti), *Maqtal al-Islambuli wa-Rifaqihi*, audio; `Azzam, *al-Gazw al-Fikri*, audio no. 2.

9. Cf. *Minbar al-Sharq* (Egypt), no. 7 (May 1993), 132 ff.

10. S. Hawwa, *Hadhihi Tajribati* (Cairo, 1987); R. Ghannushi, interview with *Egypte/Monde Arabe*.

11. `Issam al-`Iryan speaks of Tilimsani's impact upon him in his videotaped lecture *al-`Amal al-Tulabi al-Islami*; S. al-Hawali, *Qira'at min al-Dasatir al-`Arabiyya*, audio.

12. See the articles by left-wing contributors to the Cairo monthly *Minbar al-Sharq* (published by Hizb al-`Amal).

13. S. Abu Isma`il, *al-Mukhatatat al-Isti`mariyya*, audio; `A. Kishk, audios nos. 422, 515/516.

14. Kishk, audio no. 373.

15. A. al-Qattan, *al-`Afan al-Fanni*, audio no. 4 in the series; idem, *al-Fasad fi Kuwayt*, audio; idem, *Tarbiyyat al-Abna'*, audio no. 5 in the series.

16. A. al-Qattan, *Khutbat al-Mu'tamar al-Islami fi Amrika*, audio.

17. A. B. Tamimi, *Fada'il al-Ard al-Mubaraka*, audio.

18. `A. Belhadj, audio no. 34; B. Jarrar, *Khutbat Yawm al-Isra'*, audio.

19. N. al-Albani, *Ahdath al-Khalij*, audio; Kishk, *al-Kabira al-Thalith*, audio.

20. A. Nawfal, *Utruhat*, audio; H. al-Bitawi (HAMAS), *Humum wa Ma'asi al-Muslimin al-Yawm*, audio; R. Salah (Israel), *al-Quds wa l-Aqsa*, audio; B. Jarrar, *Thawrat al-Buraq*, audio.

21. F. Shqaqi, sermon, audio.

22. Introduction to his *Aqlam `Arabiyyat al-Huruf*, audio.

23. A. al-Jundi, *al-`Uruba wa al-Islam* (Beirut, 197(?)); `A. al-`Ulwan, *al-Qawmiyya fi Mizan al-Islam* (Amman, 1982); `A. B. al-Baz, *al-Qawmiyya wa al-Islam*, (3d ed., Beirut, 1978).

24. R. Ghannushi, "al-`Uruba wa al-Islam," *Minbar al-Sharq* (May 1993).

25. R. Ghannushi, *al-Hurriyyat al-`Amma lil-Dawla al-Islamiyya* (Beirut, 1993), esp. introduction.

26. A. Yasin, *al-Manhaj al-Nabawi* (3d ed.; Beirut, 1994), quotation from 151–152.

27. Ibid., 55–57.

28. Introduction to the 2d. ed. of *al-Harakat al-Siyasiyya fi Misr* (Cairo, 1982); Interview with *Egypte/Monde/ Arabe*, (CEDEJ, Cairo), 7 (1991): 128–129.

29. Interview with *al-`Alam*, March 1994. Cf. M. al-Sulh, *al-Islam wa Harakat al-Tahrir al-`Arabiyya* (Beirut, 1973, and introduction to the 1979 edition); A. `Abd al-Malik in a discussion published by *al-Mustaqbal al-`Arabi*, December 1980.

30. Interview with *al-`Alam*, July 3, 1993 and cf. *al-Da`wa* (Pakistan/Egypt), February 10, 1994, 33.

31. Interview of Turabi in *Qira'at Siyasiyya*, 2/3 (Summer 1992); resolutions of the 2d Congress in *al-Ra'id* (Syrian Muslim Brethren), 158 (January 1994).

32. H. al-Turabi, "al-Sahwa al-Islamiyya wa al-Dawla al-Qutriyya fi al-Watan al-`Arabi," in *al-Sahwa al-Islamiyya: Ru'ya Naqdiyya min al-Dakhil* (Beirut, 1990), 75–108 (quotation from 104). Cf., idem, "al-Bu`d al-`Alami lil-Haraka al-Islamiyya: al-Tajriba al-Sudaniyya," in `A. al-Nafisi (ed.), *al-Haraka al-Islamiyya: Ru'ya Mustaqbaliyya* (Cairo, 1989), 77–98. An analogous viewpoint is presented by Rif`at Sayyid Ahmad, former Nasserist turned Islamic militant, in the Egyptian Labor party and director of its monthly *Minbar al-Sharq*. Ahmad admits, however, that his views of the compatibility between Islam and Arabism-as-cultural-component diverge from those of radical Muslim associations, e.g., the Jihad organization. See his *al-Harakat al-Islamiyya fi Misr wa Iran* (Cairo, 1989); and his paper translated in *Egypte/Monde Arabe*, 15–16 (1993): 407 ff.

33. `A. Belhadj, audio no. 38 (also no. 1); B. Jarrar, *Thawrat al-Buraq*, audio.

34. `A. Belhadj, audio no. 19; H. al-Bitawi (HAMAS), *Humum wa Ma'asi al-Muslimin al-Yawm*, audio.

35. A. al-Qattan, *Nusrat Sha`b Lubnan wa Filastin*, audio.

36. Cf. *Majzarat Sarajevo wa al-Bosna* (sermons and songs), audio. R. Salah (mayor of Umm al-Fahm, Israel), *Majazia al-Sirb*; `A. `Azzam, *al-Gazw al-Fikri*. Cf. J. Shabib on Bosnia in *Filastin al-Muslima*, May 1994, 54–55; *Sawat al-Haqq wa al-Hurriyya* (Israel), 1992–1994, passim.

37. A. al-Qattan, *Maqtal al-Islambuli*, audio.

38. M. al-Hashimi al-Hamidi, "al-Ta`rib Qadiyya wataniyya wa-Islamiyya," *al-`Alam*, Sept. 15, 1993; H. Sabra, *al-Shira'* (Beirut), Aug. 15, 1994.

39. B. Jarrar, *al-Quds wa al-Aqsa*, audio. Cf. A. M. al-Gharib, "Awda Ila al-Islam min Jadid" (Cairo, 1992) presents the *jama`at* arguments against TV and the movie industry.

40. A. al-Qattan, *al-`Afan al-Fanni*, audio, esp. nos. 3, 4.

41. Y. al-`Azm, *Aqlam*, audio.

42. Ibid.; M. H. Fadlallah, interview with *al-`Alam*, March 1994.

43. See A. Nawfal, *al-Nizam al-`Alami al-Jadid*, video. Cf. J. al-Banna, "Nahwa Atar la-Markazi," *Minbar al-Sharq* (March 1993): 94–101.

44. `A. Belhadj, audio no. 6.

45. Idem, audio no. 41.

46. A. Nawfal, *al-Tariq ila Filastin*, audio. The orange tree is a PLO (and leftist) symbol, e.g., in the literary work of Ghassan al-Kanafani.

47. B. Jarrar, *al-Sakina*, audio. Cf. his *al-Quds Qalb al-Sham*, audio.

48. "Al-Dawla al-Islamiyya wa al-Dawla al-Qutriyya," 97–98, 102 ff; Yasin, *al-Manhaj al-Nabawi*, 26.

49. Husayn, interview with *al-Fajr* (Tunis), Feb. 28, 1990.

50. J. al-Banna, "Nahwa," esp. 99–100.

51. See Ghannushi, *al-Hurriyyat al-`Amma*, chapter 2.

52. A. al-Mahalawi, *al-Fitna al-Ta'ifiyya fi Misr*, audio.

53. Kishk, audio nos. 410, 422; Jarrar, *Thawrat al-Buraq*, audio; `A. Belhadj, audio no. 38; J. `Abd al-Hadj, *Akhta' fi al-Ta'rikh*, audio; `Azm, *Aqlam*.

54. Qattan, *al-Tasammun fi Filastin*, audio; idem, *Hiwar ma`a Nasrani*, audio; M. Hasan, *Salb al-Masih*, audio.

55. Ibid.; Tamimi, sermon (1983), audio.

56. *Shaykh `Umar `Abd al-Kafi, al-A`yad*, audio; idem, *Dars lil-Nisa'*, audio.

57. *I'tirafat Qasis*, 3 audios; Fawzi al-Mahdi, *Kuntu Nasraniyyan*, audio; Shaykh `Umar `Abd al-Rahman, *Tafsir Surat al-Kahf*, audio; M. Fawzi, `*Umar `Abd al-Rahman* (Cairo, 1993), 61–62. The attitudes of the various radical currents on the Coptic question are presented in M. I. Mabruk, *Muwajahat al-Muwajaha* (Cairo, 1994), 140–175.

12. The Other Arab Nationalism: Syrian/Arab Populism in Its Historical and International Contexts

1. Ministère de la Défense, Vincennes (hereafter MD) 4H114/695. Renseignements, n.d.; MD 4H114/4/662. Cousse to Gouraud, 8 July 1920; MD 4H114/4/691. Cousse to Gouraud, 13 July 1920; MD 4H114/5/282–283. Cousse to Gouraud, 15 July 1920; Foreign Office, London (hereafter FO) 371/5037/E8509/74. Mackereth to FO, 16 July 1920; MD 4H114/5. Cousse to Gouraud, 20 July 1920; FO 371/5037/E8880/80. Mackereth to FO, 23 July 1920; MD 4H60/1. Bulletin Quotidien 1270, 23 July 1920. Ghalib al-`Iyashi, *al-Idahat al-siyasiyya wa asrar al-intidab al-Faransi `ala Suriyya* (Beirut, 1955), 105–106; Hasan al-Amin, *Dhikrayat* (Beirut, 1973), 27; Ihsan al-Hindi, *Ma`rakat Maysalun* (Damascus, 1967), 59–60.

2. FO 371/5039/E10316/38. J. B. Jackson (Aleppo), 30 July 1920; India Office, London (hereafter IO) L/PS/10/802/P5841. GHQ (Egypt) to War Office, 24 July 1920; Sulayman Musa, *al-Murasalat al-ta'rikhiyya, 1920–1923* (Amman, 1978), 144; Jules Kersante, "Syrie: l'occupation d'Alep," *Petite relations d'Orient* 6 (November 1920): 173; Mahmud Charkas, *al-Dalil al-musawwar lil-bilad al-`arabiyya*, vol. 1 (Damascus, 1930), 119–121; As`ad Daghir, *Mudhakkirati `ala hamish al-qadiyya al-`arabiyya* (Cairo, 1956), 122, 139–142; Muhammad `Ali al-`Ajluni, *Dhikrayat `an al-thawra al-`arabiyya al-kubra* (Amman, 1956), 98.

3. Interview with Muhammad Rida al-Khatib, Damascus, 6 January 1990; Interviews with Kamil Daghmush (Damascus, 2 November 1989) and Abu Ribah al-Jaza'iri (Damascus, 15 November 1989), veterans of the Battle of Maysalun; al-Hindi, *Ma`rakat Maysalun*, 113.

4. Duggan's speech was later published under the title "Syria and its Tangled Problems" in *Current History* 13:2 (February 1920): 238–248. Note: unless otherwise indicated, "Syria" refers to the area that comprises present-day Syria, Lebanon, Jordan, Israel and the Occupied Territories, and western Iraq.

5. White, "Interpretation in History," in *Tropics of Discourse*, 51–80.

6. I have borrowed this phrase from Winifred Barr Rothenberg, *From Market-Places to a Market Economy: The Transformation of Rural Massachusetts, 1750–1850* (Chicago, 1992).

7. See, inter alia, Roger Owen, *The Middle East in the World Economy, 1800–1914* (London, 1981), 153–179, 244–272; James Anthony Reilly, "Origins of Peripheral Capitalism in the Damascus Region, 1830–1914" (Ph.D. dissertation, Georgetown University, 1987); Linda Schatkowski Schilcher, *Families in Politics: Damascene Factions and Estates of the 18th and 19th Century* (Stuttgart, 1985), 60–86.

8. See Leila Tarazi Fawaz, *Merchants and Migrants in Nineteenth-Century Beirut* (Cambridge, MA, 1983); Philip S. Khoury, *Urban Notables and Arab Na-*

tionalism: The Politics of Damascus, 1860–1920 (Cambridge, 1983); Rashid Khalidi, "Society and Ideology in Late-Ottoman Syria: Class, Education, Profession and Confession," in John Spagnolo (ed.), *Problems of the Modern Middle East in Historical Perspective: Essays in Honour of Albert Hourani*, (Reading, 1992), 119–131.

9. Anderson, *Imagined Communities*, 12.

10. For an analysis of the meaning of rituals in Faysali Syria see James L. Gelvin, "Demonstrating Communities in Post-Ottoman Syria," *Journal of Interdisciplinary History* 25:1 (Summer 1994): 23–44.

11. *al-'Asima*, 7 May 1919, 1–2. For the division of Syrian society into two sorts, see, for example, *al-Kawkab*, 27 May 1919, 9; *al-Kawkab*, 3 June 1919, 8–9; *al-'Asima* 17 June 1919, 1–2; *al-'Asima*, 11 September 1919, 6; *al-'Asima*, 16 October 1919, 1–2.

12. *al-'Asima*, 28 August 1919, 6. For the origins and financing of *al-Kawkab* see Durham University, Wingate Files 143/2/167(AB202). Arbur to Sirdar (Khartoum), 13 November 1916.

13. *al-'Asima*, 28 August 1919, 6. See also *al-'Asima*, 5 February 1920, 5; *al-Kawkab*, 11 November 1919, 11; *al-Kawkab*, 13 January 1919, 11.

14. *al-Kawkab*, 28 October 1919, 7–8. See also *al-'Asima*, 11 September 1919, 1–2; and the account of Gertrude Bell's visit to the "School for the Daughters of Martyrs"(*madrasat banat al-shuhada*) in Damascus: IO L/PS/10/802. Gertrude Bell, "Syria in October 1919," 15 November 1919, 11.

15. See *al-Kawkab*: 30 September 1919, 7–8; 21 October 1919, 7–8; 28 October 1919, 7–8; *al-'Asima*: 7 May 1919, 1–2; 16 June 1919, 1–2; 25 August 1919, 1–2; 28 August 1919, 5–6; #24 (n.d.). The quote is from a front page editorial entitled, "A Danger Threatens our Domestic Life," in *al-'Asima*, 11 September 1919.

16. Wajih al-Haffar, "al-Hukumat allati ta'aqabat 'ala al-hukm fi Suriyya," *al-Shurta wa al-amn al-'amm* 11:10; Archives Diplomatiques, Nantes (hereafter AD) 2374/938/CP/Dossier TEO Zone Ouest: Adm., Cabinet Politique. 29 April 1920; *al-'Asima*: 29 April 1920, 4; 3 May 1920, 5; 31 May 1920, 1; 12 July 1920, 1. Similar attitudes toward Westernized women were expressed during the Palestine Great Revolt of 1936–1939. See Ted Swedenburg, "The Role of the Palestinian Peasantry in the Great Revolt," in Edmund Burke III and Ira Lapidus (eds.), *Islam, Politics, and Social Movements*, (Berkeley, 1988), 192.

17. See Reilly, "Origins of Peripheral Capitalism," 120, 155–158; Sherry Vatter, "Militant Journeymen in Nineteenth-Century Damascus: Implications for the Middle Eastern Labor History Agenda," in Zachary Lockman (ed.), *Workers and Working Classes in the Middle East: Struggles, Histories, Historiographies* (Albany, 1994), 1–19; Linda Schatkowski Schilcher, "Violence in Rural Syria in the 1880s and 1890s: State Centralization, Rural Integration, and the World Market," in Farhad Kazemi and John Waterbury (eds.), *Peasants and Politics in the Modern Middle East*, (Miami, 1991), 50–84.

18. Charles Tilly, Louise Tilly, and Richard Tilly, *The Rebellious Century, 1830–1910* (Cambridge, 1975), 50, 253–254.

19. Schilcher, "Violence in Rural Syria," 76; Eric R. Wolf, *Peasant Wars of the Twentieth Century* (New York, 1969), 282, 292–294; James L. Gelvin, "The Social Origins of Popular Nationalism in Syria: Evidence for a New Framework," in *International Journal of Middle East Studies* 26 (1994): 645–662.

20. Ministère des Affaires Etrangères, Paris (hereafter MAE) L:SL/12/32–38. Cousse to Haut Commissionaire, 6 April 1919; AD 2344/Cl/305–306. Cousse to Picot, 31 October 1919; AD 2344/Cl/311. Cousse to Picot, 3 November 1919; AD 2430/Dossier Confidential—Départ/325–326. Cousse (?) to Haut Commissionaire, 10 November 1919; AD 2375/Chemise Division de Syrie 1919–1920/ 442/2. Arlabosse to Gen. Cmdt. Div. Syrie, 25 January 1920; AD 2375/Chemise Division de Syrie 1919–1920/445/2. Haak to Cmdt. en Chef l'AFL, 26 January 1920.

21. See MD 4H58/2. Rapport hebdomadaire 503 (29 July-4 August 1920); Khoury, Syria, 180, 191; Jean-Paul Pascual, "La Syrie a l'epoque ottomane (Le XIXe siècle)" in Andre Raymond (ed.), La Syrie d'aujourd'hui, (Paris, 1980), 39.

22. See Sarah Graham-Brown, "Agriculture and Labour Transformation in Palestine," in Kathy and Pandeli Glavanis (eds.), The Rural Middle East: Peasant Lives and Modes of Production, (London, 1989), 53–55; Swedenburg, "Palestinian Peasantry," 184, 189–193.

23. Unless otherwise cited, information about the composition and activities of the Higher National Committee, the branch committees, and the committees of national defense was obtained in the "Lajna al-wataniyya" and "Lajnat al-difa`" files preserved in the Salafiyya Library, Cairo (SL: LW, SL: LD).

24. See Swedenburg, "Palestinian Peasantry."

25. See James L. Gelvin, "Popular Mobilization and the Foundations of Mass Politics in Syria, 1918–1920" (Ph.D. dissertation, Harvard University, 1992), 232–237, 459; IO L/PS/10/802/16–17. Gertrude Bell, "Syria in October 1919," 15 November 1919.

26. Victor Turner, "Social Dramas and Ritual Metaphors," in Victor Turner (ed.), Dramas, Fields, and Metaphors: Symbolic Action in Human Society (Ithaca, 1974), 46–47.

27. al-`Asima, 17 November 1919, 1–2; SL: LW. "Nizam al-lijan al-wataniyya al-far`iyya fi bilad Suriyya," 17 November 1919; al-Kinana, 15 July 1920, 2, 3. See also leaflets and transcriptions of leaflets contained in AD 2345. 5 March 1920; AD 2372/Dossier Propagande Anti-Française. 8–9 March 1920.

28. FO 371/3054/227658. Clayton to Sykes, 28 November 1917; IO L/PS/11/140/P497/1918/P1171. "Appreciation of the Situation in Syria, Palestine, and lesser Armenia by Colonel Sir Mark Sykes," 15 November 1918; FO 371/3385/191237/277. Wingate to Balfour, 18 November 1918; FO 371/3385/191229/190. Clayton to FO, 18 November 1918; FO 371/4178/7094. Hogarth to CPO, EEF, 18 December 1918; AD 2368/10/2/66. Cousse to Haut Commissionaire, 9 January 1919; AD 2326/Dossier du Hedjaz. "Extraits de la lettre 94m de M. Bensaci, Envoye du gouvernement de la Republique a la Mecque," 16 May 1919; MAE L:SL/15/324/22–23. Picot to Pichon, 18 July 1919; AD 2358/Dossier Emir Fayçal. "Mystification Cherifienne," 13 September 1919; MAE L:AH/7/1429–30. Picot to MAE, 29 October 1919; MD 4H114/2/132. Cousse to Gouraud, 19 February 1920.

29. Keith Wrightson, "Estates, Degrees, and Sorts: Changing Perceptions of Society in Tudor and Stuart England," in Penelope J. Corfield (ed.), Language, History, and Class (Oxford, 1991), 44–47.

30. al-Difa`, 13 January 1920, 1.

31. SL: LW: "Nizam al-lajna al-wataniyya al-`ulya fi al-`asima al-suriyya," and "Nizam al-lijan al-wataniyya al-far`iyya fi bilad Suriyya," 17 November 1919.

32. Angus Stewart, "The Social Roots," in Ghita Ionescu and Ernest Gellner (eds.), *Populism: Its Meaning and National Characteristics* (London, 1969), 187.

33. *al-Kinana*, 15 July 1920, 2.

34. Paul W. Drake, "Requiem for Populism?" in Michael L. Conniff (ed.), *Latin American Populism in Comparative Perspective*, (Albuquerque, 1982), 236.

35. Ernesto Laclau, *Politics and Ideology in Marxist Theory: Capitalism—Fascism—Communism* (London, 1977), 177–179.

36. See J. B. Allcock, " 'Populism': A Brief Biography," *Sociology* 5 (1971): 372.

37. Kenneth Minogue, "Populism as a Political Movement," in Ionescu and Gellner, *Populism*, 200.

38. Laclau, *Politics and Ideology*, 101–102, 164–165; Margaret Canovan, "Two Strategies for the Study of Populism," *Political Studies* 30 (1982): 552; Donald MacRae, "Populism as an Ideology," and Peter Worsley, "The Concept of Populism," in Ionescu and Gellner, *Populism*, 153–165, 212–250.

39. See Robert Wuthnow, *Communities of Discourse: Ideology and Social Structure in the Reformation, the Enlightenment, and European Socialism* (Cambridge, 1989), 13–15, 553, 555.

40. T. S. di Tella, "Populism and Reform in Latin America," in C. Veliz (ed.), *Obstacles to Change in Latin America* (Oxford, 1962), 182.

41. Stewart, "Social Roots," 187; Laclau, *Politics and Ideology*, 148–149.

42. Rosa Luxemburg, "The Mass Strike, the Political Party, and the Trade Unions," in Mary-Alice Waters (ed.), *Rosa Luxemburg Speaks* (New York, 1970), 153–218.

43. See Gelvin, "Popular Mobilization," 431–432; Swedenburg, "Palestinian Peasantry," 193–194.

44. Kedourie, "Pan-Arabism and British Policy," 213–235.

13. Arab Workers and Arab Nationalism in Palestine: A View from Below

1. I discuss this issue in "Railway Workers and Relational History: Arabs and Jews in British-Ruled Palestine," *Comparative Studies in Society and History* 35 (1993): 601–627, and more fully in *Comrades and Enemies: Arab and Jewish Workers in Palestine, 1906–1948* (Berkeley, 1996), chapter 3.

2. This episode is detailed in Arkhiyon Ha`avoda Vehehalutz, Makhon Lavon Leheker Tnu`at Hapo`alim (the Histadrut archives, hereafter cited as AA), 208/321, Haifa Workers' Council to Histadrut executive committee, July 1932. See also the Palestine Communist Party's Arabic-language organ *Ila al-Imam*, May 1933.

3. Exceptions in the English-language literature include Rashid Khalidi's work on Palestinian peasant resistance to Zionism; Johnson, *Islam and the Politics of Meaning*; and Ted Swedenburg, *Memories of Revolt: The 1936–1939 Rebellion and the Palestinian National Past* (Minneapolis, 1996). Some Palestinian scholars and activists have sought to incorporate nonelite strata into the historical narrative—for example, `Abd al-Qadir Yasin, Musa Budeiri, and Ghassan Kanafani—but much more remains to be done.

4. Gelvin, "Demonstrating Communities," 23.

5. See my "Railway Workers," cited earlier; " 'We Opened Up their Minds for Them': Labor-Zionist Discourse and the Railway Workers of Palestine, 1919–1929," *Review of Middle East Studies* 5 (1992): 5–32; and "Exclusion and Solidarity: Labor Zionism and Arab Workers in Palestine, 1897–1929," in Gyan Prakash (ed.), *After Colonialism: Imperial Histories and Postcolonial Displacements* (Princeton, 1994), 211–240.

6. To insist that we need to unpack and analyze the complexities of Palestinian nationalism is not to deny its historical reality as a form of identity, nor to invalidate the national aspirations of the Palestinian people today or their right to self-determination. Nor am I suggesting that historians should treat Palestinian nationalism any differently than we treat Zionism or any other movement or ideology.

7. *al-Karmil*, October 10, 1925.

8. See *Ittihad al-'Ummal*, October 21, 1925.

9. AA, Center for Oral Documentation, transcript of interview with Avraham Khalfon, January 29, 1976, 12.

10. October 21, 1925. The Arabic term that *al-Karmil* used for "guild" was *niqaba*, which was already by this time the standard term for a labor union in Egypt but in Palestine still apparently retained its older guild-related connotations.

11. See for example *Filastin*, August 19, 1927.

12. On this question see Rachelle Taqqu, "Arab Labor in Mandatory Palestine, 1920–1948" (unpublished Ph.D. dissertation, Columbia University, 1977), 95.

13. Central Zionist Archives (hereafter CZA), S25/2961, Zaslani to Hoz, October 14, 1934 (emphasis in the original); AA, Center for Oral Documentation, transcript of interview with Eliyahu Agassi, February 29, 1972; CZA, S25/3107, Zaslani to Hoz, September 24, 1934.

14. See *Filastin*, July/October 1934.

15. See Anita Shapira, *Hama'avak Hanikhzav: 'Avoda 'Ivrit, 1929–1939* (Tel Aviv, 1977), 229–33, and Stephen Glazer, "Propaganda and the Histadrut-Sponsored Pickets for 'Hebrew Labor', 1927–1936" (Ph.D. dissertation, Georgetown University, 1991).

16. *Filastin*, December 18, 1934.

17. CZA, S25/2961, "Din veheshbon shel Agassi veZaslani," November 20, 1934.

18. AA 250/436, Zaslani to Agassi, November 25, 1934.

19. AA, Center for Oral Documentation, interview with Eliyahu Agassi, February 29, 1972.

20. On the strike of February/March 1935, see *Filastin*, March 5, 6, 8, 1935, and Jabra Niqula, *Harakat al-Idrabat bayna al-'Ummal al-'Arab fi Filastin* (Jaffa, 1935), 10–14. On the findings of the 1935 Jaffa labor committee, see Taqqu, "Arab Labor," 96–98, and CO 733/292/3, High Commissioner to the Colonial Secretary, April 11, 1936. See also Israel State Archives, Jaffa Port, 28/1, 158/35, January 16, 1935; on political and security concerns, see FO 371/17878, C.I.D., July 14, 1934.

21. AA 208/4495; AA 205/6, meeting of the Histadrut's Arab Committee, November 11, 1936; CZA, S25/2961, Agassi to the Political Department, February 15, 1937.

22. See George Mansur, *The Arab Worker Under the Palestine Mandate* (Jerusalem, 1938), 59–61; *Filastin*, February 21, 1936; *al-Difa'*, February 23,

1936; AA 490/2, AWS leaflet; George Mansour, testimony before the Peel Commission, in Great Britain, *Palestine Royal Commission: Minutes of Evidence Heard at Public Sessions* (London, 1937), 343.

23. *al-Difa`*, April 12, 1936.

24. For example, Yehoshua Porath fails to discuss the politically significant convergence between Arab labor and Arab nationalism described in the preceding section, either in his book on the 1930s (*1929–1939*) or in his "Social Aspects of the Emergence of the Palestinian Arab National Movement," in Menahem Milson (ed.), *Society and Political Structure in the Arab World* (New York, 1973), 93–144.

14. The Paradoxical in Arab Nationalism: Interwar Syria Revisited

1. Much of the material provided on the League of National Action and the political and economic situation in Syria at the time of its establishment appeared originally in Khoury, *Syria*, chapter 15. Portions of it have been recast to fit the purposes of this essay.

2. MAE (Ministère des Affaires Etrangères, Paris), *Rapport à la Société des Nations sur la situation de la Syrie et du Liban, 1924*; FO 371/625, vol., 19022, MacKereth to FO, 7 January 1935.

3. R. Montagne, "L'évolution de la jeunesse arabe," *CHEAM* (Centre de Hautes Etudes Administratives sur l'Afrique et l'Asie Modernes, Paris), no. 244, n. pl. (21 June 1937), 8; Roderic D. Mathews and Matta Akrawi, *Education in the Arab Countries of the Near East* (Washington, 1949), 325, 340.

4. Montagne, "L'évolution," 9; Ahmad Hilmi al-`Allaf, *Dimashq fi Matla` al-Qarn al-`Ashrin* (Damascus, 1976), 169–171.

5. There were less than 40,000 primary and secondary school students in public and private institutions in 1933, or only 2 percent of Syria's total population. MAE, *Rapport à la Société des Nations sur la situation de la Syrie et du Liban, 1924*, Appendix 4, 95; FO 371/635, vol., 19022, MacKereth to FO, 7 January 1935.

6. Zafir al-Qasimi, *Maktab `Anbar* (Beirut, 1967); Munir al-Rayyis, *al-Kitab al-Dhahabi lil-Thawrat al-Wataniyya fil-Mashriq al-`Arabi: al-Thawra al-Suriyya al-Kubra* (Beirut, 1969) 102; United States, American Consulate at Beirut, "Education in the States of the Levant under French Mandate" (Report for Office of Education, Department of Interior) (Beirut, 1 November 1933), 321.

7. Ibid; *L'Asie Française*, no. 287 (February 1931), 63.

8. Most conscious of the need to cultivate the educated youth was the National Bloc's Fakhri al-Barudi. Barudi typified the urban nationalist patron in that he came from the landed upper classes, was educated at Maktab `Anbar (though not in Istanbul afterward), joined Amir Faysal's Arab Army in 1917, served Faysal afterward in Damascus, and maintained a vast urban patronage network among merchants, artisans, and the Damascene intelligentsia. He was a dedicated nationalist, a man of sincere conviction who made the greatest pecuniary sacrifice for the cause of national independence. He was also a great humorist with charm and wit, a fiery orator, a renowned patron of the performing arts, and a popular songwriter. See Fakhri al-Barudi, *Mudhakkirat al-Barudi* (vols. 1, 2; Beirut/Damascus, 1951–1952); Nahal Bahjat Sidqi, *Fakhri al-Barudi* (Beirut, 1974); Adham al-Jundi,

Ta'rikh al-Thawrat al-Suriyya fi `Ahd al-Intidab al-Faransi* (Damascus, 1960), 555–56; Ahmad Qudama, *Ma`alim wa A`lam fi Bilad al-`Arab, vol. 1 (Damascus, 1965), 10; George Faris, *Man Huwa fi Suriyya 1949* (Damascus, 1950), 54; Virginia Vacca, "Notizie biografiche su uomini politici ministri e deputati siriani," *Oriente Moderno* 17 (October 1937): 478; Markaz al-Watha'iq al-Ta'rikhiyya (Damascus), *al-Qism al-Khass*, Fakhri al-Barudi Papers.

9. The Boy Scout movement in Syria dates from 1912 when two Indian Muslims studying at the Syrian Protestant College founded a troop in Beirut. See Anonymous, "Note sur le Scoutisme musulman en Syrie et au Liban," *CHEAM*, no. 684 (Beirut, 4 April 1944).

10. Ahmad al-Shihabi, a law student from a prominent family of South Lebanon; `Ali `Abd al-Karim al-Dandashi, a member of the Al Dandash clan of Tall Kalakh, who became the Executive Director of the Syrian Federation of Scouting; and Dr. Rushdi al-Jabi, President of the Federation. Anonymous, "Note sur le Scoutisme musulman en Syrie et au Liban," *CHEAM*, no. 684 (Beirut, 4 April 1944), 1–3.

11. In this sense, the *tajhiz* could be compared to the Lycée Louis le Grand in Paris, a major feeder school for the Ecole Normale Supérieur. A graduate of the *tajhiz* who went to Paris for higher education was Salah al-Din al-Bitar. In Paris he met Michel `Aflaq, who hailed from the same Damascus quarter, al-Maydan, but who had attended a Greek Orthodox school in the Syrian capital. Both returned to Damascus to assume teaching positions at the *tajhiz* and both were founders of the Ba`th Party with another Paris-educated school teacher, Zaki al-Arsuzi. Hanna Batatu, *The Old Social Classes and the Revolutionary Movements of Iraq* (Princeton, 1978), 724–25.

12. A. S. Bagh, *L'Industrie à Damas entre 1928 et 1958: Etude de géographie économique* (Damascus, 1961).

13. E. Epstein [Elath], "Notes from a Paper on the Present Conditions in the Hauran," *Journal of the Royal Central Asian Society* 23 (1936): 612–613; FO 371/2092, vol. 16974, 31 March 1933.

14. *Al-Mudhik al-Mubki*, no. 163 (11 March 1933), 4; no. 179 (11 July 1933), 8; no. 193 (11 November 1933), 8; no. 191 (28 October 1933), 2. Wearing the *sidara* was not only a way of criticizing the bloc but also of rejecting the fez because it was a foreign-made product, imported mainly from Czechoslovakia. Later, the league switched from the *sidara* to a more traditional Arab headdress, the *kufiyya*. M. (Raymond] O'Zoux, "Les insignes et saluts de la jeunesse en Syrie et au Liban," *Entretiens sur l'évolution des pays de civilisation arabe*, vol. 2 (Paris, 1938), 100. Fakhri al-Barudi actually tried to promote a scheme for the development of a native Syrian hat that would replace the fez. J. Gaulmier, "Congrès Général des Etudiants tenu à Hama, 1932," *CHEAM*, no. 46 (1936).

15. *Al-Mudhik al-Mubki*, no. 103 (21 November 1931), 14.

16. Akram Zu`aytir, "Ittifaq al-`Arab `ala Wada' Lubnan al-Khass," *al-Hawadith* (Beirut), no. 978 (August 1975), 66.

17. For a fuller discussion of these terms see Haim, "Islam," 287–298.

18. `Usbat al-`Amal al-Qawmi, *Bayan al-Mu'tamar al-Ta'sisi*. Pamphlet (Damascus, 24 August 1933); Muhammad Harb Farzat, *al-Hayat al-Hizbiyya fi Suriyya bayna 1920–1955* (Damascus, 1955), 138–140.

19. See Batatu, *Old Social Classes*; Porath, *1929–1939*.

20. Only 40 percent of the bloc leadership belonged to the liberal professions, three-quarters of whom practiced or taught law. For biographical data on League of National Action and National Bloc leaders see Tables 15–1, 15–2, 416–19, and Tables 10–1, 252, 10–2, 254–257, in Khoury, *Syria*.

21. Its leader was Zaki al-Arsuzi, the Sorbonne-educated school teacher of `Alawi provenance who was one of the founders of the Ba`th Party in the early 1940s. It drew most of its support from the growing Arabic-speaking intelligentsia in the towns of the Sanjaq. Although the league's principal focus was on preventing a Turkish takeover in the Sanjaq and on continuing the struggle against French rule, it was also committed to breaking the hold of the Sunni landowning class and, in particular, its dominant Turkish element, over the predominantly `Alawi peasantry. A. Alexandre, "Conflits de l'arabisme et des nationalismes voisins. Le conflit syro-turc du Sandjak d'Alexandrette d'octobre 1936 à juin 1937, vu d'Antioche," in *Entretiens sur 1'évolution des pays de civilisation arabe*, vol. 2 (Paris, 1938), 105–141.

22. Unlike in Iraq, where the ex-Sharifian officers constituted the most important element for the political elite under the monarchy and where radical Arab nationalist organizations like Nadi Muthanna aligned with factions of the officer corps in the 1930s, in Syria the army officers had little impact on interwar politics. The French dismantled the Sharifian army and jailed or exiled many Syrian officers. At the same time republican nationalists disapproved of the royalist (mainly Hashimite) proclivities of ex-Sharifian officers. In fact, for nearly a century there had been a noticeable absence of a strong military tradition in Syria. The Syrian upper classes disdained military careers and used their wealth and connections to purchase exemptions for their sons. Meanwhile, the French controlled membership in the new native officer corps of the Troupes spéciales, encouraging it to acquire a distinctive minority and rural complexion. See Michael H. Van Dusen, "Intra- and Inter-Generational Conflict in the Syrian Army," Ph.D. Dissertation, The Johns Hopkins University, 1971; for a revisionist interpretation of France's so-called minority policy for the Syrian army, see Nacklie Elias Bou-Nacklie, "Les Troupes Spéciales du Levant: Origins, Recruitment, and the History of the Syrian-Lebanese Paramilitary Forces under the French Mandate, 1919–1947," Ph.D. Dissertation, University of Utah, 1989.

23. Pan-Arabism first became a political football kicked back and forth by warring nationalist factions during the Syrian Revolt as rebels began to face military setback after setback in 1926 and 1927, and blame for the revolt's ultimate failure needed to be apportioned among its exiled leaders. See Philip S. Khoury, "Factionalism among Syrian Nationalists during the French Mandate," *International Journal of Middle East Studies* 13 (1981): 441–469.

24. Philip S. Khoury, "The Syrian Independence Movement and the Development of Economic Nationalism in Damascus," *British Journal of Middle Eastern Studies* 14 (1988): 25–36.

25. See Philip S. Khoury, "Shukri al-Quwatli," in Bernard Reich (ed.), *Political Leaders of the Contemporary Middle East and North Africa: A Biographical Dictionary* (Hamden, CT, 1990), 433–439.

26. Khoury, "Economic Nationalism," 25–36.

27. Ironically, because Dandashi had been late for an appointment on that August day, he decided to take the tram even though there was a major boycott

underway of the Franco-Belgian owned Société des Tramways et d'Electricité, which the league strongly supported. Nabih al-`Azma Papers [Syria]. File 5/274. Institute for Palestine Studies, Beirut.

28. The Lion Cubs of Arabism (*Ashbal al-`Uruba*) belonged to the league and the Steel Shirts (*al-Qumsan al-Hadidiyya*) to the bloc. See A. de Boucheman, "Les Chemises de Fer." no. 6 bis. *CHEAM* (1936).

29. al-Jundi, *Ta'rikh*, 486–487; Vacca, "Notizie," 478.

30. See Katherine Verdery, "Whither 'Nation' and 'Nationalism'?" *Daedalus*, 122 (Summer 1993): 37–46.

31. Bromley, *Rethinking Middle Eastern Politics*, 176.

32. Ibid., 174.

33. Pan-Arabism only began to manifest its radicalization in the 1930s, and especially during the Arab rebellion in Palestine in the late 1930s. See Khoury, "Divided Loyalties," 324–348.

34. Khoury, "Factionalism," and Khoury, *Syria*, chapter 22. See also Salim Tamari, "Factionalism and Class Formation in Recent Palestinian History," in Roger Owen (ed.), *Studies in the Economic and Social History of Palestine in the Nineteenth and Twentieth Centuries* (Carbondale, IL, 1982), 177–202.

Glossary of Arabic Terms

abu   father

ahl   people

`alim   a Muslim religious scholar

amir   leader, prince, commander

`ammiyya   a colloquial dialect of Arabic

`arab / `arabi   Arab (n.) / Arab (adj.)

al-ard al-muqaddasa   holy land; a traditional term for Palestine

awqaf (pl.; sing., *waqf*)   Muslim pious endowments

a`yan* (pl.; sing., *`ayn)   local notables in Arab-Ottoman society (mainly eighteenth and nineteenth centuries)

bid`a   innovation

bilad   town, land, country

butula   bravery, heroism

Dar al-Islam   the house of Islam; historically, the entire Muslim world

dars   class (in school), lesson

dawla   state, state power, power

dhimmi   protected person; historically, a non-Muslim living under Muslim rule

dhulm   oppression, tyranny

din   faith, religion

effendi / effendiyya   educated person / the modern educated urban middle class

fallah / fallaha / fallahin   peasant (m.) / peasant (f.) / peasant (pl.)

farhud   an outbreak of anti-Jewish violence in Baghdad in June 1941

fatwa   legal opinion in Muslim religious law delivered by a *mufti fida'i*   one who sacrifices oneself

Filastin / filastiniyya   Palestine / Palestinian

fitna   discord; civil strife or civil war

fusha   formal literary Arabic (in contrast to the colloquial dialects)

futuwwa   youth, adolescence; by extension, youth organizations

hadara   civilization, culture

haram   forbidden, prohibited; alternatively, holy, sacred

hijab   cover, veil; historically, the modest dress worn by Muslim women

ibn   son

ibn al-balad   son of the country; in Egypt, a person of the popular classes

iflas   bankruptcy

ikhwan (pl.; sing., *akh*)   brothers; historically, the religiously motivated warriors in Saudi Arabia

imam   leader, prayer leader

iqlim / iqlimiyya   region / regionalism

iqta`iyyin* (pl.; sing., *iqta`i)   feudalist, feudal lord

iqtisad   economy

`isamiyyun* (pl.; sing. *`isami)   self-made men

istiqlal   independence

ittihad   league, union

jadid   new, modern

jahili / jahiliyya   ignorant / ignorance, by extension paganism; historically, the period of Arab history prior to the adoption of Islam

jami`a   association, community, collectivity; in the modern era, university

jihad   religiously sanctioned effort or struggle; holy war

Ka`ba   cube; historically, the central shrine of Islam in Mecca

kha'in / khiyana   traitor / treason

khatib / khatiba   preacher (m.) / preacher (f.)

al-khilafa   the Caliphate

khitat (pl.)   projects, plans, lines of action, precepts

kufiyya   kerchief worn as a head covering, particularly in Arabia and the Fertile Crescent

Maghrib   west; the western Arab countries in northwestern Africa

mankubun (pl.; sing., *mankub*)   unhappy, wretched, victim

Mashriq   east; the eastern Arab countries (Egypt and the Arab lands in southwestern Asia)

Misr / Misri   Egypt / Egyptian

mufti   Muslim legal official who delivers an expert legal opinion or *fatwa muhafazat* (pl.; sing., *muhafaza*)   Ottoman governorate

mujahidin (pl.; sing., *mujahid*)   fighters in a righteous, generally a religiously sanctioned, cause

mujtahid (sing.) / *mujtahidin* (pl.)   qualified Muslim interpreter(s) of Muslim religious law

mukhabarat (pl.)   notices, notifications; historically, the Egyptian security services

mushtaghibun (pl.; sing., *mushtaghib*)   troublemakers, agitators

mu'tamar   congress, conference, assembly

mutanawwirun (pl.; sing., *mutanawwir*)   men of culture

mutasarrifiyya   Ottoman administrative unit

nahda   awakening, revival renaissance; historically, the Arab cultural revival of the modern era

niqaba   guild, labor union

nukta   joke, pun

qabadayat (pl.; sing., *qabaday*)   local strongmen or bosses in urban quarters

qadim   old, ancient

qawm / *qawmiyya*   ethnic group, nation / nationalism

rukud   stagnation

sabr   patience, forbearance

sada (pl.; sing., *sayyid*)   tribal chiefs; alternatively, descendants of the Prophet Muhammad

sanjaq   Ottoman administrative district; subunit of a *wilaya* or province

sha`b   people

shabab   youth

shahid   martyr

shakhsiyya   personality

al-Sham   greater Syria; the lands of the western Fertile Crescent

shari`a   Islamic religious law

shaykh   elder, local leader or tribal chief, religious dignitary

Shi`i, Shi`ism   party, faction; historically, one of the two main denominations of Islam

shuhada (pl.; sing., *shahid*)   martyrs

shu`ubiyya   an anti-Arab cultural movement in early Islam; by extension, any local nationalist orientation or tendency

sidara   cap worn by the Iraqi military in the interwar period

Sunni, Sunnism   custom, tradition; historically, one of the two main denominations of Islam

Suriyya   Syria

tajhiz   preparatory school or college

ta'ifiyya   sectarianism

tamsir   to make something Egyptian

tarbiyya   education

tarbush   conical headgear worn by the educated classes in the early twentieth century

ta'rikh   history

thaqafa   higher culture, literate culture, civilization

thawra   revolution

thuwwar (pl.; sing., *tha'ir*)   revolutionaries

tilmidh   student, pupil

`ulama (pl.; sing., *'alim*)   Muslim religious specialists

al-`ulum al-`aqliyya   the rational sciences

umm   mother

umma   historically, the community of Muslims; in the modern era, also used for nation

`ummal (pl.; sing., *'amil*)   workers

`uruba   Arabness, Arabism

`usba   league, association

ustadh   teacher, master

vilayet (Turkish)   province of the Ottoman Empire (Ar. *wilaya*)

wahda   unity

waqf   Muslim pious endowment

watan / wataniyya   homeland / patriotism or nationalism

wilaya   sovereign power, rule; historically, an Ottoman province

za`im   leader, commander

zajal   rhymed prose

Works Cited in the Text

`Abd al-Sami', A. *al-Mutatarrifun: Nadwat wa Dawa'ih Hiwar.* Cairo, 1993.

`Abduh, Ibrahim. *Ruz al-Yusuf.* Cairo, 1961.

Abdul Rahim, Abdul Rahman. "The Ottoman Rule and Its Effects on Egyptian Society." *Journal of Asian and African Studies* [Japan] 13 (1977): 57–75.

Abou El-Haj, Rifaat Ali. "Social Uses of the Past: Recent Arab Historiography of Ottoman Rule." *International Journal of Middle East Studies* 14 (1982): 187–195.

Abrash, I. "Hawla Hudud Istihdar al-Muqaddas fi al-Umur al-Dunyawiyya: Mulahazat Manhajiyya." *al-Mustaqbal al-`Arabi*, no. 180 (February 1994): 4–20.

Abu Ghuayma, Z. *al-Haraka al-Islamiyya wa Qadiyyat Filastin.* Amman, 1985.

Abu Manneh, Butrus. "Jerusalem in the Tanzimat Period: The New Ottoman Administration and Its Notables." *Die Welt des Islams* 30 (1990): 1–44.

———. "The Rise of the Sanjak of Jerusalem in the Late 19th Century." In Gabriel Ben Dor, ed., *The Palestinians and the Middle East Conflict* (Ramat Gan, 1978).

Abu al-Naml, H. *Qita` Ghaza 1948–1967: Tatawwurat Iqtisadiyya wa Siyasiyya wa Ijtima`iyya wa `Askariyya.* Beirut, 1979.

Abukhalil, Asad. "A New Arab Ideology? The Rejuvenation of Arab Nationalism." *Middle East Journal* 46 (1992): 22–36.

`Afif, Ahmad Jabir. *al-Haraka al-Wataniyya fi al-Yaman.* Damascus, 1982.

Ahmad, Rif`at Sayyid. *al-Harakat al-Islamiyya fi Misr wa Iran.* Cairo, 1989.

Ajami, Fouad. *The Arab Predicament.* Cambridge, MA, 1981.

———. "The End of Pan-Arabism." *Foreign Affairs* 57 (Winter 1978–1979): 355–373.

al-Ajluni, Muhammad `Ali. *Dhikrayat `an al-Thawra al-`Arabiyya al-Kubra.* Amman, 1956.

Akrawi, Matta. *Curriculum Construction in the Public Schools of Iraq.* New York, 1943.

al-'Allaf, Ahmad Hilmi. *Dimashq fi Matla' al-Qarn al-'Ashrin*. Damascus, 1976.

Almond, Harry J. *Iraqi Statesman: A Portrait of Mohammed Fadhel Jamali*. Salem, OR, 1993.

al-Amin, Hasan. *Dhikrayat*. Beirut, 1955.

Amin, Jalal. *al-'Arab wa Nakbat al-Kuwait*. Cairo, 1991.

Anderson, Benedict. *Imagined Communities: Reflections on the Origins and Spread of Nationalism*. 2d ed. New York, 1991.

Anis, Muhammad. *al-Dawla al-'Uthmaniyya wa al-Sharq al-'Arabi*. Cairo, n. d.

———. *Madrasat al-Ta'rikh al-Misri fi al-'Asr al-'Uthmani*. Cairo, 1962.

Antonius, George. *The Arab Awakening*. London, 1938.

Arab Unity Research Center. *Wahdat al-Thaqafa al-'Arabiyya*. Beirut, 1993.

Armstrong, John. *Nations Before Nationalism*. Chapel Hill, 1982.

al-'Asali, Kamil. *Makhtutat Fada'il Bayt al-Maqdis*. Amman, 1984.

'Awad, 'Abd al-'Aziz Muhammad. "Mutasarrifiyyat al-Quds, 1874–1914." In *al-Mu'tamar al-Dawli al-Thalith li-Ta'rikh Bilad al-Sham: Filastin*, multivols. (Amman, 1983), 1:204–223.

Ayalon, Ami. *The Press in the Arab Middle East*. Oxford, 1995.

Ayyub, M. A. *Al-Bina' al-Tabaqi lil-Filastiniyin fi Lubnan*. Beirut, 1978.

'Azmah, A. "Fakk al-Irtibat bayna al-'Uruba wa al-Islam." *al-Naqid*, no. 33 (March 1991): 19–21.

al-Baghdadi, 'Abd al-Latif. *Mudhakkirat 'Abd al-Latif al-Baghdadi*. 2 vols. Cairo, 1983.

Baram, Amatzia. *Culture, History, and Ideology in the Formation of Ba'thist Iraq, 1968–1989*. London, 1991.

———. "Territorial Nationalism in the Middle East." *Middle Eastern Studies* 26 (1990): 425–448.

Baron, Beth. "The Construction of National Honour in Egypt." *Gender and History* 5:2 (1993): 244–255.

———. "Mothers, Morality, and Nationalism in Early Twentieth-Century Egypt." In Rashid Khalidi et al., *The Origins of Arab Nationalism* (New York, 1991), 271–288.

———. "Readers and the Women's Press in Egypt." *Poetics Today* 15:2 (1994): 37–51.

———. *The Women's Awakening in Egypt: Culture, Society, and the Press*. New Haven, 1994.

al-Barrak, Fadil. *al-Madaris al-Yahudiyya wa al-Iraniyya fi al-'Iraq*. Baghdad, 1984.

al-Barudi, Fakhri. *Mudhakkirat al-Barudi*. 2 vols. Beirut/Damascus, 1951–1952.

Batatu, Hanna. *The Old Social Classes and the Revolutionary Movements of Iraq*. Princeton, 1978.

al-Baz, 'A. B. *al-Qawmiyya fi Mizan al-Islam*. 3d ed. Beirut, 1978.

Be'eri, Eliezer. *Army Officers in Arab Politics and Society*. London, 1970.

Beinin, Joel. *Was the Red Flag Flying There? Marxist Politics and the Arab-Israeli Conflict in Egypt and Israel, 1948–1965*. Berkeley, 1990.

———. Beinin, Joel, and Zachary Lockman. *Workers on the Nile: Nationalism, Communism, Islam, and the Egyptian Working Class, 1882–1954*. Princeton, 1987.

Bernier, T. "Naissance d'un nationalisme arabe a Aden." *L'Afrique et l'Asie*, no. 44 (1958): 25–41.

Bhabha, Homi. K., ed. *The Nation and Narration*. London, 1990.

Binder, Leonard. *The Ideological Revolution in the Middle East*. New York, 1964.

al-Bishri, `Abd al-`Aziz. *al-Tarbiyya al-Wataniyya*. Cairo, 1929.

Boulatta, Issa J. *Trends and Issues in Contemporary Arab Thought*. New York, 1990.

Breasted, Charles. *Pioneer to the Past: The Story of James Henry Breasted, Told by His Son Charles Breasted*. New York, 1947.

Breuilly, John. *Nationalism and the State*. 2d ed. Chicago, 1994.

Bromley, Simon. *Rethinking Middle East Politics*. Austin, 1994.

Brugman, J. *An Introduction to the History of Modern Arabic Literature*. Leiden, 1984.

Budeiri [Budayri], M. "Ta'rikh Filastin al-Ijtima`i al-Hadith." In L. Turki, ed., *al-Mujtama` al-Filastini fi al-Daffa al-Gharbiyya wa Qita` Ghaza*. Acre, 1990.

Buheiry, Marwan. "Bulus Nujaym and the Grand Liban Ideal, 1908–1919." In Marwan Buheiri, ed., *Intellectual Life in the Arab East, 1860–1939* (Beirut, 1981), 62–83.

Bulliet, Richard W. *Islam: The View from the Edge*. New York, 1994.

Burrowes, Robert. *The Yemen Arab Republic, the Politics of Development, 1962–1986*. Boulder, 1987.

Busch, Briton. *Britain, India, and the Arabs, 1914–1921*. Berkeley, 1971.

Carapico, Sheila. "From Ballot Box to Battlefield: The War of the Two `Alis." *Middle East Report*, no. 190 (Sept./Oct. 1994): 24–27.

Carter, Howard, and A. C. Mace. *The Tomb of Tut.Ankh.Amen Discovered by the Late Earl of Carnarvon and Howard Carter*. 3 vols. New York, 1963 reprint.

Charkas, Mahmud. *al-Dalil al-Musawwar lil-Bilad al-`Arabiyya*. Damascus, 1930.

Chatterjee, Partha. *The Nation and Its Fragments: Colonial and Postcolonial Histories*. Princeton, 1993.

———. *Nationalist Thought and the Colonial World: A Derivative Discourse?* London, 1986.

Chejne, Anwar G. "Egyptian Attitudes Toward Pan-Arabism." *Middle East Journal* 11 (1957): 253–268.

———. "Some Aspects of Islamic Nationalism." *Islamic Literature* 8 (1956): 434–445.

———. "The Use of History by Modern Arab Writers." *Middle East Journal* 14 (1960): 387–398.

Chelhod, Joseph, et. al. *L'Arabie du Sud: Histoire et civilization*. 3 vols. Paris, 1984.

Choueiri, Youssef. *Arab History and the Nation-State*. London, 1989.

Clements, Frank. *The Emergence of Arab Nationalism: From the Nineteenth Century to 1921, A Bibliography*. Wilmington, 1976.

Cleveland, William L. *Islam Against the West: Shakib Arslan and the Campaign for Islamic Nationalism*. Austin, 1985.

———. *The Making of an Arab Nationalist: Ottomanism and Arabism in the Life and Thought of Sati` al-Husri*. Princeton, 1971.

Cohen, Amnon. *Political Parties in the West Bank Under the Jordanian Regime, 1949–1967*. Ithaca, 1982.

Cohen, Hayyim J. "The Anti-Jewish Farhud in Baghdad 1941." *Middle Eastern Studies* 3 (1966–1967): 2–17.

———. *Ha-Pe`ilut ha-Zionit be-`Iraq*. Jerusalem, 1969.

Commins, David. "Religious Reformers and Arabists in Damascus, 1885–1914." *International Journal of Middle East Studies* 18 (1986): 405–425.

Coudougnan, Gerard. *Nos Ancêtres les Pharaons: L'histoire pharonique et copte dans les manuels scolaires* (Cairo, 1988).

Coury, Ralph M. "Egyptians in Jerusalem: Their Role in the General Islamic Conference of 1931." *Muslim World* 82 (1992): 37–54.

———. "The Politics of the Funereal: The Tomb of Saad Zaghlul." *Journal of the American Research Center in Egypt* 39 (1992): 191–200.

———. "Who 'Invented' Egyptian Arab Nationalism?" *International Journal of Middle East Studies* 14 (1982): 249–281 and 459–479.

Daghir, As`ad. *Mudhakkirati `ala Hamish al-Qadiyya al-`Arabiyya*. Cairo, 1956.

Dawn, C. Ernest. "The Formation of Pan-Arab Ideology in the Interwar Years." *International Journal of Middle East Studies* 20 (1988): 67–91.

———. *From Ottomanism to Arabism: Essays on the Origins of Arab Nationalism*. Urbana, IL, 1973.

———. "The Origins of Arab Nationalism." In Rashid Khalidi et al., *The Origins of Arab Nationalism* (New York, 1991), 3–30.

Dawson, Warren R., and Eric P. Uphill. *Who Was Who in Egyptology*. 2d ed. London, 1972.

Deutsch, Karl W. *Nationalism and Social Communication*. Cambridge, MA, 1953.

Dhikra Istiqlal Suriyya. Damascus, 1920.

Douglas, Alan, and Fedwa Malti-Douglas. *Arab Comic Strips: Politics of an Emerging Mass Culture*. Bloomington, 1994.

Douglas, J. Leigh. *The Free Yemeni Movement, 1935–1962*. Beirut, 1987.

Dresch, Paul. "A Daily Plebiscite: Nation and State in Yemen." *Revue du Monde Musulman et de la Mediterrannée*, no. 67 (1993): 67–77.

———. *Tribes, Government, and History in Yemen*. Oxford, 1989.

Duggan, Stephen P. "Syria and Its Tangled Problems." *Current History* 13:2 (February 1920): 238–248.

al-Durrah, Mahmud. *al-Harb al-`Iraqiyya al-Britaniyya 1941*. Beirut, 1969.

Edmonds, C. J. *Kurds, Turks, and Arabs: Politics, Travel, and Research in North-Eastern Iraq, 1919–1925*. London, 1957.

Egger, Vernon. *A Fabian in Egypt: Salamah Musa and the Rise of the Professional Classes in Egypt, 1909–1939*. New York, 1986.

Egypt, Ministry of National Guidance. *Majmu`at Khutub wa Tasrihat wa Bayanat al-Ra'is Jamal `Abd al-Nasir*. Multi-vols. Cairo, n. d.

Entretiens sur l'evolution des pays de civilization arabe. 2 vols. Paris, 1938.

Eppel, Michael. "The Hikmat Sulayman-Bakir Sidqi Government in Iraq, 1936–1937, and the Palestine Question." *Middle Eastern Studies* 24 (1988): 25–41.

———. *The Palestine Conflict in the History of Modern Iraq: The Dynamics of Involvement*. London, 1994.

Farag, Nagwa. "Illustration: To Whom Is It Addressed?" In *Images d'Egypt: De la fresque a la bande dessinée* (Cairo, 1991), 285–290.

Farah, Tawfic E., ed. *Pan-Arabism and Arab Nationalism: The Continuing Debate.* Boulder, 1987.

—, ed. *Political Behavior in the Arab States.* Boulder, 1983.

Faris, George. *Man Huwa fi Suriyya 1949.* Damascus, 1950.

Farouq-Sluglett, Marion, and Peter Sluglett. "Labor and National Liberation: The Trade Union Movement in Iraq, 1920–1958." *Arab Studies Quarterly* 5 (1983): 139–154.

Farzat, Muhammad Harb. *al-Hayat al-Hizbiyya fi Suriyya bayna 1920–1955.* Damascus, 1955.

Fawaz, Leila Tarazi. *Merchants and Migrants in Nineteenth-Century Beirut.* Cambridge, MA, 1983.

Fawzi, M. `Umar `Abd al-Rahman.* Cairo, 1993.

Fawzi, Mahmud. *Thuwwar Yulyu Yatakallimu.* Cairo, 1988.

Friedman, Isaiah. *Germany, Turkey, and Zionism, 1897–1918.* Oxford, 1977.

Gabra, Sami. *Chez les derniers adorateurs de Trismegiste: la Necropole d'Hermopolis Touna El Gebel.* Cairo, 1971.

Gellner, Ernest. *Nations and Nationalism.* Ithaca, 1983.

Gelvin, James L. *Contesting Nationalisms and the Birth of Mass Politics in Syria.* Berkeley, 1997.

———. "Demonstrating Communities in Post-Ottoman Syria." *Journal of Interdisciplinary History* 25:1 (Summer 1994): 23–44.

———. "The Social Origins of Popular Nationalism in Syria: Evidence for a New Framework." *International Journal of Middle East Studies* 26 (1994): 645–662.

Gendzier, Irene. "James Sanua and Egyptian Nationalism." *Middle East Journal* 15 (1961): 16–28.

———. *The Practical Visions of Ya`qub Sanu`.* Cambridge, MA, 1966.

Gershoni, Israel. "Arabization of Islam: The Egyptian Salafiyya and the Rise of Arabism in Pre-Revolutionary Egypt." *Asian and African Studies* 13 (1979): 22–57.

———. *The Emergence of Pan-Arabism in Egypt.* Tel Aviv, 1981.

———. "The Emergence of Pan-Nationalism in Egypt: Pan-Islamism and Pan-Arabism in the 1930s," *Asian and African Studies* 16 (1982): 59–94.

———. "The Evolution of National Culture in Modern Egypt: Intellectual Formation and Social Diffusion, 1892–1945." *Poetics Today* 13 (1992): 325–350.

———. "The Muslim Brothers and the Arab Revolt in Palestine, 1936–1939." *Middle Eastern Studies* 22 (1986): 367–397.

Gershoni, Israel, and James Jankowski. *Egypt, Islam, and the Arabs: The Search for Egyptian Nationhood, 1900–1930.* New York, 1986.

———. *Redefining the Egyptian Nation, 1930–1945.* Cambridge, 1995.

Ghannushi, R. *al-Hurriyyat al-`Amma lil-Dawla al-Islamiyya.* Beirut, 1993.

Ghareeb, Edmund. *The Kurdish Question in Iraq.* Syracuse, 1981.

al-Gharib, A. M. `Awda ila al-Islam min Jadid.* Cairo, 1992.

Ghaylun, Burhan. *Le malaise arabe.* Paris, 1991.

———. *Mihnat al-`Aql.* Beirut, 1985.

Ghorbal, Shafik [Shafiq Ghurbal]. *The Beginning of the Egyptian Question and the Rise of Mehmet Ali*. London, 1928.

Gibb, H. A. R. "Toward Arab Unity." *Foreign Affairs* 24 (1945–1946): 119–129.

Goldschmidt, Arthur, Jr. "The Egyptian Nationalist Party, 1892–1919." In P. M. Holt, ed., *Political and Social Change in Modern Egypt* (London, 1968), 308–333.

Gomaa, Ahmed M. *The Foundation of the League of Arab States*. London, 1986.

Gordon, Joel. *Nasser's Blessed Movement: Egypt's Free Officers and the July Revolution*. New York, 1992.

Graham-Brown, Sarah. "Agriculture and Labour Transformation in Palestine." In Kathy and Pandeli Glavanis, eds., *The Rural Middle East: Peasant Lives and Modes of Production* (London, 1989), 53–69.

———. *Images of Women: The Portrayal of Women in Photography in the Middle East, 1860–1950*. New York, 1988.

Greenfeld, Liah. *Nationalism: Five Roads to Modernity*. Cambridge, MA, 1992.

al-Habashi, M. S. *Aden*. Algeirs, 1964.

Haddad, Mahmoud. "Iraq Before World War I: A Case of Anti-European Arab Ottomanism." In Rashid Khalidi et al., *The Origins of Arab Nationalism* (New York, 1991), 120–150.

Haim, Sylvia G. *Arab Nationalism: An Anthology*. Berkeley, 1962.

———. "Islam and the Theory of Arab Nationalism." In Walter Z. Laqueur, ed., *The Middle East in Transition* (New York, 1958), 280–307.

Hall, Stuart. "Ethnicity: Identity and Difference." *Radical America* 23:4 (Oct./ Dec. 1989): 9–20.

Halliday, Fred. *Arabia Without Sultans*. Harmondsworth, 1974.

———. "Bringing the 'Economic' Back In: the Case of Nationalism." *Economy and Society* 21:4 (November 1992): 483–490.

———. " 'Orientalism' and Its Critics." *British Journal of Middle Eastern Studies* 20:2 (1993): 145–163.

———. *Revolution and Foreign Policy: The Case of South Yemen, 1967–1987*. Cambridge, 1990.

———. "The Third Inter-Yemeni War." *Asian Affairs* 26:2 (June 1995): 131–140.

Haj, Samira. "The Problems of Tribalism: The Case of Nineteenth-Century Iraqi History." *Social History* 16 (1991): 45–58.

Hamdi, Walid M. S. *Rashid Ali al-Gailani and the Nationalist Movement in Iraq 1939–1941*. London, 1987.

Hammuda, S. *Shaykh `Izz al-Din al-Qassam: al-Wa`i wa al-Thawra*. Jerusalem, 1986.

Hamrush, Ahmad. *Qissat Thawrat 23 Yulyu*. 5 vols. 2d ed. Cairo, 1983.

Hamza, `Abd al-Latif. *Adab al-Maqala al-Suhufiyya fi Misr*. Multi-vols. Cairo, 1953–1962.

al-Hasani, `Abd al-Razzaq. *Ta'rikh Wizarat al-`Iraqiyya*. Multi-vols. Sidon, 1953–1967.

Hawwa, S. *Hadhihi Tajribati*. Cairo, 1987.

Haykal, Muhammad Hasanayn. *Li-Misr la Li-`Abd al-Nasir*. Cairo, 1987.

———. *Milaffat al-Suwis*. Cairo, 1986.

———. *Sanawat al-Ghalayan*. Cairo, 1988.

Haykal, Muhammad Husayn. *Mudhakkirat fi al-Siyasa al-Misriyya.* 2 vols. Cairo, 1953.

Heikal, Mohamed Hassanein [Muhammad Hasanayn Haykal]. *The Cairo Documents.* New York, 1973.

al-Hindi, Ihsan. *Ma`rakat Maysalun.* Damascus, 1967.

Hobsbawm, Eric. *Nations and Nationalism Since 1780.* Cambridge, 1983.

Hobsbawm, Eric, and Terence Ranger, eds. *The Invention of Tradition.* Cambridge, 1983.

Hopwood, Derek. *The Russian Presence in Syria and Palestine.* Oxford, 1969.

Hourani, Albert. "*The Arab Awakening* Forty Years After." In his *The Emergence of the Modern Middle East* (London, 1981), 193–215.

———. *Arabic Thought in the Liberal Age, 1798–1939.* Oxford, 1962.

———. *A History of the Arab Peoples.* Cambridge, MA, 1991.

———. "How Should We Write the History of the Middle East?" *International Journal of Middle East Studies* 23 (1991): 125–136.

Hurvitz, Nimrod. "Muhibb al-Din al-Khatib's Semitic Wave Theory and the Emergence of Pan-Arab Ideology in the Interwar Period." *Middle Eastern Studies* 29 (1993): 118–134.

Husayn, `Adil. *al-Harakat al-Siyasiyya fi Misr.* Cairo, 1982.

al-Husri, Sati`. *Mudhakkirati fi al-`Iraq.* 2 vols. Beirut, 1966–1968.

Husry, Khaldun S. "King Faysal I and Arab Unity, 1930–1933." *Journal of Contemporary History* 10 (1975): 323–340.

al-Hut, Bayan Nuwayhid. *al-Qidayat wa al-Mu'assasat al-Siyasiyya fi Filastin, 1917–1948.* Beirut, 1981.

al-`Iyashi, Ghalib. *al-Idahat al-Siyasiyya wa Asrar al-Intidab al-Faransi `ala Suriyya.* Beirut, 1955.

Jabir, Afif, and Said el-Attar. *Le Sous-Developpement economique et sociale du Yemen.* Algiers, 1964.

Jankowski, James. "Egyptian Responses to the Palestine Problem in the Interwar Period." *International Journal of Middle East Studies* 12 (1980): 1–38.

———. *Egypt's Young Rebels: "Young Egypt," 1933–1952.* Stanford, 1975.

———. "The Government of Egypt and the Palestine Question, 1936–1939." *Middle Eastern Studies* 17 (1981): 427–453.

Jawhar, Sami. *al-Samitun Yatakallimu.* Cairo, 1975.

Johnson, Nels. *Islam and the Politics of Meaning in Palestinian Nationalism.* New York, 1982.

al-Jundi, A. *al-`Uruba wa al-Islam.* Beirut, 197(?).

al-Jundi, Adham. *Ta'rikh al-Thawrat al-Suriyya fi `Ahd al-Intidab al-Faransi.* Damascus, 1960.

Kamil, `Ali Fahmi. *Mustafa Kamil Basha fi 34 Rabi`an.* 9 vols. Cairo, 1908–1911.

Kanafani, G. "Thawrat 1936–39 fi Filastin: Khalfiyyat wa Tafasil wa Tahlil." *Shu'un Filastiniyya,* no. 6 (Jan. 1972): 45–77.

Karnouk, Liliane. *Modern Egyptian Art: The Emergence of a National Style.* Cairo, 1988.

Karpat, Kemal. "The Ottoman Ethnic and Confessional Legacy in the Middle East." In Milton J. Esman and Itamar Rabinovich, eds., *Ethnicity, Pluralism, and the State in the Middle East* (Ithaca, 1988), 35–53.

al-Kayyali, A. *Ta'rikh Filastin al-Hadith*. Beirut, 1970 (translated as *Palestine: A Modern History* [London, 1978]).

Kazziha, Walid. *Revolutionary Transformation in the Arab World*. London, 1975.

Kedourie, Elie. "The Break Between Muslims and Jews in Iraq." In Mark R. Cohen and Abraham Udovitch, eds., *Jews Among Arabs: Contacts and Boundaries* (Princeton, 1989), 21–63.

———. "The Iraqi Shi`is and Their Fate." In Martin Kramer, ed., *Shi`ism, Resistance, and Revolution* (Boulder, 1987), 135–158.

———. "The Kingdom of Iraq: Retrospect." In his *The Chatham House Version and Other Middle-Eastern Studies* (London, 1970), 236–285.

———. *Nationalism*. 2d ed. New York, 1961.

———. "Pan-Arabism and British Policy." In his *The Chatham House Version and Other Middle-Eastern Studies* (London, 1970), 213–235.

Khadduri, Majid. *Political Trends in the Arab World: The Role of Ideas and Ideals in Politics*. Baltimore, 1970.

Khalidi, Rashid. "`Abd al-Ghani al-`Uraysi and al-Mufid: The Press and Arab Nationalism before 1914." In Marwan Buheiry, ed., *Intellectual Life in the Arab East, 1860–1939* (Beirut, 1981), 38–61.

———. "Arab Nationalism: Historical Problems in the Literature." *American Historical Review* 96 (1991): 1363–1373.

———. *British Policy Toward Syria and Palestine, 1906–1914*. London, 1980.

———. "Contrasting Narratives of Palestinian Identity." In Patricia Yaeger, ed., *The Geography of Identity*. Ann Arbor, 1996.

———. "Palestinian Peasant Resistance to Zionism before World War I." In Edward Said and Christopher Hitchens, eds., *Blaming the Victims: Spurious Scholarship and the Palestine Question* (New York, 1988), 207–233.

———. "The Role of the Press in the Early Arab Reaction to Zionism." *Peuples Mediterraneans/Mediterranean Peoples* 20 (July–Sept. 1982): 105–124.

———. "Society and Ideology in Late-Ottoman Syria: Class, Education, Profession, and Confession." In John Spagnolo, ed., *Problems of the Modern Middle East in Historical Perspective: Essays in Honour of Albert Hourani* (Reading, 1992), 119–131.

Khalidi, Rashid, Lisa Anderson, Muhammad Muslih, and Reeva S. Simon, eds. *The Origins of Arab Nationalism*. New York, 1991.

Khoury, Philip S. "Divided Loyalties: Syria and the Question of Palestine, 1919–1939." *Middle Eastern Studies* 21 (1985): 324–348.

———. "Factionalism among Syrian Nationalists during the French Mandate." *International Journal of Middle East Studies* 13 (1981): 441–469.

———. *Syria and the French Mandate: The Politics of Arab Nationalism, 1920–1945*. Princeton, 1987.

———. "The Syrian Independence Movement and the Development of Economic Nationalism in Damascus." *British Journal of Middle Eastern Studies* 14 (1988): 25–36.

———. *Urban Notables and Arab Nationalism: The Politics of Damascus, 1860–1920*. Cambridge, 1983.

Khuri, Yusuf. ed. *al-Sihafa al-`Arabiyya fi Filastin, 1876–1948*. Beirut, 1976.

Kimmerling, Baruch, and Joel Migdal. *Palestinians: The Making of a People*. New York, 1993.

Klein, Menahem. "Arab Unity: A Nonexistent Entity." *The Jerusalem Journal of International Relations* 12 (1990): 28–44.

Kramer, Martin. "Arab Nationalism: Mistaken Identity." *Daedalus*, 122 (Summer 1993): 171–206.

Labib, Pahor. *Lamahat min al-Dirasat al-Misriyya al-Qadima*. Cairo, 1947.

Lachman, S. "Arab Rebellion and Terrorism in Palestine, 1929–1939: The Case of Shaykh Izz Al-Din Al-Qassam and His Movement." In Elie Kedourie and Sylvia G. Haim, eds., *Zionism and Arabism in Palestine and Israel* (London, 1982), 52–99.

Lacouture, Jean. *Nasser*. New York, 1973.

Lacouture, Jean and Simonne. *Egypt in Transition*. New York, 1958.

Lesch, Ann Mosely. *Arab Politics in Palestine, 1919–1939: The Frustration of a National Movement*. Ithaca, 1979.

Lewis, Bernard. *The Middle East and the West*. New York, 1964.

Lockman, Zachary. *Comrades and Enemies: Arab and Jewish Workers in Palestine, 1906–1948*. Berkeley, 1996.

———. "Exclusion and Solidarity: Labor Zionism and Arab Workers in Palestine, 1897–1929." In Gyan Prakash, ed., *After Colonialism: Imperial Histories and Postcolonial Displacements* (Princeton, 1994), 211–240.

———. "Imagining the Working Class: Representations of Society and Class in Egypt Before 1914." *Poetics Today* 15:2 (1994): 157–190.

———. "Railway Workers and Relational History: Arabs and Jews in British-Ruled Palestine." *Comparative Studies in Society and History* 35 (1993): 601–627.

———. " 'We Opened Their Minds for Them': Labor-Zionist Discourse and the Railway Workers of Palestine, 1919–1929." *Review of Middle East Studies* 5 (1992): 5–32.

Mabruk, M. I. *Muwajahat al-Muwajaha*. Cairo, 1994.

al-Mad`aj, `Abd al-Muhsin Mad`aj. *The Yemen in Early Islam: A Political History*. London, 1988.

Mandel, Neville. *The Arabs and Zionism before World War I*. Berkeley, 1976.

Mansur, George. *The Arab Worker Under the Palestine Mandate*. Jerusalem, 1938.

al-Mar`ashli, Tawfiq. *al-Tarbiyya al-Wataniyya*. Cairo, 1928.

Mar`i, Sayyid. *Awraq Siyasiyya*. 3 vols. Cairo, 1979.

Marr, Phebe. "The Development of a Nationalist Ideology in Iraq, 1920–1941." *Muslim World* 75 (April 1985): 85–101.

———. *The Modern History of Iraq*. Boulder, 1985.

Matar, Fu'ad. *Bi-Saraha an `Abd al-Nasir: Hiwar ma`a Muhammad Hasanayn Haykal*. Beirut, 1975.

Mathews, Roderic D., and Matta Akrawi. *Education in the Arab Countries of the Near East*. Washington, 1949.

Mayer, Thomas. "Egypt and the General Islamic Conference in Jerusalem in 1931." *Middle Eastern Studies* 18 (1982): 311–322.

———. *Egypt and the Palestine Question, 1936–1945*. Berlin, 1983.

————. "Egypt and the 1936 Arab Revolt in Palestine." *Journal of Contemporary History* 19 (1984): 275–287.

————. "Egypt's 1948 Invasion of Palestine." *Middle Eastern Studies* 22 (1986): 20–36.

McCarthy, Justin. *The Population of Palestine: Population History and Statistics of the Late-Ottoman Period and the Mandate.* New York, 1990.

Me`ir, Yosef. *Ha-hitpathut ha-hevratit-tarbutit shel Yehudei `Iraq me`az 1830 ve-ad yameinu.* Jerusalem, 1989.

el-Messiri, Sawsan. *Ibn al-Balad: A Concept of Egyptian Identity.* Leiden, 1978.

Miller, Ylana. *Government and Society in Mandatory Palestine.* Austin, 1985.

Mitchell, Richard. *The Society of the Muslim Brothers.* New York, 1969.

Mitchell, Timothy. "The Limit of the State." *American Political Science Review* 85:1 (1991): 77–96.

Muhyi al-Din, Khalid. *Wa al-An Atakallimu.* Cairo, 1992.

Musa, Sulayman. *al-Murasalat al-Ta'rikhiyya, 1920–1923.* Amman, 1978.

Muslih, Muhammad. *The Origins of Palestinian Nationalism.* New York, 1988.

————. "The Rise of Local Nationalism in the Arab East." In Rashid Khalidi et al., *The Origins of Arab Nationalism* (New York, 1991), 167–185.

Naji, Sultan. "The Genesis of the Call for Yemeni Unity." In B. R. Pridham, ed., *Contemporary Yemen; Politics and Historical Background* (Beckenham, Kent, 1984).

Najib, Muhammad. *Mudhakkirat Muhammad Najib: Kuntu Ra'isan li-Misr.* Cairo, 1984.

Nakash, Yitzhak. *The Shi`is of Iraq.* Princeton, 1994.

Nasser, Gamal Abdel. *The Philosophy of the Revolution.* Buffalo, NY, 1959.

Nasr, Marlene. "al-Qawmiyya wa al-Din fi Fikr `Abd al-Nasir." In Sa`d al-Din Ibrahim, ed., *Misr wa al-Qawmiyya wa Thawrat Yulyu* (2d ed.; Cairo, 1983), 53–81.

————. *al-Tasawwur al-Qawmi al-`Arabi fi Fikr Jamal `Abd al-Nasir, 1952–1970.* Beirut, 1982.

————. "Tatawwur al-Qawmi al-`Arabi." In Sa`d al-Din Ibrahim, ed., *Misr wa al-Qawmiyya wa Thawrat Yulyu* (2d ed.; Cairo, 1983), 93–101.

Nimni, Ephraim. *Marxism and Nationalism.* London, 1991.

Niqula, Jabra. *Harakat al-Idrabat bayna al-`Ummal al-`Arab fi Filastin.* Jaffa, 1935.

Novick, Peter. *That Noble Dream: The "Objectivity Question" and the American Historical Profession.* Cambridge, 1989.

Nuseibeh, Hazem Zaki. *The Ideas of Arab Nationalism.* Ithaca, 1956.

Nüsse, A. "The Ideology of Hamas: Palestinian Islamic Fundamentalist Thought on the Jews, Israel, and Islam." In R. Nettler, ed., *Studies in Muslim-Jewish Relations* (Oxford, 1993), 97–125.

Nuwayhid, `Ajaj. *Rijal min Filastin ma bayna Bidayat al-Qarn hatta `Amm 1948.* Amman, 1981.

Ostle, Robin. "Modern Egyptian Renaissance Man." *Bulletin of the School of Oriental and African Studies* 57 (1994): 184–192.

Owen, Roger. *The Middle East in the World Economy, 1800–1914.* London, 1981.

————. *State, Power, and Politics in the Making of the Modern Middle East.* London, 1992.

Pascual, Jean-Paul. "La Syrie a l'Epoque Ottomane (Le XIXe siecle)." In Andre Raymond, ed., *La Syrie d'Aujourd'hui* (Paris, 1980).

Peters, R. *Islam and Colonialism: The Doctrine of Jihad in Modern History.* The Hague, 1979.

Piscatori, James. *Islam in a World of Nation-States.* Cambridge, 1986.

Piterberg, Gabriel. "Domestic Orientalism: The Representation of 'Oriental' Jews in Zionist/Israeli Historiography." *British Journal of Middle Eastern Studies* 23:2 (December 1996).

Porath, Yehoshua. *The Emergence of the Palestinian Arab National Movement, 1918–1929.* London, 1974.

———. *In Search of Arab Unity, 1930–1945.* London, 1986.

———. *The Palestinian Arab National Movement, 1929–1939: From Riots to Rebellion.* London, 1977.

———. "Social Aspects of the Emergence of the Palestinian Arab National Movement." In Menahem Milson, ed., *Society and Political Structure in the Arab World* (New York, 1973), 93–144.

al-Qasimi, Zafir. *Maktab ʿAnbar.* Beirut, 1967.

Qudama, Ahmad. *Maʿalim wa Aʿlam fi Bilad al-ʿArab.* Damascus, 1965.

Rabinovich, Itamar. "Inter-Arab Relations Foreshadowed: The Question of the Syrian Throne in the 1920s and 1930s." In *Festschrift in Honor of Dr. George S. Wise* (Tel Aviv, 1981), 237–250.

Radwan, Fathi. *72 Shahran maʿa ʿAbd al-Nasir.* Cairo, 1985.

al-Rafiʿi, ʿAbd al-Rahman. *Mustafa Kamil: Baʿith al-Haraka al-Wataniyya, 1892–1908.* 5th ed. Cairo, 1984.

al-Rayyis, Munir. *al-Kitab al-Dhahabi lil-Thawrat al-Wataniyya fi al-Mashriq al-ʿArabi: al-Thawra al-Suriyya al-Kubra.* Beirut, 1969.

Reid, Donald M. "Indigenous Egyptology: The Decolonization of a Profession?" *Journal of the American Oriental Society* 105 (1985): 233–246.

Rejwan, Nissim. "Arab Nationalism: In Search of an Ideology." In Walter Z. Laqueur, ed., *The Middle East in Transition,* (New York, 1958), 145–165.

Rifʿat, Muhammad, and ʿAbd al-ʿAziz al-Bishri. *al-Tarbiyya al-Wataniyya.* Cairo, 1943.

Riyad, Mahmud. *Mudhakkirat Mahmud Riyad, 1948–1978.* 3 vols. Cairo, 1985–1986.

Rosenthal, E. I. J. *Islam in the Modern National State.* Cambridge, 1965.

Roy, Olivier. *The Failure of Political Islam.* Cambridge, MA, 1994.

Russell, Malcolm B. *The First Modern Arab State: Syria under Faysal, 1918–1920.* Minneapolis, 1985.

Said, Edward. *Culture and Imperialism.* New York, 1994.

———. *Orientalism.* New York, 1978.

———. *The Politics of Dispossession.* London, 1992.

Sakhnini, I. "Damm Filastin al-Wusta ila Sharq al-Urdun, 1948–1950." *Shuʾun Filastiniyya,* no. 40 (December, 1974): 56–83.

Sakakini, Khalil. *Filastin baʿd al-Harb al-Kubra.* Jerusalem, 1925.

Salibi, Kamal. *A House of Many Mansions: The History of Lebanon Reconsidered.* Berkeley, 1988.

Salih, M. M. *al-Tayyar al-Islami fi Filastin wa Atharuhu fi Harakat al-Jihad, 1917–1948.* Kuwait, 1988.

Sayegh, Fayez A. *Arab Unity: Hope and Fulfillment.* New York, 1958.

al-Sayih, `Abd al-Hamid. *Muzaqarat: Filastin, La Salatta Tahta al-Hirab.* Beirut, 1994.

al-Sayyid Marsot, Afaf Lutfi. "The Cartoon in Egypt." *Comparative Studies in Society and History* 13 (1971): 2–15.

Schatkowski Schilcher, Linda. *Families in Politics: Damascene Factions and Estates of the 18th and 19th Century.* Stuttgart, 1985.

———. "Violence in Rural Syria in the 1880s and 1890s: State Centralization, Rural Integration, and the World Market." In Farhad Kazemi and John Waterbury, eds., *Peasants and Politics in the Modern Middle East* (Miami, 1991), 50–84.

Schölch, Alexander. "Britain in Palestine 1838–1882: The Roots of the Balfour Policy." *Journal of Palestine Studies* 22 (1992): 39–56.

———. *Palestine in Transformation, 1856–1882: Studies in Social, Economic, and Political Development.* Washington, 1993.

Seale, Patrick. *The Struggle for Syria: A Study of Post-War Arab Politics, 1945–1958.* Oxford, 1965.

al-Shahid `Izz al-Din al-Qassam: Hayatuhu wa Jihaduhu. Damascus, n. d.

Shamir, Shimon. "Self-View in Modern Egyptian Historiography." In Shimon Shamir, ed., *Self-Views in Historical Perspective in Egypt and Israel* (Tel Aviv, 1981), 37–49.

Sharabi, Hisham B. *Nationalism and Revolution in the Arab World.* Toronto, 1966.

Shawkat, Sami. *Hadhihi Ahdafuna.* Baghdad, 1939.

El-Shayyal, Gamal El-Din [Jamal al-Din al-Shayyal]. *A History of Egyptian Historiography in the Nineteenth Century.* Alexandria, 1962.

al-Shayyal, Jamal al-Din. *Ta'rikh al-Tarjama fi Misr fi `Ahd al-Hamla al-Faransiyya.* Cairo, 1950.

———. *al-Ta'rikh wa al-Mu'arrikhun fi Misr fi al-Qarn al-Tasi` `Ashr.* Alexandria, 1958.

Sidqi, Nahal Bahjat. *Fakhri al-Barudi.* Beirut, 1974.

Simon, Reeva S. "The Education of an Iraqi Army Officer." In Rashid Khalidi et al., *The Origins of Arab Nationalism* (New York, 1991), 151–166.

———. "The Hashimite 'Conspiracy': Hashimite Unity Attempts, 1921–1958." *International Journal of Middle Eastern Studies* 5 (1974): 314–327.

———. *Iraq Between the Two World Wars: The Creation and Implementation of a Nationalist Ideology.* New York, 1986.

———. "The Teaching of History in Iraq Before the Rashid Ali Coup of 1941." *Middle Eastern Studies* 22 (1986): 37–51.

Sivan, Emmanuel. "The Arab Nation-State: In Search of a Useable Past." *Middle East Review,* Spring 1987, 21–30.

Smith, Anthony D. *The Ethnic Origins of Nations.* New York, 1986.

———. *The Ethnic Revival in the Modern World.* Cambridge, 1981.

———. *National Identity.* London, 1991.

———. *Theories of Nationalism.* 2d ed. London, 1983.

Smith, W. C. *Islam in Modern History.* Princeton, 1957.

Somekh, S. "The Neo-Classical Arab Poets." In M. M. Badawi, ed., *Modern Arabic Literature* (Cambridge, 1993), 36–81.

Starkey, Paul. *From the Ivory Tower: A Critical Study of Tawfiq al-Hakim*. London, 1987.

Stephens, Robert. *Nasser: A Political Biography*. New York, 1971.

Stookey, Robert. *Yemen, The Politics of the Yemen Arab Republic*. Boulder, 1978.

al-Suwaidi, Jamal, ed. *The Yemeni War of 1994*. London, 1995.

al-Sulh, M. *al-Islam wa Harakat al-Tahrir al-`Arabiyya*. Beirut, 1973.

Swedenburg, Ted. *Memories of Revolt: The 1936–1939 Rebellion and the Palestinian National Past*. Minneapolis, 1996.

———. "The Role of the Palestinian Peasantry in the Great Revolt." In Edmund Burke III and Ira Lapidus, eds., *Islam, Politics, and Social Movements* (Berkeley, 1988), 169–203.

Talhami, Ghada Hashem. *Palestine and Egyptian National Identity*. New York, 1992.

Tamari, Salim. "Factionalism and Class Formation in Recent Palestinian History." In Roger Owen, ed., *Studies in the Economic and Social History of Palestine in the Nineteenth and Twentieth Centuries* (Carbondale, IL, 1982), 177–202.

Tarbush, Mohammad A. *The Role of the Military in Politics: A Case Study of Iraq to 1941*. London, 1982.

Taylor, John H. *Howard Carter: Before Tutankhamun*. New York, 1992.

Tibawi, A. L. *Arab Education in Mandatory Palestine*. London, 1954.

———. *British Interests in Palestine*. Oxford, 1966.

Tibi, Bassam. *Arab Nationalism: A Critical Enquiry*. Translated by Marion Farouq-Sluglett and Peter Sluglett. New York, 1981.

al-Turabi, H. "al-Sahwa al-Islamiyya wa al-Dawla al-Qutriyya fi al-Watan al-`Arabi." In *al-Sahwa al-Islamiyya: Ru'ya Naqdiyya min al-Dakhil* (Beirut, 1990), 75–108.

———. "al-Bu`d al-`Alami lil-Haraka al-Islamiyya: al-Tajriba al-Sudaniyya." In `A. al-Nafisi, ed., *al-Haraka al-Islamiyya: Ru'ya Mustaqbaliyya* (Cairo, 1989), 77–98.

Tütsch, Hans E. *Facets of Arab Nationalism*. Detroit, 1965.

al-`Ulwan, A. *al-Qawmiyya fi Mizan al-Islam*. Amman, 1982.

`Umar, Sultan Ahmad. *Nazra fi Tatawwur al-Mujtama` al-Yamani*. Beirut, 1970,

Uways, Sayyid. *L'Histoire que je porte sur mon dos: Memoires*. Cairo, 1989.

van den Berghe, Pierre. *The Ethnic Phenomenon*. New York, 1979.

Vatikiotis, P. J. *The History of Modern Egypt*. 4th ed. Baltimore, 1991.

———. *Nasser and His Generation*. London, 1978.

Vatter, Sherry. "Militant Journeymen in Nineteenth Century Damascus: Implications for the Middle Eastern Labor History Agenda." In Zachary Lockman, ed., *Workers and Working Classes in the Middle East: Struggles, Histories, Historiographies* (Albany, 1994), 1–19.

Vaucher, Georges. *Gamal Abdel Nasser et son Equipe*. Paris, 1959.

Verdery, Katherine. "Whither 'Nation" and 'Nationalism'?" *Daedalus* 122 (Summer 1993): 37–46.

Vereté, Mayir. "The Balfour Declaration and Its Makers." In Norman Rose. ed., *From Palmerston to Balfour: Collected Essays of Mayir Vereté* (London, 1992), 1–38.

von Grunebaum, G. E. *Modern Islam: The Search for Cultural Identity*.New York, 1964.

Wasserstein, Bernard. *The British in Palestine: The Mandatory Government and the Arab-Jewish Conflict, 1917–1929*. 2d ed.; Oxford, 1991.

Wendell, Charles. *The Evolution of the Egyptian National Image: From Its Origins to Ahmad Lutfi al-Sayyid*. Berkeley, 1972.

Wheelock, Keith. *Nasser's New Egypt*. New York, 1960.

White, Hayden. *The Content of the Form*. Baltimore, 1987.

———. "The Fictions of Factual Representation." In Angus Fletcher, ed., *The Literature of Fact* (New York, 1976), 21–44.

———. "History, Historicism, and the Historical Imagination." *History and Theory* 14 (1975): 48–67.

———. *Metahistory*. 2d ed. Baltimore, 1993.

———. *Tropics of Discourse: Essays in Cultural Criticism*. Baltimore, 1978.

Wilson, John A. *Signs and Wonders Upon Pharaoh: A History of American Archeology*. Chicago, 1974.

———. *Thousands of Years: An Archeologist's Search for Ancient Egypt*. New York, 1972.

Woolbert, Robert G. "Pan-Arabism and the Palestine Problem," *Foreign Affairs* 16 (January 1938): 309–322.

Yasin, A. *al-Manhaj al-Nabawi*. 3d ed. Beirut, 1994.

Yasin, S. *al-Harb al-`Isabat fi Filastin*. Cairo, 1967.

al-Yusuf, Fatima. *Dhikrayat*. Cairo, 1953; reprint 1976.

Ziadeh, Nicola A. "Recent Arab Literature on Arabism." *Middle East Journal* 6 (1952): 468–473.

Zu`aytir, Akram. "Ittifaq al-`Arab `ala Wada' Lubnan al-Khass." *al-Hawadith* (Beirut), no. 978 (Aug. 1975): 64–66.

Zu`aytir, Akram, and Darwish al-Miqdadi. *Ta'rikhuna bi Uslub Qissasi*. Baghdad, 1939.

Zubaida, Sami. "Community, Class and Minorities in Iraqi Politics." In Robert A. Fernea and Roger Owen, eds., *The Iraqi Revolution of 1958: The Old Social Classes Revisited* (London, 1991), 197–210.

———. *Islam: The People and the State*. London, 1989.

———. *Race and Racism*. London, 1978.

Zurayk, Costi K. "The Essence of Arab Civilization." *Middle East Journal* 3 (1949): 125–139.

Contributors

Beth Baron is Associate Professor of History at the Graduate School and the City College of the City University of New York. She is the coeditor, with Nikki R. Keddie, of *Women in Middle Eastern History* (Yale University Press, 1991) and the author of *The Women's Awakening in Egypt: Culture, Society, and the Press* (Yale University Press, 1994).

Musa Budeiri is Associate Professor of Political Science and Director of the Center for Area Studies at Al Quds University, East Jerusalem. His publications include *The Palestine Communist Party, 1919–1948: Arab and Jew in the Struggle for Internationalism* (Ithaca Press, 1979).

William L. Cleveland is Professor of History at Simon Fraser University. His publications include *The Making of an Arab Nationalist: Ottomanism and Arabism in the Life and Thought of Sati` al-Husri* (Princeton University Press, 1971); *Islam Against the West: Shakib Arslan and the Campaign for Islamic Nationalism* (Texas University Press, 1985); and *A History of the Modern Middle East* (Westview Press, 1994).

James Gelvin is Assistant Professor of History at the University of California at Los Angeles. He is the author of *Contesting Nationalisms and the Birth of Mass Politics in Syria* (University of California Press, 1997).

Israel Gershoni is Professor of History in the Department of Middle Eastern and African History at Tel Aviv University. He is the author of *The Emergence of Pan-Arabism in Egypt* (Shiloah Center for Middle Eastern and African Studies, 1981) and coauthor, with James Jankowski, of *Egypt, Islam, and the Arabs: The Search for Egyptian Nationhood, 1900–1930* (Oxford University Press, 1986), and *Redefining the Egyptian Nation* (Cambridge University Press, 1995).

Fred Halliday is Professor of International Relations at the London School of Economics and Political Science. His publications include *Arabia Without Sultans: A Political Survey of Instability in the Arab World* (Vintage, 1975); *Iran: Dictatorship and Development* (Penguin, 1979); *The Making of the Second Cold War* (Verso, 1986); *Revolution in Foreign Policy: The Case of South Yemen, 1967–1987* (Cambridge University Press, 1990); and *Islam and the Myth of Confrontation* (I. B. Tauris, 1996).

James Jankowski is Professor of History at the University of Colorado at Boulder. He is the author of *Egypt's Young Rebels: Young Egypt, 1933–1952* (Hoover Institution Press, 1975), and the coauthor, with Israel Gershoni, or *Egypt, Islam, and the Arabs: The Search for Egyptian Nationhood, 1900–1930* (Oxford University Press, 1986) and *Redefining the Egyptian Nation, 1930–1945* (Cambridge University Press, 1995).

Rashid Khalidi is Professor of History and Director of the Center for International Studies at the University of Chicago. His publications include *British Policy Toward Syria and Palestine, 1906–1914* (Ithaca Press, 1980), *Under Siege: PLO Decision-Making During the 1982 War* (Columbia University Press, 1986), and *Palestinian Identity: the Construction of Modern National Consciousness* (Columbia University Press, 1997). He is the coeditor of *The Origins of Arab Nationalism* (Columbia University Press, 1991).

Philip S. Khoury is Professor of History and Dean of the School of Humanities and Social Science at the Massachusetts Institute of Technology. He is the author of *Urban Notables and Arab Nationalism: The Politics of Damascus, 1860–1920* (Cambridge University Press, 1983) and *Syria and the French Mandate: The Politics of Arab Nationalism, 1920–1945* (Princeton University Press, 1987). He is the coeditor, with Joseph Kostiner, of *Tribes and State Formation in the Middle East* (University of California Press, 1990) and, with Albert Hourani and Mary C. Wilson, of *The Modern Middle East: A Reader* (University of California Press, 1993).

Zachary Lockman teaches in the Department of Middle Eastern Studies at New York University. He is the author of *Comrades and Enemies: Arab and Jewish Workers in Palestine, 1906–1948* (University of California Press, 1996); the editor of *Workers and Working Classes in the Middle East: Struggles, Histories, Historiographies* (State University of New York Press, 1994); and the coauthor, with Joel Beinin, of *Workers on the Nile: Nationalism, Communism, Islam and the Egyptian Working Class, 1882–1954* (Princeton University Press, 1987).

Gabriel Piterberg is a Lecturer in the Department of Middle Eastern Studies at the Ben Gurion University of the Negev. He is the coauthor, with Elan Pappe, of *The Politics of History in Israel* (Cambridge University Press, 1997).

Donald M. Reid is Professor of History at Georgia State University. His publications include *The Odyssey of Farah Antun: A Syrian Christian's Search for Secularism* (Bibliotheca Islamica, 1981); *Lawyers and Politics in the Arab World,*

1880–1960 (Bibliotheca Islamica, 1981); and *Cairo University and the Making of Modern Egypt* (Cambridge University Press, 1990).

Reeva S. Simon is Assistant Director of the Middle East Institute, Columbia University. She is the author of *Iraq Between the Two World Wars: The Creation and Implementation of a Nationalist Ideology* (Columbia University Press, 1986) and *The Middle East in Crime Fiction: Mysteries, Spy Novels, and Thrillers from 1916 to the 1980s* (Lilian Barber Press, 1989). She is the editor of *The Middle East and North Africa: Essays in Honor of J. C. Hurewitz* (Middle East Institute, Columbia University, 1990) and the coeditor of *The Origins of Arab Nationalism* (Columbia University Press, 1991) and of the *Encyclopedia of the Modern Middle East* (Macmillan, 1996).

Emmanual Sivan is Professor of History in the Faculty of Humanities at the Hebrew University of Jerusalem. His publications include *Interpretations of Islam: Past and Present* (Darwin Press, 1985); *Radical Islam: Medieval Theology and Modern Politics* (Yale University Press, 1985; enlarged edition, 1990); *Mythes Arabes Politiques* (Editions Fayard, 1995); and, with J. Winter, *War and Remembrance* (Cambridge University Press, forthcoming).

Index